Robert Manning Strozier Library

AUG 6 1989

Tallahassee, Florida

UNIVERSITY LIBRARIES
FLORIDA STATE UNIVERSITY
Tallahassee, Florida

The Coming Explosion in Latin America

BY GERALD CLARK

DAVID McKAY COMPANY, INC.
New York

THE COMING EXPLOSION IN LATIN AMERICA

COPYRIGHT © 1962, 1963 BY GERALD CLARK
AND PUBLISHED SIMULTANEOUSLY IN CANADA
BY THE MUSSON BOOK COMPANY LTD., TORONTO

All rights reserved, including the right to reproduce this book, or parts thereof, in any form, except for the inclusion of brief quotations in a review.

F
1414
.C55
1963

309.18
C593c

LIBRARY
FLORIDA STATE UNIVERSITY
TALLAHASSEE, FLORIDA

LIBRARY OF CONGRESS CATALOG CARD NUMBER: 63-13174

MANUFACTURED IN THE UNITED STATES OF AMERICA

VAN REES PRESS • NEW YORK

To my mother

FOREWORD

WE TEND TO ASSOCIATE the word *revolution* with Latin America since governments there are overthrown with greater frequency than in other parts of the world. However, revolution has many meanings. For Europeans and North Americans the Industrial Revolution changed a pattern of life a century ago; in more modern times social structures have been altered by ideological upheavals. But the significance of fundamental change, in the relationship of man to man, has hardly been felt in Latin America. With the exceptions mainly of Mexico and Cuba, revolutions of a profound nature are unknown.

This condition is now bound to end. Whether the first action will take place in the Peruvian Andes, where Indians exist in virtual peonage, or in the Northeast of Brazil, a starving land by itself, is impossible to foretell. Celso Furtado, a brilliant Brazilian economist, categorizes the Northeast now as in a pre-revolutionary state. If—or more aptly, when—it blows up, its echoes will make the Cuban experience fade into triviality.

I started my trip with the intention of examining the broad forces at work in Latin America, subject by subject, rather than country by country. That is, I was primarily interested in common denominators, such as the mood of landless peasants, the role of armed forces—whether in Argentina, Venezuela, or Nicaragua—and the dynamism of students whose influence is far more meaningful than is usually understood in North America.

Many other topics have come into this book. Obviously, in this context, a chapter or section was planned on Fidel Castro and the impact he has had on the rest of Latin America. But in the writing of the book I found that Castro's name crept in almost from page one. It appears, it will be noted, not merely in a single chapter but throughout the book as a steady, almost pervasive reminder that Castro cannot be dismissed in a few pages. For Fidelismo has become the greatest single subject, the greatest single force in this society of 200 million people.

The reason for the pervasiveness of Castro's name, and the movement he introduced, is not difficult to comprehend. Even taking into account obvious differences in the character of twenty countries, in almost all there is a uniform, dominant pattern: massive poverty contrasted with extreme and exclusive wealth. There is also a new awareness that man is entitled to some degree of respect and security as his basic right. Therefore the word *dignidad,* the dignity of the human being in striving for what he believes to be justice, will occur almost as often as Fidelismo. For reasons set forth in the following pages, Fidelismo has an appeal where one of its parents, communism, failed to incite pressures of any substance.

North Americans are inclined to regard the resolution of the Cuban missile crisis as a severe setback for Castro in the eyes of Latin Americans. Suddenly, it is argued, the man who was identified as a Cuban patriot, defying the mighty Yankees, turned out to be nothing more than the pawn of another great power, Russia; he was pushed to one side and ignominiously ignored by Khrushchev when it came to dismantling the bases in response to a firm demand by the United States.

There is, of course, some validity in talking about a loss of prestige for Castro, but the question of degree must be considered. Castro's personal popularity in Latin America was on the decline even before there was evidence that he had allowed himself to become a tool in the cold war. I have quoted Latin Americans to show the reasons for this decline; at the same time I have emphasized that even if Castro as an individual no longer has unlimited prestige abroad, it is the movement to which he has given his name that is important. It will long outlast the man himself.

For a brief moment, following the withdrawal of Soviet offensive missiles, it appeared that a rise in United States prestige might result in a little more borrowed time, crucial for any tranquil transformation in Latin America. "If a free society cannot help the many who are poor it can never save the few who are rich," President Kennedy has said. These words, wise and probably prophetic, underlie the philosophy of the Alliance for Progress. But the Cuban crisis has had little effect in converting "the few who are rich" to the idea of hastening reforms, relinquishing parochial privileges, and moving with urgency. Wealthy Latin Americans have shown little more faith today than in the past; they continue to send money to the safekeeping of Swiss banks. Meanwhile, Washington is confronted with a growing demand to rescue countries from bankruptcy while Alliance funds are not getting down to the grass roots where they might stave off upheaval.

The blame is not entirely on Latin-American shoulders. Partly it rests with North Americans who consider capitalism, of the North American version, as the salvation for underdeveloped nations. To the masses in Latin America capitalism, if it is thought about at all, is linked with a closed, feudal, aristocratic society; for this is precisely what Latin-American capitalism has been in its refusal to evolve into modern forms.

There are many people to whom I am indebted for help during a survey that embraced 50,000 miles of travel and brought me in close contact with peasants and presidents, generals and priests, Communists and conservatives, intellectuals and laborers, and other representatives of the economic, political, and social complex of the continent. I would like to make two specific acknowledgments. One is to the Berlitz instructors who, in a concentrated course of drilling, gave me a grasp of Spanish that enabled me to get by without total reliance on interpreters and so opened informal roads of contact that otherwise would have been lost. I would also like to express my appreciation to John G. McConnell, President of *The Montreal Star,* who gave me the encouragement to spend more than a year on this project.

FEBRUARY, 1963. GERALD CLARK

Contents

1

The Open Door of Tequendama

MANY, MANY CENTURIES AGO, a legend of the Chibcha Indians relates, a fierce storm raged across a fertile plateau of what is now known as the Cordillera Oriental of Colombia. Greedy and heartless torrents drowned the crops of maize and potatoes, swept away huts, and destroyed man and beast alike. The flood waters continued to rise more and more, while the terrified and bewildered people fled to higher ground. From these isolated little islands in the Andes, the chanted prayers of the people, appealing to their gods for deliverance, sounded above the roar of the roiling waters. Suddenly, there appeared the god Bochica to rescue the doomed Chibchas. With his gold wand he struck hard on the mountains that dammed in the waters; and, all at once, while thunder punctuated the shrill chanting, the mountains parted. Desperately, the evil waters sought an outlet and swelled through the opening, plunging far down the mountainside. Thus were the people of the Chibchas, and their land, saved from total disaster. Today, not far from Bogotá, the new capital established by white men, the wild and dramatic Tequendama Falls still plunge nearly five hundred feet to the river below, keeping alive the ancient Chibcha legend of Bochica and the flood. In Chibcha language *Tequendama* means "open door."

SOME SIXTY MILES SOUTHEAST OF BOGOTÁ, sheltered quietly on the slopes of the Cordillera Oriental or eastern range of the Andes, is the small community of Viotá. The people who dwell there are descendants of the Chibchas. Like highland folk in the rest of Colombia—and, for that matter, in Peru, Bolivia, and other countries—they struggle with the soil for subsistence living, without benefit of education, proper nutrition, or hygiene. Coffee is the main crop, and tilling the precipitous hillsides is difficult and dangerous. Both the coffee trees and the tall shade trees, usually banana palms, require constant attention. When the coffee cherries are bright red, the farmer's entire family, including children of six or seven years, select the ripest from dawn to sunset; the next day they return to pick those that have ripened in the meanwhile. The women cook meals over a wood fire and collect water from a spring or shallow well. The only lighting at night is from homemade tallow candles; even during daytime, light seldom penetrates the windowless and airless adobe hovels. The dry mud walls of a hut are topped by a palm-thatched roof, but the floor is of bare earth, and pigs are able to wander inside from what resembles a vegetable patch.

Under a system of peonage, which the early Spanish settlers introduced along with coffee cultivation, the highlanders grew to realize that the land of their forebears, a sedentary agricultural people, no longer belonged to them. Four landowners in the twentieth century, for instance, controlled the entire region around Viotá and its population of 20,000 men, women, and children. Viotá, located in a valley of subtropical foliage, has a rather hot, unpleasant climate, and two of the landowners preferred the surroundings of Bogotá, with its bracing altitude of 8,600 feet and luxury imports from Europe and the United States. They left their *fincas* in the hands of salaried managers, who, in common with the other two plantation owners, paid a *campesino* thirty cents a day for his family's output of coffee. Moreover, the *campesino,* or peasant, had to show, on demand, an identity card issued by the landowner; if he failed to have the card on him he forfeited his produce without compensation.

This was a degrading practice that involved more than economics alone; not only did it take from a man food for his children, but it also denied him the most fundamental of human rights, the freedom to move elsewhere. For, in an alliance of self-interest, no plantation boss would hire a *peón* belonging to a neighbor, and simple existence itself hovered around the identity card. It may be argued that illiterate and barely articulate peasants could hardly comprehend the symbolism of the identity card. The same was argued in another part of the world of which few of the Colombian Indians to this day have ever heard: South Africa. And yet an instinctive, universal urge to break loose from unwarranted abuse impelled the Africans of Sharpeville to make a bloody and massive demonstration in March of 1960. When I saw the men and women of Sharpeville they were still counting their dead—but they were also heaping on bonfires the hated passbooks, which, like their equivalents 7,000 miles distant, tied them to overlords, robbed them of human dignity, and threatened to engulf them forever.

Bochica reached South Africa later than he returned to the Valley of Viotá, for the *peones* tore up their identity cards in the 1930's. Without realizing it, they were in the forefront of a movement that is sweeping through South America. It has a common root in South Africa and other countries that shriek of man's inhumanity to man. In some instances the movement has behind it organizers who are skilful, dedicated, and knowledgeable, but usually the movement springs from within, with spontaneity and suppressed fury. Viotá, in its time, was rather exceptional. About thirty years ago an unheralded stranger from another district arrived and promised the *campesinos* some land and an end to the evil waters that were drowning them. Such is the irony that no one I met could recall the name of the modern Bochica, but in fact he was a Communist organizer, and Viotá had been chosen as a test ground for Communist advances.

Cleverly led and agitated, the peasants and sharecroppers simply began squatting on their employers' *fincas,* gradually taking over some of the properties for themselves. National guardsmen were sent down by Bogotá in an attempt to evict them; but vigilante groups had sealed off all entries to the area—an easy feat when you see the cliffs and mountain passes and know that in those days there were only dirt paths, with no road wide enough for motorized vehicles. There was not much shooting, and so far as anyone can remember only two persons were killed, one a *campesino,* the other a soldier. That was the end of government action. Viotá was left alone, like an inflamed but insignificant pimple that would vanish if ignored.

Viotá, however, refused to disappear from public attention. The *campesinos,* under the guidance of the Red Bochica, proclaimed a new name for Viotá: "Republic of Tequendama." The door opened onto a new vista, thousands of hectares of land that the old owners were once and for all compelled to vacate and that the *campesinos* now divided "legally," according to their definition. For, did not the freshly printed pieces of paper give them the titles to the land? The Republic of Tequendama also printed its own money and bonds, operated its own law courts, and started its own schools. The central government in Bogotá was forced to concede to the rule of the hills, until, in 1954, it decided that the highlanders were sufficiently mellow to accept another change. Bogotá built a paved road linking Viotá with the outside; and, more importantly, it enacted a special land reform law that recognized the *campesinos'* right to the land they had seized.

Now, in 1962, driving through the onetime enclave of

communism in the heart of Colombia, I found it physically no different from other impoverished parts of Latin America. Emaciated women scrubbed clothing in brooks that trickled down from the hilltops; and barefoot children, some of them with the bloated bellies of malnutrition, scampered, along with hogs, in and out of the adobe huts. What, then, had communism meant to them? When I asked this of an oldtimer, a man who had received two hectares, not quite five acres, in 1934, he rubbed his fingers over the gray stubble on his chin, appeared puzzled, and then shrugged his shoulders. I rephrased the question: "Who are the Communists?"

"Ah," he murmured, a glint of recognition in his eyes. "The Communists? They were men who gave away land."

This definition was confirmed by a young parish priest, Hector Osorio, who said: "The people of Viotá do not understand, and have never understood, the meaning of communism. To them it was simply a thing that distributed land and allowed them to tear up their identity cards. This, I suppose, was enough for them to know."

I drove along the primitive dirt road that goes high into the hills surrounding the town of Viotá. And at one place I stopped because I was attracted by a crudely lettered sign on the side of the road. The sign, of cardboard, read: "Helsinki, Seat of the 8th World Festival of Youth for Peace and Friendship." It was nailed to the wall of a frame hut that, as I discovered, doubled as a soft-drink stand and home for a woman and her sixteen-year-old daughter.

"Where," I asked the girl, "did the sign come from?"

She said that a man had ridden by on his burro and had stuck it there. Yes, she had seen him before, but not too often because he lived a good kilometer or two away. I asked if she knew what country Helsinki was in, and she shook her head. But why was the sign here?

The mother now replied: "It is to show that poor people

are having a meeting so they can live better." Under Communist auspices? The woman did not understand the word Communist. I asked the daughter if she had ever heard of Fidel Castro.

"Yes," she said, "he is a courageous man." Where had she heard that? The man on the burro had said that, and he had read it in *El Tiempo,* the big Bogotá newspaper. The girl could not read, and was, of course, unaware that *El Tiempo* was very distinctly anti-Castro. What country did Fidel Castro live in? The girl again moved her head in consternation. Peru, Colombia, Chile, Cuba? She simply did not know.

"But he is a good man, is he not?" she said.

This was fairly representative of the degree of political sophistication I found in Viotá. There are still in the district a few Communist propagandists, such as the elusive man on the burro; and obviously some of their words have had an impact. Occasionally, too, an outdoor rally is called in order to incite people to vote for leftist candidates in municipal elections. But it is a listless, disinterested crowd that attends; and the majority of officeholders belong to the traditional Liberal and Conservative parties of Colombia. Over the years the character of Viotá has swung back to an older way of life, and the Communists have no real following.

"The trouble," explained a man named Milciades Nova, "was that they tried to make the *campesinos* into Communists, when the *campesinos* for many generations had been Liberals or Conservatives." This, however, was not the entire explanation, as Nova's own case history indicated. Milciades Nova had been one of the first to get a few hectares of land, and he admits that he once applied to himself the term "Communist." But later he sold part of his landholdings in order to buy a grocery store—a rather pathetic business with a few shelves of packaged cereal and row upon row of chewing gum. Two developments have marked

Nova's career. First, he no longer is in bondage to any estate owner, as he was in his youth. Second, and more significantly, he is now a tiny capitalist. Around Viotá there are many other men who have manipulated the property that was handed them some thirty years ago, so that their direct interest in land goes beyond any conception of communism.

If there is a message to the story of Viotá, it is a quietly dramatic one. Communism's appeal is not on ideological but on practical grounds. If initially it offers land, it also offers hope for the future. But once the cravings for land and dignity are satisfied, the potential of communism is weakened. The Republic of Tequendama, embracing only 20,000 people, disappeared when a central government finally recognized its mood and needs. But such recognition is not being applied on a full scale in Colombia, nor in the rest of the continent. There are nearly 200,000,000 people in Latin America, and there will be many more Tequendamas. The question is whether the ending will be quite so simple as it was in Viotá.

In Brazil they are called *favelas,* in Argentina they are *poblaciones callampas,* in Colombia they are *bohilas,* in Venezuela they are *ranchos,* in Peru they are *barriadas,* and they all mean the same: slums. One third to one half of the people in the principal cities of each of these countries live in a nightmare of depression and squalor unequaled even in Shanghai.

El Montón (the heap) is an example of a *barriada* in Lima. Built atop an old garbage dump, it stretches perhaps a mile in each direction, and if you jab a stick anywhere beneath its sandy surface you will hit rusty tin cans, bottles, and other refuse deposited by Peruvians of generations past. El Montón is one of a dozen *barriadas* in and around Lima, and in them subsist 400,000 souls. Children, with festering sores on their bare legs, play in the exposed garbage; adults forage through it, picking out bits of cardboard or strips of metal to patch their shanties. El Montón lies almost under the shadow of San Cristobal, the hill crowned with a cross of pilgrimage and affording a sweeping panorama of the capital. The early Spaniards who came in search of Inca gold selected a splendid site for the haven of their viceroys, for the Andean foothills creep toward the nearby sea, and the air is crisp and clean, so long as you avoid El Montón. This is easy enough to do; discreetly erected mud walls cut El Montón off from the view of casual visitors, and you can wander instead through Lima's old plazas with their handsome colonial palaces or go out to the luxurious suburbs of Miraflores and San Isidro, there to see mansions so sumptuous that they are rarely matched in Europe or in the affluent United States.

Still, it is not always possible even for the *ricos,* the wealthy residents of Lima, to forget El Montón. Occasional breezes carry with them the odor of decayed garbage, which comes to the surface and mixes with the dry earth spilling from the unpaved alleys and the excrement of the open sewage. The gulf between rich and poor is never so wide that the stench is isolated completely. The walls help you shut your eyes to the haphazard jungle of paper shacks and the scrawny bodies of babies left untended by working mothers; it is difficult to close your ears to the moans of older folk dying of malnutrition; but this can be achieved as you find distraction in the screeching of sea gulls that somehow seem to have wandered off course and found El Montón oppressive. However, you can never get rid of the fetor, the stink that clings to your clothing and makes you want to retch and rush to your shower and send everything quickly, immediately, to the cleaners or to the fire.

Twenty-five thousand human beings are huddled in El Montón, yet in a fashion they boast an advantage over a similar district I saw 2,500 miles away in Recife, Northeast

Brazil. In Recife, where people live alongside a swamp, they must pay for their drinking water brought around by human carriers (one third of a cent a pail). But at least in El Montón a few community water taps have been linked with the main city supply. Actually, it is not necessary to go as far afield as Recife to see a mass of supposedly city dwellers living in bestially primitive conditions, without benefit of water or light or any of the amenities taken for granted even in China's overcrowded centers. A few miles from El Montón, on the outskirts of Lima, is Pampa de Comas, the largest of the *barriadas*, with a population of 80,000. Private vendors earn a sketchy livelihood selling water by the barrel; a fifty-gallon keg fetches four soles (sixteen cents), and a family will make this last for a week of drinking, cooking, and washing.

Walking through the dirt lanes of Pampa de Comas, and watching the water vendors hauling their carts while they shrilly proclaimed the sustenance they had to offer, I could not but think back to Shanghai in 1958. At that time a Communist guide escorted me through some of the worst quarters, and I remember the pride with which he motioned toward the rows of freshly installed communal water taps at street corners. In a way it was pathetic to find that water could take on such a precious meaning, but the taps did point up the advances of New China; and the water was free of harmful bacteria, and free of cost. Squads of sanitation inspectors and students also taught the rudiments of child care, with such startling results that a team of visiting British physicians was able to report in *The Lancet,* the medical journal, that in eight years the infant mortality rate in Shanghai had been cut by two thirds, so that it now stood at about thirty per 1,000 births: not much higher than the British figure of twenty-five. In the Western Hemisphere slums of Lima half the children are dead before the age of one.

Pampa de Comas takes its name from the *hacienda* it faces just across the highway. This privately owned plantation, right on the city border, covers 4,000 acres and draws its labor from the convenient *barriada*. At daybreak the workers walk across the paved road, into fields of cotton and maize, and at night they trudge back into nothingness, the men enriched by seventy-two cents each for thirteen hours of labor, the women by thirty-six cents. Other *haciendas* extend forty kilometers, through the Valley of Chillon, to the sea; and the workers of Pampa de Comas spend sixteen cents daily on bus transportation to get there; in all, there are six landowners, giving each an average farm five miles long and three miles wide.

Some of the residents of Pampa de Comas, of course, seek employment in the city itself. Roberto Huapaya, aged thirty-five, earns $36 a month as a stonemason hired by construction firms for Lima's new skyscrapers and tourist hotels. A thin, rather wan individual, Roberto told me: "I came down from the mountains to escape starvation and to find work." The same motive, according to a survey by a Canadian Catholic mission, is given by eight out of ten of the menfolk in the *barriada*. Most of the migrants from the Andes are Indians or *mestizos* (half-breeds of part-Indian, part-European blood). And it is quite true, as the *ricos* argue defensively, that the migrants' living conditions and hopes for advancement are somewhat better in a *barriada* than they were in the rocky hills. It is equally true that huge and costly housing developments would be required to match the influx into the city that has taken place in the last few years, and little has been done about this problem.

What makes the Roberto Huapaya of the city different from the Roberto Huapaya of the highlands is not merely economics or physical betterment. Indeed, Roberto and his family have today a little more security than yesterday. For instance, the Canadian church mission, composed of a priest and three nuns, runs a health clinic inside Pampa de Comas, so that Roberto's three surviving children (two died in infancy) can claim a greater than even chance of living beyond the age of forty-one, which is the life expectancy for the half-castes of Peru, and certainly in excess of the thirty-two years fated to the Andean Indians or the mulattoes of Brazil's shocking Northeast.[1] However, Roberto's real change is in his state of mind. "In the *sierra*," he said, "I was just one man. Now I am many men."

What he meant was this: Isolated in the Andes, removed from the impact of communications and world forces, Roberto felt that the individual had no power. In the year since his arrival in Pampa de Comas he has become aware of group strength. Sometimes in the evenings he and his neighbors sit around a kerosene lantern and discuss the phenomenon of what happens when men do band together. "In El Montón," Roberto recounted firmly, "they received taps for drinking water because they said they must have taps." (The residents of El Montón threatened to descend en masse on another open Lima site, where pipes were already laid, and to take over the land by squatting; municipal authorities, to prevent what might have developed into an ugly event, agreed to install a few community taps in the *barriada.*)

Roberto said: "We decided last night that we will demand water here, and electricity as well." I could not stay long enough to find out whether Roberto and his friends have had their demands accepted. The concessions, in any case, would not be significant, because even today there is no sense of urgency on the part of Peru's oligarchic rulers, partly because of unbelievably stupid blindness, partly because men such as Roberto have not yet become drunk with the power

[1] Just two years more than life expectancy in Roman times. In the United States today it is seventy years.

they have suddenly discovered. There is a slow, slow fuse beginning to burn; but Roberto, for one, still retains a kind of Indian stoicism and fatalism, which imply patience and resignation.

And yet there is conflict within him, for he has been brought, for the first time, in contact with strange but somewhat appealing ideas. Students from the University of San Marcos have, from week to week, dropped around to make studies of the people of Pampa de Comas, and told them, as Roberto relates it, "that socialism will bring us a better life." Roberto cannot describe socialism or communism. But, since there are a few radios in the *barriada*—and there were none in the Andes—he has finally heard of a man named Castro in a country called Cuba. "I have heard," he said to me, "that socialism in Cuba means liberation."

The liberation he talks about is liberation from want; for Roberto is starting to sense, according to the interpretation I gave his words, that abject poverty and indignity and hunger are not necessarily ordained. Somewhere in the remote outer world are men who have managed to evoke promises of more plentiful attainment—if not for themselves at least for their children. And Roberto, it must be remembered, has three children. The older son is twelve, and he works in the city as a messenger to help feed the family. Roberto's own wage of nine dollars a week does not pay fully for the beans and potatoes they eat regularly, with perhaps once a week a piece of fish, and for the barrels of water, the bus to town, and the rent of his hovel. Another highlander, who came down a few years ago, actually owns the hut.

It is a one-room shack; the room, about twelve feet by eight feet, is used for cooking and sleeping and all purposes; the walls are made of flattened tin containers; the stove in a corner is a pile of rocks cemented together. A crate serves as a table, and the only other furniture is a single bedstead, without mattress, on which Roberto and his wife sleep. The children sleep on sacking, which covers the earthen floor. There are no windows in the hut; but another piece of coarse sacking, across the doorway, can be drawn open to let in air and let out smoke from the stove. Roberto's younger son, Carlos, who is seven years old, goes to school, a squat adobe structure with benches but no desks. If the pattern for the majority of Peruvian children holds true, Carlos will spend no more than one year in school, because after that he will be needed to earn money. The middle child, a girl of nine, spends her hours searching in the rubbish of the *barriada* for scraps of metal that can be sold to salvage dealers, or she simply idles in the dust and garbage.

The stench lingers on your clothes and in your heart when you drive away from Pampa de Comas or El Montón. It is a short drive to San Isidro and the Country Club, and there you can inhale deeply and sit beside the immense pool and watch other children splash about eagerly and in ignorance of Roberto Huapaya's children. An ingenious concrete bridge spans one end of the pool, and tots, accompanied by nannies in starched uniforms, clamber onto it. Or they sit at tables set with linen and silverware, dipping their manicured fingers into platters of cream cakes and other goodies. A stunning woman, attired in clinging vivid green slacks and a dramatic pink silk blouse, leads three magnificent Great Danes on a multiple leash; as they cross the immaculate lawn, there are shrieks of delight from the children.

In all Latin America there are similarly striking contrasts of wealth and poverty, of vulgar opulence in a sea of misery. The degree varies, as I saw, from Rio de Janeiro to Managua, from Buenos Aires to Santo Domingo, from Caracas to Santiago; but the fundamentals are the same. Peru, however, possibly stands out as a classic example of a country with the elements of revolution, having inherited the rigid class structure of the old Inca Empire and the more recent tyrannies of Spain. It is said that no more than two dozen families control the wealth of a nation of twelve million; and, if this is a statistical inaccuracy, it is no exaggeration to say that 2 per cent from the rarefied upper strata are dominant; only a small middle class serves as a buffer between it and the huge indigent class.

In Lima I visited the home of a man who proudly showed me his art collection, including several paintings by Matisse and Picasso—and one of the biggest assemblages of privately held Inca gold objects in existence, worth between $5 million and $10 million. The early Spaniards, in their lustful looting of Inca temples and palaces, treasured golden masks and religious ornaments and golden breastplates, not for their beauty but for their material value. These precious items were melted into bullion and shipped to Spain. Some, however, survived in the original form; and now my host ushered me through a hall filled with showcase after showcase of golden necklaces and armor, of goblets and figurines. Speaking of the present-day descendants of the Incas, he said: "They are human cattle." (This was a phrase I heard also in the Northeast of Brazil, in reference to the mulattoes, and in other areas where men of power described the serfs they commanded.)

"Unfortunately," said my host, dryly, "we Peruvians were not born equal and never will be."

He spoke of the Indians today as being better off than they ever were in the past, though he also admitted, as an absentee landlord who owns a sugar plantation larger than all of Luxembourg, that they form a plentiful supply of cheap labor. I asked him what he thought of the feasibility of land reform. "Land reform," was the reply, "is big propaganda from Cuba and Russia. If we had land reform in Peru, we would grow less cotton and less sugar."

But does not the United States, in speaking of the Alliance for Progress, call for essential agrarian reform in South America? My host glanced through the window, into the spacious gardens below, and observed: "Much of the harm that is being done in South America today is the fault of North American news agencies, which use false figures, such as eighty dollars a year in Peru, to report on per capita income. This is nonsense, and dangerous." [2]

"Do you think," I asked, "that there might be a revolution here?"

"It could happen," he said, "because the masses are being propagandized by Cuba and Russia."

This, as I learned in five months of travel through the continent, was a gravely oversimplified statement. Cuba and the Soviet Union are indeed active in spreading propaganda; but communism, as we understand it, is not the immediate curse. Communist parties in most Latin American countries are small, disunited, and relatively powerless. There is no evidence that they are responding, or are even capable of doing so, to cunning master plans developed in the Kremlin and transmitted by push button. The situation would be perhaps easier to grasp, and more in keeping with our preconceived notions, if we could hear an omnipotent, remote voice saying: "Let there be a revolution tomorrow in Peru . . . or in Chile . . . or in Ecuador." The situation, in fact, is far more subtle than this, and therefore the more difficult to comprehend and to alter.

In isolated hamlets in the Peruvian Andes half the Indians have never heard of Peru, much less of communism. And yet, like their cousins of Tequendama, they have moved in on farmland that they felt they should possess, have been shot at and killed by state police, and stubbornly managed to hold on to the land. In the Northeast of Brazil, where a cane cutter earns fifteen cents a day and pays twelve cents for a pound of black beans, there is chronic hunger. There

[2] In fact, the per capita income in Peru is $119 a year.

are also humble men unknown to the outside world, among them priests, teachers, lawyers, who have started to organize the region's twenty-five million Negroes and mulattoes in a primitive drive for human rights. I met the same kind of men in a score of countries. These men are not Communists; in most cases their movements have sprung up spontaneously. Their label should be "social reformers." But they will tell you, bluntly, that if the present order will not provide essential, rudimentary needs, then they will look to any promising system, whether it is called fascism, Fidelismo, or communism.

This is the real danger. The United States government is well aware of it, and through the Alliance for Progress—a superb but handicapped plan—is willing to lavish billions of dollars on Latin America. No outpouring of generous wealth, however, will have any substantial meaning, or penetrate deeply enough, unless Latin America's own members of the aristocracy and oligarchy undergo a basic transformation in mentality. The dilemma no longer is whether these men will change but whether there is time.

In the old colonial center of Quito, Ecuador, I visited a famous cemetery filled with elaborate and expensive family vaults, ornate statuary, and chapels. This has none of the somber atmosphere expected in a cemetery, and in fact is a tourist attraction. Alongside it, and beyond the same main gate, is the burial ground for *los pobres* (the poor), as my guide, a student, pointed out. There the grass is untended, and the weeds almost hide the wooden crosses or simple stakes. "Even in death," said my guide wryly, "life is different for the rich."

2

Palace Revolts, Flour, Semantics

WHEN PRINCE PHILIP, the Duke of Edinburgh, made a tour of South America last year, he put his finger—perhaps unwittingly but more likely with his well-known sense of deviltry—on one of the continent's lesser though significant evils. Introduced to a Venezuelan farm-union leader, Philip stepped back and said, "Come now, you're not in agriculture: your hands are too soft."

There is a disdain for manual labor inherited from the original Spanish noblemen, and prevalent today not only among the upper class but among those in the middle category who aspire to emulate or join their social and economic peers. In this respect, Latin America as a whole can claim a kinship with pre-Communist China; the old-style mandarins also frowned on any kind of toil that soiled the fingers.

But other parallels are even more ominous. Lavish United States gifts of food for Chinese flood and drought victims, before 1949, often did not reach their intended recipients, ending instead on the black market. In 1960 the southern part of Chile suffered a disastrous earthquake that killed 2,500 men, women, and children, and left tens of thousands homeless and without nourishment. Prompt loads of flour and other essentials were airlifted from the United States. Long after, almost two years later, I was having dinner in the home of a foreign diplomat in Santiago, when his wife murmured to me: "You will enjoy these hot biscuits more, I am sure, than you would have the last batch." She explained: Her cook was in the habit of ordering flour by the sack, and one day a shipment arrived with the stenciled exhortation that this was a gift from the United States of America and not for sale. In Latin-American terms, as formerly in Chinese, this was far from an isolated example of relief supplies moving through corrupt official channels to commercial vendors.

Another likeness is discouraging. In China, men of means transferred their funds to banks in Switzerland and the United States, denuding their homeland's economy and self-confidence, and contributing to Chiang Kai-shek's downfall. In Latin America today, despite massive United States dollar assistance and loans, the exodus of capital is greater than the inflow. At the same time, not a single Latin-American country makes it a criminal offense to evade income taxes.

Behind much of Latin America's malaise is an egotistical philosophy introduced by the Portuguese and Spanish *conquistadores,* an attitude of mind repugnant to present-day North Americans. North America once had its robber barons who lived on a greedy, irresponsible basis. Today, however, whether because of force of society or inner compulsion, there is a code of social responsibility: so-called "American capitalists" contribute to welfare agencies; their wives do volunteer work. This code of social responsibility is lacking in Latin America, which, while pushing into the industrial era, has yet to graduate morally into the twentieth century.

Historians have an explanation for it; the sociologists rationalize about it. In almost every book I read before first visiting the region, I noted recurrent references to one attractive feature bequeathed by the Portuguese and Span-

civil war, into a single and powerful nation. A smaller group of Spanish colonies, following their break from European control in the first quarter of the nineteenth century, showed anarchist tendencies, engaged in a series of boundary disputes and wars among themselves, to emerge as a score of relatively small and weak nations. Only Portuguese Brazil, which had undergone a less rigorous colonial policy, managed to cling together as a unit.

The leaders of the new states acted with far less self-assurance than the Founding Fathers of the United States. They had taken no part in political affairs during the centuries of viceregal dictates, and, with only a minor say in running municipalities, lacked experience in public administration. Only a small percentage of the inhabitants were of European descent; the rest, who needed direction after generations in serfdom or slavery, composed a heterogeneous and ragged collection of *mestizos* and Indians, Negroes, and mulattoes. In a milder fashion the plundering *conquistadores* were replaced by another breed of exploiters, ambitious and impatient businessmen of Western Europe and the United States. This was the shape of Latin America.

I was determined to explore the issues and aspirations of Latin America not as a North American, but, theoretically, as a Latin American might like to see his present problems and the reasons for them. Obviously, it is impossible for an alien to project himself with whole success into a foreign environment; and, no matter how good the intentions, there are bound to be areas where understanding is not accompanied by sympathy; there are inescapable times when a North American finds himself behaving and reacting like a North American.

For example, what excuse can be laid at history's door for the callous attitude toward the waifs who wander the streets of Santiago and Bogotá? There are hundreds of them, homeless and parentless, who roam the cities by day and night in complete abandonment, misery, and dirt. Like stray cats, boys and girls of six years and upward forage through dumps or sniff for scraps of food. In the traffic jams of rush hour they dart among the halted cars and wipe windshields in the hope of collecting a few *centavos*. In the night rain, half-naked and shivering, they stand outside theaters with hands outstretched. And then they retreat to their cardboard and tin shacks, or simply wrap themselves in newspapers and huddle in doorways for a few hours of sleep. In Bogotá they are known disdainfully as *gamins,* though the purists in language prefer to call them *pelafustanillos* (little hoboes). "Look, fellow," said an eleven-year-old, "everybody hates us, nobody wants to take care of us. The only thing we can do is to beg and be bothersome."

In Santiago a North American resident told how she had seen a boy, possibly aged ten, prostrate in the gutter, ashen faced and gasping—showing every appearance of grave illness. She begged passers-by to help, but they ignored her—and the boy. Finally she got hold of a policeman and asked him to call an ambulance. The policeman glanced at the boy, said that probably he did not possess a health card and therefore was not entitled to assistance, and anyway the likelihood was that he was going to die. The North American retreated, feeling helpless and bewildered and indignant.

Shortly after hearing of this episode, I went to LAN Chilean Airlines to pick up a ticket for La Paz. The girl behind the counter said that I could not claim my reservation until I produced a vaccination certificate; so I returned to my hotel to hunt for it. The girl explained that the airline might be heavily fined if documents were not absolutely in order.

I cited this incident several times in my travels to point out to Latin Americans what I considered odd values; a boy could be left to die, but on the other hand there had to be

iards: a lack of a color line. It is true that the majority of people are of mixed blood and that, in theory, hue of complexion is no restriction to advancement. But in practice, most of the men of influence, of the aristocracy, are "white" and make a point of preserving the family lineage by marrying women of the same eugenic and economic backgrounds. Brazil is often held up as an example of a country with an enlightened racial harmony, because the tones range from pure white to *amarelinho* (high yellow), *caboclo* (white-Indian), and *cafuso* (coffee-brown) to plain *preto* or black. But no *preto* ever considers walking up to the registration desk of Rio's luxurious Copacabana Palace Hotel. On the Copacabana itself, the famous public beach that offers miles of free sand and sunshine, the tacit understanding is that no "white" man will deign to show himself after two-thirty in the afternoon; that is the time for the descent of hordes of Negroes and mulattoes. In Rio I was told by a cynical but observant Brazilian: "A Negro washes the car, a mulatto chauffeur opens the door, and a white man steps inside."

The historians are right about one thing. Latin America is sometimes unjustly condemned by North Americans who think of their own pioneers and fail to take into account a different ancestry and motive for settlement in the New World. The Pilgrim Fathers sailed from Plymouth to seek freedom of worship; and those who followed were prepared to work constructively and industriously, to shape a future *on* the land which they dug themselves. The *conquistadores* who arrived in Hispanic America were no less brave; they fought hostile forces, and tropical diseases, and difficult terrain unknown even to the early North American settlers (one has only to drive through the mountains of Mexico or Peru to marvel how Spanish soldiers, weighted by armor breastplates, were able to penetrate them). But here the similarity ends. The Spanish conquerors came to wrest *from* the land, to pillage the treasure houses, and to ship their gains back to the Old World at the expense of the New. They, too, were motivated partly by religion: a zeal to evangelize, to spread Roman Catholicism beyond the shores of Europe. But the clergy who accompanied the nobility together formed the same wealthy upper classes as in Spain, and neither could be said to possess the ideals of liberalism finding shape among the Anglo-Saxons.

The sixteenth-century traditions and values the Spaniards brought with them were already beginning to lead to decay and decrepitude in Spain itself. Spain had emerged triumphantly from a long series of wars, but an idle nobility was fostering political disorder and living on administrative graft while others provided cheap labor. The essence of life was quick gain; frequently it was through bad and corrupt government or despotic repression. Huge landed estates in Spain, *latifundios,* which concentrated farming and grazing in a few hands, held back the growth of a middle class and hindered economic development. Summing up this period, J. Fred Rippy [1] says: "Spanish contempt for manual toil, Spanish love of display and fondness for military adventure and official position, profoundly influenced the character and history of the colonies."

Rippy argues that the record was not entirely negative; the Spaniards taught the Indians skills, built cities, and transplanted culture. It can also be argued, however, that they destroyed a thriving Inca civilization. Their main economic effort as they hacked their way up and down the Pacific coast was to search for the sacred lake of El Dorado (the Gilded One), the elusive Indian chieftain who was thought to throw gold objects into the waters. This quest could hardly be considered capital investment in more

[1] *Latin America, A Modern History,* The University of Michigan Press, 1958.

lasting forms of production. The first Spaniard to record his sight of Cuzco, the great Inca capital, spoke not of Indian achievement but of a city ablaze with gold. As a sample, he reported he saw a "quadrangular building... measuring three hundred and fifty paces from corner to corner, entirely plated with gold; of these gold plates [we] took down seven hundred which together weighed five hundred pesos of gold...."

Failing to locate El Dorado himself, the Spaniards looked for large concentrations of subdued Indians who could be transformed into slave laborers.[2] Some of the Indians were forced down from the Andean plateaus to perish on tropical *latifundios;* others were pushed up from the coast to die as miners. In an incredibly short period, millions were dead, and the Spaniards wrecked one of the most elaborate agricultural organizations in history. The Inca highland empire had provided abundant support for twenty-five to thirty million people, largely through scientific strip contour farming. An intricate network of warehouses kept food in reserve for times of drought or crop failures, so that while Indians may go hungry today, they had security and were amply fed five hundred years ago.

The Incas did not know of the horse or the wheel, but communications were better then than they are in many parts of present-day Peru or Ecuador. Swift *chasqui*-couriers could run messages in relays between Quito and Cuzco, a distance of 1,250 miles at an altitude ranging between 6,000 and 17,000 feet, in five days. Today in the Andes a letter between two similar points takes up to three weeks, if it is delivered at all. Under Inca engineers many types of *chacas,* or bridges—suspension, pontoon, cantilever, of wood and rope—spanned the deep ravines. The most noted was

[2] Meanwhile the Portuguese, whose first white settlers included criminals or unwilling conscripts, were importing African slaves into their more thinly populated territories on the Atlantic coast.

the fiber-cable structure over the formidable gorge and river of the Apurimac; it has entered literary history as *The Bridge of San Luis Rey.* Under the Spaniards the *chacas* were left in disrepair or used until they simply decomposed, and in a way the collapse of the bridge of San Luis Rey is symbolic of the whole wanton colonial period.

Driving through hundreds of miles of the Peruvian valleys, in the midst of what had once been a wonderland of agriculture, I could now see primitive instead of advanced Indians working on pathetically tiny individual plots or turning the soil in obscurity for the big landowners in the cities. At Macchu Picchu, the mountaintop sanctuary of the Inca rulers and probably the most awe-inspiring sight in South America, I looked down upon hanging gardens carved in the sharp hillsides; in the fifteenth century they were watered by aqueducts, to yield *sara,* or corn, and other crops. The feat of building Macchu Picchu high in the Andean clouds was never matched by any material accomplishment of the Spaniards. All up and down the Pacific coast it is the same story of senseless plunder and disintegration.

What was the legacy of the Spaniards? Whenever I asked this question of Latin Americans, I was told almost invariably: "They left us a good language; that is all." There were, of course, grandsons and great-grandsons of the *conquistadores* who revolted against Spain, but not necessarily because of social evils. Their fight was against an absolute monarchy that functioned through such institutions as the viceroyalty, the captaincy general, and the *audencia* (royal judiciary), and was far more despotic than any rule experienced by the thirteen English colonies to the north. Aside from any divergence in the character of the peoples involved, the big difference between the struggles in North America and Latin America was this: the thirteen English colonies finally united, after a period of political strife and civil war, into a single and powerful nation. A smaller group of Spanish colonies, following their break from European control in the first quarter of the nineteenth century, showed anarchist tendencies, engaged in a series of boundary disputes and wars among themselves, to emerge as a score of relatively small and weak nations. Only Portuguese Brazil, which had undergone a less rigorous colonial policy, managed to cling together as a unit.

The leaders of the new states acted with far less self-assurance than the Founding Fathers of the United States. They had taken no part in political affairs during the centuries of viceregal dictates, and, with only a minor say in running municipalities, lacked experience in public administration. Only a small percentage of the inhabitants were of European descent; the rest, who needed direction after generations in serfdom or slavery, composed a heterogeneous and ragged collection of *mestizos* and Indians, Negroes, and mulattoes. In a milder fashion the plundering *conquistadores* were replaced by another breed of exploiters, ambitious and impatient businessmen of Western Europe and the United States. This was the shape of Latin America.

I was determined to explore the issues and aspirations of Latin America not as a North American, but, theoretically, as a Latin American might like to see his present problems and the reasons for them. Obviously, it is impossible for an alien to project himself with whole success into a foreign environment; and, no matter how good the intentions, there are bound to be areas where understanding is not accompanied by sympathy; there are inescapable times when a North American finds himself behaving and reacting like a North American.

For example, what excuse can be laid at history's door for the callous attitude toward the waifs who wander the streets of Santiago and Bogotá? There are hundreds of them, homeless and parentless, who roam the cities by day and night in complete abandonment, misery, and dirt. Like stray cats, boys and girls of six years and upward forage through dumps or sniff for scraps of food. In the traffic jams of rush hour they dart among the halted cars and wipe windshields in the hope of collecting a few *centavos*. In the night rain, half-naked and shivering, they stand outside theaters with hands outstretched. And then they retreat to their cardboard and tin shacks, or simply wrap themselves in newspapers and huddle in doorways for a few hours of sleep. In Bogotá they are known disdainfully as *gamins*, though the purists in language prefer to call them *pelafustanillos* (little hoboes). "Look, fellow," said an eleven-year-old, "everybody hates us, nobody wants to take care of us. The only thing we can do is to beg and be bothersome."

In Santiago a North American resident told how she had seen a boy, possibly aged ten, prostrate in the gutter, ashen faced and gasping—showing every appearance of grave illness. She begged passers-by to help, but they ignored her—and the boy. Finally she got hold of a policeman and asked him to call an ambulance. The policeman glanced at the boy, said that probably he did not possess a health card and therefore was not entitled to assistance, and anyway the likelihood was that he was going to die. The North American retreated, feeling helpless and bewildered and indignant.

Shortly after hearing of this episode, I went to LAN Chilean Airlines to pick up a ticket for La Paz. The girl behind the counter said that I could not claim my reservation until I produced a vaccination certificate; so I returned to my hotel to hunt for it. The girl explained that the airline might be heavily fined if documents were not absolutely in order.

I cited this incident several times in my travels to point out to Latin Americans what I considered odd values; a boy could be left to die, but on the other hand there had to be adherence to inconsequential regulations. The response varied, depending on the position of the person with whom I was talking. Wealthier people, *ricos,* said the boy in the gutter was almost certainly pulling an act to arouse sympathy and gain a handout; reformers agreed that it was an example of what was wrong in Latin America, a need for proper social consciousness. Others merely shrugged their shoulders and said, "What could we do about it?" They had problems of their own.

Underlying the attitude, however, is a disregard for human life as we think of it in North America, unless the life is that of a family member. In this respect another parallel can be drawn with China, where honor, brothers, and cousins must be protected no matter what the sacrifice; otherwise, life is cheap. In Nicaragua I met a man whose brother had had six bullets pumped into him by a political foe. Miraculously he survived; but the would-be assassin, said the Nicaraguan with a sly grin, later was found butchered to death. "I, of course," he said with another knowing smile, "had nothing to do with it."

In Rio de Janeiro one day, sitting in the back seat of a taxi, I saw a pedestrian struck by a car in the lane next to us; the man was flung against our fender. The car that had hit him did not pause, and other vehicles simply swung past the crumpled form on the road. I shouted at my driver to halt. He picked up speed, instead, and later explained he did not want to be bothered by questions from the police. In Brazil, as in some other countries, the law says that the first man on the scene of an accident is held responsible unless he can prove his innocence.

There are indeed strange values in this part of the world. Some of these values revolve around the word *vivo,* which means "shrewd" or "sharp." A Canadian, visiting the home of a prominent industrialist in Buenos Aires, was treated to a story: The Argentine's son Arturo, aged twelve, was bicycling along the street one day with a friend when they spotted in the curbside what looked like a 500-peso bill. Arturo leaped off his bike, snatched up the object, crumpled and tossed it back contemptuously, and said to his friend: "It is only a scrap of paper." It was in fact a 500-peso bill. Later, when his friend had gone, Arturo returned to the spot and retrieved the money.

The father proudly recounted the incident in front of his son, tapping the boy's forehead and commenting, *"Vivo."* The moral was that it was better to take a chance, and gamble that no one else would meanwhile stumble on the money, than to consider sharing.

The main paradox of Latin America is this: the men who are expected to introduce basic reforms, members of the oligarchy and government in each country, would in the process be committing financial suicide. They go through the motions of saying that they accept United States requirements such as agrarian and income-tax reforms, and giving assurances that United States funds will not end in already heavily laden individual pockets, but in practice they conduct themselves much as in the past. Since 1945 Brazil has had ninety-two land reform bills before its Congress; every one of the bills, including the most recent in response to the Alliance for Progress, has been killed by land-owning members of Congress.

It is, admittedly, unreasonable to lump together all Latin America. Marked economic differences exist even within a single country. In Brazil's Northeast the *flagelados* (those who are whipped) live off cactus in times of drought; but in the rich agricultural and industrial heartland of São Paulo millions of people have already crossed the subsistence threshold. Latin America cannot be considered even a geographic unit, let alone a political one. It includes not only South America (with the exception of British Guiana, Surinam, and French Guiana) but also Mexico, which is part of

North America. It takes in all Central America, aside from British Honduras, and several of the Caribbean islands. In the process it spans every type of climate known to man. Elongated Chile, for instance, has deserts in the north and ice fields in the south. Sixteen of the twenty independent republics are situated entirely or mainly in the tropics, a point residents are quick to make when they talk of depressing heat, matted jungles, and pestilent insects that debilitate them and not North Americans. (In fact, however, many of these states have large areas at invigorating high altitudes.)

The term Latin America, or Hispanic America, alludes to the influence of Spain and Portugal, but even here there must be an exception: the language of Haiti is neither Spanish nor Portuguese; it is French. And even where Spanish is spoken, as it is in eighteen of the countries, it not only differs widely from the Castilian of Spain but from the version used by a neighboring state. In the illiterate Andean lands of Bolivia, Ecuador, and Peru entire Indian and *mestizo* populations are unable even to speak the official tongue. About the only thing that can be said without qualification is that Latin America is big, covering one sixth of the earth's land surface. Brazil alone is almost as large as the United States; Chile's border would stretch from New York to San Francisco; Bolivia is the size of Texas and California combined.

The variety in physical shapes is accompanied by multiplicity in human energy and sometimes in temperament. The half-literate *cariocas* of Rio de Janeiro, with a handsome beach at their elbows, are happy-go-lucky in the midst of political crises; and if Brazil overextends herself, by assembling automobiles uneconomically or erecting Brasília at the price of near-bankruptcy, so what? On the other hand, the people of Argentina, who are largely a cultured middle class of European origin, have managed to attain much the same industrial production and per capita income as Canada of a generation ago.

Brazilians and Argentines, rivals for a position of pre-eminence on the continent, speak loathingly of one another. Erudite Colombians, who are jealous of the more prosperous oil-endowed Venezuelans, say sneeringly: "Venezuelans fell out of trees into Cadillacs." Paraguay and Bolivia as recently as 1935 fought a war that killed 100,000 of their young men and left their economies impoverished. Bolivia, while I was there, was still arguing—this time with Chile—over the rights to a waterway, the Lauca River; the dispute set off street riots in La Paz and a break in diplomatic relations. The disparities among Latin Americans, in many directions, are indeed noteworthy, as they themselves hasten to emphasize in trying to arouse a North American understanding that each country is distinctive.

And yet, despite the variations, some common denominators are paramount, because they touch on explosive social problems in almost every one of the twenty republics. More than half of Latin Americans are chronically undernourished and hungry, and some of them live under conditions worse than any I saw in China a few years ago. Most people possess nothing but their simple clothing (half the Brazilians have no shoes) and a decrepit chair or two; any hope of owning more is necessarily slight among human beings with a per capita income of only $280 a year. But even this figure is deceptive, since the statisticians divide among the many the billions of dollars owned by the few. At least half, and probably closer to two thirds, do not rank in the statistics as consumers at all; these are the men and women in the rural areas who exist on what they can grow on minuscule patches, and in the cities, on what they pick up in scrap heaps.

Although 60 per cent of all Latin Americans are engaged in agriculture, the bulk of the arable soil—three quarters of it—is owned by a landlord class numbering 2 per cent. Similarly, the mines, the oil fields, the utilities, when not under the control of foreign investors, are owned mostly by a thin layer of wealthy families. In essence, the feudal design created by the *conquistadores* persists, with minor modifications, to this day. Six out of every ten Latin Americans cannot read or write (in Haiti, nine out of ten) and most children do not go beyond second grade in school. "Even if there was a classroom," said a harassed woman in Guatemala, "how could I send my daughter? She has no clothing to wear."

If there are few schools, there are many tanks and guns and jet fighter planes. Some states spend half their budgets on the armed forces; Argentina got an aircraft carrier, so Brazil had to get one. "Our country is not in any danger of attack," said a Peruvian. "The real function of the army is to protect the oligarchy from the people." Peruvian officials argue that their soldiers are put to use building roads, and this only points up another glaring deficiency. All Latin America has a smaller network of highways than France alone; Bolivia has only a three-hundred-mile paved stretch, built with United States funds. Canada, with one tenth the population, boasts more cars than the whole of South America. Brazil's tiny, ramshackle railway system runs over fewer miles than Belgium's; it operates on five different gauges, and most of the engines burn wood.

South American reformers talk lustily of the immense wealth that lies inland for the taking, once communications are put in order. Great untapped reservoirs of energy are to be found in oil and hydroelectric power; the continent can claim the biggest storehouse of timber in the world, uncalculated deposits of virtually every chemical required by industry, of every metal, base or rare. It has at least three times as much fertile land, per head, as Asia. But the men with money, in control, consider it far more agreeable to draft blueprints for a factory than to tackle the obstinate burden of an archaic and inefficient land-tenure system; it is less hazardous to manufacture textiles, or even refrigerators, than to venture into the uncertain and uncomfortable tropical belts where the real frontiers await opening. After all, in São Paulo or Caracas or Santiago you can make from 24 to 36 per cent interest a year on your capital.

Wealthy Brazilians and Venezuelans and Chileans say they must insist on a quick return for unreliable currency; and it is true that inflation sometimes cuts profits in half, leaving still an appreciable amount. In Chile the cost of living rose fourteenfold from 1953 to 1962; in Argentina ninefold. But why the inflation? In part it is because of chaotic politics and planning, but it is also because governments refuse to enforce equitable tax measures that would affect their oligarchic members.[3] Some countries have simply printed more and more money to meet their needs. Even in those states that have succeeded in keeping their currency reasonably stable, the hangover from inflationary days lingers; the rich have yet to be convinced that it is patriotic or wise to invest in their nation's long-range development. If it comes to smaller yields they prefer the safety of banks abroad.

Ironically, the *ricos* are afraid of the future because the same spiraling prices that have made them richer have made the poor poorer and spread more germs for social disorder. In the few weeks I was in Brazil, the *cruzeiro* dropped 30 per cent in value. A night watchman spent one quarter of his wage merely getting to and from work. Bank clerks in Rio, few of whom were Communists or even sympathizers,

[3] In Venezuela in 1962 a man with a personal income of $100,000 paid $8,000 in taxes; in Canada or the United States he would have paid more than $50,000.

went on strike bearing placards: "Less whisky for the rich, more bread for the poor."

In Bolivia's capital, La Paz, a local journalist arranged a midnight meeting for me with Mario Gutiérrez, the leader of the rightist Falange Party. It was not exactly a cloak-and-dagger affair; but, since Gutiérrez, a strident opponent of the government, had only two weeks previously returned from exile, he said he had to be careful. And so the rendezvous was in the apartment of a third party, up some creaky stairs and through a darkened hallway. Gutiérrez covered, in two hours, complaints ranging from the reform policies of President Paz Estenssoro to what he called the "Communist" attitude of the United States in fostering reform ideas. At the end, he took a flashlight from his pocket.

"I closed all the lights in my house," he explained, "because this afternoon in Congress I said some nasty things about the government, and maybe someone is waiting to beat me up. It is better to enter unseen." Then, from his other pocket, Gutiérrez extracted an automatic and tested the safety catch.

The point about the story was not the quiet drama but the fact that a political enemy had indeed come back from banishment, and, although still a little uneasy, was able to function at all. Contrary to North American misconception, Latin-American politicians do not always execute their rivals, nor do they bear grudges. There is a great degree of sophistication involved, largely out of self-protection; no political chief really knows today whether he will be out tomorrow. And the ground rules take this into account.

General Gustavo Rojas Pinilla was a vain and despised dictator of Colombia; he was deposed on May 10, 1957, and promptly flew to the sanctuary of Spain. A year later, believing he still had a following, Rojas returned to Bogotá. A similar act in a European country just recovering from the effects of a corrupt and brutal rule would have been considered foolish, at the least, and more likely suicidal. But Rojas was simply stripped of "political rights," which meant that he could not run for any office. Instead, in the 1962 presidential contest, he actively campaigned on behalf of his former minister of the interior, who had also been chief of the hated secret police and, like Rojas, had experienced foreign asylum. Rojas' man lost, but Rojas received 47,842 write-in votes, though they were invalid and he himself could not vote. Such, to North American despair, are the caprices of Latin-American politics.

Another dictator, Manuel Odría of Peru, outlawed the country's strongest party, APRA, among whose noted disciples was Dr. Luis Alberto Sánchez. While in forced seclusion in Chile, Sánchez received word of his father's death in Lima. He telegraphed the Peruvian minister of the interior for permission to return home for the funeral. Twenty-four hours later the minister, a first cousin, wired back: "Obviously there is not enough time now for your return. Deepest sympathy and best regards." In telling me of this incident, Dr. Sánchez, who became rector again of the venerable University of San Marcos in a change of government, said: "I carry no enmity. I see Odría, and even my cousin, quite often socially. We like to think we are civilized in Peru."

Semantics, quite obviously, take on distinctive vagaries in Latin America, and this applies to several phases of political and social life. One of the first diplomats I met, a Pole, said: "The best advice I can give you is to forget all the definitions that obtain in other parts of the world, such as 'right wing' or 'left wing.' " This, as I soon discovered, was shrewd counsel. There is in our sense no methodical way of placing a label on ideological elements in Latin America, nor on loyalties.

Oswaldo Filho threw many alleged Communists in jail

when he was chief of police in Recife a few years ago. Later, as a congressman representing this principal city in Brazil's Northeast, he began preaching radical reforms. Asked why he now talked like the men he once imprisoned, he grinned and replied: "I've grown up." The inconsistency may be attributed to expediency, but it may also be nothing more than a revision of definitions. Early in 1961 a Brazilian cabinet minister assured a North American envoy that communism was no threat in Brazil; what he feared more, he said, were upheavals in Paraguay, Uruguay, or British Guiana which could sweep across the border and infect Brazil. Six months later, during the crisis caused by the unexpected resignation of President Jânio Quadros, the same minister talked tremulously of government offices "riddled with Communists." Stated simply, a man who is against what you stand for is often a "Communist," or, conversely, an "imperialist reactionary." In each case he may be, by our terms of reference, a genuine liberal; but this does not matter.

Alfonso López Michelsen, head of the left wing of Colombia's Liberal Party, put it this way: "Our wealthy class does not really understand what communism means. If the maid walks off with the silver, they say she is a Communist. In the same way, 90 per cent of the people of Latin America haven't the slightest idea of what the United States means by capitalism, or at least the kind that exists in the United States. To them, from experience with their own capitalists and some North Americans, the word just stands for exploitation." One must even be careful with the use of "nationalize." In North America or Europe the expression usually connotes a public takeover of industries or utilities. A Latin American who talks about "nationalization" often signifies he is in favor only of controlling foreign holdings in his country, not domestic. Thus a "nationalist" in Brazil is neither a socialist nor a rabid fanatic but someone who believes that the billion-dollar Canadian-owned Brazilian Traction Company should be made purely Brazilian.

The word *democracía* is also misleading and is covered by sham and a façade. Aside from Paraguay, all South American countries are supposed to be democracies. But in Brazil there are only twelve million eligible voters in an adult population of more than thirty-five million; the others are barred because of literacy tests and various devices deliberately invoked by upper echelons to keep their own command secure. In Chile, voters are required to register four months in advance of an election. Some *fundo* owners who disapprove of their laborers' political leanings do not give them the necessary time off for registration; other people are penalized when they move from the countryside to the cities in search of jobs. The result is that in a nation that is considered one of the most advanced politically in Latin America, some 30 per cent of Chileans are disfranchised.

It can be argued, of course, that elections in our sense are meaningless anyway, since governments are replaced more by military coups than they are by the electorate. Even the Spanish word *revolución* has nothing of the English implication of fundamental change. With the exception of Mexico, which started its social transformation a half century ago, Bolivia which began in 1952, and, more recently, Cuba, the revolutions that have taken place in Latin America have been political rather than benevolent or ideological. Mostly they are "palace revolts" or "barracks rebellions" or other mutinies which involve changes in personnel and not changes in beliefs or values. The switch is carried out entirely within the existing system. Tiny Ecuador, for instance, has had some thirty presidents and ruling *juntas* in the last twenty-five years, but has yet to demonstrate a capacity to change the old order.

One group moves out, another group moves in, and with constant repetition of the process it is not surprising that government stability is rare. And, since Latin Americans are prone to nepotism, massive shifts in the civil service sometimes accompany alterations in leadership. Relatives as well as supporters must be given jobs. But again it is an error to think of a "civil service" in North American or European terms. France averaged a new government every six months for several years after World War II, but the state apparatus was so ingrained, public administration had so impressed its characteristics on the whole structure of the country, that dislocations were slight. The strength of France is that it is able to survive one crisis after another because of its permanent civil service. In Latin America generally the army is the only agency with any sort of continuity.

One inevitable result is waste and inefficiency. A United Nations expert, sent to Colombia to help streamline government office operations, reports that staffs are about half as productive as their North American counterparts. The poor quality of work begins with the selection; in Bogotá each ministry hires its own people; there is no coordination of standards or requirements through a central bureau. It ends in the cult that scorns "manual" labor; no stenographer will dishonor herself by carrying a file from one side of the room to the other; this has to be done by a menial, a messenger.

A lack of proper organization cuts into virtually every phase of Latin America's public administration. A Scotland Yard officer, on a tour to advise on police operations, told me of a simple but graphic example: Not a single South American country maintains a central bureau for criminal records. What happens, for instance, in Peru or Bolivia is that town and rural police keep their own records, but copies are not sent to the capitals. When a suspected criminal is picked up in Lima or La Paz there is no way of checking on his past, short of despatching a message to scores of police stations scattered through thousands of miles of hinterland.

If the bureaucratic machine is inefficient, it is at any rate big, because of the custom of rewarding friends and relatives with sinecures. Argentina, a nation of twenty millions, has 1.3 million government employees, largely the legacy of Perón.[4] Even Bolivia, despite attempts at reforms, has been unable to shake off the inordinate red tape of a civil service swollen out of all proportion to needs. In order to leave the country, I first had to go to a government department in La Paz where one man glanced at my passport, handed it to a man at the next desk who entered my name in a ledger, and, in turn, gave it to a third man who stamped it: this aside from later airport formalities. Part of the explanation rests in the hard fact of life that wages are so low that a man must hold down two or even three jobs simultaneously if he is to survive, and the state provides an easy outlet.

This leads to the unavoidable question of corruption. If in La Paz your house is robbed, the police arrive and say: "Well, we have no car. If we had a car, or even a motorcycle, we might be able to chase the burglars. Would you care to make a contribution toward a motorcycle?"

Asked about this hardly subtle form of extortion, an official replied: "What can you expect when a policeman doesn't earn enough to feed himself, let alone his wife and children?"

Customs officers in most countries are so frugally compensated that they regard bribes not as indecent but as indispensable. A United States television team, arriving in Rio de Janeiro to film a program about Brazil, underwent a commonplace experience. The network had been assured by the Brazilian Embassy in Washington that since its cameras and equipment would be taken out of Brazil, there

[4] Canada, with a slightly smaller population, has 440,000 federal and provincial employees.

would, of course, be no entry duty. Customs men on the spot did not dispute this point; they simply said they would require "time" to examine the equipment to be certain it did not include any contraband. Ten days elapsed, and the examination still had not taken place; every day of lost work was cutting into scheduled shooting and therefore represented a financial loss. Finally, the North Americans tumbled to the rites; a bribe of one hundred dollars was slipped to a customs inspector, and the television crew drove smartly away with their cameras.

Even when legal duties are called for and have been met, you still pay extra if you want prompt action. Some North American firms doing business in Argentina and Venezuela budget as high as 20 per cent of operating costs for necessary handouts; they figure this is cheaper than having supplies tied up in customs warehouses. But the big payoffs extend through cabinet ministers to presidents. While I was in one country, an indignant North American manufacturer of machinery told me how a presidential aide had approached him for an additional 5 per cent kickback, *after* a government contract had been signed. "I guaranteed enough in advance," said the businessman; "I'll be damned if they get more now." Then, calming down, he said reluctantly, "I suppose if I want to do business in the future I'd better go along with them."

The system works all the way up and down the line. I learned in Peru not to affix expensive stamps to airmail letters if I wanted to ensure delivery; underpaid postal clerks, who take their cue from higher officials, were likely to steal them (hotels provide meter machines for foreign guests). In Peru, universities collect part of their revenue from a special tax on imported Scotch whisky. Dr. Luis Alberto Sánchez estimates that ten times as much Scotch is consumed today as in 1946, when he was first rector of the University of San Marcos; but tax revenue is only about half as much. In other words, the bulk of whisky, at a lower price than the official, is smuggled into the country.

A Brazilian, whom I met at a cocktail party in Rio's fashionable Leblon district, openly traffics in contraband. His comment: "If an employee sees his boss engaged in smuggling millions of *cruzeiros'* worth of stuff into the country, he won't report it to the authorities. He hopes one day to be in a similar position where he can make some easy money." The Brazilian was saying in effect that a sense of public responsibility is lacking not only at the top but at the bottom of the economic or social ladder.

Smuggling began early on the continent; sixteenth-century seadogs and corsairs engaged in it as well as in piracy. By the seventeenth century the Portuguese alone were shipping out from Europe about two hundred vessels a year filled with contraband cargoes destined particularly for Spanish America. The hazards were slight, because Spanish governors not only accepted bribes but set up their own exclusive agencies to peddle the illegal articles. In some countries today the corruption can be said to be reasonably equitable, since it is spread among many officials at many levels; in this way it may be likened to the old Chinese system of "squeeze" which was relayed from the humblest *hsien* functionary along a chain to the emperor's men in Peking, with everyone sharing. But in other states there is a kind of centralization of graft. Nicaragua in 1962 was notable. No one made a move or considered setting up an industry without a direct payment to a representative of the ruling Somoza family, which ran Nicaragua like a private estate.

The corruption in Latin America is pervasive and digs its roots in history and economics. But, like all other statements dealing with this turbulent part of the world, there are exceptions. Costa Rica is situated next to Nicaragua, which has the most venal and depressing regime of Central America. And yet little Costa Rica is clean and refreshing, a Switzerland in an alien sea. Except for the Spanish language, you hardly feel you are in Latin America. There is honesty, self-discipline, and orderliness; the country is well administered, and past presidents do not wind up abroad with huge fortunes.

Costa Rica inherited none of the racial complexities of its bigger cousins to the south, but this is not the only reason for its stability and enlightenment. When I asked Ricardo Castro, editor of *La Nación,* for an explanation of why his country was different from the others, he pointed out that the *conquistadores* knew that El Dorado was not to be found here, and so they moved on, toward Venezuela, toward Peru. The Spaniards who colonized Costa Rica thought of it as a future home, not as a fortune chest to be smashed open. Costa Rica was free from the imprints of governors who introduced greed and theft, which have lingered to this day in most governments.

Ricardo Castro related an apocryphal but telling story of a viceroy in Peru who, questioned on how he was able to get away with so much graft, said simply: "The King is too far distant, and God is too high."

When I visited the United States Embassy in Caracas, workmen were still busy repairing the building that had been marred by a skilfully planted bomb only a few weeks earlier. The bomb was left in a seventh floor washroom adjacent to the ambassador's office. It went off to tear a hole in the wall, so that unplanned daylight streamed jarringly onto the sixth and seventh floors. No one, miraculously, was hurt, but the impact on morale was considerable. U.S. Marine guards now subjected all visitors to intensive scrutiny; no stranger could ascend any more with a bulky briefcase to the seventh floor, or to any other floor. The bomb was thought to be of Communist or possibly student origin, as a protest against anti-Castro action by the United States. But its derivation was not really as important as the point it made. Embassy people and the United States were reminded once again that the revived "good neighbor" policy does not carry with it an automatic guarantee that Latin Americans can forget the past.

Only one salient feature was different. A few decades ago even the stoning of a junior embassy official might have brought about armed reaction from the United States. Today the United States, at least in theory, proscribes the use of force in interhemisphere affairs. But for many Latin Americans, particularly students and intellectuals, pronouncements of nonintervention are to be distrusted, especially since the thinly disguised invasion attempt of Cuba in 1961. For these Latin Americans the shadow of U.S. Marines still seems more ominous than any threat from Fidel Castro. This is an intricacy that North Americans must bear in mind in trying to look logically at the moods and sensibilities of the people. The discontent of Latin Americans revolves not only around their own deficiencies but around all forces they consider to dominate them, including the United States.

The reasons for doubting United States intentions are steeped in history and are varied. Mexicans still talk of "the lost territories of the North," Texas, New Mexico, and other parts of the United States Southwest, annexed by the United States in the nineteenth century; they talk of "aggression" in this century when President Wilson, responding to a misguided American moment of pique because some United States sailors had been arrested by Mexicans, ordered the occupation of Vera Cruz; two hundred Mexican soldiers and twenty-one U.S. Marines died as a result. Colombians speak of the "treachery" of President Theodore Roosevelt in promoting a revolution in Panama, which declared itself independent of Colombia, so the United States could get its hands on the Canal Zone. And the people of Guatemala,

Nicaragua, and the Dominican Republic cry out about the neo-colonialism of the United States, which installed governments or manipulated their affairs to some degree even in the second half of the twentieth century. Ecuador still accuses the United States of forcing it to cede the equivalent of almost half its territory to Peru in 1942, after an invasion by its far stronger Andean neighbor.

Whether or not these historical complaints are justified in full, the one inclination Latin Americans have in common is that they blame the United States; anti-Americanism is possibly the only area in which they are all united. They feel that United States policy, with the exception of the Franklin Roosevelt "good neighbor" policy and *maybe* the current Kennedy one, has been totally to dominate the hemisphere. The Monroe Doctrine, in their eyes, is an artifice so designed that the United States can intrude in domestic affairs without giving Latin Americans a chance to summon aid and stand up to intervention.

Where armed might is not in the background, there is the accusation of economic aggression. Here, too, the arguments are diverse. In some instances, the United States is condemned because it invested too much in a country so it could possess it like a colony; or it did not sink enough money in a country so it could keep it underdeveloped and compliant. This anti-Americanism translates itself in absurd yet significant details. A Chilean market researcher, making a survey in 1961 on why relatively little Coca-Cola was sold in Santiago, found that the product was unpopular because it was identified with "Yankee imperialism." Pepsi-Cola, a newer entrant in the market, was not so stigmatized.

The story of United States business practice is not nearly as sordid as it is depicted by many Latin Americans. Giant United States corporations have introduced to the republics efficient production and, even more importantly, wage scales and benefits far superior to those of domestic rivals. However, the fact remains that the record is marked by destructive blemishes. While United States private investments, now totaling eight billion dollars, have improved conditions for some groups, individual firms too often have been indifferent to the distribution of this wealth or whether it has led to the construction of schools and hospitals, roads, and homes. The most tragic example, of course, was Cuba. It is being repeated to a measure today in Venezuela. Venezuela receives oil royalties of nearly one billion dollars a year, enough for a substantial down payment on a generous welfare program. And, though Venezuela is held up by Washington as a great hope in Latin America, the rate of illiteracy is 70 per cent, elements of wealth and poverty are as sharp as elsewhere, and extreme insufficiencies make this one of the most explosive places in an explosive continent.

The blame, obviously, cannot be laid exclusively on North American entrepreneurs interested in quick gain without a concern about the future. Until Castro, the United States government itself showed little interest in the lot of ordinary Latin Americans; nor did it care if the prevailing system continued forever, so long as it did not hinder United States operations. The United States, busy thinking of the more obvious zones of unrest, and implicitly the inroads of communism, paid its attention first to postwar Europe, then to such areas as Quemoy and Matsu, and Laos. From 1945 to 1960, of the billions in loans and grants the United States delivered to the world, scarcely 2 per cent of the total went to Latin America, less even than to the Philippines. And then one day Washington, to its horror, awoke to discover there were masses of people next door who were discontented and restless and volatile. Castro, as he himself continues to remind his fellow Latin Americans, was quite a blessing for them. The aid from Washington at last began to move southward, and with it came a realistic look at the regimes and an insistence that reforms be carried out, reforms that only a couple of years previously were considered "socialist" and that might easily have saved Cuba from extremism.

The questions whether much can be retrieved in the way of good will and whether effective reforms can be hoped for will be examined in a later chapter. But one thing can be said with certainty: the United States is in for a difficult time, no matter what it does, no matter how lofty its motives or generous its offers of assistance. Much of the anti-American sentiment of Latin America can be traced to a recognizable and understandable spirit of patriotism and a fear that gunboat diplomacy may one day be dominant again. But the more I talked with Latin Americans, including presidents and political leaders, the more convinced I was that an entire continent is suffering from a form of split personality. On the one hand it needs and wants United States financial and technical aid; on the other hand it is resentful and suspicious of the aid.

Despite all efforts to remember the rationale, some of the sensitivity emerges as unreasonable and perverse and irritating even to a Canadian visitor. In La Paz, I had a long interview with Bolivia's minister of economics, Alfonso Gumucio. A calm, orderly individual, Gumucio made some intelligent points in outlining United States–Latin-American relations. He explained, for example, that South Americans would require a long time to forget past administrations, up to and including Eisenhower's, which tried to keep the continent as a producer of raw materials and a dumping ground for United States products. But he also said that the new team under Kennedy appeared to be taking a more enlightened and hopeful course.

I questioned Gumucio about the Alliance for Progress. Suddenly he stopped me and said: "You have been referring to 'aid.' For us it is not aid, only time drafts that we are now collecting." What did he mean? Gumucio continued: "During the war, when it was not our war, we made an effort to help the United States. We sold our tin to the United States at one sixth the price the United States and Germany were offering on the neutral Lisbon market. On this basis, the United States is indebted to us for an additional $400 million. Since 1954, the United States has put $180 million into Bolivia. Therefore it still owes us $220 million."

There are some men who are tolerant, trustful, and balanced in their views about the United States. Among them is Alberto Lleras Camargo, one of Latin America's most respected statesmen, whom I met shortly before his retirement as President of Colombia. When I confessed that at times I found myself annoyed by Latin-American postures, and cited the above Bolivian example, Lleras reflected for a moment. "Bolivia's attitude is understandable," he finally said, "but how wise is it?" For instance, he went on, he could stand up and denounce the United States because Colombia has lost several million dollars in coffee sales in the last few years. But what are the reasons? Because Brazil and other countries are producing more and there is greater world competition.

"Can you reasonably expect the United States," Lleras asked, "to pay two or three cents a pound more in order to sustain Colombia's coffee economy when other countries are jockeying among themselves, rejecting agreements, and throwing more coffee on the market?"

Lleras, as a moderate, is one of the exceptions in a continent of passionate partisans.

In almost every capital someone sooner or later produced a chart for me to study. The chart showed two critical curves: first the birth rate, second the gross national product. Latin America has the highest rate of population growth in the world. In the thirty years after 1920 its population soared by more than 80 per cent; countries of Southeast Asia, in that period, increased only 63 per cent. At present, Latin America's population is about the same as the United States and Canada combined. By 1975 it will be an estimated 300 millions. In thirty-seven years, when Anglo-Americans will number approximately 300 millions, Latin Americans will number 600 millions.

The statistics need not be disquieting; on the contrary, they could be looked upon optimistically, if one could visualize this massed human energy working constructively toward a life of fulfillment. But the trend is the other way. Discontent grows with the growth in numbers. It is not that space is lacking. In Britain seven hundred and fifty people live in every square mile, in the United States fifty, in South America only eleven. But among landless peasants there is land hunger. And, ironically, the one practical gift left by the Spaniards, skill and energy in building cities, proves a burden on the continent's economy. With few opportunities to sustain life in the interior, and with no sign of any appreciable expansion of pioneer frontiers, more and more people continue to move into the urban centers. A third of Argentina crowds into Buenos Aires and its suburbs, a quarter of Chile into Santiago. The new arrivals squat in cardboard hovels, search fruitlessly for jobs, and contribute to the already prevalent and grave social unrest.

The second curve on the chart completes the disturbing picture. Production of goods is not keeping pace with the increase in population; some authorities reason that per capita output not only has stopped growing but has started going down. "Those republics that are running as fast as they believe to be within their power," comments *The Economist* of London, "only succeed in holding their positions. And those that are failing to spurt, drop further and further behind."

Latin Americans themselves tend to argue that their part of the world is only now embarking on its industrial revolution, and one should be hopeful about the future. "You must make comparisons not with Europe of today," a state planner told me, "but with Europe during the Industrial Revolution." This point might be considered valid, were it not for the fact that Europe's industrial revolution took place in the nineteenth century, and not, as Latin America's, in the twentieth. Today there are social forces unknown a century ago, there are such factors as communications—which transmit the power of example—and there are men who preach what should be expected in man's relations to man. For the first time, all Latin America is echoing to cries for a substantial *revolución.*

Adlai Stevenson has called it "the revolution of rising expectations." But how will it end? What will be the ultimate impact of 600 million Latin Americans on half their numbers to the North? In the face of social injustices and inequalities, the portent to someone from the outside seems obvious. All over the world—in Africa, the Middle East, the Far East—changes are coming about, some of them through violence. But nowhere, I believe, will the explosions be as severe or as contagious as in Latin America, unless there are urgent and drastic reforms.

To me, one of the most baffling questions remains without satisfactory answer. Wherever I talked with landowners, industrialists, politicians—men of wide travel and knowledge, of intelligence—I asked: "Surely you see the writing on the wall, surely you know what has been happening in the rest of the world. Why don't you modify the extremes and make social improvements before time runs out?" In many cases I received this kind of reply: "Nothing will happen here; our people are not violent." In Brazil I heard over and over again the familiar saying: "God is a Brazilian."

(He will protect us.) Generally, the idea is that maybe your house will catch on fire, but never mine.

In Rio de Janeiro I met a perceptive, understanding member of the aristocracy. He said: "It is better to give up the rings on your fingers than to lose your fingers." But he, tragically, spoke almost alone.

3

Students and Intellectuals

MY FIRST CONTACT with university students in South America was at Pontificia Universidade Católica do Rio de Janeiro. I had been told by a Brazilian businessman, just that day at lunch, that most universities were of the left, having heavy infiltration by Communists. Catholic University, whose faculty was made up mainly of Jesuit priests, hardly conformed to this label, though one of the first students I spoke to, a pretty and sweet girl named Ana Carolina Valenca, aged nineteen, promptly informed me that she knew of at least one undergraduate who was in the pay of the Communists. Why was she so certain? "Whenever we have a discussion," said Ana, "he tries to agitate for his point of view." And what was that point of view? "Different from ours," said Ana.

Ana was studying law, following the example of her father, a prominent advocate. She found herself, by her own admission, quite confused about what beliefs to hold in politics. For example, she had placed great faith in Jânio Quadros; and when he walked out as President of Brazil, she was terribly let down. "I thought he would give us stability," said Ana with a sigh, "and instead he caused more confusion. I do not know what to believe any more."

At this point another student, Sergio Monteiro, joined the conversation. Sergio, twenty-three, the son of an admiral, was taking philosophy and journalism; he intended to combine a career in journalism with politics. Sergio said the only hope for Brazil was a dictatorship by the military; the best fifteen years of Brazil's history were during the dictatorial rule of Getúlio Vargas with the blessing of a *junta* of generals. Sergio added: "Salazar is not doing a bad job in Portugal." Since Sergio had also identified himself as a "democrat," I asked if he thought there was democracy in Portugal. "There is no democracy in Brazil," he replied, "so what is the difference?" Ana, who had been silent the while, now commented that she did not like any kind of dictatorship; but, if there had to be one, she preferred it to be of the right rather than the left.

Sergio was secretary general of the Students' Council, a post he won along with other "rightists" (his own terminology) over so-called "leftists" on the campus. It was a narrow victory, because even in this privately endowed Catholic University, the wealthiest in Brazil, the "rightists" carried the election with a majority of only twenty-eight out of a total enrollment of 2,500. Ana said: "We should really divide the student body into Communists and non-Communists." But how could there be many Communists, I asked, among students who originated from obviously high-income levels? Should they not perhaps be classified as "socialists" or "reformers"? Ana shook her head in puzzlement.

A third participant in our talk, Luiz Oscar Dubeux Pinto, had come along. Luiz, whose father is a civil engineer, said: "On the right we want reform, too; but we must use intelligence."

They were showing me through the university; and now

we stood on the roof of the main building, a handsome, modernistic structure, ten storeys up. In the background were Rio's beautiful mountains and Corcovado Peak with its extraordinary statue of Christ surveying the city. But not far off, on the edge of the campus in fact, and almost directly beneath us, was a *favela*. Laundry fluttered from lines strung between the slum shacks; lifting toward us were the piercing notes of children chasing one another, barefoot, through the dirt lanes.

Sergio volunteered: "It is not very pretty, is it? It will have to change." But by what means?

Luiz answered: "We will start land reform and other reforms." But how much time will be required?

"It does not matter," Sergio said. "We must study the problems of reforms and do things in a constitutional way."

A question of legality had arisen previously, when President Quadros resigned and the generals tried to prevent the vice-president, supposedly "leftist" João Goulart, from following the rules and assuming the chief executive's office. Nearly every college and university in Rio de Janeiro and São Paulo went on strike to protest against the army's attempted violation of the constitution; the sole exception was Catholic University. Ana declared: "I am for the constitution, but not when it came to Goulart."

At the time, an assembly was held at Catholic University to vote whether or not to join students of other universities in the demonstrations. As Sergio recalled it, "There was such a tumult at the meeting; the Communists caused such an uproar in demanding the floor that it was impossible to hold a vote." Instead, Sergio and fellow members of the Council convened privately and decided the issue. I asked if undergraduates at other universities might have considered this a rather high-handed action. Sergio said: "They respect us because they think we are rich here."

From Catholic University I drove over to the offices of

the Brazilian Students' Federation, the national organization that speaks for the majority of students in Latin America's most populous country. The president of the Federation, Aldo Arantes, had organized the proconstitution strike that resulted in an all-night street battle when police were ordered to disperse students with tear-gas bombs and batons. Police set out to arrest Arantes; but, tipped off in advance, he fled to the home of friends in Rio Grande do Sul. Now Arantes, aged twenty-two, greeted me with an apology for the shabby appearance of the Federation building: chipped plaster, scribblings on the wall, a couple of patched-up chairs in the lobby. Arantes explained that money for student activities, in common with other public activities in Brazil, was lacking. I assured him that student headquarters of my university days bore the same battered trademarks, although this was not exactly so. Student chambers at home can look abused and informal, but here there was plain deterioration.

The majority of the officers of the Federation, from middle class backgrounds, were studying at state universities. Arantes, however, was in law at Catholic University. When I told him I had just come from his school, where it was suggested a Salazar-type regime would provide the answers for Brazil's problems, Arantes threw his hands up in disgust. If this was not enough of a gesture, he removed his eyeglasses and waved them very emphatically. "Salazar?" he echoed. "Horrible!" He said that the Federation had long ago passed a resolution condemning the dictatorships of António de Oliveira Salazar and Francisco Franco.

"What would be a good form of government for Brazil?" I asked.

Arantes was decisive: "Socialist." A half-dozen of his colleagues, who sat around the office while we chatted, nodded in agreement. There was a clear distinction in Arantes' mind between social democracy and communism.

"If I thought communism would work, I would be a Communist," he said. "But I am not a Communist. I am a Catholic and a democrat." What he wanted was this: "Socialism in Brazilian style: it must be based on Brazilian reality." Something on the pattern of Sweden or Britain under socialist governments? "No," he said, again with determination. "It is bad for Brazil always to be trying to follow others; we must create a country that has its own personality."

He went on: "We have a low cultural and economic life because we have always looked elsewhere, and for this reason the student mission today is more important than it would be, say, in Canada or the United States. The most important class is the student class because we are clean; other groups have interests that are dirty. Students have the responsibility to show the people of the country what are the real issues, the right ideals. First, there is something wrong when other countries are always trying to exploit us. These countries—yes, especially the United States—try to sell us clothing, Coca-Cola, and cars. They spread the word through advertisements; and people think it is good to buy Coca-Cola, without considering whether it is good for the country. Sixty per cent of the pharmaceutical companies here are foreign. Foreign investors are against us developing our own steel industry because they wouldn't get immediate returns. They don't want Brazil to wake up."

I said: "But do you really think Brazil could have advanced, even as far as she has, without foreign investments?"

"The results have not been good for the Brazilian people: only for the top ones who make the profits."

"What, then," I said, "should be done?"

Arantes had his answer ready: "The first fundamental is agrarian reform, because Brazil is mainly an agricultural country. Most of the land is in the hands of rich men who don't do anything to help the nation as a whole. Banks don't lend money to poor people; they lend it to the rich, and the terrible thing is that much of the land in these few hands is not even being put to use. The government should take over *all* the land and pay for it over a long period. Those owners who have hung onto land but never cultivated it would be compensated the last. The land would be distributed among the peasants who would own it because they would pay for it through financial assistance from the government."

With hardly a pause, Arantes made his second point: "We must also have a planned economy, and this means state ownership of the basic industries: transportation, steel, and so on. Foreign capital should be applied by the state, never by private industry, and this includes loans from international banks."

His third point: "Half our people are illiterate because they have been kept that way deliberately by men who feel that mass ignorance gives security to their rule, that once a person gets an education he begins to demand improvements in life. We really haven't a national conscience in Brazil; and so one of the first things is to educate people, to put them to study, to help them develop a national conscience."

I asked Arantes what he thought of Fidel Castro and the Cuban revolution.

"The Cuban revolution," he said, "was a good thing; the history of Cuba called for it. It represented the beginning of freedom in Latin America. It is essential to believe in the revolution of Cuba; otherwise, if it is defeated, it will represent a defeat for all Latin America."

I said he had evaded my direct question about Castro. He denied this, saying, "The revolution is the fundamental thing. Fidel is incidental. Only by revolutionary process can our own needs be reached."

"At the expense of bloodshed?"

"We shall aim for revolution without bloodshed, but we shall not reject it because of bloodshed. We already have bloodshed. What else do you call it when children die from starvation or disease?"

Quadros?

"Quadros had the courage to go against the established interests, but it is limiting to put all hopes of a country in one person. Maybe Quadros could be a leader, maybe not."

Goulart?

"He always worked for the people, but in a weak way, thinking of his own interests. He has had a paternalistic approach to the solution of Brazil's problems, as did Vargas. But Goulart has never been in a revolutionary mood."

Disenchanted by Goulart?

"Yes, but this doesn't mean that he alone is guilty."

United States–Brazilian relations?

"They should be based on coordination, not subordination. We want dialogue with all countries of the world, on the same level."

Arantes' conclusion: "In the situation in which we are living, anything can happen at any hour. The political crisis over Quadros brought about a new consciousness among the people. The government that came out of this crisis has the contradictions of Brazil; it will not be able to solve our problems. Two classes appear as the revolutionary ones: first the students because they have no commitments to the old setup, second the city and farm workers who have the most to gain."

I have quoted Aldo Arantes at length, partly because he was chosen as spokesman by 75 per cent of the entire student body of Brazil, and partly because his views coincide remarkably with those I heard in a score of other vulnerable nations. His beliefs, his complaints, his desires, his demands for advances, and the forms to be taken have more in common with those of students in Chile and Venezuela and Guatemala than with classmates in his own Catholic University. There is, as we shall see, some disillusionment with Castro as an individual; but this does not alter the unyielding support for the Cuban revolution itself. There is a recognition that some leaders may be trying, but they are incapable of making basic changes because of ingrained patterns and opposition power. There is a universality to student thinking in Latin America, much of it based on intense nationalism and therefore, by indirection, intense anti-Americanism. And above all, there is a fervent insistence on social revolution, by force if necessary.

Latin America's students are in a category of their own. Whether they spring from impoverished or wealthy homes, they are for the most part restless and radical. They are also influential far beyond their numbers. When Peruvian police punished a few University of San Marcos demonstrators by throwing them deliberately into cells with common criminals and homosexuals, the public outcry was so loud that the minister of the interior, responsible for policing, was forced to resign. But the authority of students manifests itself in much more dramatic, more cogent ways. Within the same fortnight students in two widely separated states, Ecuador and the Dominican Republic, touched off disorders that led to the downfall of governments.

A student in Quito was killed when police, with drawn sabers, charged a university parade protesting against the demagogic policies of President José María Velasco. The bloodletting, coming at the height of a political crisis, sent Ecuadorian students into the streets for two days of battle; in short order, army units were pitted against one another, and thirty-five persons, many of them students, lay dead; Velasco, realizing his time was up, fled the country. Fifteen hundred miles away, in Ciudad Trujillo, students behind barricades held off riot squads by heaving at them rocks and cast-iron water-meter covers, eventually being driven off themselves by machine-gun bullets; but in the process they generated enough turmoil to cause the flight of the last of the Trujillo clan and give the Dominican Republic its first taste of freedom in thirty-one years.

Student weapons are not always so prosaic as sticks and stones, as I discovered in Caracas. At Universidad Central de Venezuela, the largest in the nation, there are secret caches of pistols, tommy guns, and Molotov cocktails, used frequently in the last few years. Venezuelan students are possibly the most violent in Latin America; certainly they have been at the forefront of recent disturbances. In order to visit Central University I first had to pass through a police checkpoint and show my credentials. The place was under a state of siege.

Like many other Latin-American seats of learning, Central University has extraterritorial rights; police, at least in theory, cannot enter the grounds without permission from the rector. And, again in common with similar state-financed institutions, which draw mainly from white-collar families, it reflects the moods and politics of articulate young people. Sixty per cent of the undergraduates have elected as executive of the Students' Federation a combination of Communists, socialists, and other left-wing elements. Thirty per cent could be classed as "moderate" or "conservative"; the rest are scattered in sentiments.

The university became officially leftist shortly after the overturn, in 1958, of Venezuela's dictator Marcos Pérez Jiménez. From the early days of his rule, which began in 1950, students had made up the hard core of opposition and helped lead the revolution that finally threw him from office. But Pérez Jiménez meanwhile had managed to suspend the university's autonomy and to stack its faculty with sycophants. The new provisional government, headed by Admiral Wolfgang Larrazábal, set out in 1958 to evict the Pérez

Jiménez appointees from professorships and administrative jobs. Larrazábal also restored the traditional *claustrum* found in other universities in Latin America: a sort of electoral college, composed of student representatives, faculty members, and alumni, who have the power to choose the university rector, who, in turn, has a say in selection of key staff personnel. Under leftist direction, the university soon found itself a fresh command post against higher authority, this time against the government of President Rómulo Betancourt, who, the students and faculty members said, was far from the liberal reformer he claimed to be.

The initial anti-Betancourt demonstration erupted in 1960, when Venezuela supported the San José Declaration, which gave Castro his first gentle rap on the knuckles by Latin American neighbors. Students barricaded themselves on university grounds while riot troops, forgetting about the inviolability of the campus, moved in and tried to quiet them. For three days a couple of hundred youths, holed up in a dormitory they called "Stalingrad," peppered away at their besiegers with rifles, submachine guns, and Molotov bombs. One result, aside from bloodshed, was a split in the Betancourt coalition, with the socialist U.R.D. (Republican Democratic Union) breaking away from the government.

The next year an even more gruesome series of student-inspired outbursts took place, first over Venezuela's break in diplomatic relations with Cuba's Castro regime, then over the announcement of a visit to Caracas by President Kennedy, and finally, spilling into 1962, over the Punta del Este conference, which declared Castro an outlaw in the hemisphere.

The Punta del Este riots cost at least thirty-five lives, among them two students, with hundreds more wounded. Betancourt suspended some constitutional rights, shut down leftist newspapers, and ordered the arrest of eight hundred opponents, including former U.R.D. members of his coalition government, and three hundred and fifty students. The university's administrative council—the rector, the vice-rector, and all eleven deans of the various colleges—resigned in protest; the university automatically shut down. This gave the students something else to storm about; but now the police, using more refined tactics, kept off the grounds. They waited outside the main gates, ready to pounce on any student who ventured in or out of the hallowed territory.

The university had been closed three weeks when I drove up; where normally 17,500 young men and women wandered through the sprawling campus or into the stunningly modern buildings, only thirty diehards were on hand, and they were busy writing antigovernment and pro-Cuban literature. I spoke with two of the remaining leaders, the president of the Students' Federation himself being in jail. Frederick Muñoz, an economics student, was vice-president of the Federation and a proclaimed Communist. Victor José Ochoa, a law student, was treasurer and a member of the socialist U.R.D. They, and their couple of dozen comrades, slept on camp cots in the paper-littered student offices, surrounded by walls covered with posters that said: "Kennedy *fuera*" (Kennedy get out) and *"Cuba si! Yanqui no!"* There were also quotations from Lenin.

The "insurgents" were fed at the University Medical College Hospital and between meals churned out, on mimeograph machines, leaflets with such headings as *"Por la defensa de Cuba"* and *"Contra la fascista represión political."* Muñoz and Ochoa said it was necessary to print these leaflets because downtown newspapers were under instructions not to publish any statements by the Students' Federation. They argued righteously that President Betancourt employed military planes to drop leaflets exhorting the public to show up for government rallies while the right to assembly was denied opposition parties. Any argument that Betancourt might have been compelled to ban other meetings, to prevent further bloodshed, was brushed aside with contempt.

Muñoz and Ochoa struck me as being quite fanatic. They ushered me into the Room of Martyrs, an office lined with photographs of six students who had been killed in street fights in the last three years. One of the portraits was of Livia Gouverneur, a young, attractive girl who died in 1961 with a bullet in her back. The story is still hidden in mystery. The known facts are that some students, armed with tommy guns, raked a Caracas house occupied by anti-Castro Cuban exiles; the Cubans returned the fire. Next morning Livia's body was brought around to her parents by two students in a Volkswagen; they claimed she had been killed by the Cubans, but it is equally likely that in the melée she was accidentally shot by one of her colleagues.

"Where do you get your arms?" I asked Muñoz.

Muñoz smiled and said that most weapons bear a Venezuelan mark—that is, they once belonged to the army and were issued to students in 1958, after the overthrow of Pérez Jiménez, by the Larrazábal *junta* "to defend the constitution." Some weapons, he admitted with a grin, were retained when they should have been returned to the army. But there is also no doubt that arms smuggling is common, and for a price you can obtain an automatic or a rifle brought over the border from Colombia; the government claims, too, that weapons come across the Caribbean from Cuba.

"I don't deny that we have arms," said Muñoz, "but they are necessary for our defense."

Having heard this fairly standard rationalization in other parts of the world before, I asked the students what their ambition was for Venezuela.

Ochoa, the U.R.D. youth, answered: "To free ourselves from imperialism, the economic control of the United States."

But what about the Alliance for Progress, which is far from an imperialist concept?

Muñoz, the Communist: "The Alliance is still Yankee imperialism. Its aim is to try to stop the work that has been done in Cuba and to put up a future barrier against Cuba."

Ochoa, the socialist: "Under the Alliance the United States does not speak of industrialization of our country. The imperialists of the United States are not interested in letting Latin Americans produce their own goods because this would destroy markets."

And all the investments the United States has put into Venezuela, including the oil industry, which accounts for 90 per cent of Venezuela's foreign exchange?

Ochoa: "It should be one of our objectives to nationalize the oil industry."

Muñoz: "Nationalization is indispensable for our independence. And there is no need for compensation. The United States oil monopolies have taken out more money than they have given Venezuela."

The remarks by Muñoz were predictable. Socialist Ochoa is frowned on by older U.R.D. leaders as being an extremist; U.R.D. itself does not call for a takeover of the oil industry. Ochoa, nevertheless, is worth recording because he delineates the attitude of other students in Venezuela and elsewhere, youth who do not necessarily follow the line advocated by their elder statesmen. It should be remembered that political parties in Latin-American universities are more than junior branches of national parties. Political disciples on campuses south of the United States border are far more active than their opposite numbers in Cambridge, Mass., or Berkeley, Calif. They are included in national party committees, they plan strategy, and they organize demonstrations that are often crucial in general elections. The national parties, in turn, devote substantial effort and funds to student elections; at the same time, bowing to the strong student feeling for autonomy, they avoid dictation. For its part, the public, recognizing the influence of student thinking, follows campus campaigns closely; press, radio, and television provide wide coverage.

Students sometimes take their cues from adults, and then spurt ahead of them. The case history of the University of San Marcos is illustrative not only because of the rejection of an older philosophy but because of the development of something more powerful: Fidelismo. Lima's San Marcos, founded in 1551, though not constructed until twenty-five years later, claims to be the oldest university of the Americas. In the early days its students came only from the aristocracy or privileged classes. But gradually wealthier families sent their sons to Europe, and more recently to the United States for higher studies. Some moneyed students still attend; but San Marcos, like other state institutions on the continent, draws mainly from what passes as the middle class: shop-keepers, artisans, professionals, technicians, who have moderate incomes and have managed to save their children from the same fate as the mass of poor who seldom emerge beyond the first couple of grades of primary school. Though fees are nominal, life in San Marcos is often a great economic burden; and many students are in their late twenties because they step out alternate years to work. Some who study law or medicine or economics hope to improve their financial positions, but others look to a profession as a stepping stone to a career in politics.

San Marcos has long been a sounding board for new political and social ideas. Forty years ago a youth named Victor Raúl Haya de la Torre conceived, along with fellow students, the dynamics of a party that was to become known as APRA (American Popular Revolutionary Alliance). Flowering in the old palm-shaded patios of San Marcos, APRA was radically leftist; it declared itself against "imperialism" and the "oligarchy"; it declared itself for land distribution and a better break for the Indian population. APRA, though anti-Communist, stood for many of the features of Marxism. But Marxism was a foreign ideology, born in a German mind and nurtured on Russian soil. APRA was the first genuine Latin American movement tailored to the Latin-American mentality and needs. It spread its branches to several other countries and grew quickly in strength, so much so at San Marcos that no one could think of holding student office without membership in the party.

Apristas, using methods later attributed to Communists, infiltrated trade unions and government posts and were not beyond employing political terrorism to shock people into support. Despite the fact that it was the greatest political force in the country, APRA could never gain a real foothold in the face of oligarchic resistance; it degenerated into a rabble-rousing movement, and in 1948, after attempting a rebellion against the government, was outlawed. By now founder Haya de la Torre, imprisoned and exiled at various stages, and the focus of much controversy, was becoming a middle-aged revolutionary; the party was regarded by some students as feeble and without purpose.

The major disaffection occurred in 1956, when national leaders instructed APRA followers to support a conservative presidential candidate, banker Manuel Prado, in an exchange deal that would legalize the party and give some of its members cabinet posts. Prado, with the help of APRA votes, won the election; but four years later his government was still conservative (or, to use a student term, "reactionary") and most of the Apristas had been dropped from the cabinet.

The timing was to prove of possibly lasting significance, because it was just about then that a new star was beginning to shine brightly—the 26th of July Movement of Fidel Castro. This again had the required ingredients: Latin American in concept, reformist, and, as an appealing added measure, a challenge to the dominance of the United States.

APRA moved toward the right, Fidelismo moved toward the left.

It is said that Communists in San Marcos promptly took advantage of the students' disillusion with APRA and maneuvered skilfully behind the scenes to build up Fidelismo even before it was identified with communism. While some such performance would be standard procedure, it by no means explains away the tremendous pull of the Cuban experience. The story, simply told, is that San Marcos students were revolutionary in spirit, and Castro's revolution gave a fresh outlet to this spirit. A new party, Revolutionary Student Front, composed of adherents to the principles of the Cuban revolution, built up quick strength at the expense of APRA and a third party, the Christian Democrats; with 80 per cent of San Marcos' 15,000 students taking part in campus elections, the Fidelistas won a substantial plurality in 1960, to control the Students' Council; they increased their figures in the succeeding two years.

And what about other universities, such as Lima's private Catholic University, which is populated mainly by "conservative" students from upper-income categories? By 1961 "leftists" dominated the Students' Council, in sharp contrast to the previous five years when Christian Democrats led the elections. One of the members of the Council, Enrique Bernales, a twenty-two-year-old law student, turned out to be something of a tragic figure. He had been expelled, along with nineteen others, by university authorities, for supporting a pro-Cuban resolution at a national congress of the Federation of Students of Peru. The Lima press stuck on Bernales the tags "Marxist" and "Communist." Bernales, with a heritage of wealth and privilege, is not a Communist. He is, so far as I could judge from talks with his professors, a sincere and middle-course reformer.

"Was the expulsion justified?" I asked Bernales.

"It was not a just decision," he said quietly, "because

not enough attention was paid to the text of the resolution. We were referring to historic reasons for the Cuban revolution and the need for reform. We were not necessarily approving the later methods of the revolution."

What are the main points about the Cuban revolution?

"One of the things that impresses us a great deal," said Bernales, "is the general mobilization against illiteracy in the countryside, putting students into field work. This would be even more important in Peru than in Cuba, since our illiteracy rate is higher. I am not referring to the kind of textbooks in Cuba, with Marxist orientation, but to the main idea of creating a mystique about work with peasants, an effective mystique about work."

Land reform?

"We disagree with the Cuban method because we try to apply the teachings of the Church, which respects private property. But land reform is absolutely indispensable in Peru. We must not only distribute land belonging to the present handful of the ruling class—paying for this land, not confiscating it as in Cuba—but we must also give technical aid and education to the people who would have the land. Without such reforms I am convinced there will be a horrible revolution."

And the negative features of the Cuban revolution?

Bernales pondered for several moments before answering: "Among the negative elements are the person of Castro himself and the attitude of the United States government under the Eisenhower administration. This United States attitude helped Marxist influence in Cuba to become more decisive."

Here, I think, were the salient clues to the reasoning of young Latin Americans. There are, of course, students who violently resent Castro and all he signifies. The bulk, however, can be said to favor in one way or another the Cuban revolution. This group can be broken down roughly into two categories: those who unhesitatingly applaud Castro and everything he has done; and those, like Bernales, who understand the circumstances of the revolution but became increasingly upset by Castro's behavior as time went on. Bernales, for instance, was shocked by the wave of executions of political prisoners; such killings were in violation of the Latin-American code of political ethics. Bernales also disapproves of the extreme approach to nationalization, but here there is some attempt to justify it on the grounds that the United States pushed Castro into communism.

What it adds up to is this: Whether or not Castro stays in the picture, whether he lives or dies, he is no longer important. Fidelismo, with its promise of changes, its challenge to the Colossus of the North, has caught on. It has a firm grasp on students and will, I believe, continue to dominate their thinking. This does not imply that they have disowned democratic principles of personal and economic freedom, but it does suggest that they have been unable to accept the existing social inequalities and are prepared to risk even these liberties to alter course.

I sat in with a half-dozen graduate students at the Institute of Economics, University of Chile. The institute, akin to the London School of Economics, is the best of its kind in Latin America and attracts from all over the continent young men and women who intend to enter government work or industry. It was a serious, sober group, with not a "rightist" among them, nor, for that matter, a Communist; the conversation, too, was impressive, because everything they had to say was related to reform; and nothing was said in sloganeering language. We held an impromptu poll of opinion, and there was unanimous agreement that on balance the impact of Fidelismo was positive rather than negative. Here are some of the comments:

Fernando Mateo of Argentina: "The main thing is that Castro captured the imagination of the people. Cubans are on the move, living more intensely than ever before."

Juan Prado of Bolivia: "Fidelismo isn't just a Cuban matter. It is a correct and just solution to Latin American problems. In Bolivia we also had a social revolution but the plans were half-hearted and the results unsubstantial. So far, the Cuban revolution is the only solid road that has been found in Latin America. I do not relate this to Castro's demagoguery, because this is vague, but to the fact that he has solved desperate, pressing problems."

Julio Funes of Argentina: "The measure of support that Castro has in Latin America is a direct measure of the frustrations of the working classes; they see the present ruling classes as ineffectual. Fidelismo is showing the way democracy could work, too, if it wanted to work properly."

Does all this sound repetitious, monotonous? If so, it is the theme I found throughout this vast expanse of the world. Here are some more jottings from my notes gathered from one end of Latin America to the other, in places as far apart as 5,000 miles.

In Santiago, Chile, Sonia Gallegos speaks: "None of our countries can solve their problems without total, planned economy. Partial solutions are no good."

In Panama City, Lillian Mijares judges: "There is despair among students; our relations with the United States will always be bad so long as we are cheated out of revenue from the Panama Canal."

In Quito, Ecuador, Milton Burbano: "Cuba trading one master for another? Nonsense. In the case of United States–Cuban relations, the means of production were owned by United States companies. Now, in Cuba, deals with Russia are made on a government to government basis."

In Mexico City, a medical student: "We like the money from the Alliance for Progress but not the conditions that go with it. Look at Argentina; it breaks relations with Cuba and immediately gets a loan of $25 million."

In Bogotá, Colombia: "We are making the United States

rich because they buy our products at low prices, then pay us back with loans that we have to repay with interest; and all the while they make us feel we are taking charity."

The same mood prevails in Argentina, despite the fact that the country stands apart from most of the others on several grounds. For one thing, the extremes of wealth and poverty are not as blatant as elsewhere; moreover, trade unionism is strongly organized; and, no matter how poor conditions have been, the average worker has never starved. In this rich, meat-producing land, the per capita consumption of beef is a pound a day; *gauchos* average two and a quarter pounds each. But there are anomalies. While other countries may talk vaguely of state ownership of some basic utilities, Argentina has reversed the process. Under the government of former President Arturo Frondizi, it denationalized the oil industry in an effort to attract more United States private investors. "This was done," said Daniel J. Divinsky, "at the expense of our independence."

Divinsky, aged twenty-one, is a law student and son of a prosperous physician. He accused Frondizi of betraying Argentina by promising reforms and not delivering them. "He mounted the horse from the left, and he descended from the right," said Divinsky. But the main complaint was that Argentina was getting deeper into the orbit of what Divinsky, along with other students, called "foreign economic imperialism." One evening, after a two-hour talk over drinks and dinner, I asked Divinsky bluntly: "If I had a million dollars, and invested it in Argentina, in my own business here, would you take it from me?"

He sipped his liqueur, looked at me steadily and replied: "It is unfortunate, but I am afraid I would take it from you."

Yesterday's students are today's intellectual leaders. When they reach this mature status, they may lose their physical vehemence, their urge to plunge headlong into bloody street marches. But they attain something else: the respect and attention of a calm audience drawn to them by the printed word, the drama of a stage setting, the power of flashing wit, of deep thinking. For these are the *pensadores,* the men to whom Latin America has always looked for its intellectual guidance: the authors, the critics, the political scientists, the moralists, the sociologists, the men who analyze the whole social spectrum as they see it, who look into the uncertain future bearing in mind the influence of the past.

They occupy a position of authority of far greater importance than the writers and analysts of North America. In bygone days there were such sages as Esteban Echeverría, who a century ago sang of Argentina: "The great thought of the revolution has not been carried out. We are independent, but we are not free. The arms of Spain do not oppress us; but its traditions still weigh us down." Or Domingo Faustino Sarmiento who told Chileans in 1849 of his terror of industrial and international rivalry: "Against the violence and injustice of the Yankees there is no appeal on this earth." And, of course, Cuba's José Martí who declared: "I am not a man speaking, but a people protesting."

The basic perplexities have not changed much in the twentieth century. Today's *pensadores* are concerned with their own national identities and a search for answers to some distinctive problems, and yet, underlying this groping, there is a common quandary: how to develop, how to live with the United States, what form the relationship should take, what should be made of Fidel Castro, or rather of the movement he unleashed. If disciplined orderliness has replaced student unruliness, most of the intelligensia, it can be stated safely, are still on the left. Some are Communists; the bulk fall into a more moderate though reformist class. Some justify the extreme measures of Cuba; others are disturbed by them. But all feel the need for changes in Latin America.

I have assembled here a cross section of contemporary thought as it was expressed to me informally:

PLAYWRIGHT

Vinicius de Moraes was renowned in Brazil as a poet and playwright long before his *Black Orpheus* reached foreign screens and won the 1959 Grand Prix at Cannes. De Moraes, with characteristic Latin fascination for the soul and heart of man, took the ancient, legendary Orpheus and made him into a Rio streetcar conductor. Eurydice is his love, and together they go down from a *favela* in the high bluffs above the city to celebrate the riotous carnival in the streets below. There her enemy, who is Death, finds her and carries her away.

De Moraes is still interested in allegory, and now he ties it to Jânio Quadros. "He was our great hope," de Moraes says, "and the shock of his resignation was overwhelming, as though a trusted father had gone." Sitting, drinking gin and tonic, he points to our glasses and says, "when Jânio was here, as leader, we would drink in pleasure and relaxation, with no worries about the country back of our minds. Now I do not drink with the same ease, the sheer joy, as one should when one is being sociable." De Moraes feels that Quadros was pushed out by right wingers. This view is not accepted by others who claim that the president was attempting an ill-conceived political move to gain more power. Nevertheless, de Moraes says he is going to write a play with a "religious undertone . . . almost like Christ surrounded by men who did not understand him or what he was trying to do. Quadros will emerge with a universal flavor as a man who attempts to change the established order but is crucified by other men who fear him because they do not understand him . . . a tragic figure."

In a broad sense he feels, too, that Brazil tragically is caught up in the squeeze between East and West. "One of the troubles," he says, "is that our neighbors to the North think with a Protestant mentality, forgetting we are Catholics. There are different backgrounds, and these must never be overlooked. I remember seeing in Florence several paintings of the Nativity Scene. You could always tell which painters were Protestants; all the figures were looking outward, at the artist. But in the paintings by Catholics they were all looking at the Child. Here was a difference of tenderness in inner feeling." In other words, the concept of "soul" is important; but then, with some reluctance, de Moraes says that perhaps Brazil's greatest trouble is that "we are suffering from a fatal disease which I call politicism, brought about by inept, corrupt, selfish, unprincipled men in politics who have no sense of social responsibility."

CULTURAL DIRECTOR

Manuel Benjamín Carrión is one of Ecuador's most distinguished men of letters. As director of the state-financed but autonomous House of Culture, he determines the subsidies to be paid struggling authors, magazines, and literary reviews. "The mass of people are for Castro," he says. "If Castro came here he would receive an overwhelming reception. If Kennedy came he would receive a courteous reception. That is the difference." But how does Dr. Carrión regard the bloodshed in Cuba? "The Cuban revolution is the most economical revolution of all time," he says. "More than one million died in the French revolution. Even Colombia, which officially has not had a revolution, has seen between 200,000 and 300,000 dead in recent years; in Cuba there were perhaps seven hundred killed. All revolutions are violent, this was the least violent of all."

ECONOMIST

Claudio Veliz, a prominent Chilean economist, says the definition of private enterprise as it is practiced in the

United States is different from the version in Latin America. "In the United States," he says, "there is genuine competition ensured by antitrust laws; here private enterprise is simply a cover for monopoly." For instance, in Chile, he avers, industries ranging from copper and steel to processed food and cigarettes are monopolies. "At one time," he goes on, "we had several breweries, but gradually they were almost all absorbed by one giant. Only one man held out, and the giant made a deal to have him produce a trickle of beer so that the public would be lulled into imagining it had a choice. A beer vendor tried to make a test case by complaining to the Department of Commerce, and an official feigned horror and said if a monopoly existed it would have to be stopped. Everyone has always known about the beer monopoly here; but hypocrisy exists in industry, even to the official's reaction. Of course, nothing has been done."

Veliz is anti-Communist. In his writing for *Ultima Hora,* the socialist newspaper, he urges radical reform as a safeguard against communism. Veliz, whose father is a landowner, also talks about the pernicious disdain for manual toil prevalent in the middle and upper classes. Once he was on a farm with a North American visitor, watching a *campesino* guide a single-blade plow and horse. The American said he would like to try plowing; the furrow came out very jagged. Claudio also tried, unsuccessfully. His father happened by and was horrified, saying, "First, you must never do menial work; second, in effect, you lose face, because a peasant must always believe that you can do anything better than he can."

While a student, Veliz was shocked during a visit to a *fundo,* where he saw the owner step accidentally into a puddle, and automatically snap his fingers at a peasant. The peasant ran over and used his own shirt to wipe the mud from his master's boots. "From that moment on," says Veliz, "I knew there would have to be changes here."

Social Scientist

Universities around the world have heard lectures by Gilberto Freyre, Latin America's most noted social scientist. Educated in the United States, he is a Brazilian constantly pondering about his country, its past and future, its culture, and its race. He is an anthropologist and sociologist but prefers to be called simply a "writer," understandably, since his works have been translated into several languages. At the age of sixty-two, Freyre is possibly the most hopeful and patient of the many intellectuals with whom I have spoken. "I do not think the situation in Latin America is a desperate one," he says. "But we are going through a tremendous crisis of leadership. Young men, instead of entering politics, are gravitating toward industry. There are some very able men in industry, but they have too much of a private vision of things—profits, technical developments—instead of a public vision. As industrial leaders they are not interested in leading politically. This trend is apparent in Argentina and Mexico, but in an acute way in Brazil. The political leaders of the nineteenth-century Brazil were far superior to the leaders of today. They were statesmen as well as responsible leaders. At the present there is not a single political leader in Brazil who could be described as a statesman. Quadros was a dramatic man, but not a statesman or even a leader."

Would it be fair to say that Latin America is at the same development stage as Europe, or North America, in the mid-nineteenth century, the difference being, of course, that this is now the twentieth century?

"It is difficult to generalize," replies Freyre, "because even in each nation there are different groups living in different times. In Brazil, for example, the elite live in the twentieth century. At the same moment, some Indian tribes live as they did when Brazil was discovered four hundred years ago. Between these two extremes there are gradations. In the

Northeast you can find a change that began only fifty years ago, when the old colonial sugar mills became industrialized. But with this industrialization of mills you had a preservation of bad feudal traits and a loss of the good ones. At least, previously, mill owners were also planters, and they had a sense of paternalism because they lived close by their workers. If a worker or cane cutter was sick, the patron was there to make sure someone took care of him. But now the plantation and mill owners live far away, in Rio de Janeiro, and have lost all sense of social responsibility."

What is the prognosis for the Northeast, Brazil's most troubled region?

"Owners will not voluntarily make the necessary changes; they have had a chance, and they ignored it. What is needed is social legislation. Without it, there are seeds for violence."

Moralist

Until recent times—ten years or so ago—the trend in Chilean literature was toward folklore and history. But now it is changing. The extreme leftists write about farm and labor conditions, and the urgency for reforms. Even in the center or right, where writers tend to describe the society they know best, the implicit message is that things are not going too well. A good example of the latter school is Jorge Edwards, who is thirty years of age. Edwards is the scion of one of Chile's oldest and wealthiest families. He writes short stories and works at the foreign ministry (only one or two of the older, more established writers live completely on authorship). Edwards does not write bluntly of the need for social and land reforms, since he believes an artist should not preach but, rather, should let the moral tell itself. He feels strongly, however, that reforms are necessary, along with an altered attitude among the oligarchy.

And so he deals primarily with familiar subjects, such as the dilemma in which his own society finds itself. One of his persistent themes is about members of the oligarchy who lose their money because of poor investments and prove incapable of adjustment. The point is that "menial work" (and this often includes any form of effort short of living off invested capital) is still considered degrading "and they stoop to dishonest practice or thievery in order to maintain their old positions." A sample short story by Jorge Edwards: A young man of the impoverished nobility finally accepts a senior post in a bank, at a good salary. Over a period of two years he embezzles a fortune. It is what he does with the money that makes the tragedy; he uses it to pay accumulated debts at the fashionable country club his family helped to found, to hire once again a valet, in short to preserve, vainly, his social position.

"The mentality of the old aristocracy must change," Edwards says simply. "The aristocracy must learn not to look down on those of us who try to adjust to the transformation in life around us."

Academician

Gerardo Molina is rector of Bogotá's Universidad Libre, a small and dynamic university founded by liberals forty years ago. A man of fifty-four, lean and handsome, with close-cropped gray hair and a fair skin, Molina looks like a campus type from the United States Midwest. But he is much more than a small-town college figure; he is widely accepted as the leader of the intellectual left wing of Colombia. Molina is an anti-Communist Marxist. He says that communism denies liberty and freedom of action, and therefore the road to progress is through socialism. Questioned about Cuba, and the fact that only one political party exists there, he answers by saying Cuba's case is unusual: "There are refugees in Miami, the former oligarchy who would, by devious means, attempt to take over in Cuba if any kind of election were held at the moment." (The same reasoning is heard today in Havana.)

On the bigger question of United States–Latin-American relations, he says: "The United States must understand that the problems of Latin America will not be solved by money alone. We want more than money: independence, respect, the choice to negotiate and avoid alignment with any bloc. I am a neutralist."

When I ask him to amplify the meaning of "independence," he says it goes beyond political or economic matters; it involves, also, culture. "Students take their higher studies in the United States," he comments, "and come back with North American mentalities. The United States has a 'technical' mentality; our thinking is much closer to that of Europe, and I would prefer to see more of our young people interested in France, Britain, Germany, or Italy."

On the political side, he considers that perhaps Mexico, Brazil, and Chile are independent of United States domination, but not Colombia, nor Venezuela, nor Peru, nor most of the other countries: "It is wrong for the United States to think only in terms of communism and anticommunism. Life is wider than that. It is for this reason that the United States does not understand the revolt in Latin America: a revolt very near socialism, but not communism, since it is based on national conditions."

Architect

One of the world's great architects, and designer of virtually every major building in Brasília, Oscar Niemeyer is a pleasant, soft-spoken man with receding black hair and dark complexion, which give him an almost ethereal appearance. He is a Communist, but a rather naïve one despite his fifty-four years; for he talks in clichés and slogans that fell out of fashion a generation or more ago. For instance, he describes a visit to Moscow several years ago, when he found that "the Soviet Union is a haven for architects, because here we work only for the rich, while there they work for all the people." However, occasionally he breaks away from a set patter to cite a telling detail: "There is such poverty in the Northeast that the people cannot even afford a simple casket in which to bury their dead."

The problem, he says, is not created by men but by the system: "Kubitschek (the president who built Brasília) was a good human being; Quadros was a clever man. But neither could be of much use when you have a system such as exists here."

Niemeyer has been neither to Cuba nor Red China (he is frankly afraid of air travel) but he says the proper answers will be found there: first socialism, then communism. "In Russia," he adds, "there will be real communism in a few years, with free food and shelter for all. This is the kind of revolution we need in Brazil and the rest of Latin America."

JOURNALIST

Alberto Zalamea, thirty-one, is editor of *La Nueva Prensa,* a Colombian political and cultural weekly something of the order of Britain's *New Statesman.* Young, alert, progressive, he would be termed by British standards a Gaitskellite but certainly no further left. Despite the fact that he believes in mixed economy, and sees foreign investments of benefit to Colombia, his magazine falters along on a circulation of 15,000, with flimsy advertising, because the big companies consider him "radical" and impose a boycott.

"In your opinion," I ask Zalamea, "why does the United States look on Colombia and Venezuela as 'good' examples in Latin America?"

"Because the presidents of these countries," he replies, "are ideologically in tune with the president of the United States, rather than with their own national interests. They talk of democracy, but actually there is no such thing as democracy in Venezuela or Colombia. The governments of these countries assume that problems here can be solved the same way as problems in the United States a hundred years ago. They think in abstracts."

"What is your view of the Alliance for Progress?"

"It is well intentioned but it is going to end badly. Perhaps President Kennedy believes the ruling classes will make a revolution of sorts, but in practice they will not. Besides, look at the financial figures. The Alliance talks of twenty billion dollars in ten years, but half of this is to be provided by Latin-American countries and by private enterprise. Think of the one billion dollars from the United States each year divided by twenty countries; it means fifty million dollars apiece, and this is not enough. International banks are lending more than this amount now, so that nothing is really changed except the name."

"Then what is the forecast for Latin America?"

"If nothing more is done, different forms of Communist governments will creep up. Castro was never a Communist; he was forced by circumstances into taking a position with communism. We shall have right-wing governments trying to preserve their interests, and then there will be a reaction against them, with extremism of the left. In any event, in underdeveloped countries, 'right' and 'left' have no meaning. The term should be 'nationalism,' not of the pattern of old-fashioned European nationalism, with one country against the next, but along the lines of modern Europe, with integration in the national interest."

"And how do you see the Cuban revolution?"

"If the United States had adopted a different policy, Castro could have made a national revolution similar to Nasser's in Egypt. It's too late now; Cuba is firmly on the other side. I don't favor the Cuban revolution as it is today; but I fight for the right of any country to have what it wants, whether it is fascism or communism. Twenty years ago, in

North American eyes, it was wrong to be a Nazi; now it is wrong to be a Communist. Maybe in twenty years the vision will change again, and it will be wrong to be a democrat. We should think historically, not ideologically."

A Mexican Voice

The young and well-known Carlos Fuentes is one of Mexico's most outspoken novelists and political commentators. His background is of the old nobility; his father was a diplomat. Fuentes, in his early thirties, identifies himself as a Marxist but non-Communist. He is aware that in his kind of pursuit, which demands complete intellectual freedom, he would be one of the first to suffer under communism. Nevertheless, he supports Castro, arguing that Fidelismo was inevitable, that Cuba, "a colony of the United States," had to swing to the other extreme: not only because it was pushed by Washington into awkward reliance on Russia but because Cuba's geographic position made it imperative for the island to get as far away from the United States, psychologically, as possible.

Fuentes is not repulsed by the executions in Cuba. Bloodshed and violence are understood by students of the Mexican revolution. "After all," he says, "we had our Zapata and his firing squads." He dismisses as "naïve" the concept that some Mexicans frown on the Cuban revolution because it did not retain its original distinctive character, as did the Mexican forerunner, at least in its early years. "World conditions have changed since Mexico's revolution," he points out. "Since ours was before the Russian revolution we had no recent experience to emulate and no one with whom to align ourselves. In fact, we adopted an outmoded and unrealistic constitution that went back to the last big revolution in the world, in France."

While intellectuals in republics south of Mexico are preoccupied with the desire for fundamental social revolutions in their own areas, Fuentes' grievance about his country is more subtle. His principal complaint is that Mexico's revolution, now fifty years old, is faltering, "that a new moneyed class has been created, and that the money is once again unevenly distributed." Three per cent of Mexicans, he estimates, own 50 per cent of the wealth. A new bourgeoisie has been created, the bulk of whose members are settled and content with their lot. But the life of the peasant and the city worker, he believes, is steadily becoming worse. This gives rise to a new ideological conflict inside Mexico, a conflict preceding Fidelismo by at least a few years. Fuentes fears that "rightists" are gaining in strength because of the fate of all revolutions: after a while indifference and stagnation set in.

A recent novel by Fuentes, *Where the Air Is Clear,* was translated into English and published in the United States (by Obolensky, New York). It is a big book and it talks about the shades of splendor and squalor, about the smugly satisfied in contrast to those desperately searching for new meanings in what should be a continuous revolutionary age. One character says: "How can we keep it from sinking, a country where instead of poetry, men read ads that proclaim the need to use antisweat cream on pain of losing your sweetheart, to gargle with chlorophyll on pain of being unpopular? Paradox, metaphor, imagination, to what a chasm you lead!"

There is the character Rodrigo Pola, a writer whose father, a member of Zapata's army, was executed by another revolutionary leader, Huerta; and there is Ixca Cienfuegos, a journalist and the modern conscience of Mexico, who assails both young and old for their apathy.

Rodrigo says:

> "You learn when you are very young. I had learned. Afterward, I always knew that I was what I had felt myself to be then: a spy. That is to say, a looker-on, destined to make

my life of the lives of others. And that was all. And I made something shoddy, because of my ability to understand all my defects, my inability to rise above them."

"You resemble the nation," said Ixca.

"No, Ixca, no. Why did my father know how to throw himself into the struggle, to overcome his defects, and I haven't known? Why was there a path of honorable action open to him and his men, while for us there is only conformity, burning inside and secretly, and the goddamned hopelessness? I tell you, from the time I knew anything about anything, I knew that I am less his son physically than morally, and that today I ought to act, that I have better reasons than he had, that he *would* act today, one way or another, that he wouldn't live at second hand. . . ."

4

A Warning from Pliny

The incontestable fact is that the struggle between the Communist and non-Communist countries, notably between America and the Kremlin dictatorship, is not over the capitalist industrialized nations in Europe or elsewhere, but over the under-developed or peasant countries in Asia, Africa, and Latin America. Having failed to persuade, beguile, or drive the proletarian in industrialized countries into revolutionary uprisings, the Kremlin leaders are concentrating their attention, now as never before, on the peasant in the backward areas of our planet. We are indeed living in an age not of proletarian but peasant revolutions.[1]

—Maurice Hindus

PRESSED BETWEEN THE huge walls of the Andes to the East and the Pacific Ocean to the West, long and thin Chile appears on a map to be simply a ribbon decorating the edge of Argentina. But potentially Chile is one of the richest agricultural areas in the world. The central valley, the heartland of the country, rests in the shelter of the Andean ranges and is easily irrigated by the melting snows that tumble from the hilltops. About two thirds of Chile's eight million inhabitants live in this fertile belt stretching a few hundred miles

[1] *House Without a Roof,* Doubleday, Garden City, 1961.

from north of Santiago down toward Concepción. Wheat, corn, barley, beans, potatoes, lentils, grapes, and a variety of other fruits, as well as prize-winning horses, cattle, and hogs come from the bountiful valley, and yet Chile each year finds it is less able to feed itself. It spends nearly $100 million annually, largely from United States loans and grants, to import foodstuffs. The anomaly, created by a medieval mentality as much as by inefficient farming, is accompanied by an ever-increasing gap beween the standard of living of *fundo* owners, the handful of men who control the land, and the *inquilinos,* the hired hands who labor on it.

Armando Garcia, now thirty, grew up as an *inquilino*; he works for the same *fundo* as his father before him. He is paid the equivalent of ninety cents a day, of which forty-five cents are deducted as rent for his mud hut and personal vegetable patch. In return, he provides not only his own labor five days a week; his wife, working in rotation with other *inquilino* wives, spends every second week in the big *fundo* home as a cleaning woman without additional pay; the Garcia children, aged six and eight, are too young for heavy toil; but they are on call for free services whenever the *fundo* owner so requires. The Garcias eat beans and bread every day and meat once a week; they take their drinking water from an irrigation ditch. About half the farm workers in Chile, one of the most advanced countries of Latin America, live in similar fashion.

Garcia's employer is a woman whose family has held the same couple of thousand acres for something like two hundred years; she maintains a town house in Santiago, where she spends most of her time. It was at a reception in the city that I met her and also received an invitation to drive down to the *fundo* to see for myself "how content everyone really is." When I enquired about the food allotment for *inquilinos,* she said, rather heatedly as she fingered her four-strand pearl necklace, "You do not understand customs here.

They eat beans and bread because they don't like anything else." Was there a danger, I asked, that "customs" might change, that landless peasants might be caught up in the swirl that has enveloped much of the globe? After all, in the most recent revolutions of significance—notably in China and Cuba—the appeal was directed at masses of peasants rather than at any other groups.

The reply was made with firmness and a degree of primitive dignity: "If the Communists have to come, I will wait for them and let them seize my property. I will never relinquish it of my own will." Another landowner, who had been a silent member of our group, now spoke: "Give the *inquilinos* land? You have to have human material capable of running the land. These are no better than animals. They work only a few hours a day, they get drunk on weekends."

There was an element of truth in this statement, applying not only to Chile but to every country where the majority of farm people are not owners of the land they work. (The generic term is *colono*, but the local name is different in different countries: *inquilino* in Chile, *conuquero* in Venezuela, *huasipungo* in Ecuador, *yanacona* in Peru.) The reasons for the so-called indolence and drunkenness, however, are not always as pictured by the owners. Sociologists with whom I spoke in almost every republic produced medical evidence to prove that the average peasant is so badly undernourished that he is incapable of sustained, intensive labor. Andean Indians take to *chicha,* a crude corn liquor, to deaden stomach cramps; or they chew the leaf of the coca plant, from which cocaine is derived, as a more effective killer of hunger pains. Any argument that proper agrarian reform might improve living standards as well as satisfy a basic emotional want is dismissed with contempt by most members of the oligarchy (but not by all, as we shall see later). A fairly representative remark was made to me by Hernándo de Lavalle, a onetime Peruvian presidential candidate, who referred to agrarian reform as "the big cancer of Latin America."

Armando Garcia, standing outside his hut in Chile's central valley, was not so forceful in his language. He said simply, "I cannot buy shoes" and "my children have no clothes." As he was speaking, a group of children sauntered down the road, chanting, "Fidel, Fidel." They had no real idea who Fidel was, except that, vaguely, he stood for some sort of Latin Robin Hood. Garcia could not enlighten them in their ignorance. He did know, however, beyond the fact that he was tied to another's land, that something else was lacking. Some people from the big city had come along and asked him if he was receiving the federal family allowance to which he was entitled. Garcia had never heard of a family allowance, but the people from the city now made him suspect that his *fundo* owner was collecting it from the government but not distributing it, as she should, among the *inquilinos*. His suspicion was probably well founded, because one newspaper advertisement I saw for a *fundo* up for sale boasted not only of its size but of the income from family allowances: about six thousand dollars a year.

There are two main troubles with the land-tenure system in Chile. First, only 14 per cent of the nation's arable land is cultivated. Second, three quarters of this cultivated land is divided into large *fundos* whose owners (2 per cent of the population) find it more profitable to speculate in land than to farm it properly. Between the extremes of large landowners and *inquilinos* is a third group of smallholders whose *minifundios*, averaging twelve acres apiece, are not big enough to sustain family life. The *minifundios* represent a scratched-out existence based on every form of destructive farming with no measure for preservation of the soil. The net outcome is that Chile, which twenty years ago was able to export more agricultural products than she imported, now has a huge deficit consuming a quarter of her foreign exchange. Unless there is a basic change in policy and attitude, the situation can only grow more ominous; food production is increasing by only 1.6 per cent a year while population grows more than 2 per cent. From time to time, various governments, with different degrees of sincerity, have gone through the motions of revitalizing land tenure, of considering equitable and more economic distribution; but not a single administration has been able to break through the aristocratic wall of conservatism.

"Maybe my son will have a different life," Armando Garcia said. Garcia's employer has told me that he, like other *campesinos,* was fatalistic and taciturn; and yet his attitude belies this comforting notion, for Garcia at least thinks in terms of advancement for his children if not for himself. Interestingly enough, too, Garcia in the last election exercised for the first time a vote of his own choice. Previously, the *inquilinos* in his district were handed ballot slips by their *patrones,* who told them precisely how to use them, with the result that a Conservative representative to Congress was always elected. In 1961 a man named Salvador Allende, about whom we shall hear considerably more, ran on a socialist platform and decided to buck the system of elections in Garcia's area. Allende hired a bus, equipped it with loudspeakers over which he urged peasants to vote without fear of reprisal, and displayed charts and photographs that pointed up the difference in standards between *fundo* owners and *inquilinos.* More pungently, Allende pointed up the lesson that the *campesinos* in Cuba, according to him, are now better off than ever before. Allende won the election, and Garcia in his own way indicated that he was not quite so "taciturn" as his employer would wish to believe.

Latin America, as I have mentioned previously, cannot be tied together as one unit. In some countries the elements of feudalism are not as great as in others; Mexico was the earliest of Latin American countries to start land reform; and while after many years controversy still rages about the results, there is no doubt that *peones* achieved a large measure of emancipation; in Brazil's Northeast, on the other hand, plantation workers live virtually as slaves. Purists may quibble about references to "feudalism" or "slavery." In the classical sense, it is true that Latin America was never feudalistic in the fashion described by Henri Pirenne and other experts on the Middle Ages. But in practice it makes little difference what terminology is applied; the important factor is that a traditional society—feudalism, semi-feudalism, modified slavery—survives to this day in much of Latin America, the statistics concerning which are shocking. And again common denominators creep through the graphs and figures.

In a few republics it appears that there is a large proportion of owner-cultivators. Statistically, for instance, Guatemala has great numbers of landowners; but this record is deceptive. Ninety-seven per cent of the farms are of the handkerchief size, much of the land so depleted it barely produces enough to compensate the tiller for the seeds he has planted. But at the other end of the scale there are 516 Guatemalan families who control 41 per cent of the best agricultural land. Half the farm land of Brazil is in the hands of 1.6 per cent of the owners. Since, for historic reasons, these *latifundios*, or large estates, embrace the most desirable soil, it automatically follows that what is left over is both minute and unproductive. In Colombia some 325,000 farms average one acre, and a further 500,000 average five acres. In Peru, Ecuador, and Venezuela 90 per cent of the *minifundios* fall into the same bracket of hand-to-mouth farming; and, since they hardly feed the immediate occupiers, are outside the market economy.

"Picture to yourselves the social and political effects—the political dynamite—of hundreds of thousands of tiny, exhausted holdings persisting side by side with tremendous estates that, as often as not, are uncultivated and managed more or less efficiently (usually less) for absentee landlords."

The man who made this shrewd observation was hardly a wild revolutionary or an extremist. He was, instead, Lester D. Mallory, Deputy Assistant Secretary for Inter-American Affairs, U.S. Department of State. Another point raised by Mallory: "The land problem and land-reform movements are nothing new. They are not something invented by Communist agitators; much less is the desire to solve them a Communist ideal. They are, in point of fact, as old as history and have been at the root of political and military conflicts since time immemorial." [2]

Another wise observer of the Latin American scene, Dr. Solon Barraclough, of the United Nations Food and Agricultural Organization, put it this way: "There is no reason that the Communists should take all the credit for supporting land reform. After all, one of the most devastating criticisms to be found anywhere of the system of large semi-feudal estates is to be found not in Marx but in Adam Smith's *Wealth of Nations*."

The quotations can be drawn from farther back in antiquity. In Athens, in the seventh century B.C., Solon made efforts to limit the amount of land controlled by any individual; his denunciation of the wealthy landowners and their failure to release men from bondage could be translated with ease into a contemporary accent. In Rome, in the first century A.D., Pliny the Elder looked fearfully at the strongly entrenched system of estates and wrote: "*Latifundia* will be the ruin of Rome." Some modern historians echo Pliny's words and say that the Roman obsession with big, privately held farms drove landless peasants into the cities, overcrowding facilities and contributing to Rome's decline. Re-

[2] *Department of State Bulletin,* November 28, 1960.

gardless of this point, the *latifundia* pattern itself survived and was handed down to later Latin kings who, in old Roman style, rewarded faithful followers and *conquistadores* with immense tracts of land; Latin America, in the middle of the twentieth century, is unwilling to relinquish the system; and as a consequence agrarian reform is unquestionably the most burning issue of today.

It was so, as well, in China of 1949 and Cuba of 1958. The message is obvious; and yet it has not sunk in where it is most required, in the minds of the strongly entrenched members of the oligarchy. Mao Tse-tung, in his appeal to four fifths of the Chinese, the peasantry, bypassed cities in the early stages of the battle with the Kuomintang and concentrated on the countryside, dividing the land as he went along and recruiting his soldiers from among the peasants; what happened later—the state takeover of the land and the establishment of communes—was cynically incidental, because by then the Chinese Communist revolution had established itself solidly. Fidel Castro also received much of his initial support from *campesinos,* who remain among the strongest supporters of the Cuban revolution.

Today, under the stimulus of dangerously warm breezes from Cuba and strong urgings from Washington, some of the Latin-American governments appear to be entering the road toward reform, but at a stumbling pace and over hurdles carefully erected in some instances by the governments themselves and continually by the landed gentry. If a few leaders are aware that farm problems must be faced squarely, there is a multitude of other leaders ready to push these problems to the background, either in self-interest or an effort to gain the moneyed support of the aristocracy. Fundamentally lacking is the will to give even a minor concession, lest it lead to a major concession. Many of those who talk about land problems, especially to impress the United States and qualify for funds under the Alliance for

Progress, refuse to concede that a solution to those problems must by necessity entail some sacrifice.

There are no simple or inexpensive answers to questions involving agrarian reform, as any Mexican or Bolivian authority can verify. The concept of land reform in itself is a controversial and academically fascinating subject. The narrowest definition implies simply redistribution with education (so peasants can learn how to get the best use from their soil), with credit facilities (so peasants can borrow money for seeds and farm implements), with marketing arrangements (so they can get a fair return for their efforts) and a hundred other details, including irrigation schemes, research, and so on.

Land reform means different things to different countries. It does not automatically signify seizure of the big estates or plantations and division into hundreds of thousands of small units. *Minifundios,* as we have already noted, do exist in Latin America, but generally they are characterized by limited capital and manpower and cannot provide sustenance even for their owner-families. Bolivia knew the most extreme form of concentration of big estates (92 per cent of the land was in the possession of fewer than 6 per cent of the people); and in the chaos following the 1952 revolution the land was fragmentized haphazardly into *minifundios,* so that today there is actually a decline in over-all production of commercial crops.

Every expert with whom I have discussed the problem comes to the same broad conclusions: Agrarian reform must be tackled diligently and scientifically. In some instances, co-operative farming is the solution; in others, especially those of sugar plantations, which cannot be subdivided with any economic sense, a form of outright state ownership with state management might provide the answer; in still other cases, *minifundios,* so long as they are sufficiently sizable, would be acceptable. But two main points remain paramount. First, there is the immediate need to satisfy land hunger of landless peasants; Bolivia has had 175 revolutions in its short history as a republic, approximately one a year; but—despite the drop in commercial crops—the one that was really meaningful took place in 1952. Second, there is the equal need to make better use of available land. Some Latin Americans, especially the largeholders, claim that only 5 per cent of all the continent is suitable for cultivation. Even accepting this figure, it works out to one and a half acres a person; on a comparative basis, this is three times as much arable land as Asians can place their hands on. But the big trouble, as illustrated by Chile, which utilizes less than one sixth of its cultivable soil, is that *fundo* owners retain title to surrounding territory, out of greed or a desire to keep investments in property, without putting a plow to it. In other words, much of Latin America is wasted.

And so the key to agrarian reform, regardless of the variants or details, rests ultimately in the grip of each of the Latin-American governments and the people who make up the governments. No matter how the key is twisted it must turn on a measure of self-denial. Before any scientific planning can be contemplated, the door must first open on the central problem of the present land tenure. States can carve up or in other ways make economic the overextended and often idle estates in one of two methods: either by expropriating the land or altering the tax system so that owners no longer find it profitable to neglect useful soil. In most countries, land taxes for the big estate owners are extremely low, but laws already exist giving governments the authority to penalize the wastrels and even, under certain circumstances, to take over their holdings. What the laws do not do is to convert hyprocrisy into solemnity.

If the intentions of Peruvian governments, for instance, were honest or sincere, degrees of land reform could have been pushed through years ago. There have long existed on the statute books regulations that say that any *hacendado*, or estate owner, who has thirty or more *yanacona* children in his domain is required to provide a school and a teacher. This law is observed by United States-owned estates and companies, some of which employ as many as sixty teachers; but most Peruvian *hacendados* in the mountains ignore it. A large number of their *haciendas* are so marginal and inefficient in operation that the added expense of a teacher would force them out of business; one North American agriculture expert in Lima gave me his estimate that as many as 90 per cent of the Andean estates could, in this fashion, be taken over painlessly by the government. While I was in the capital, a reform-inclined deputy actually had the audacity to stand up in Congress and suggest that the law be applied; he was shouted down by landowner deputies.

Peru, however, insists, for propaganda purposes, that its intentions are good. Typically, the government brought over in 1961 an Italian land expert as a much-heralded adviser; the publicity value was believed to be considerable, especially since the same man had helped to design Italy's postwar agrarian reform program. But within four months he quit in disgust, reporting that the Peruvian government and oligarchy simply did not have the will to alter the *status quo*. Again while I was in Lima the Congress went through maneuvers of debating a land-reform bill; because of intricate legislative rules, the bill would have to be debated two years in a row, and because of complex constitutional changes involved, the earliest any effective action could take place would be in 1964, if then.

Peru, of course, is not alone in such exercises, designed largely for Washington's benefit. Brazil has a clause built into its constitution that prohibits any takeover of land without prior payment in cash. Therefore, as matters stood in 1962, no government could introduce the first necessary step: a bond issue, redeemable over a period of several years, to pay off the big existing landowners. During my visit, the government had ten university committees working on various problems of land tenure and reform. Nine of the reports came in sooner than the government expected. Awaiting the tenth, obviously without impatience, an official told me: "Well, I suppose it will be in next month. Then, naturally, we will have to take two or three years to examine and study the reports." It was with similar cynicism that Brazil's Congress had previously discarded the scores of agrarian reform bills submitted by individual deputies. Ironically, one of these Brazilian presentations formed the basis for Cuba's radical land scheme.

A sensitive point about agrarian reform hinges on the question of how owners should be compensated for expropriated property. In Chile, for example, the three parties, so-called Liberals, Radicals, and Conservatives, which formed the coalition government in 1962, agreed in principle that land changes were necessary, but a major blowup ensued over the form of payment. A joint committee recommended twenty-year bonds. But Old Guard Liberals of the upper class rejected the committee's exhortation, and instead demanded cash, knowing that the government could not raise sufficient funds to meet any immediate and major bills. Finally, young Liberals, whose eyes had been opened by the growing influence of Fidelismo and who were well aware that Chilean socialists and Communists in a new alliance might easily win the next election, swung their elders to accept the notion of bonds. "You have swept away the right of ownership," cried an indignant Old Guard. However, at this writing a substantial Chilean land-reform scheme has yet to be put into motion.

Colombia at least is ahead of Chile, having enacted an agrarian reform bill on November 22, 1961. But even here only time will determine its effectiveness. As far back as 1936 Colombia's Congress passed a law allowing for the expropriation of unproductive territory; but nobody was ever able to define what "unproductive" meant. In 1957 another bill was approved dividing arable land into four classifications; but nobody could ever figure out which classification was which. The newest act came about as a result of the efforts of President Alberto Lleras Camargo, who had some disturbing figures gnawing at him: Colombia spends $30 million a year to bring in food while most of the nation's *campesinos* grow only enough for their own needs, with nothing to spare for city markets; at the same time, 40 per cent of the land is held by 1 per cent of the landowning class, who leave much of this 40 per cent uncultivated. By rectifying the maldistribution and increasing acreage under cultivation, Colombia in a few years could become self-sufficient in agriculture.

Lleras' bill, by any standards except Colombian, was moderate. It set up an Agrarian Reform Institute to resettle a modest 50,000 *campesino* families in four years—mainly on expropriated large holdings of more than five thousand acres that are not under proper cultivation. In return for relinquishing this type of unused property to the state, owners are to receive twenty-five-year bonds at 2 per cent annual interest. But where land is "partly" cultivated, owners are to get cash: 20 per cent outright, and the balance in eight yearly installments. It so happens that much of Colombia's uncultivated land belongs to families of relatively humble means with insufficient capital to develop it; they simply pass their properties down from one generation to another. It is this group that is the hardest hit by the legislation, while the really big and wealthy landowners, who have managed to find loopholes in the past, may be expected to take token steps "partly" to cultivate their unused land, thereby receiving cash settlement, or, since the treasury is limited, avoiding all state intervention.

Still, such is the emotional depth surrounding any event

that might indicate the beginning of the end of traditional rights that, when Lleras' bill reached the House of Representatives, right-wing Conservatives hysterically went into a near riot. As the clerk of the House started to recite a section of the bill, a Conservative Congressman leaped to his feet, attempting interruption by launching into an entirely different subject. The speaker of the House rebuked the Congressman, who then yanked the microphone off his desk and hurled it at the clerk. Other Conservatives joined in, and proceeded to rip out all microphone wires so the clerk would be silenced. When this tactic failed (the clerk continued to read without benefit of the public address system), the mutineers contrived to turn off all the lights. Decorum was eventually reestablished, but not before a Conservative, in a last stand, hauled an automatic from his pocket and threatened to shoot Congressmen who supported the bill. Eventually, a union of Liberals and less fanatic Conservatives succeeded in pushing it through the House.

Leftist parties also denounced the bill, but for not going far enough. What stood out, however, was the lesson that even as mild a reform as this is sufficient to arouse oligarchic passions in Latin America. President Lleras, a middle-of-the-roader who firmly believes in constitutional democracy, spoke wisely when he confessed that his bill was the best that could be expected under the political circumstances. A Colombian economist, with the memory of past measures that failed, said: "This could be a good agrarian reform law—if our people want to make it good."

It is clear that agrarian reform cannot be evaluated in immediate or practical results alone. An intangible yet vital factor enters into it: the promise of a better life for the multitude who up to now have had no reason to hope. This psychological element was brought out in Bolivia in the 1950's, and more recently in Venezuela. In many ways, Venezuelan reform is something of a test case. Its history does not follow the violence of the Bolivian or Mexican or Cuban pattern, but is an outgrowth of an active campaign by the party of Rómulo Betancourt, who fought verbally from election platforms. Venezuela's new land program had its official beginning in March, 1960, before there was any talk of reward from the United States through the Alliance for Progress. Today Washington looks upon it optimistically as an example to other countries that want to solve basic agricultural and social problems through peaceful and harmonious means. The hope for advancement still existed among Venezuelan *campesinos* when I was there last year, but, tragically, signs of political discord were also creeping in because progress was not rapid enough.

I drove out from Caracas, with its spectacular skyscrapers and white-faced buildings, along a six-lane expressway complete with toll booths and billboards reminiscent of North America. There was a choice between Philip Morris cigarettes and Kool, between U.S. Royal and Firestone tires, between Coca-Cola and Pepsi-Cola, or 7-Up. In this atmosphere of speeding cars and flashing signs, it was strange to know first that this was South America, and second that the consumer market could hardly benefit from the advertising, since it really takes in only a minority of the population. The bulk could hardly afford any of these U.S.-inspired products, and, in fact, live beneath any monetary economy and with far fewer than the minimum calories required for adequate health. But on and on, for a hundred kilometers to the bustling city of Valencia with a myriad of modern factories: electronics, a Ford assembly plant, Colgate-Palmolive. And still on and on, for another hundred kilometers, into the countryside, where live the majority of Venezuelans, as ill fed and as primitively housed as the peasants on the Delhi plain in India and worse off even than some of the *fellahin* of the Nile delta.

It is toward the advancement of these Venezuelans that Betancourt's agrarian reform program is primarily directed. The land allocated to them is from a variety of sources; some has simply been confiscated from cabinet ministers and other officials of the evicted government of dictator Pérez Jiménez; some is old state property; in a few instances, *latifundios* have been purchased from wealthy owners, with up to $30,000 of the value in cash, the balance partly in cash and partly in bonds.

One of my stops was at El Topo, formerly a private *hacienda,* in the state of Cojedes. Here dwelt fifty-two *campesino* families in a kind of collective life. Each had two or three hectares (five to seven and a half acres) for individual farming, but the main hours were spent working in the vast community fields. Before the state scheme, men such as Nicolás Bolivar and Pedro Pérez had been classified as *conuqueros,* nomadic laborers or squatters on badly cleared subsistence farms to which they did not have titles. Bolivar could never really claim the security of even borrowed land; he toiled merely for a few cents a day and a handout lunch provided by his *patrón.* Pérez at least had possessed a *minifundio* of one hectare, on which, as he put it, "my wife and my two children starved."

I asked Pérez if his life was any better today. "Better?" he echoed, and, not bothering to answer by words, he led me across the fields into a neighboring estate still held by a private owner. He pointed to a cluster of huts, some of mud heaped on frames of small poles lashed together with thongs, and palm leaf roofs, others of primitively thatched sidings which at least allowed a breeze to circulate. But around all were scrawny chickens and hogs, freely entering the dwellings and sloshing through the human and animal excrement. Pérez, still in silence, escorted me into one of the airless *adobes,* one room with no furniture of any kind. Then, as we walked back across the fields, he said: "I lived in that kind of house. My wife carried water from a spring, five hundred meters away, three times a day." Now he showed me his new home; it was far from lavish but it was at least neat and trim, its cement walls freshly whitewashed, its roof of proper construction. The two bedrooms and the combination dining room-living room boasted furniture: a couple of chairs and a table, and real beds instead of the mats on which Pérez and his family used to sleep. Possibly the most dramatic feature was the bathroom, with indoor toilet and shower.

Pedro Pérez built his home with his own hands and the help of neighbors, and, more importantly, under the direction of a government man who knew something about building. It cost five thousand bolivars (about $1,000), the credit extended by a government agency, Banco Agricola y Pecuario. Pérez' repayment is four dollars a month; but, working in the communal fields, he can figure on an income of nearly two dollars a day, a far cry from the old days when he existed virtually outside the money system. The bank also provided El Topo with enough funds to buy two threshing machines (the first mechanical equipment any of the peasants had ever enjoyed), deducting installments from revenues from the marketing which it handles for the community. For the first time, there is a school for the Pérez children, and a dispensary attended by a state doctor every Tuesday.

But the main impact of modern El Topo is that it has aroused hope in Pérez and the other former serfs; Pérez eventually will have title to his house and two hectares of soil, on which he has started to grow his own vegetables and raise some plump chickens. I questioned him about Fidel Castro. "A dangerous man," said Pérez. Previously, he confessed, he had given some sympathetic thought to Castro's words, but now he believes the Cuban approach to reform would make no sense for Venezuelans. "We are tired of slavery," said Pérez in a reference to the almost unbroken series of dictatorships that governed Venezuela in the last century.

Pérez, better informed than most *campesinos,* can express intelligibly why he supports Acción Democrática, the country's leading political party headed by Betancourt. Many peasants idolize Betancourt, and for good reason, because he at least made an effort to deliver some of his campaign promises. Pérez' friend, Nicolás Bolivar, not so sophisticated politically, frankly admitted that he did not know why he had been given his particular plot of land. Someone, he recalled, had just come up to him and said: "That bit is yours." But what Bolivar could understand and resent was the neglect by previous administrations of the well-being of *conuqueros.* "Year after year," he said, "I worked my *conuco,* and never had enough to eat. Did anyone care if I lived or died?"

But the story does not quite end with a flourish of triumphal trumpets. Rather, the question now is: Was Betancourt's plan a recurrence of the tragic "too little and too late"? Betancourt himself, a onetime vocal socialist, was beset by a series of ailments common to any dedicated reformer in Latin America. For one thing, he inherited a distorted economy left by Pérez Jiménez, who found graft easier to extort from industry than from agriculture; Pérez Jiménez concentrated on fraudulent public works in the cities, neglecting irrigation and other essentials that would make food more plentiful. Betancourt quietly told me: "Pérez Jiménez poured concrete into Caracas. I have gone mainly into the countryside."

But Betancourt's main problem was extremism; on one side were military and oligarchic figures strenuously opposed to changes of any kind; on the other side were Communists demanding sweeping and speedy dismemberment of the prevailing land tenure. "It was," said Betancourt, "like being a fakir lying on a bed of nails, with pricks from a hundred directions at once." Betancourt's admittedly cautious approach to land reform, he assured me, was not dictated by compromise or expediency but by a genuine belief in gradual process. "Otherwise," he said, "I call it an erosion of good things. If you do things too quickly, they can spoil."

What the Betancourt plan has been trying to do, in essence, is to create a class of small landowners or capitalists to replace the idle movement of men who were reduced to shifting from one piece of unused land to another; these squatters, who still exist in droves, are at the mercy of title holders who can appear at any moment and demand their removal. But the idea now is to give them, in stages, legal rights to the land on which they have struggled to achieve some degree of livelihood and dignity. The alternative is organized land invasion by impatient *campesinos* and a Fidel Castro type of collectivism. That the threat is a real one was indicated in May and June of last year when government forces had to put down a series of revolts by garrisons of marines, and a few leftist civilians, who, Betancourt charged, were attempting to lead a "Cuban-style rebellion."

And so the success or failure of Venezuela's agrarian reform really hovers on the precariousness of time. From El Topo and its optimistic air (El Topo is exceptional, and a showpiece for visitors) I descended into other areas filled with the blight and depression that mark most of Latin America. *Campesinos* were listless and confused; their lives had not yet been remotely touched by the charts and graphs drawn up by the National Agrarian Institute, which employs some five hundred planners in Caracas. The target is to resettle or to give financial assistance to approximately 400,000 farm families by 1970. The government claims that in the first year of operation land grants were made to 30,000 families; opposition economists with whom I spoke said the realistic estimate was no more than 15,000; and at the present rate, taking into account normal population growth, at least fifty years will be required to complete agrarian reform.

This gloomy forecast, in turn, is rejected by government officials who argue that Venezuela is proceeding not only with the purchase of *haciendas* but with schemes to open up virgin territory. But "colonization" of far-off land runs afoul of two main problems: the difficulty in convincing large numbers of people to move into new and remote areas and the enormous cost of building roads and other facilities to get them there. I heard the cry for "colonization" in every Latin American republic, almost invariably uttered by large landowners who have used the same chant in the past as a diversionary move to forestall fundamental changes in land tenure. Chilean landowners supported in 1935 the establishment of *Caja de Colonización*, a government agency empowered to finance settlements on state property; in twenty-six years new farms were set up for the benefit of only 3,300 of Chile's 200,000 landless rural families.

What are the chances for peaceful, democratically planned land reform in Latin America? An authority, Thomas F. Carroll of F.A.O.'s Latin American Regional Office, gives his answer:

> The available evidence is not encouraging. In fact, on the basis of past experience alone, an outlook of pessimism is warranted. With the possible exception of Venezuela, policy tends to polarize on one side in a "do nothing" attitude and on the other in a radical, revolutionary stance. The former group may tinker with some land settlement or tax reforms, and is likely to appoint commissions to "study the problem"; it may even pass some laws—which, however, are likely to remain on the books. With this group, in general, the hope is that the problem will go away. Where, on the other hand, land reforms have been imbedded in violent revolutions, there is either a nearly complete neglect of the technical and

developmental aspects (as in Bolivia) or a tendency toward political excesses (as in Cuba)....[3]

Dr. Carroll goes on to say that the picture is not without hope, partly because of pressures by the United States on Latin-American governments, partly because of some realization by ruling elements that the impact of Fidelismo must in some way be offset. The conjunction of these influences, he concludes, may eventually lead to meaningful land reform over wide areas of Latin America. Time is still the intangible ingredient, and possibly the final word is from another F.A.O. man who told me: "The average peasant, used to the domination of an overseer on horseback, wouldn't care much if he worked on a collective farm with a party officer telling him what to do—especially if he got more out of it."

"Social Security" de luxe

As far back as a half century ago a prominent Brazilian jurist, Ruy Barbosa, said: "Brazil has the finest laws in the world, but it needs one more to make the others operate." The reference was not only to criminal and civil codes but to social legislation; for Brazil, like Latin America as a whole, can be said to possess advanced labor and welfare rules—if not for the peasantry at least for industrial workers. Indeed, by United States terms of reference, many of the republics today can almost be called "Communist" because of their cradle-to-the-grave mentalities. In several instances they are much farther ahead even than such European countries as Britain and Sweden, which implement some genuinely socialistic principles of welfare. This phenomenon is interesting for two reasons: First it points up the fact that radical thinking in Latin America is nothing new and certainly is not the result of a fledgling ideology known as

[3] *Latin American Issues,* The Twentieth Century Fund, 1961.

Fidelismo. Legislators have long been aware of the sentiments of the growing industrial and labor classes, and have catered to their moods—in theory. Chile, for instance, has no fewer than forty-eight separate social-security funds covering various categories of workers. But the second part of the story is equally significant: Few of the ambitious schemes of Chile and other states are put into practice, partly because governments default in payments, partly because of inefficiency and gross bureaucracy, partly because of corruption. In virtually every republic free education and a free health service are provided—on paper. But these facilities are rarely translated into actuality.

In Argentina it is theoretically possible for a railway employee to retire at the age of fifty, and to go on receiving three quarters of his wages. In Uruguay a miner who started to work when he was eighteen can, again in theory, retire when he attains the ripe old age of forty. The fact that law provides, but practice refutes, does not unduly disturb government officials. "You Anglo-Saxons don't understand us," said a Chilean. "When we have a law it is not necessarily that we say that this is what we are going to do. Rather, it is an ideal toward which we will strive." In Chile for every active army officer there are five on pension. But out of every hundred factory workers only one receives a pension. Trade unionism in Chile supposedly is strong, but not nearly as strong as military unionism. People who have made contributions toward retirement funds must wait in line, hoping to collect after welfare agencies have met their immediate overhead expenses; usually there is nothing left over. People also cure themselves, or die, before vaunted medical help reaches them.

Brazilian and Argentine businessmen complain, sometimes with justification, that they cannot run efficient establishments because government labor regulations cripple them. In Brazil you cannot dismiss an employee without "fair reason" and without severance pay amounting to one month's salary for each year's work. There are, of course, dodges. In São Paulo I met a textile-mill owner who confessed the following: He had overproduced, and his warehouses were jammed with unsold goods. But he could not lay off workers because he could not afford the huge labor compensation. And so he simply called in a couple of union leaders and slipped them a private packet of money. The next morning workers were pulled out on "strike." Curiously, the "strike" lasted until the mill's stockpile was down to normal.

It is hardly any wonder that even though Brazilian law provides for collective bargaining, only 10 to 15 per cent of industrial workers bother to join unions. "What is the use?" said a typically dismayed Paulista. "The syndicates just steal, or get involved in politics." In Brazil, as in most other countries, the fanciful scheme for social benefits is run by a number of semiofficial organizations, to which unions, employers, and government contribute. Much of the syndicate money assessed from members is unaccounted for; while the government itself is billions of *cruzeiros* in arreas. "We have been betrayed," said a Brazilian. "Our money is squandered, and there is none left for our old age." I spent an evening in his company, along with five of his mates who were trying to establish what they called a benevolent syndicate to take over from the existing big confederation of labor. It was a pathetic group, comprising, by their own definitions, two "Trotskyites," two "democrats," and two "anarchists." Anarchists are not new to the Latin-American labor scene. They helped establish Argentina's first unions, back in 1870. They, along with Communists, dominated trade unions in Brazil until Getúlio Vargas came along in the early 1930s and transformed the syndicates into state instruments, just as Perón did several years later in Argentina. Labor affairs have been mixed with confusion, ineptitude, and dishonesty ever since.

On a continent where social improvement is so obvious and desperate a necessity, undelivered paper promises only add to the appeal of Fidelismo, whose advocates talk of social security equitably and honestly delivered. Uruguay's social security system may be too idealistic and therefore impossible to put completely into effect (there are one hundred and twenty-two laws of social legislation). But the tiny state does prove what can be done without the abuses of communism. Its government is truly democratic, being run by an efficient nine-man council representing the major parties. Its utilities are almost all state owned. You ride to work on a state bus, you watch state television, you fill your car tank with gasoline refined by the state and sold in state service stations. The chances are you spend your vacation at a state hotel, and, perhaps most comforting of all, you never really fear hunger because you collect a pension when you are entitled to it.

Uruguay's attitude was summed up last year by its president, Eduardo Victor Haedo, when he told a group of visiting United States businessmen: "You are capitalists; we believe more in socialism. But we like your ideas of freedom." And that is the essence, and the need: a respect for *dignidad* and liberty, but also a pride in social legislation that effectively provides a measure of security in a neighborhood of mounting insecurity. Uruguay is not terribly ebullient by Latin-American standards, but it is stable, and it has a place for everyone.

The Bandidos of Colombia

Colombians tell a bitter-sweet joke about a backwoods prefect who, informing Bogotá about a local election, telegraphed: "Voting going smoothly. Order prevails. Only nineteen dead." Apocryphal or not, it sums up a situation little known to the outside world, yet perilous to Colombia's stability. While newspapers in the United States and elsewhere were devoting headlines to bloodletting in the Congo and Algeria, more people were being killed every day through senseless violence in Colombia than in either of those two countries. What began as an undeclared civil war degenerated into family and political feuding, aggravated by sheer banditry and undertones of Castro-like action in the hills. In the last fifteen years, some 300,000 Colombians have been hacked or shot to death: a greater number than the total battle toll of all United States forces in World War II.

La violencia, as Colombians have learned to call it with fatalism and resignation, has its roots in the old hatred, jealousy and antagonism between Colombia's two traditional parties, Liberals and Conservatives. Murders had long marred Colombian politics; but the current warfare broke out in earnest on April 9, 1948, after the assassination of a Liberal leader. The Liberals accused the Conservatives of the killing; the Conservatives denied it. Rioting swept the capital, Bogotá, with hundreds of victims. The Conservatives, who were in office, drove Liberals from their farms; Liberals retaliated by organizing guerrilla bands and seizing Conservative property. From that time on both sides were obsessed only with the thought of slaughtering one another. Whole villages were wiped out because the inhabitants were known, for generations back, to have Liberal or Conservative sentiments. Individual communities themselves were divided by barricades. In the Andean town of Libano, for example, more than 8,000 of a population of 60,000, lay dead after nine years of skirmishes; one third of the homes and buildings were in ruins.

By 1957 the nation was understandably weary of decimation; it was also disenchanted with the dictatorship of General Gustavo Rojas Pinilla, who had come to power four years previously in a coup d'état pledged to restore peace and establish prosperity. Rojas' inept leadership only accelerated the chaos. The Liberals and Conservatives finally joined forces to throw him out; they agreed to an armistice in which the parties would alternate the presidency and divide evenly all government offices down to the level of municipal councillors. The arrangement, unwieldy as it was, worked to a point. At least the massive onslaughts ended. But now the habit of killing was so prevalent that even in 1962 lawlessness still dominated five of Colombia's seventeen departments. Despite martial law in these areas, at least one hundred persons continued to be slaughtered every month.

If the immediate reasons were not political, the origin could be found in politics. Bands of armed youths, left homeless and parentless through earlier killings, roamed the mountain passes, setting up ambushes for travelers or simply descending on farms to rob, rape, and butcher the *campesinos.* In one representative day last year, a bus was forced to halt because of a roadblock on a lonely rural road. Gunmen sprang out from behind rocks and bushes, removed the money from passengers as they dismounted, and then decapitated them one by one with machetes; hours later the same *bandidos,* led by a self-styled "Captain Poison," invaded the isolated *finca* belonging to Miguel Antonio Villegas, murdered him, raped and then killed his wife and two daughters, leaving behind a badly wounded farm hand to tell the story. By the time police heard it, three days later, Captain Poison was off in the hills striking another *finca.*

There are scores of similar bands whose chieftains boast such names as "The Avenger" or "Captain Trigger." Occasionally revenge is the motive, for the Liberal-Conservative feud has left bitter memories recalling *lex talionis,* the law of retaliation, which disfigured early Italian history. So ingrained is political hatred in some villages that attempts at "mixed marriages" between offspring of Liberal and Conservative families end in Romeo-and-Juliet tragedies. Some of the marauders wear army uniforms, which they have stolen or bought from indifferent quartermaster sergeants, and are believed to be Fidelistas, determined to emulate in the Andes the example of Castro in the Sierra Maestra. But most today are nonpolitical, content to hijack coffee crops or confiscate the belongings of entire villages. No construction has gone on in the town of Sevilla for a decade because those with the means have fled to the somewhat safer environs of Bogotá. Bogotá itself is free from danger by day, but few residents consider venturing into the surrounding countryside by night. On any excursions I took outside the city I was warned to return by dusk.

When Lleras Camargo became the Liberal president in 1958 he offered amnesty to all *bandidos* who would turn in their weapons. He also established a special antiguerrilla army unit known as the *Lanceros* to root out those still in the hills. The difficulty here is that you think back to Malaya, where it took the British, with modern equipment and scores of thousands of troops, nine years to eliminate Communist guerrillas from the jungles. In Colombia, the handful of *Lanceros* have two helicopters at their disposal; usually when they or the police arrive at the scene of a raid they can do little more than count the bodies. In some of the more fearsome areas the troops refuse to leave their vehicles.

Still, the moves by Lleras met with some success; in 1958 the estimated number of *bandidos* was 100,000; four years later the figure was calculated at 60,000. But Lleras, in keeping with the political armistice, retired from office, to be replaced by a Conservative president, Guillermo León Valencia. This led to a fresh outbreak of shootings by resentful extremists among the Liberals. Aside from the steady and expensive toll in lives, Colombia's little-publicized violence costs the economy untold millions of pesos annually, retards development of some of the nation's richest countryside, and could resume its former massive scale at any time.

A Common Market?

Many of Latin America's new political leaders have, at least in theory, a sensible and enlightened awareness of the hazards implicit in the gross inequality of wealth that endangers the continent's social and economic stability. But, as *The Economist* of London points out, nowhere, except in Cuba, has the redistribution of income yet been seriously thought about as a primary means to avert this danger. Instead, the governments tend to pin their hopes on projects for increasing the total wealths of their countries in the belief that by a simple process of arithmetic all the people will eventually have more. "This, however," says *The Economist*, "is not an automatic development. The mathematical division of export earnings stops short long before it reaches the people most urgently in need of relief. The bulk of profits are divided between the producing companies often owned by foreign interests, and the governments, which need most of the money they can collect from taxation on exports to keep their civil services and their armies in being. What is left percolates through to industry, to commerce, and to the local labor employed by export industries." But the vast disparity in the wages earned in the main export industries and by the ordinary urban worker is in itself a disrupting social factor; a Chilean copper miner, for example, earns the equivalent of $90 a week compared with the average industrial wage of $14.

Most of the Latin-American countries that have been largely dependent on one-item economies (coffee, in the case of Colombia; tin, in the case of Bolivia) are now aiming at more diversified economies. But will industrial development, if allowed to run its own course, necessarily result in a more equitable division? *The Economist* asks this question and then answers: Probably not, for two reasons. First, trade-union organizations in Latin America are very weak and are unable to have their voices heard above the din of conflicting interests. With the exception of Argentina, where trade unionism is based on Peronism, and to a smaller degree in Chile, the labor organizations do not compete with any effect against the most powerful pressure groups: the armies, the church, the foreign companies, property owners. Second, as industrial expansion goes up, agricultural production is faltering, and agriculture still acounts for the occupation of nearly two out of three Latin Americans; unless investors get rid of their notion of quick profit in industry, and fortify agriculture with better use of the land, any industrial growth is not likely to remove the disparity in income, and may even increase it.

With this danger in the background, Latin-American countries—some with ambitious five- and ten-year programs of economic planning—have nevertheless plunged into what, on the face of it, appears a noble aim: the creation of a common market. The enormity of this project can be better understood if the twenty republics are considered in the same light as the many European countries, with different nationalities, conflicting frontiers, and a variety of other problems. But here the comparison with Europe takes another direction and becomes a contrast. European countries, even before their own common market, traded among themselves. Trade among Latin-American neighbors has been almost nonexistent, largely because of mutual political mistrust. Trade routes traditionally have been from each country to its European or United States market: a shipment out of raw materials, such as coffee and cotton and minerals, and a shipment back of industrial and consumer supplies.

A striking example of Latin America's economic separateness, as described by *The Reporter*, is to be found in the northern regions of Chile and Argentina. In northern Chile the mining town of Antofagasta is located in arid desert; just across the Andes, linked by a railroad, is the fertile Argentine region of Salta, whose fruits and vegetables are isolated from the markets of Buenos Aires. The sensible arrangement would be to have Salta send its produce to Antofagasta, where it would be appreciated. The idea was voiced a couple of years ago, with several disturbing results. For one, it was discovered that the rail link between the Chilean and Argentine system had never been completed. Approximately fifty yards separated them: a defense, it was argued, against invasion. The two railroads had no agreement for the exchange of freight cars, each fearing the other would never return them. Moreover, there were no telegraph lines between Salta and Antofagasta; messages had to go via Buenos Aires and Santiago, a detour of several thousand miles. Banking arrangements followed the same impractical route. When steps were taken to overcome these hurdles, a great cry went up from Chilean farmers in the agricultural central and southern valleys. Although they had never been able to ship perishable fruits or vegetables to Antofagasta in any event, this was a *Chilean* market and not Argentine territory. Soon, they complained, Argentina would think of annexing northern Chile. ("It is not only the United States that is accused of imperialism," comments *The Reporter* wryly.) The idea of supplying a Chilean desert community with fresh Argentine produce was finally pushed aside, to await development of a common market.

European planners, of course, ran into the same kind of parochial obstructions when they first sought to establish their common market. But the trade patterns for Latin America are more rigid than Europe's, and no one believed it would be an easy task to create a system of communications between countries accustomed to ignoring one another. However, with prodding and encouragement from the United Nations Economic Commission for Latin America (ECLA) nine republics (Argentina, Brazil, Chile, Colombia, Ecuador, Paraguay, Peru, Uruguay, and Mexico) formed the Latin American Free Trade Association in 1961. They agreed to eliminate all tariffs between members within twelve years, at a minimum annual rate of 8 per cent.

The treaty, on paper, is a weak instrument, interwoven generously with escape clauses. Plainly, it will work only as well as its subscribers want it to work. But the logic in favor of trade among neighbors is there, especially in view of the fact that Europe bought 30 per cent of Latin America's exports before forming its own economic union; and now Latin Americans fear the Europeans will give a preference to products from African states. "Faced with the European Common Market, the Latin Americans are only now beginning to realize how isolated they really are," a vaguely optimistic ECLA official told me. One indication that the republics might now be willing to forget old differences and to compromise came six months after the treaty: members consented to 2,500 mutual tariff cuts averaging not 8 but 27 per cent each.

To finance their economic plans, the republics are turning first to private investment, and then, when this is not available, to international loans and credits. *The Economist* adds a note of caution:

> The reliance on foreign capital illustrates one of the basic shortcomings of nearly all the plans: the fact that they do not probe deeply into Latin America's failure to raise more of its own money for development.... Nowhere is there a radical attempt to divert the money that flows into salaries, defence and food imports. So the problem twists back, as do most economic and social problems in Latin America, to the weary tangle of under-employed land and a weak and discriminating tax system. The admonitions of self-help and

self-discipline that roll forth these days from Washington find little response in the economic development plans. The plans themselves are bold and imaginative exercises; they run the risks of toppling over unless the structure on which they are built is strengthened.

5

Another White Cross—and Vicos

STRETCHING UP from Chile, the great *cordillera* of the Andes forms a massive barrier between Peru's coastal desert and the eastern plains of the Amazon River. The loftiest Peruvian peaks are almost as high as Mount Everest, and the canyons are tremendous, some nearly twice as deep as Grand Canyon. In many places the rivers pass through narrow gorges with vertical rock walls. Roads, a few of them built by the ancient Incas, are carved like winding shelves on these awesome parapets left by Nature.

The Incas were a clever people, and well advanced in civilization. Five hundred years ago they could perform intricate brain operations. The only trouble with the Incas is that they never thought of inventing the wheel, so that no matter how marvelous were their engineering feats in hacking a road on the face of perpendicular rock they did not visualize man in speedy locomotion. The Incas, who had good nerves, went by foot around the steep and blind curves, or used llamas as beasts of burden.

There is a modern version of the llama, and it is called a *colectivo*. A *colectivo* is a kind of taxi: that is, an old sedan boasting four wheels, a motor of sorts, and a horn. The name comes from the connotation that it is a pool operation; the driver takes off for a journey up into the Andes when he has four or five passengers.

I started out in good faith for the community of Vicos, high in the *sierra*. It was four in the morning, an ideal time to vacate a hotel room in Lima, the comfortable and sophisticated capital of Peru. But I was anxious to visit Vicos because of an experiment conducted there among the Indians by Cornell University, a grass-roots effort that anticipated the United States Peace Corps by nine years. The Cornell representative in Lima, Dr. Henry Dobyns, assured me it would be a pleasant and scenic trip.

Now, I should not malign my friends from Cornell. The scenery for three hundred miles was indeed varied and picturesque. At first my *colectivo* driver, *a mestizo* whose name was Garcia, pointed out that the smooth surface we were on belonged to the Pan-American highway, which runs a good length of the continent. This felt like a fine flat road, and we clipped along it merrily in the dark.

And then, in the first glimmering of dawn, I saw that we had reached the coastal desert: a pretty sight, except that on the right side of the road shifty sand dunes spilled a bit over our path, and on the left there was nothing but a clean drop of several hundred yards directly into the Pacific Ocean below.

Garcia disapproved of vehicles ahead of him. So, with the precipice and the sea to the left, he passed a few cars at about seventy miles an hour. I had to estimate the speed; the speedometer, which had known better days ten years ago, was not functioning.

Suddenly, Garcia, coming around a curve, jammed on the brakes. The car rolled, but finally stopped. A hill of sand had cascaded right across the highway. Maybe if we had hit it the sand would have acted like a cushion; or maybe it would have been like a billiard table and we would have bounced into the sea. For a moment I thought of asking Garcia's opinion, but decided instead I urgently needed fresh air.

Waiting for a bulldozer to clear the road, I made my way along the edge of the cliff, and it was then that I noticed for the first time the white crosses. There were three of them, in a neat row, planted on the roadside and confronting the Pacific.

I retreated to the *colectivo*. Two of my fellow passengers were Indians who spoke the Quechua language of their Inca ancestors and no Spanish. The fourth occupant was an agriculture student from Lima en route to visit his family in the town of Carhuas. "What," I asked him, dreading the answer, "is the meaning of the white crosses?"

"Cars," he said. "Cars that went over the edge. One cross for each car. It is a nice kind of remembrance."

He glanced obliquely at me with an amused gleam in his eye. "Nervous?" he asked.

"Not at all," I protested.

"We Andeans," he said, "are quite used to this kind of driving and living."

For the next hour or so I was able to forget the white crosses and the fact that I had foolishly examined our tires and found them pathetically bald. The barren desert with its treacherous sand was gone, and we were driving through the richly green landscape of tropical valleys. Cotton plantations intimately nestled between quiet streams; and, even though the road had a dirt surface, it was straight and clear.

It occurred to me after a while that where you have valleys you usually find mountains, and here they were—breathtakingly beautiful—all around us, complete with snowcaps. We then began the climb, higher and higher.

It was only after we were on the Andean road for about twenty minutes that I realized that the surface was still of dirt but the width was cut down to a single lane. The beauty of the mountains vanished. The road twisted and wound in an endless series of S's, except that the bends were shaped more like Z's. Garcia honked his way past the blindly fearsome corners without slackening his pace.

On one side was a rocky mountain wall straight up; on the other side was an escarpment straight down, a sheer plunge in places of about half a mile, with no trifling bushes to break the view—or the fall. Garcia was obviously a man of aesthetic spirit; he kept peering over his shoulder at the spectacular scenery, guiding the 1950 Chevrolet at fifty miles an hour by instinct and horn. At one particularly steep decline he thought prudently enough to shift into second; but the gear refused to hold, and slipped into neutral.

The car gathered speed. Garcia steered with his left hand while he continued to wiggle the lever with his right hand, until the gear clicked into position.

I found myself stammering in my Berlitz Spanish: "Are you sure your brakes are good?"

Garcia swung around to answer. "We used them on the Pan-American road. They worked, didn't they?"

Since there were tortuous curves every fifty yards or so and Garcia insisted on answering by looking at me instead of the road, I withheld further questions. A few white crosses flashed by. I leaned toward the agriculture student and said, "What happens if a car comes from the opposite direction?"

He made a resigned shrug of the shoulders and said, "There's no room for two cars."

Actually we did encounter a few *colectivos* and trucks coming the other way. I am still not sure of the rules of the Peruvian road, whether the car on the ascent or descent is expected to give ground. But Indian drivers must have a code of signals of their own. After a few honks and a toot we backed up until we reached a patch wide enough for the other vehicle to go by.

This was an interesting operation. In order to get better

vision while he twisted and navigated backward, Garcia opened his door. As a result I got a much clearer view of the toylike bottom of the ravine. The open door also provided a magnificent frame for photographs of the white crosses.

By the time we had gone twelve hours and risen to 14,000 feet I felt I was in a rarefied and almost holy atmosphere. I thought: if I have to commit suicide I would prefer it by my own hand and not the hand of a stranger named Garcia whose Inca blood gives him courage but not necessarily a knowledge of the wheel.

Garcia, as though reading my mind, murmured something about having to be on the lookout for *huaycos,* avalanches; this was the height at which they sometimes occurred, and there was no telling when boulders might tumble on the road. I said to the agriculture student: "When a car goes over the side, can they ever find the wreckage in the depths below?"

Gently he patted me on the shoulder. "There are far more accidents on the Pan-American highway; it is wide and people drive faster." Then, noticing the numb expression of my face, he said in what was intended to be a reassuring tone: "These mountain drivers are very experienced."

What he did not mention, and what, unfortunately, I remembered from incidental research, was that the life expectancy of the average Andean is thirty-two years. Garcia was thirty-five years old, at least three years overdue.

At the end of the line, in Vicos, I was greeted by two young Cornell archaeologists, Gary Vescelius and Nicholas Asheshov. They asked me how I had enjoyed my trip. I told them that not even wartime shellfire had left me so terrified and shaken.

The Cornell men promptly decided I needed a drink.

"You may wonder," said Vescelius, "how we managed to get ice."

I had not wondered

"Remember," Vescelius said, chidingly, "there are no refrigerators in this part of the world."

My mind, I made it clear, was not on refrigerators or ice.

"Glacier ice!" Asheshov announced, undaunted. "That's million-year-old ice in your drink, sir. We've an Indian who chops a chunk for us once a week."

"Under no circumstances," I said, "will I return to Lima the way I came."

The two archaeologists considered this amusing. Could I suggest an alternative way?

A few days high on the shoulders of the Andes, living with stoical and simple Indians, can be wonderful for your nerves. Perhaps the paucity of oxygen affects your reasoning power. In any event, the decision suddenly appears very simple: either you stay there or you go back. My driver this time was much older than Garcia. He was at least thirty-seven, and therefore more mature and experienced. But he had more Indian in him, and his eyelids gave the impression of being mongoloid and half closed. I was not really certain whether he was awake at the wheel.

As we started out, shrouded in the clouds that grace the heights of the Andes, he confessed that he had just driven the three hundred miles from Lima and had managed to snatch only an hour's siesta. His breath also broadcast the stale odor of *chicha,* the devastating corn liquor first brewed by the Incas hundreds of years ago.

But he was resourceful. He stopped at a stream and dipped his head in the icy water. This gave him the uncanny ability to maneuver the car through a herd of llamas clogging the road. Every once in a while he repeated the performance at a stream, returning to the driver's seat dripping wet but at least refreshed.

We had only two near misses. The first took place just outside a quaint village where the adobe huts clung to the mountain ledge. We were proceeding toward a curve at the leisurely speed of forty-five miles an hour, with nothing between us and the chasm but a thin native horn. Honking! Screeching of brakes! A car from the other direction! We halted two inches apart.

As I glanced at the scenic wonders about a quarter of a mile underneath us I choked and said to the driver: "Would you kindly drive a bit more carefully?" Those may not have been the exact words. Still, there is nothing more effective in a foreign country, if you want to establish rapport with the people, than to speak their language.

The next time around a turn we touched bumpers with an oncoming car. It was one of the few places in hundreds of miles where the outside rim of the road was protected by jutting rock. In the slamming of brakes, our car skidded on the dirt surface; the rear end jammed into the protuberance and held fast. Visualizing what otherwise would have been a swift drop into the abyss, I again used my "impeccable" Spanish.

The driver shouted back: "But I honked my horn, didn't I?"

Obviously, I made Lima. I reported immediately to the Cornell office and asked Dr. Dobyns why I had not been warned about the shattering adventure that befalls anyone ignorant enough to scale the Andes. Dobyns, a rather shy professorial type, grinned and said: "If I had told you, would you have gone? We want publicity for our project."

He settled back slowly in his chair and reminisced. "As a matter of fact," he said, "I made the trip to Vicos myself two weeks ago in my station wagon (I would never trust a *colectivo*). And do you know, as I was coming around one of the bends I saw a crowd on the road; and a policeman stopped me. He asked if I wouldn't mind taking four bodies to the nearest mortuary. A car had gone over the cliff, landing, fortunately for the relatives I suppose, in a place people could get at.

"Anyway I couldn't argue. They loaded the back of the station wagon with the bodies."

Another car, another white cross.

Vicos is situated in a spectacularly beautiful valley, Callejón de Huaylas, under the peaks of the White Cordillera. It is here that the Andes reach their greatest average height; the twin towers of Huascarán, perpetually covered with snow, soar to 21,000 feet and dominate Vicos' setting. Vicos itself, an old *hacienda* of about 35,000 acres, rises and falls in levels ranging from 9,000 to 14,000 feet. The higher slopes are devoted to pasture for sheep and cattle; the lower, hilly fields are turned to maize, potatoes, wheat, barley, beans, and quinoa. Vicosinos live in primitive *adobes* and get about by foot or burro, sometimes visiting the glacier above the high plateau or, even more occasionally, descending through the clumps of eucalyptus into the valleys below them. The life of the people of Vicos is—or rather, was—the same as that of millions of other highland Indians through Peru, Bolivia, and Ecuador: one of physical isolation, neglect, and insecurity, accompanied by deep-rooted distrust and suspicion toward the outside world.

No one knows precisely how many "Indians" make their homes in the *sierra* of the three principal Indo-American countries, which, because of the "Indian problem," stand apart from the rest of South America. Estimates run anywhere from five to fifteen million. In Ecuador 60 per cent are supposed to belong to the purely Indian proportion of the population, in Bolivia 55 per cent. Peru classifies as "Indians" only 3.5 million of its twelve million inhabitants, though almost everyone has some Indian blood in him. None of the figures is especially meaningful, since by definition "Indian" is open to dispute. In practice, it is an economic and cultural classification rather than a racial one. The label "Indian" cannot be applied on the basis of physical characteristics, such as skin color, in contrast to the clearer interpretation of "Negro" in the United States.

With the biological mixture becoming increasingly more complex every year since the arrival of the first Spaniards, many ethnologists feel that racial differences between the two originally divergent groups, "whites" and Indians, have largely disappeared. Some exceptions are to be found in remote villages where 100 per cent Indians do exist and in the cities where European migrants have come over in the last few decades. But generally the lines have been drawn more and more around habits, education, and wealth. A man who speaks only Quechua or the other major Indian language, Aymara, wears a homespun *poncho,* and chews coca leaf, automatically is stigmatized as "Indian." If the same man moves from the *sierra* into an urban or coastal area, learns a little Spanish and discards coca for Coca-Cola, his *poncho* for Western-style garb, he may earn the more desirable title of *mestizo* (mixed ancestry), especially if, in the process, he also receives cash for his services. At the top of the status hierarchy, and centered in the towns, stands the minuscule upper class elite that calls itself *blanco,* or pure white.

The imputed "inferiority" of the Indian goes back to colonial times, and each of the two "superior" castes strives to keep the "Indian" in his place, arguing that he is incapable of accepting advancement. In turn, those discriminated against have, over a period of four hundred years, learned hostility and insularity. This is aggravated by economic backwardness that ties millions of landless and unpaid *peones* or serfs to the big *haciendas.* The "Indian problem" is a very real and explosive social issue; it should more accurately be called the "*sierra* problem," for it is in the mountains where the most withdrawn of the people live.

Bolivia was the first, and thus far the only one, of the Indo-American countries in South America (as distinct from

Mexico), to alter appreciably the social structure, following its revolution in 1952. This revolution had been aimed not only against a previous government but against the institutions and traditions that enabled an oligarchic regime to stay in power. Yet, even before the new president, Víctor Paz Estenssoro, could introduce land-reform measures, chaos and lawlessness swept the *altiplano,* the high plateau (12,000 feet) with the densest population. Frustrated and impatient Indian *peones,* many of them armed, drove landowners off their estates and simply occupied these *haciendas* as their own.

This was a genuine peasant uprising, but the situation, with overtones of a war of extermination between "Indians" and *blancos,* became critical. Paz Estenssoro quickly decreed the abolition of *latifundios* and the redistribution of the land. Economic disaster followed. Ignorant peasants, in their hunger and release from restraint, killed off cattle indiscriminately, thereby destroying breeding stock; other capital investments deteriorated. During the first few years farm production fell by almost one third, or at least that portion of the marketable crops reaching the cities. Urban areas are still feeling the food pinch, though it is likely that *campesinos* themselves are eating better than they did before 1952. Land distribution is nearly completed, with some 100,000 farm families the beneficiaries.

The revolution, inevitably, was accompanied by abuses; former landowners have received almost no compensation, and the dangerous extension of *minifundios* has not yet been offset by sufficient state aid in scientific planting or irrigation. Nevertheless, the *psychological* advances have been profound. With the disappearance of an entire class of wealthy, largely absentee landowners, Bolivians have begun to throw off the inferior and depressing status imposed on them and to experience a new sensation of power and dignity. It was the President of Bolivia himself, Paz Estenssoro, who pointed out to me a telling detail: for the first time, the faces of Indians are appearing on billboards and in advertisements as worthy consumers. The country, stated simply, has formed a national consciousness and sense of purpose.

This is not so in the case of Ecuador or Peru, though the topic holds the attention of some political leaders and many sociologists and writers. Jorge Icaza is one of Ecuador's most famed authors. A book he wrote in 1934, *Huasipungo,* won him international recognition and was translated into a half-dozen languages. In this slim volume, Icaza described the events that impelled a group of Indian peasants to rebel against their *latifundista,* or landlord, and how they asserted their claim to the soil. I asked Icaza whether conditions today are much different from those twenty-eight years ago. "Basically, no," he said. "The point, though, is that the only people who talked about the burdens of the Indians in 1934 were Communists or others considered extremists. Today everyone with a conscience talks about agrarian reform and the need to rehabilitate the Indians. It is not a problem of the Indians but a problem for all of us, involving economic, social, and psychological changes. People who still say that the Indians refuse to change their ways, simply do not understand them."

Icaza, who describes himself as "a progressive reformer," does not advocate violent revolution. But he is frankly pessimistic about the chances for social improvements to evolve peacefully. Ecuador, for instance, is speculating about the possibility of transforming *comunidades* into modern co-operatives or collectives. *Comunidades,* common to other Andean countries, are throwbacks to the days of the Incas. Members of them work in a vague kind of community effort, but without incentive or effective leadership or group action. Their land is usually the poorest, and without benefit of capital investment. Thus the system in its present shape reflects a stagnant type of agriculture, as much as the *hacienda,* a Spanish innovation, represents the extreme in autocracy.

Is there, possibly, a happy blend, a way to encourage peasants in self-improvement? Can they be made to drop their enmity toward *blancos* and strangers, to confound the skeptics and the extremists, to enrich themselves spiritually and physically without violent upheavals? Vicos is a remarkable example of what can be done by a handful of men —in this case, North American and Peruvian anthropologists—to engender a spirit that knocks down mental barriers and builds up confidence and economic gain.

Vicos possessed all the negative elements of thousands of similar mountain *haciendas.* It had undergone few changes since it was first established in the colonial period four centuries ago. A lone *patrón,* in the style of a feudal baron, manipulated the lives and fates of some three hundred and sixty families, 1,850 Quechua-speaking Indians. They were attached to the land, but owned none of it. The peasants worked in the main fields on commercial crops four days a week without pay, except for the occasional gratuity of one sole (four cents) to buy coca, the mild narcotic leaf. In addition, the men and their wives were compelled to do labor service in the "big house," the home of the *hacendado,* or estate owner; sometimes only one adult of each family had to meet the obligation for the remaining three days of the week; at other times the entire family moved over to fill the roles of cooks, grooms, watchmen, or shepherds. This effort, too, went unpaid. The only reward to the *peón* laborer was a tiny plot of rocky land supposedly sufficient to feed his family and leave a little produce for sale in the market. But, if he failed to execute all his liabilities, he stood to forfeit to the *hacendado* his tools, his animals, and even his sliver of land.

Vicos, like many other comparable properties, belonged

to the state. It was auctioned every ten years or so—ironically through an agency known as the Public Benevolent Society of Huarás—for lease to the highest bidder. The average annual rent for the 35,000 acres, complete with serfs, was $1,400. Vicos has had some particularly evil *patrones* and some relatively good ones. Recalling a few of them, a middle-aged Vicosino, León Stelso, told me about Señor Manuel Lostonoa: "He rented us to other *haciendas* as if we were cattle." For this unquestioned right, the *patrón* gained for himself some handy extra income, about twenty cents a day for every body rented out; if he did not lease them to neighboring *hacendados,* he leased them to the mines at Pompey or Huamaná. One of the worst *patrones,* Stelso remembered, was named Schereiber, who took from an elderly Vicosino his only cow, because the elderly man, while on duty with the *hacienda* herd, had allowed a wild dog to bite one of Schereiber's cows. Under Schereiber, most of the peasants fell desperately in debt for lost livestock; if a sheep strayed from the flock or was slain by a fox, the shepherd doing his labor service at the time had to make good. On the other hand, there was Señor Basagoitia who once in a while doled out grain and other food to the children.

"But when the *patrones* were bad, what could you do?" I asked Stelso.

Stelso gave me a quizzical look, as though this was a pointless question. Then he said: "We did not complain, because if we complained we were punished more. Sometimes the *patrón* beat us with sticks, or the *mayoral* (foreman) did it for him. Once, I did object to a beating, and I shouted at the *mayoral.* He ran to the *patrón,* and the *patrón* had me taken to jail in Carhuas. The *patrón* told the police I stole some vegetables from the big house, and I stayed in jail for two weeks."

Such was the oppression and depression around *Quebrada Honda,* or "Deep Broken Place," the ice-rimmed area in which Vicos' Andean valley is located. It was here that Dr. Allan R. Holmberg, Professor of Anthropology at Cornell University, looked in 1952 when he cast around for a typical highland community in which to undertake a systematic program of study and development; the objective was to determine how an Indian population would react to a sympathetic endeavor to introduce it to a more modern kind of existence.

Some facts and figures about Vicos were already known; for the previous three years a noted Peruvian anthropologist, Dr. Mario Vásquez, had conducted research there. Vicos was impaired by the usual decays: its people were listless, its habits ingrained from centuries of repetition; life's trials were insoluble because of "the will of God"; the world beyond the valley was alien and unfriendly. Only static conditions could be expected, and anyone who would attempt to change them must be looked upon as a fool or a dangerous devil. The United States, North Americans? Half of the Vicosinos had never heard of the Peru in which they lived, much less a foreign country or another system.

For diplomatic as well as practical reasons, Holmberg enlisted at the start the collaboration of government officials and the Indigenous Institute of Peru, so that his experiment could be called the Cornell-Peru Project. From the beginning, it had modest proportions; at no time were more than two North American and two Peruvian experts present at the site; only small grants, mostly from the Carnegie Corporation of New York, were available, and much of this money was used to sublease Vicos from the existing *hacendado*. The rest of the funds went toward simple equipment and salaries of the few trained technicians who could direct integration of four major areas of development: agronomy, health, education, and social organization. The underlying philosophy was one of self-help—the individual did have power to elevate himself—so that at no point were the peasants given financial handouts.

Holmberg soon realized that many of the abuses of the *hacienda* system were stupidly uneconomic and could easily be eliminated, to the advantage both of the owner and the *peones*. The peasants did not deplore so much the time they had to devote to the *hacienda* fields in exchange for their plots of land; what irked them was the extra service demanded. A *campesino* wife might have to go off to cook in the "big house" when she was needed urgently to care for her own children; a man might have to work as a shepherd for a few days when his lone cow was ailing and required attention. These were the prevalent annoyances that caused resentment, and feelings in the community often ran high. The simple and obvious solution was to abolish the canon of free service and to pay wages to men and women who were willing to assume a real responsibility toward domestic jobs. Holmberg came up with a particularly graphic illustration of how abolition of the established order could be beneficial for all:

The heights above Vicos, *Quebrada Honda,* were grazing areas not only for the *hacienda*; pack trains making the three-day journey from mines on the other side of the glaciated canyon also had to rely on *Quebrada Honda* to provide at least one night's pasture for their animals. For this public use of his territory, the *hacendado* charged a small fee. *Peones,* performing unpaid duty, stationed themselves at the narrow mouth of the canyon which served both as a collection point and a check point to prevent theft of the *hacienda's* cattle. But, since the *peones* received no direct reward, and in fact were sacrificing time that could be spent on their own chores, they saw justice in making deals with muleteers who were allowed to "steal" cattle. Even if the *hacendado* attempted to penalize them by demanding replacements, he often took a loss; many *peones* simply did not have livestock of their own, and sufficient cash was unknown to them. Project people discovered that by posting a permanent collector at the check point, and letting him keep the toll as his wage, the rustling was drastically reduced. The *hacienda,* as a result, saved money, and the *peones* saved time.

Not all the transitions were so relatively effortless. Holmberg and his colleagues were confronted with far deeper problems when they attempted to persuade the peasants to alter their agriculture methods. Tradition and suspicion were the two main obstacles. Peasants employed ancient, unproductive farm techniques, such as row spacing; they had never heard of insecticides against plant diseases; adequate fertilizers were nonexistent; seeds were old and impotent. In short, Vicosinos, like other highlanders, abided by the fatalistic formula of "plant and pray." Aside from poor soil and even poorer habits, they were handicapped by bigoted mistrust of any advice or ideas that came from the exterior.

Fate, in a way, assisted the Cornell group. Soon after the Vicos project was launched, blight knocked out the Indians' mainstay, the potato crop. Technicians tried to convince the farmers that not only could the blight be controlled but the potato crop actually could be multiplied if they would follow a few simple rules involving adequate preparation and fertilizing of the soil, planting of healthy seed, and periodic spraying with insecticide.

"Presented with this formula for increasing their potato yields," Holmberg recounted rather soberly, "the Indians did not immediately scramble to adopt the practices suggested." Many clung to their superstitions about alien intervention. Others, more amenable but outside a money economy, simply lacked funds to buy the necessary supplies. Finally, the project announced a scheme to extend credit so the Indians could buy the supplies, repaying at the end of the season with part of the increased crops. Still, the response was far from overwhelming. But a few of the *peones* figured they had nothing to lose, and so, on a small scale, Vicos farm reform was inaugurated.

The results were dramatic. For these few adventurous Indians, yields of potatoes more than doubled in the first year. Within the next two years almost the entire community accepted the formula, and yields in some instances rose by 400 per cent. Within another couple of years *peones* found that where they had once been able to grow only enough potatoes for their immediate families, they now had surpluses that they could sell in the markets of Carhuas, sixteen kilometers away. Vicos, in fact, grew more potatoes per head than any other region in Peru. Vicosinos entered the monetary economy, buying little household items previously unattainable. More impressively, they were able to entertain what was once an inconceivable notion: the thought of buying title to the land on which they had always been serfs.

Under Cornell sublease the *hacienda* fields continued to be worked by the community as a whole. But now, instead of four days a week, a *peón* put in only one day, with the rest of the time for his own plot. Startlingly, the *hacienda* crops, too, were bigger than ever before. In part, there were practical reasons; *peones* no longer were rented out to neighboring estates or to the mines, and so the lost man-hours were devoted to Vicos itself; and, of course, a measure of scientific farming helped. But another factor overrode all others, and León Stelso, the simple Vicosino, provided its clue: "Now we did not mind working, because we were not treated as cattle." Formerly, they resisted showing up in the *patrón's* fields before eight in the morning; under the project they chose to be there at six-thirty. It paid them, for after the project met its immediate expenses a portion of the *hacienda* crop went toward the *peones'* communal bank account.

By 1958 the fewer than 2,000 Indians of Vicos had saved enough to put down a deposit on the *hacienda*. By late 1961 they had $20,000—and then possession of the title! It was the first time in Peruvian history that Indians were ever in a position to buy a big *hacienda*; individuals, of course, had owned uneconomic *minifundios* of a couple of acres apiece, but nowhere else could you find such a large expanse independent of overlords or *patrones,* glowing with a refreshing air of hope.

Vicosinos continue, by any standards, to lead primitive lives. Even while I was there—well after emancipation—few families could boast a net income of more than two or three dollars a month. Diet to this day consists of potatoes or boiled wheat, and for the children *mazamorra* (corn meal and sugar pap). The children, barefoot as usual, spurt in and out of mud huts, which are thatched with *ichu* grass and closed off from sunlight. The women, following tradition, wear floppy, wide-brimmed fedoras indoors and outdoors, and wash their heavy dark robes at streams—and then only for *fiestas* three or four times a year. But there are differences, substantial ones. Infants do not die in quite such heavy numbers as before; the mud huts and the plots that go with them belong to the families; and Vicos runs its own affairs.

From the start, the project was concerned with transferring power to the community, not with retaining it in the grand manner of a *patrón*. But this, by necessity, had to be a cautious and gradual process. The only Vicosinos with any vague sort of experience in administration or leading other people were the *mayorales,* the half dozen foremen of the *hacienda*. Though chosen by the *patrón* to represent his interests, *mayorales* commanded respect. They were old men, and therefore considered by the rest of the community to be wise men. As a first step, Holmberg invited the *mayorales* to sit in with project experts while they discussed the economic and social problems of Vicos. After a while the *mayorales* were given the responsibility of settling small issues, such as disputes between peasants over boundaries. From here the graduation was toward policy decisions affecting the whole group, so the *mayorales* could broaden a onetime parochial outlook. Now the *campesinos* themselves were introduced to the rudiments of democracy; after weekly project-*mayoral* sessions, members of the entire community gathered to discuss resolutions and to offer amendments. From their ranks came men assigned to build a new schoolhouse, to spread some basic lessons of hygiene, to organize political discussion meetings, and in general to assume creative leadership in community affairs.

Seven years after initiating the project, Holmberg and the handful of other Cornell scientists were able to withdraw from direct control or even supervision of Vicos' affairs. Dr. Mario Vásquez, the Peruvian anthropologist, stayed on to study the process of social change and to advise the Vicosinos whenever they so requested. The only Cornell men who show up now, such as the two youthful archaeologists who offered me glacier-chilled drinks, are engaged in pure research; they have no authority. The community council, expanded from six to thirteen representatives and chosen by a popular vote of all the adults, includes younger men who demonstrate an aptitude for self-rule and self-reliance. This is not to suggest that the Vicos council in any way reflects the sophistication of a Western-style institution. In one session I attended there was a simple but touching discussion about whether the community could afford to buy, rather than rent, a truck to haul produce to the market (this, incidentally, now goes directly to Lima, where it fetches a better price than in nearby Carhuas). The councillors, fresh from the fields and cloaked in dirty homespun garments, sat on roughly planked benches in a hut with a pounded mud floor. But it was in the same hut, just a few years previously, where they had reached the momentous decision to buy the *hacienda* and to prove after centuries of serfdom that they could be their own masters. Today they deferred judgment on expenditure for a truck; this would be considered again next week. But they agreed unanimously that work must be done immediately to remove some of the rocks from the bumpy and treacherous dirt road to Carhuas.

"It is truly hard to recognize in the new Vicos the bedraggled and hopeless village where our project first began its studies," comments Holmberg, who still manages to pay a visit every summer. Holmberg sums up:

> This is simply one example of what can be done through a bootstrap operation to raise both the economic level of the Indian household and the production of food. When we examine the important increases in food production that can be brought about in Peru and elsewhere through the patient and careful introduction of more modern methods, the *sierra* of Peru no longer stands out as the area of poor resources that it has always been considered. The Vicos experience indicates so far that dramatic results can be achieved at a relatively small cost. They can be attained, however, only if careful attention is given, not only to the problem of modern techniques, but also to the people and their culture. For this reason, from the very start the Cornell-Peru project has given careful thought to the problem of developing a spirit of independence, responsibility, and leadership in community affairs—a spirit that had never existed before. . . . Our experience at Vicos indicates that, if granted respect, the Indian will give respect. If allowed to share in the making of decisions, he will take responsibility and pride in making and carrying them out. . . . An approach to the *sierra* people along

these lines can lead them into a dynamic and progressive society.[1]

Vicos is operated on semicommunal lines. While individual peasants are allowed a couple of hectares of land each, the main fields are held by the community and profits go into a common treasury. On the surface it even resembles a Chinese commune. Houses are scattered through the countryside, but people gravitate toward a kind of village compound that takes in the main buildings: the school, the clinic, a makeshift hostel for visitors, a "club" or community center for women. There is obvious pride in this development, for walls of these large *adobes* are whitewashed and, as in Communist China, exteriors are covered with hand-lettered slogans. But here the similarity fades away. In Hsushui commune, Hopei Province, I read such phrases as: "Chairman Mao thinks of our welfare," and, "One Hand on the Hoe, One on the Rifle." In Vicos the quotations were from the United Nations Declaration of Human Rights: *Todos los seres humanos nacen libres e iguales en dignidad y derechos!* All human beings are born free and equal in dignity and rights. Hsushui, backed by government resources and autocratic direction, was far more efficiently managed than Vicos, a rather disturbing message until one remembers that Vicos retains dignity and individuality. The option of whether Hsushui or Vicos will set the future pattern for Peru remains with the government in Lima.

There is no evidence that the Peruvian government was ever enamored of the concept of Vicos. On the contrary, though Holmberg discreetly avoids any such references in his writings, the indications are that if Lima had suspected any widespread social undertones to the project, it might never have permitted its start. But the dictator Manuel

[1] *Social Changes in Latin America Today,* published for the Council on Foreign Relations by Harper & Row, 1960.

Odría was in power at the time and eager to make a favorable impression on the United States. One of the ways in which he could appear cooperative was to allow a small group of harmless United States professors to conduct an experiment in the remote Andes; at least the established order was not in any sense in jeopardy. Later, when the practical results of Vicos became known, the government took the propaganda line that it was trying to help peasants, and, to prove it, would establish on its own five similar projects.

Significantly, however, Vicosinos have the United States President's youngest brother, Edward M. Kennedy, to thank for the title to their land. Ever since making their down payment in 1958 on the purchase of the *hacienda* they had appealed to the state-controlled Public Benevolent Society of Huarás to relinquish the title. The society held back, even after the community could guarantee full payment; the supposition was that Vicos was a dangerous embarrassment because its unfettered ideas were spreading to other *haciendas*. Kennedy, on a visit to Vicos in 1961, heard of the plight of the Vicosinos, and on his return to Lima put pressure on Peru's president, Manuel Prado, to issue orders to the "Benevolent Society." Again because a government wanted to keep in well with Washington, a small request—involving a justified land title—was granted.

Much of the battle the Vicosinos have learned to fight for themselves. Long before the first Cornell men showed up, Vicos had a schoolroom, yet not a single child of primary school age could read or write. In the entire population of 1,850, only four persons were literate, and just barely so. Not more than a few men had even a smattering of spoken Spanish, an essential if contact was ever to be made with the world beyond the valley, and they had learned this during compulsory army service. The reasons for the backwardness were general throughout the highlands. For one thing, the *hacendado,* or *patrón,* who was responsible for education, simply did not desire to see it pursued. "I come from a country," cried the great *pensador* Domingo Sarmiento after a nineteenth-century visit to the United States, "where education is everything, where education has succeeded in establishing true democracy, making races and classes equal!" In the minds of *patrones,* even in the twentieth century, it was precisely this risk of democratization that was to be avoided; for them, *peones* were a plentiful source of cheap unskilled labor that might be lost if they were given an opportunity to acquire knowledge and new values. At the same time, nescient parents did not press for the education of their children; if God would command it, fine; otherwise, why bother? Besides, on the rare occasions when a teacher did make an appearance, she would, being a *mestizo,* treat Indian children as inferiors and usually put them to work as servants in her house rather than in the classroom. If this was the case, their labor efforts were of greater value at home.

It did not take the Cornell people long to convince Vicosinos that they were entitled to reasonable instructors and that education would mean an improvement in their living standards. The Peruvian ministry of education was persuaded to send out a teacher, and by the end of the first year thirty children were in attendance in the classroom. In the second year, men of the community set out to build the first wing of a modern schoolhouse; thirty-five boys and girls were now using it. By the third year a second wing was being erected, including an auditorium, and enrollment had jumped to eighty-five. In 1961 two hundred and seventy children were registered, but the Vicos community council, now in command and feeling novel confidence, was not satisfied with the caliber of the teachers. The *mestizos* sent out by the government came from faraway areas, bringing with them the old prejudices against Indians; some children found themselves assigned to the menial chores of former days.

The council attempted, unsuccessfully, to get the ministry of education to hire teachers from the region, men and women who would take a more understanding attitude toward their charges. When the government failed to respond, the council simply voted to hold a strike, and for a week the children stayed away from school. The council made its point, and today the Vicos school boasts seven state teachers from nearby towns, one teacher for each of the classrooms. The average Vicosino child is likely to receive seven years of primary school education, a far longer course than in the rest of Latin America.

Moreover, Vicosinos speak proudly of the two children, the first ever, who have been transferred to high school in Carhuas. The community pays for their room and board away from home, and the intention is that after graduation the children will become teachers in their own village.

Girls, who previously were considered unfit for education, are beginning to appear at the Vicos school along with the boys. One reason for the constantly increasing enrollment is eminently practical. Cornell men, in swinging Vicosinos toward education, used as bait a free meal; that is, children would be given a nutritious hot lunch if they attended classes. This stimulus had natural appeal among desperately poor families for whom the feeding of every mouth was a burden. The tradition of free meals goes on, but now the community itself maintains the kitchen at the schoolhouse. Another Cornell-inspired lure is employed in passing out some simple lessons in child care. The women of Vicos are fascinated by the five Singer sewing machines that adorn one of the two rooms in the whitewashed *adobe* which serves as a clubhouse. They arrive in large numbers to learn how to handle the machines and mend their garments; while there, a "seamstress," herself barely qualified, coaxes them into the adjacent room where they are given homely lectures on hygiene and other measures designed to cut the infant mortality rate. In 1952, 60 per cent of Vicos' children were dead before the age of five; the figure is still shocking, but at least it has declined to 40 per cent.

A state doctor also calls around once a week at the clinic (he had not shown up for several weeks before my visit, and the community council was drafting a strong protest). Many Vicosinos continue to abide by old superstitious medical rules: When sick, take a guinea pig and rub it against your chest; this will transfer your sickness to the guinea pig. But, slowly, they are accepting Western medications. Some of the adults, too, are taking night courses in reading and writing, so that today about 10 per cent have a glimmering of Spanish and the United Nations inscriptions on the wall are becoming meaningful.

One of the delicate problems of the original project hands was to introduce the Indians to the higher standard of living enjoyed by Spanish-speaking *mestizos* but at the same time protect them against *mestizo* mentality, which tries to copy the upper classes in thinking that physical labor is undignified. The *mestizo* group acts as a hindrance rather than a help in any effort to bring the Indians into communication with outer civilization. The Indians themselves have sensed this, especially after watching Cornell *blancos,* or "white" men, dig into the soil with their own hands or otherwise pick up filth while demonstrating farm techniques. *Mestizo* technicians, sent occasionally by the state, have not been similarly inclined. A curious result is that Vicosinos, who have seen fewer than thirty North Americans in the last ten years, have discarded their ancient suspicion and fear of strangers,[2] and now place more confidence in *blancos* than

[2] I, for instance, was treated with great courtesy, and continually called "doctor," a tribute to the anthropologists and other deserving academic types who had come to Vicos before me.

in *mestizos*. Dr. Vásquez, the benevolent social scientist on the site, and himself a *mestizo,* recognizes this denouement, rather sadly but with sympathy. He can quite understand why Vicosinos, who were hardly aware of the existence of the United States before 1952, have asked, through their elected council, for help from the United States Peace Corps. After a taste of instruction and education they want more: someone to teach accountancy so the community books can be better kept, to teach animal husbandry, and even English!

The Vicos project, with its encouraging years of results, is the greatest single justification I know for the work of the Peace Corps and similar agencies that have men and women willing to live among and labor with indigent people.

The terrible irony is that the Peruvian government itself has done little to move the human resources into rewarding channels. The five integration programs it has started elsewhere in the Andes, based on the Vicos experience, embrace only a few hundred families and have more a publicity than a practical value. The main talk in Lima is about "colonization," an escapist formula to shift peasants into the virgin Amazon jungle; this is no substitute for basic agrarian reform of existing cultivable soil, which Vicos proved could be made fruitful beyond expectation. The example of Vicos has spread far and wide by word of mouth. Dr. Vásquez, who is familiar with the mood of the countryside, believes ardently that unless Lima moves rapidly to satisfy the aggravated frustration of *peones* the outcome will be one of violence. He says:

> In the highlands they know nothing about politics—nothing about communism or even their own government. But one day they could well know about communism; people from here sometimes move to the cities, and when they come back on visits they explain what is happening in the outside world. The Indians may be ignorant and illiterate, but there

is an instinctive hunger for land and freedom. One way or another, they will get it. It would be better if they got it the way Vicosinos got it.

The sum of Vicos is that it is the most inspiring phenomenon I met in all Latin America. Here is a simple and clear case of how a people, previously oppressed but now treated with respect, can, given the opportunity, pull themselves from endless misery by their own energies. They might have languished in the hills or drifted off to the slum poverty and degradation of the Lima *barriadas*. Instead, they are attaining a better life with dignity and self-confidence.

Near the rolling lands of Vicos, and in the same valley, Callejón de Huaylas, are other *haciendas* where the peasants for centuries accepted their lot. Touchingly, once the Vicosinos began to feel secure, they engaged in their own informal "Point Four" program, passing on to neighbors their new farm techniques. But for some of the recipients information by itself was not enough. They wanted land. Adjacent to Vicos was the *hacienda* known as Huapra. In accordance with a medieval custom, the descendants of the original title-holder leased Huapra, over a period of hundreds of years, to the church. A group of forty-five Indians, realizing that a huge portion of Huapra was uncultivated, went to their parish priest. Their spokesman said: "Here is unused land. We wish to farm it. We will save the money we make from the crops, and one day we will buy the land, the way the Vicosinos bought their land." The priest gave his permission and his blessing.

But overlooked was the archaic specter of a *hacendado* somewhere in the background—that is, a man who technically could claim to be the owner since the title was still in his family's name, regardless of the fact that the church, and not the family, had been administering the estate for generation upon generation. The *hacendado,* characteristic of his caste, did not believe that Indians should be permitted to step an inch out of predestined line. He drove to the regional prefect's office and demanded that fifteen national guardsmen accompany him back to Huapra to evict the "squatters." Once on the fields, the *hacendado* pointed to the Indians he felt were the leaders of the group. Guardsmen moved closer, to make arrests. But the other Indians shouted that if one or two were going to be killed, they would all have to be killed. A youthful guardsman, frightened by the uproar, leveled his rifle and fired. The rest of the soldiers fell into a chain reaction and also opened fire. Within seconds, three Indians lay dead and five were critically wounded. It may have been a quirk of timing, or, more precisely, a sign of the times, that the incident at Huapra took place shortly after police in Sharpeville, South Africa, slaughtered other men appealing for their rights.

As at Sharpeville, the local authorities claimed they had to act in self-defense; in this case they said they were attacked by a savage mob of two hundred heavily armed Indians. In fact, there were forty-five Indians, all unarmed. The episode might have ended there, but for the presence of three witnesses from the Cornell project at Vicos: Carlos Tolentino, a Peruvian student writing a thesis on agrarian reform; Ralph Klein, a New York psychologist; and Norman Fine, a New York medical student. Fine, hearing that guardsmen were on their way to Huapra, mounted a horse and raced over to the *hacienda.* He saw the soldiers take aim and then heard the shots, but assumed they were blanks until a bullet landed in the dust beside him and he had to hold his horse from bolting. The three students gave first aid to the wounded; Carlos Tolentino, protesting in heated Spanish the viciousness of the guardsmen, was arrested on the spot. Soldiers also tried but failed to confiscate film taken by Klein. Unaware of the eyewitness accounts, authorities in Lima later asserted that the Indians, "led by outside agitators," charged an army outpost. Cornell people made up a booklet of photographs, together with statements from the three students, to prove the true sequence; and Lima finally called for the resignation of the district prefect.

The Huapra event pointed up the fact that "serfs" are no longer submissive; the survivors of the shooting did not flee, as might be expected (nor did the men and women of Sharpeville decide to cease agitating after some of their numbers were killed). To this day the Indians are "squatting" at Huapra, but now the *hacendado* dares not call out the national guard. Huapra was simply one of twelve known similar incidents in the Peruvian Andes, within a year, in which there were deaths. What makes it different is that it is the best documented massacre of Indians on record.

Other violent occurrences pass without the clear-cut testimony of neutral observers. In October, 1961, the first of some four thousand Indians began squatting on the pastures of five large *haciendas* in the copper-mining area of Cerro de Pasco, high in the Andes. The Indians were from the community of Yanahuanca, which suffered from the usual complaints that landless peasants were going hungry while absentee landlords ignored them. Without warning, on March 3, 1962, a national guard battalion of three hundred soldiers arrived at Yanahuanca to expel the Indians. The date is undisputed. The rest is lost in conflicting accounts. According to one of the peasants, Fermín Espinoza,

> It happened after the shepherds had brought their flocks together and everyone was resting and happy, drinking a little *chicha* and playing their *quenas* (reed flutes) and singing. Suddenly, mounted guards appeared and started shouting for us to go away. When we refused, they began to use tear gas. Everyone ran in confusion, women and children crying. They set fire to our huts. Some of the men refused to leave,

> saying "Let's hold onto this land. It is truly ours." But the guards broke us up with their horses, beat us with their sabres, and fired into us, and that is how several were killed and many more were wounded.[3]

The official report, issued 110 miles away in Lima, gives a different version. It quotes General Humberto Quea, of the national guard, as saying that his men, on their way to one of the estates, were attacked without provocation by a hostile band of Indians armed with shotguns, knives, and slingshots. When the soldiers threw tear gas, Quea said, the Indians really started the bloodshed by rolling boulders down the steep hillsides and firing their guns and slingshots. The guardsmen then retaliated, said Quea, by opening fire with their own rifles.

Whichever interpretation was correct, eight Indians who had died of bullet wounds were buried on a rocky mountainside near Yanahuanca. At the funeral, Yanahuanca's mayor, Eladio Lobatón, called them "the first heroes of the agrarian reform." The government, meanwhile, published another bulletin claiming that the drama was part of an extremist campaign intended to exploit Peru's Indians and create turmoil under the cry for agrarian reform. This glib dismissal of an ugly shooting covered up the grave features of a deeply significant trend. There was no evidence that the Indians of Yanahuanca had been subjected to external influences. But there is also no doubt that leftist reformers from Lima are now making use of the mood of peasants, moving among them, and even setting up farm unions. Part of the appeal to Indians is that the *haciendas* are actually their lands, taken from their ancestors centuries ago by the Spanish *conquistadores*. Implicit in this approach is an effort to establish a pan-Indian or pan-peasant movement, as in Bolivia, which

[3] Quoted in *Time*, Latin-American edition, March 16, 1962.

would seize control of the government and usher in radical reform. In this connection, it is interesting that the loudest shouts of a new chant, *"A la cubana!"* (the Cuban way), I heard in the chill mountain air of Cuzco, the former capital of the Inca empire.

6

The Frock and the Uniform

It was by sheer chance that I met Padre Antônio Costa. Along with an interpreter in Portuguese, I had stopped near the village of Cabo, in the Northeast of Brazil, to ask a farmer for directions to a nearby sugar plantation. He jumped into our car and guided us in person. Later he suggested that we visit the village priest, who, he said, could tell us many interesting points about the area.

Brazilian newspapers, it turned out, had already caught sight of Padre Costa and published articles about him, in the expectation that he might become a national figure. My own impression is that he well might, if only because of the strength of his personality. A man of twenty-eight, with flashing brown eyes and a marvelously expressive face, Padre Costa has the gifts of fervor and rhetoric. One of my first questions was about Francisco Julião, the founder and leader of the Northeast's growing and revolutionary chain of Peasant Leagues. Did the people believe in him?

"They do not believe in Julião, they do not believe in the Church, they do not believe in anything," said the padre, with a flourish of the hands. "They are too hungry to believe."

Padre Costa, a member of the Secular Order of Brazil, does not preach politics in church, but he does hold informal open-air meetings near the railway station. He also teaches school. While he was speaking to me in the schoolroom, about thirty children, ranging in age from about eight to thirteen, clustered outside the open door, obviously savoring his words and looking on with undisguised admiration.

Three things, he said, are indisputable about present living conditions: "First, everyone accepts that there is a problem. Second, everyone says something must be done about it. Third, no one does anything." In Brazil's Northeast, which has more inhabitants than all of Argentina, there is massive peasant poverty, unemployment, and malnutrition—and enough discontent to create a half-dozen Cubas. To Padre Costa the cure for the chronic ailments is manifestly simple, yet it would involve a measure of magnanimity by landowners and other greedy oligarchs. "We need land reform and education immediately," he says. "The rest can come later." The rest? The padre speaks almost with a Gandhian philosophy: "We can think of industrialization after we have fed the people and given them the knowledge with which to work. We have the greatest machinery in man's two hands, but first we must give him hope."

The reference to industrialization is an oblique criticism of Sudene, a Brazilian government agency that is attempting an ambitious program of rehabilitation in the Northeast, with part of the emphasis on expanding the few existing factories. Padre Costa looks upon this as a dodging of the real issue: land. What he wants primarily is for the state to take over the large plantations and estates, with compensation, and to spread the land among the peasants. As a result, the planters call him a "Communist." This does not bother Padre Costa. He makes the point: "If changes are not made, then surely the Communists will win."

Thousands of miles away, high in the Andean hills around

Vicos, I ran into another type of parish priest. Indians complained bitterly that they saw him only once every few weeks, for important funerals, and he would not conduct the service unless he was paid. The priest chanted the Requiem with one hand outstretched. As soon as the flow of coins ceased, so did the service.

Between the two extremes is the story of the Roman Catholic Church in Latin America. The hierarchy in general, and many parish priests, cling to a Middle Ages mentality that supports the traditional landowners and preaches that man's reward comes in afterlife. That this approach creates contradictions is attested by some statistics. In Brazil, which is almost entirely Catholic, fewer than 10 per cent attend Sunday Mass; in Argentina, according to a Church survey, "an average of Catholics who make their Easter duty would not be above 5 per cent." [1] The same kind of figures prevail throughout the continent.

The Church in Latin America has long been characterized by ambivalence. Under the system of royal patronage, the cross and the sword moved alongside one another over the seas and into the New World. The cry was for conquest equally in the name of God and King, and to the religious orders fell the task of converting and taming the Indians brought into line by the *conquistadores*. The Church, which was dominated by the royal authorities, became a handy instrument for controlling the population and fostering expansion. In this alliance, priests took on some of the worst features of their military partners: a buildup of exploitation and a greed for wealth and power. Some of the missionaries, notably the Jesuits, defended the Indians against abuse, establishing inland cooperative colonies and teaching them how to farm on scientific lines; in this role they themselves were hounded by the colonizers. But on the whole the

[1] *Latin-American Catholicism*, by Father William J. Coleman, M.M., World Horizon Reports, 1958.

Church remained aloof from the material problems of its converts and opposed to social changes. In the process it amassed a great fortune. By the nineteenth century the Church, through gifts, tithes, and other revenues, owned between one third and one half of all the private property in the colonies. It also directed education.

Since the Church had been an arm of the Spanish and Portuguese empires, members of the hierarchy, with minor exceptions, opposed the colonies' emancipation movements of the early 1800's. After independence, there was a bitter struggle and an attempt by high Church officials to set the Church free from the control of the State and make it a servant of the Church. In the end, the functions, privileges and wealth of the Church were reduced in the interests of the State. "In most instances," according to Rippy, "all that the people obtained from the expensive, bloody and prolonged conflict was a little more freedom in religion—in which they were not seriously concerned, since they were content to remain Roman Catholics—and somewhat broader opportunities for education.[2] The Church properties taken over by the State were not widely distributed; they fell into the hands of the oligarchy and continued to be almost as immune from taxation as they had been under the Church, and almost as inalienable."

Even after the loss of some of their riches, many priests continued to identify themselves with oligarchs and ultraconservative elements. Today, however, just as two or three hundred years ago, encouraging exceptions are to be found. How many priests are there like Padre Costa, dedicated to social advances as well as to religion? How much freedom have they when their attitude runs counter to the hierarchy?

[2] Today the constitution of every Latin-American country sets up the state as the sole educator. Of the twenty republics, only six—Argentina, Brazil, Colombia, Costa Rica, Haiti, and Peru—have religious and moral education in the public schools. The Church, however, is permitted to run its own private schools and colleges in all countries except Cuba.

Padre Costa answers the latter question by saying that his bishop never interferes with what he has to say; and, moreover, he expects to obtain permission to write for the press. Padre Costa, by his own admission, is in a minority; the bulk of priests in Brazil, as elsewhere, are at the extreme right or in the center, and say nothing to change the established order. And yet Padre Costa is joined in a crusade in his own troubled Northeast by such men as Bishop Eugenio Salles and Padre António Melo. The dynamic Bishop Salles operates a legal-advice bureau for sharecroppers and carries into court their complaints against avaricious landlords. Padre Melo is busily engaged in organizing, in some ninety towns and villages, peasant syndicates to offer the hope without the extremism of Francisco Julião's Peasant Leagues.

Some of the priests sound more communist than the Communists. One padre in the Northeast, helping the peasants to establish cooperatives after illegal squatting on plantations, told them in a sermon: "You should raise a goat to provide milk for your children. If the landlord comes and tries to punish you by killing your goat, he is menacing the lives of your children. You must not let him kill your goat. You must kill him first." And on another part of the continent, Father Salomón Bolo, who is known as "chaplain of the Peruvian revolution," a rather premature title, busily tells open-air rallies that "when the guerrillas begin to fight in Peru, I will be with them to give them the sacraments." Father Bolo, most active around Cuzco, the old Inca capital, has defied his Church superiors and has been declared in a state of disobedience, but he goes on to proclaim his support of a Cuban-style revolution, blaming the United States and its partnership with the Peruvian oligarchy for his nation's social and economic ailments.

These priests launched into their campaigns long before there was any official guidance in the form of 1961's historic encyclical *Mater et Magistra* (Mother and Teacher), which summed up progressive Church policy on social reform. In his lengthy document, Pope John noted "the sorrowful spectacle of . . . a harsh and offensive contrast . . . between the extreme poverty of the great majority and the wealth and the unbridled luxury of the privileged few." Since one third of the world's Roman Catholics live in Latin America, the words can be assumed to be aimed at that area as well as at other regions. The Pope was concerned not only with pointing out social injustices. "From instruction and education," he urged, "one must pass on to action." If Father Bolo's response has been overly militant, it is sadly counterbalanced by inactivity on the part of other ecclesiastics. Few Church publications in Latin America bothered to reprint in full the 25,000-word encyclical, and few priests have read more than brief summaries. The digests in many countries have been so edited as not to disrupt the prevailing notions of local Church officials. "The trouble," as a foreign diplomat, himself a Roman Catholic, put it to me in Rio de Janeiro, "is that the Church is in league with conservative elements. Too many priests take a posture of charity, of giving handouts to the faithful. Instead, they should be telling the governing classes that it is their duty to establish reforms, that everyone is entitled not to charity but to a decent and dignified standard of living."

Much of the attitude of fatalism, or defeatism, of the backwoods people of the continent can be attributed to the parochial preachings they, and their ancestors, have heard over many generations. "Our destiny," said an Indian in the Peruvian Andes, "is decided by divine will. Because God wills it, some are rich, some know how to read and write, some are masters while we are the servants. When God does not will that we be elevated, then we can never become anything in life though we might desire it with the greatest intensity." Here is a woman, five of whose nine children died in infancy: "I was very moved to see my children die so soon after they were born. But then I felt easier, because I remembered the priest saying that young children who die go directly to heaven because they have committed no sins."

The lesson that God's reward is in the hereafter is often appended to the more immediate understanding that the Church will perform a service for a fee. Priests argue that since the state takeover of Church wealth a century ago they can survive only by the *cruzeiro* or peso contributions of followers. Nevertheless, some of the practices are disquieting, especially to North Americans. A United States teacher, who is the principal of schools in a company oil town in Colombia, reminisced one evening during dinner in Bogotá:

> I have seen some shocking things in my time, but one of the most shocking took place only last week. One of my pupils, a twelve-year-old boy, died, and I went around to see his parents. I asked what time the funeral service would be held at church. The father stared at me for a while, and then he said that he had six other children to support and he couldn't afford a Requiem. I was at the funeral. The coffin was just carried by some friends to the cemetery. There was no priest, and not a word of prayer was uttered. The boy was simply buried, and that was all.

In parts of Ecuador peasants have to pay merely for the ringing of funeral bells. In Ecuador, too, 25 per cent of the husband-wife couples admit to living out of wedlock because they cannot raise enough money for a marriage ceremony. In Colombia, where a church wedding costs on the average fifty pesos, or four dollars (more than most *campesinos* earn in a month), half the children are illegitimate. Corresponding figures apply to almost all Latin-American countries. Ironically, it took a natural disaster to cause several Chilean common-law marriages to be solemnized. When the Canadian government shipped in grain for the relief of earthquake victims in 1960, the rule was that heads of families would receive more than single people. But there had to be proof of marriage. Peasants, many with borrowed funds, rushed to priests to make legal a status that in some instances had existed for twenty years.

"Religion among (Chileans) has been made the instrument of despotism instead of the basis of civilization." So wrote philosopher José Victorino Lastarría in the mid-nineteenth century. The *pensadores* of old showed great hostility toward the power of the Church and were vitally concerned with organized religion's inability or unwillingness to promote the advancement of the people. "With very rare exceptions, from time immemorial, priests have been the more determined oppressors of humanity, especially of the underprivileged classes," commented Peru's Manuel González Prada at the turn of this century. "In the past, they did nothing to abolish pauperism and improve the social condition of the masses; in the present it is the same old story. They perpetuate the grossest superstitions and live petrified in an atmosphere of errors and lies. They constitute a force hostile to civilization."

Today's *pensadores,* or at least most of them, are equally harsh and caustic. There are, of course, some intellectual defenders of the Church. While I was in Santiago, a famous Chilean literary critic, Hernan Diaz, argued in the newspaper *El Mercurio* that the concept of social justice, instead of charity, is against the principles of the Church and is therefore the forerunner of communism. But more common are the outbursts in the other direction. In Bogotá, Gerardo Molina, rector of Universidad Libre, told me: "Castro has this advantage: he offers land now, the Church offers salvation in another life. What we need is education, not confession." Anticlerical Colombians claim that the Church in their country is the most bigoted in Latin America. Ecuadorians, in turn, say that theirs is worse. A Quito editor recalled an expression by liberator Simón Bolívar who, when he saw the dissolution of his visionary Confederation of Gran Colombia in 1830, said that Venezuela would always be a country of the military, Colombia would always be a country of the intellectuals, and Ecuador would always be "a convent."

The degree of Church influence and enlightenment does vary from country to country. The Church in Brazil, for example, is considered more liberal than in Argentina, where in principle it has accepted the encyclical but in practice does nothing. Argentina's hierarchy supported Perón until he threatened the Church's educational rights. His successor, President Arturo Frondizi, collaborated more closely, restoring the privilege of private Catholic universities to grant degrees, much to the distaste of state educators. Frondizi's brother, Dr. Risieri Frondizi, rector of the University of Buenos Aires, informed me flatly: "Our Church is ultraconservative, and if you are not with it, you are called a 'Communist'."

In several countries the Church is still united with the State.[3] This arrangement, in general, is frowned upon by North American ecclesiastical authorities who say it is a survival of the old system of royal patronage, which gives the State the power to intervene in the nomination of bishops, in subsidies for education, and in other activities of the Church. They prefer the more normalized relations of such countries as Uruguay and Chile, where there is a separation between Church and State. But union of Church and State more often than not works in favor of the Church. In Colombia, the Church not only controls divorces but is answerable for an immigration law that admits only Roman Catholic migrants into the country.

In Colombia, too, the Church has been—and is still—active in politics. It was responsible for the origin, in the

[3] Argentina, Bolivia, Colombia, Peru, and Venezuela.

early national period, of the two most important political parties, the Liberals and the Conservatives, the latter identified as clericals and reactionaries. As recently as 1948 village priests incited "Conservative" *campesinos* to attack neighboring "Liberal" villages, reviving old hatreds and contributing to Colombia's devastating and unofficial civil war that goes on, in a fashion, to this day. During the 1962 presidential and congressional election campaign the Archbishop of Bogotá, Cardinal Luis Concha Córdoba, issued a pastoral letter warning his people against supporting "candidates of a party that is allied to communism or shares in the ideas of the Communist Party." The exhortation by implication linked, unjustifiably, the left wing of the Liberal Party with the Communists and had only one meaning: Vote Conservative.

Interference in secular affairs is not limited to Colombia. In Brazil in 1960, Cardinal Dom Jaime Camara urged churchgoers not to vote for vice-presidential candidate João Goulart because he was, allegedly, a "Communist." In Mexico, where the state introduced stringent anticlerical measures some forty-three years before Cuba, charges are constantly being raised that the Church is attempting to overstep its bounds. Violence erupted in the summer of 1961, notably in the city of Puebla, when the hierarchy started a series of rallies in protest against a government decision to investigate the tuition rates of Church schools. Priests publicly labeled the minister of education and most of his public school teachers as "Communists." In Puebla, resentful students set fire to the office of a pro-Church newspaper, and the governor finally had to declare a state of siege.

The sensitivity regarding the Church in Mexico is acute, and most Mexicans support the 1917 constitution, which took primary education out of ecclesiastical hands and prohibited the ownership by the Church of any private property. The Church had long been held in disfavor by social reformers because of its opposition to change; and this grew into bloody reprisal in 1910 when the hierarchy plotted, on the side of landowners, against the peasant revolution. A new wave of anticlerical turbulence broke out in the 1920's when priests tried to regain some of their lost authority; many of them had to flee to the hills around Mexico City to fight off attackers; and many, too, were slain. Priests today are forbidden to walk about in public in their habits. Though this law is not strictly enforced and though Mexicans attend Sunday Mass, there is a lingering fear of the Church going beyond religious matters. I met *peones* who still recalled stories, handed down by their fathers, about irrigation ditches and springs that had their origin on Church property and would be dammed off if peasants failed to follow the dictates of their rural priests.

The statistics on slim Church attendance are somewhat misleading, since most Latin Americans still follow Roman Catholicism to one degree or another. The contradictions previously mentioned are illustrated by a simple example: in the *barriadas* of Lima 90 per cent of the children are baptized, but only 9 per cent of their parents go to Mass. If the adults feel that children should be started in a righteous direction, the same compulsion does not motivate their own later lives, particularly since formal worship involves a financial cost. In any event, they say, almost invariably, that they are "good" Catholics. But this does not mean necessarily that they are "safely" Catholic. The notion that communism, or more precisely Fidelismo, cannot make headway in Latin America because of Roman Catholicism can no longer be accepted with complacency.

Cuba, of course, is the classic example, although a rather special one. Latterday Cubans were not even as devout as Catholics in other parts of the hemisphere. The reason lies partly in history. While the rest of the continent won its independence from Spain more than a hundred years ago, the Church in Cuba was merely an appendage of Spanish imperialism until the turn of this century. Five hundred of the seven hundred priests on the island in 1961 still came from Spain, and few Cubans identified themselves with this branch of the clergy. By forcibly deporting most of the priests, Castro set out to isolate rather than destroy the Church, much as Mexico had done earlier. His measures against the Church met with some opposition but not as much as the outside world, unaware of the superficiality of religion in Cuba, might have expected.

The power of the Church to sway public opinion in other Latin-American countries has by no means disappeared; it is particularly strong among *campesinos* in rural areas, and few politicians would think of seeking local office without the support of the village priest. But there are virtually no republics today where the Church dominates community action or thought as completely as in the past. Some priests recognize this shrinkage of authority even in countries with obstinately rigid hierarchies, such as Colombia. In Viotá, the onetime enclave of communism, the thirty-year-old Father Hector Osorio spoke to me soberly and realistically of his parish's history: "Religion was not at stake: just the correcting of social wrongs." Some priests, he said, believe that communism should be tackled head on, with religious condemnation of it. Father Osorio believes, and he said that some other young priests share this view (though, by inference, not the hierarchy), that the Church should take the approach that any danger of communism can be met by economic means and that, in any case, the Church should stay outside the field of politics, otherwise it runs the risk of being foresaken. He said,

> The problem is that if we start talking against communism, then it appears that we are on the side of the rich and

against the poor. Here in Viotá I do not preach politics or ideology in church or even outside it. I am well received wherever I go, even in the homes of really true Communists. The idea is not to abandon them but to try to keep them close to the Church. I visit them not as Communists but as Catholics and Colombians. The result is that people who call themselves "Communists" come to Mass.

But Father Osorio, isolated in his own philosophy as well as by geography, is a rarity. Broadly, the most forward-looking priests are the ones who come in contact with foreign missionaries of the modern (not Spanish) variety. Half the two thousand ecclesiastics in Peru, for example, are from Europe, Canada, and the United States. The padres with whom I spoke, both Peruvian and North American, shared a common goal: to introduce liberalism not only for humanitarian reasons but to give the Church greater prestige in the contest with communism.

In Bolivia, where four hundred of the six hundred priests are from abroad, a Canadian group, the Oblate Order of Mary Immaculate, is active in the impoverished tin-mining areas. Here the miners and their families subsist on a diet of rice and potatoes, and perhaps meat once a week. The average mother gives birth to eight or nine children, but only three survive. Conditions inside the mines themselves are not too bad, and compare favorably with some in North America. Miners are issued masks and other safety devices. Nevertheless, silicosis takes a high toll, simply because miners, who have not been educated in the use of masks, keep them slung idly over their chests. The death rate adds to an inherent fatalism. "Why should I make an effort," said a typical miner, "when I know I have only ten years ahead of me?"

This somewhat primitive mentality may have hastened the inflow of communism. But the facts are that the mine unions are run by avowed Communists, and while only 10 per cent of the miners attend Mass, some 90 per cent show up for union meetings. A course in Marxist indoctrination is part of union activities. In rebuttal, the Canadian fathers do not spend their time speaking of communism in a negative way; instead, they offer the constructive alternative of health clinics, classes in child care, and adult courses in reading and writing. At one mine, *Siglo Veinte* (Twentieth Century), 12,000 feet up in the Andes, much of the educational work is conducted through a radio station the fathers operate.

On the air from five in the morning to midnight, with a generous sprinkling of music, *Pio Doce* (Pius XII) is the most popular station in the region. In July, 1961, resentful union leaders broadcast a command over their own transmitters for an attack on *Pio Doce*. The Canadians, in turn, appealed to miners to defend the station. By midnight, two thousand protectors were on hand, some armed with rifles, others with sticks of dynamite. A miner shouted at a restless mob of union-led demonstrators: "If you want the station you will have to take it over our bodies." The mob retreated. Here, as a Canadian priest pointed out to me, was a positive example of some influence of the Church. But two months later, in union elections, the Communist leaders were returned with a bigger majority than ever before.

"When it came to an attack on the station," the priest recalled quietly, "the miners looked on this, deep down and perhaps without defining it, as an attack on their faith. But when it came to work, and the promise of greater gain, they supported the Communists. Ideally, they would like to be both Catholic and Communist. Some see that the two are incompatible. Others are confused, and this is where lies the real danger."

The sword that hacked through the *montaña* of Latin America, to create a New World in the name of Spain and

Portugal, still dominates much of the continent in the name of traditional order, social progress or patriotism, depending on the individual leanings of army officers. Whatever the guise of their roles, the senior officers form a tripartite oligarchy, along with the upper clergy and landowners or industrialists. If their approach to political and economic problems is not always as orthodox as that of their partners, it leaves them, nonetheless, just as responsible for the common malaise, discontent, that affects directly or indirectly the majority of Latin America's 200 million inhabitants. With only few exceptions—Mexico, Uruguay, Costa Rica, Bolivia (and to a lesser degree Brazil, Chile, Colombia)—the armed forces today make and unmake governments, just as they did a century ago. In some instances, their motives have altered, but militarism itself remains unabated. When presidents are not actually generals in civilian clothes they are, as Argentina rediscovered last year, at the mercy of armed commanders.

At Buenos Aires' presidential *Casa Rosada* (Pink House), during an interview with Arturo Frondizi, I brought up the point some of his critics were uttering: that he had won office on a platform of liberal reforms, but, as one young man put it, while he had mounted the horse from the left he was clearly descending from the right. Could the president comment on this charge? The fifty-three-year-old Frondizi promptly replied: "I propose to get off the horse in the same way I got on, neither with the right nor with the left, but with the nation." A few short weeks later, Arturo Frondizi, who had survived thirty-five major national crises in four years, fell with a hard and sad crash, pushed by the generals and admirals. In his demise was a story not unique in Argentina but common to all Latin-American countries whose elements of ferment include a growing industrial class, a frightened middle group that sometimes passes for a middle class, an omnipotent officer corps, all mixed together in a batter of faulty or greedy economic planning. Argentina, it is obvious, had a specific hangover of Peronismo, but this only served to heighten the case history: the dilemma of any republic striving to attain sound government and to relegate the military to a function understood in North America and most of Europe—of subordination to civilian authority.

Frondizi may be condemned on many grounds; he was crafty, a master of unsavory political adroitness and expediency; he was personally austere and uninspiring as a leader; but he was, from beginning to end, an opponent of military rule. As far back as 1930, graduating in law during the regime of dictator José Uriburu, he refused to accept an honors certificate from, as he proclaimed publicly, "a government put in power and maintained by military force." Later he risked imprisonment and torture by conducting clandestine meetings against another dictator, Colonel Juan Perón, who, in 1943, had led a clique of officers to overthrow the legal government. These officers, typical of their generation, were discontented not only with civilian titular heads but with their own generals, who, they felt, were out of tune with popular needs. In other words, this was to be a benevolent and collective dictatorship, in youthful military style. But Perón, over the next couple of years, outflanked his fellow conspirators through a shrewd realization that the balance of power was shifting from the landowners and fecund plains to the great cities with their frustrated labor classes. Deliberately he built up trade unions as a balancing force against the army, so that his own strength as *caudillo* no longer would be dependent on his old comrades. But the armed forces could never be ignored; the navy, especially, with more democratic traditions than the army, showed its hostility to Perón from the start, and it was to be the navy, in September, 1955, that sparked his downfall. There were many contributing causes, including antagonism of the Church against legalized gambling and prostitution; but Perón's collapse can be linked basically with his dream of converting Argentina overnight from a pastoral economy to an industrial nation with a loyal trade-union federation backing him.

The dream had some popular appeal prevalent elsewhere in Latin America: to free the nation from dependence on foreign investors. Riding high on a wartime demand for Argentina's beef and grain, which had filled the country's treasury with foreign exchange, Perón bought out the British railway network, United States oil refineries, and other alien industries. But in trying for rapid state industrialization, the dictator violated every rule in the code book of economics, even penalizing the lifeline, agriculture, through export exchange rates. Perón won the allegiance of more and more *descamisados,* "shirtless ones," who poured into the cities in search of high, artificially fixed wages, but also the enmity of landowners, who now found it unprofitable to raise cattle and grain, and the hatred of the middle class (the only truly big one in Latin America) who were caught in a vicious inflationary spiral. Added to the anti-Peronistas were the hundreds of purged army officers just waiting for an opportunity for revenge. After more than a decade under Perón's domination, the military finally moved; Perón fled when a navy cruiser appeared ready to fire on Buenos Aires; and he left behind him a fearful legacy; an economy virtually at a standstill (in seven years the gross national product had dropped by more than 7 per cent), with three quarters of the population now living in towns and swelling state enterprises out of all reasonable proportions at the expense of a now stagnant agriculture.

What was Peronismo like? A Buenos Aires doctor gave me one answer: "I had my first experience of it as a young intern in 1953 when a man showed up at the hospital with a tiny cut on his finger. I put a Band-Aid on it; and he said, 'Well, where's the medical certificate?' I couldn't understand what he meant, and I asked him to repeat it. He practically shouted at me, 'Where's the medical certificate so I can get my seven days off from work?' I shouted back, and said I had been on duty for eighteen hours without sleep and nobody was giving me time off. I sent him on his way." This, however, was not the end of the episode. The worker appealed to his trade union, which in turn made representations at the ministry of health; and he received his week's sick leave. "I," said the doctor, "got a bawling out from the ministry for not understanding that workers' demands have to be met." The doctor fell silent for a few moments, and then said, slowly, "Perón? He left a legalized laziness."

Some of the work by Perón and his late wife, Evita, was notable. Evita established homes for the aged, for indigent mothers, for working girls; if the *caudillo* himself stifled the press and seized control of the universities, he was still a heroic figure to millions of workers; for he not only left them alone but subsidized the steaks they ate every day for lunch and made it impossible for any employer to fire them. The full tragedy of Argentina's economic ruin was never understood by the *descamisados,* but economists had merely to tally the figures to find a foreign-trade deficit of $300 million a year, a steady inflationary gallop of 50 per cent a year, and featherbedded state industries with 75 per cent surplus personnel. After a period of military receivership, Argentina elected Frondizi president in 1958, but only because he was able to enlist the Peronista vote by making a deal with the exiled *caudillo.*

Frondizi came in on a left-wing program pledged to continue the prolabor policies of Perón and to restore outlawed Peronista union leaders to control of the powerful General Confederation of Labor. Within months he was caught between two main power blocs: the armed forces who were fitfully prepared to react, almost by reflex, at any suggestion that Perón might be recouping his former hold, and the unionized masses who remembered wishfully their plushier days. Even when I arrived four years later, it was only necessary to walk along the picturesque banks of the Río de la Plata in Buenos Aires to hear the loud complaints of the Peronistas. Teamsters, pausing beside the row of *carritos,* or open-air diners, lamented that a charcoal grilled steak cost thirty pesos (thirty-five cents) while under Perón it had cost only twelve pesos.

Frondizi engaged in a juggler's act, trying to keep in perpetual motion a half-dozen spheres representing the trade unions, the armed forces, the bankers, the rival factions within his own party, the landowners, the United States. If either of the first two dropped, it would mean the end of the act. Nimble a performer as he was, Frondizi never got close to solving his country's devilish problems; he tried to appeal as a friend of labor by shuffling top military posts, and in the process deepened the already touchy suspicions of the generals; when he made concessions to the army, workers went out on strike. What was intended to be a reform program became instead an austerity program. "There are hard times ahead," Frondizi announced, "but the greater the contribution each one makes, the shorter and less painful will be the period of stabilization." But because of the stirring Peronist memories among urban workers, he dared not permit wages to find their own normal levels; industrialists and landowners nagged at him while trade remained static and uncompetitive in foreign markets. Imports, meanwhile, had to go up to satisfy the wants of the large urban groups. Argentina ended 1961 with a foreign trade deficit of $450 million.

In one area Frondizi met with more success. The International Monetary Fund made available substantial credits, and North American, French, German, and British industries resumed the investing that had dwindled during the Perón era of nationalization. Argentina became a new symbol, a testing ground for private enterprise and United States policy toward Latin America; only a month before Frondizi's downfall, Buenos Aires received a pledge of $150 million under the Alliance for Progress. Critics, among them army people, accused Frondizi of selling out to the United States; but this type of carping did not disturb him, because, as he pointed out to me, his invitation to United States oil companies to drill and produce had made the nation self-sufficient in petroleum within three years and alone saved $300 million annually in foreign exchange.

But still the national deficit remained huge, a major portion of it, for example, traced directly to the state-owned railway, which was running at an enormous loss. For a week I could not travel anywhere in Argentina by rail; everyone was out on strike because Frondizi had finally decided to chance an attack on the Perón heritage of redundancy. Canada, where conditions in terms of population and distances are somewhat similar to those in Argentina, employs 1,270 railwaymen for every million tons of freight; in Argentina the figure was 8,755. Frondizi sought to lop off 75,000 employees and to get the remaining 135,000 to work at least six hours daily, rather than the four hours of Perón practice. The strike ended in a typical compromise that achieved little for the nation.

Meanwhile, Frondizi was anxious to prove that the hold of Peronismo was not nearly as great as some of the skeptics believed. He persuaded a reluctant military command that Peronistas should be allowed to run, for the first time since their ban from office in 1955, in state and congressional elections. Frondizi, with a vision of democratic process, was at the same time confident of victory for his own candidates. But the results on March 18, 1962 were more than disturbing. Out of a total of 7,200,000 votes cast, Peronistas polled

2,500,000. It was a minority vote, but enough to take ten governorships in twenty-two states and half of the congressional seats at stake. The furious military, fearful of any gains for Peronismo, blamed Frondizi for a miscalculation, forced him to annul the results of the elections, and within twelve days deposed him. There were among the officers some who were constitutionally minded and willing to adhere to the results, as unpalatable as they were; but the more powerful generals won out. Once again Argentina went into military receivership. Soldiers and sailors covered themselves with "legitimacy" by permitting an unimpressive, minor politician, José María Guido, to be sworn in as president; but they kept for themselves the right to veto all cabinet appointments and actions. New elections were promised, but so designed that a proper civilian government could not take office before May 1, 1964.

The details were relatively unimportant. What stood out were the broad lessons: Castroism was not a direct factor in a nation that, despite its economic and political hardships, enjoyed the highest standard of living in Latin America. Argentina, with 97 per cent of its people European in origin, had a solid middle class and few of the extreme poverty problems of its neighbor to the North, Brazil. And yet there was plainly discontent that presented dilemmas not only for Argentina but for the United States. How could Washington reconcile its Alliance grant ("an indication of confidence in President Frondizi") with the claims of some voters who said they had gone against Frondizi not through any sentiment for Peronismo but through fervent opposition to any marked return of private enterprise fostered by foreign capital? How could Washington recognize a puppet government after backing so openly and strongly a democratic government? President Kennedy, speaking of the "unfortunate" election results, said: "They reveal what happens if you neglect an area for a decade." But the "neglect" included a United States attitude of catering to the military, not only in Argentina but all over Latin America, a hazardous defense policy that will be inspected in another chapter.

The sum was this: Argentina's military leaders, who had not fought a war since 1870 and yet commanded a well-armed and disciplined force of 150,000 men, were in control of the continent's second largest country. Neither they nor the Peronistas appeared willing to relinquish narrow privileges in order to consolidate prosperity in this potentially wealthy land. There were some academic questions. If a democracy was to exist, could antidemocratic elements such as Peronistas be permitted to take seats in parliament? And, conversely, what justification was there for soldiers to prevent the seating of men chosen in a fair and secret ballot by a literate electorate? Which was preferable, a popularly elected government that could move toward one form of dictatorship, or a military dictatorship determined to prevent the first? The answer, of course, is that neither was desirable. "A nation which conducts its political affairs with responsibility and common sense," said *The New York Times* in connection with Argentina's elections, "will not have to make a choice of dictatorships."

Argentina, given the strength of civilian authority, could have avoided its latest tragedy. Two out of three voters chose a non-Peronist course; it was for them to decide how the minority could be appeased or allowed rein. But curiously, with a sense of resignation, they passively accepted militarism as inevitable. At the other end of the scale, tiny Costa Rica dissolved its army because it interfered with a civilian mandate. When Costa Rica's government refused to heed the results of a 1948 vote, and called out the army to prevent a democratically elected party from assuming office, José Figueres, a fiery and dynamic patriot, led a makeshift "Caribbean Legion" in successful rebellion. One of his first legal acts, in revenge for the army's action in a nonmilitary matter, was to call for its disbandment and the conversion of the main barracks in San José into a museum of fine arts. A *guardia,* or national police force of a thousand men, was set up to handle internal security. In conversation with me many years later, Figueres, possibly Central America's greatest statesman, said, "Why should a band of professional soldiers have taken upon themselves the right to annul the popular will as expressed at the polls?"

In the interval, Figueres and other presidents in moderately socialist governments confirmed their belief that Costa Rica could manage quite well without a regular army, despite two invasion efforts against them. Antigovernment exiles in Nicaragua attempted a coup in December of 1948, and again in 1955, but were held back by volunteer forces. Prompt intervention by the Organization of American States also helped; representatives from the United States, Mexico, Colombia, and Brazil sorted out Costa Rican charges that Nicaragua was aiding in aggression, and war between the two states was averted. The moral, as Figueres himself mentions today, is that the army no longer plays a role in Costa Rica's affairs; yet the nation feels secure from external threats, and has been spared the heavy burden of military expenditures: a budgetary drain afflicting other Latin-American countries that could make far better use of their money in vital social and economic reforms.[4]

Between the two poles of Argentina and Costa Rica are various gradations of the armed forces' influence. At the beginning of this century no army in Latin America was more political than Mexico's, and yet, following the civilian uprisings of 1910, weaknesses in it began to set in. Citizen-generals, each leading large and revolutionary armies in

[4] Destitute and medieval Paraguay spends 50 per cent of its budget on the armed forces, Argentina and Brazil between 35 and 40 per cent. In most Latin-American republics the minimum is 25 per cent.

separate parts of the country, started assuming the functions of the older, similarly nonprofessional but regular officers whose social positions for centuries had given them predatory careers in enriching themselves. By the early 1920's the central government was ready to take action to curb militarism. Its first cautious move was to invite the revolutionary citizen-generals into the permanent army, with status and a generous federal payroll. Then followed an effort to instill professionalism through a new officers' training school, and afterward a ruthless but effective series of purges, executions, and banishments.

There were, inevitably, counterblows by the old soldiers, but by the 1940's the Mexican army had already taken on some of the orthodox, well-disciplined forms customary in North America. Today, Mexico's military establishment, by Latin America's yardstick, is small (around 50,000 men in a population of 32 millions); it acts neither as a drag on the economy (using only about 12 per cent of the national budget) nor a dangerous influence on politics. A generation of time has elapsed in this evolution, but Mexico has set an example that could well be followed by other republics striving to reach a balanced formula between defense needs and civilian authority. Indeed, Bolivia, after its 1952 revolution aimed at social changes, took quick measures to disband the armed forces and to replace them with a civilian militia, as a preventive against any revival of *juntas,* which, in former days, had ruled in favor of the oligarchy.

Colombia is an example of a country midway on the road toward an understanding between civilian and military leaders. As in Chile, Colombia's military men have by tradition and theory stayed apart from politics—in Chile's case since the early nineteenth century, in Colombia since the beginning of this century. Still, in modern times each country's army has intervened during periods it considered national crises, though Chile, since 1932, has been able to boast of constitutional governments elected without military pressure. The tacit agreement there is that the armed forces will not interfere in politics if the civilians, in turn, will leave the generals and admirals—and their budgets—alone. Colombia is trying to work out a similar arrangement of *quid pro quo,* but its army's last involvement in civilian affairs goes back only a few years.

In 1953, with Colombia engaged in an undeclared civil war between Liberals and Conservatives, General Gustavo Rojas Pinilla seized power, largely with popular approval. Although he pursued some welfare policies designed to appeal to the masses, Rojas ruled as a dictator, relying on the armed forces to keep him in office and drawing his key administrators from military ranks. After a series of blunders, which made him more tyrannical and created public disfavor, Rojas was finally removed by his fellow officers. Since 1957 Colombia has again been governed by civilians, an intricate and uneasy kind of coalition between Conservatives and Liberals, who have made a point of paying open tribute to the military on every suitable occasion. For their part, the generals, having had their fingers burned in trying to do a civilian job, say they prefer keeping to their traditional side of the fence. Nevertheless, within the war ministry a struggle still goes on between those who regard military service as an opportunity to serve their country and those who see it as a means of achieving power.

What is the attitude of the younger officers? The ones with whom I spoke in Bogotá gave me a distinct feeling that a new breed not only is emerging but is acquiring ideals that might provide salvation for their country. There is nothing novel about cleavages between the generations of Latin America's officer castes. Many "palace revolts" or insurrections have been brought about by young officers who scorned their seniors but at the same time revealed their own archconservative backgrounds by sneering at democracy. In former days, only scions of the propertied elite could enter officer ranks, but today many identify themselves with the urban or middle groups from which they originate. If this does not exactly make them "socialists" or reformers, it at least instills in them a healthy regard for legality. I asked a youthful Colombian air-force pilot for his reaction to the Argentine army pushing Frondizi into a break in relations with Cuba (shortly preceding the President's downfall). Without hesitating, the pilot replied: "I do not like Castro or anything about him. But the armed forces in Argentina had no business interfering in civilian matters; they acted contrary to the way armed forces should act."

The Venezuela once described by Bolívar as "a barracks" is still very much under the influence of the military, but with an altered complexion. While, previously, civilian authorities were harassed by moves exclusively from extreme right-wing generals ready to protect the oligarchy (in a century and a half of independence Venezuela had only two honest elections), today the pressure comes equally from the extreme left of the young officer elite. But there are moderates as well. Venezuela's minister of defense, General Briceño Linares, echoed the views of the young Colombian officer by saying that Argentina's army should not have meddled in the functions of a civilian government. But then he added: "However, a president should be smart and never get himself into a position where the army will have to act." My interpretation of the Venezuelan view, therefore, is that the army will respect civil government, as long as civil government goes along with the army. But this may be too cynical an estimate. Venezuela, under President Betancourt's guidance, showed a remarkable transition from 1958 to 1962. At least such a man as Linares could truly distinguish between the function of the armed forces and government: "The main role of the military is national defense, and then to provide full support for the constitutional government elected by the people. Up to now, in this government's life, we have been successful. This is the first time in Venezuela's history when a constitutional government has lasted three years and more, and I am optimistic."

Linares, a handsome, straight-speaking man of forty-seven, impressed me as being fairly open-minded. Betancourt had managed to weed out most of the Old Guard associated with former dictator Pérez Jiménez, sending some abroad as ambassadors. Linares received his post because his thoughts about democratic process for reform coincided with those of Betancourt. "I have a strong social sensibility," he told me, "but I want to see changes made lawfully. The only way to fight communism is to kill its roots—poverty and everything else that goes with it. Having a strong government backed by force will not in itself solve the problems. For that reason I want to succeed in our reforms, but there must be time. All the problems will not be solved by this government, or the next. There must be a chance for continuity."

But this philosophy alone is not what tied him to Betancourt. Betancourt shrewdly gave Linares a large budget and a free hand in military expenditures. "Pérez Jiménez, as a general, believed he knew more about military matters than his chiefs of staff," Linares recalled. "But now when the president calls us in for advice he accepts it, because he knows we are experts, and he is not. For example, during the Pérez Jiménez regime we discussed for ten years what was to be the army's biggest unit, and we never arrived at a satisfactory answer. Last year we worked out a complete plan for reorganization of the army, and we spent one afternoon discussing it with Betancourt. The next morning he signed his approval." Linares led me to a map lining one wall of his office, and pointed out the position of air bases in terms of Venezuela's valuable oil fields. "Pérez Jiménez," he said, "bought a lot of aircraft, but with an eye only to how much he would receive immediately in graft, not with any regard to strategic value. Our bases were much too far from the oil fields, which would be prime targets in the event of war. Now they are being built more sensibly."

On the face of it, it seemed like a successful cohabitation of military and nonmilitary, but in essence it added up to the major flaw that an army officer, and not a civilian, was still minister of defense and therefore the dominant partner.[5] When I questioned Linares on this point, he was firm in saying that during "the transitional period" it was preferable to have a military man as minister. But he could not specify the duration of a "transitional period," nor at what point the armed forces would consider it necessary to move to prevent what he called "leftist tendencies." In other words, Linares was prepared, and probably quite genuinely, to support reforms, but these would have to be as he defined them.

In the meantime, it was clear that the curse of militarism was far from lifted in Venezuela. Linares admitted that "there is still a group of old officers who would like to rule the country"; but they, as representatives of the oligarchy, were for the moment under control. Not so predictable was a new factor, but still a militarist one: the group of young officers who intermittently in 1962 tried to overthrow the elected government because they believed it was not going far and fast enough in reforms. One particular engagement, the second in a month, took place at Puerto Cabello, seventy-five miles west of Caracas, when a trio of officers managed to rouse seven hundred marines at a nearby base, occupy the city, and release pro-Castro civilian prisoners from jail. The marines were joined by armed students, and by the time loyal government forces put down the insurrection scores of men were dead and hundreds more injured.

[5] In South America, only Uruguay has had a long and unbroken record of civilian control of the armed forces. Uniquely, it reached this position through gradual evolution, not revolution. The defense minister is a civilian.

The possibility of civil war in Venezuela, with old soldiers taking a right-wing position and the younger ones a leftist stance, is never far from reality.

Brazil emerged from a civil war fright in 1961, shaken by a military attempt to violate the constitution but relieved that a national sense of legality finally prevailed. The position of Brazil's army is in many ways unusual in Latin America. It has been content to pose as the upholder of the constitution and to be beyond partisan politics; unlike most neighbors, whose armed forces have often put their own generals into presidencies, Brazil has been ruled almost continually by civilians since it became a republic more than seventy years ago.[6] But in practice the generals act with autonomy, above the state, ready to issue a quiet but stern ultimatum that all sensible civilians respect. It was a *junta* of generals who in 1930 handed over dictatorial power to Getúlio Vargas, an old and skilled working politician. For the next quarter of a century, until his suicide, Vargas dominated the political life of Brazil.

At the start, Vargas was well received. With the zeal of a reformer he pushed Brazil into the industrial age, improved educational facilities, instituted labor legislation and, perhaps more importantly than anything else, molded a score of quarreling, semiautonomous states (at one point São Paulo even had a formidable army of its own) into a reasonably unified nation. But at the end there was a vast and corrupt personal machine attended by nepotism and followed by political instability in a country that had grown dependent on one-man rule. In 1954-55 Brazil went through five presidents in fifteen months. Today, as part of the Vargas legacy, there are thirteen political groups that call themselves parties; but in fact, undisciplined and splintered

[6] Only three of Brazil's presidents have been military men, the last in 1914—compared with Argentina where in one period alone, between 1930 and 1957, eight out of ten presidents were colonels or generals.

even among their own ranks, they are not parties in a North American sense. It is as providers of balance, stability, and continuity that the armed services see themselves. A colonel, the chief of staff of an armored division, told me: "The intellectuals—the doctors, the writers, and so on—are influential but they haven't the organization. The military is the greatest single force in Brazil. It is popular because it is always striving to improve the country."

Oddly enough, this claim to popularity is fundamentally true. Unlike such republics as Argentina, Peru, Paraguay, Nicaragua, or Haiti, whose military leaders are either feared or loathed, Brazil's armed services have commanded respect and pride; aside from the fact that Brazil's generals and admirals promote the teaching of reading and writing among conscripts, and engage in such fruitful missions as road and bridge-building, they alone among South Americans put a force into the field (Italy) on the Allied side in World War II. But this having been said, there was a sharp division in the nation over the attitude of the high command during the Quadros upheaval. I arrived in Rio de Janeiro several weeks after the crisis had been resolved, but it had left a wound that was still deeply sensitive and continued to be the main topic of conversation. "It was the most perilous crisis Brazil experienced in its entire history as a republic," said Roberto Marinho, editor of Rio's largest newspaper, *O Globo*. "We still need to recover our self-confidence, because the equally big crisis we are suffering is that we are afraid of tomorrow."

Jânio Quadros had been inaugurated as president of Brazil in January, 1961 with the largest vote in the nation's records. He was known as a go-getter. In the 1930's and onward Brazil had undergone the "new kind of democracy" of Vargas. Then came President Juscelino Kubitschek with his "new program for national redemption: fifty years of progress in five"; Kubitschek brought massive construction but also staggering foreign debts and runaway inflation. And now Quadros flourished his "new broom" to sweep away corruption, intrigue, and economic chaos.

It was a forceful, dynamic concept, but it aroused apprehension in many circles. At home, industrialists objected when Quadros cut subsidies and tightened credit; military chieftains were stunned when he talked of trying to get closer to a balanced budget by paring their expenditures: a civilian intrusion on sacrosanct territory; Congress ignored his plans for land reform and higher taxes that would, of course, affect its members. In foreign relations, Quadros supported the fledgling Alliance for Progress but upset Washington by opposing efforts to have the hemisphere isolate Castro's Cuba; he declared a policy of *neutralismo interesado,* or "benevolent neutrality"; he moved toward restoring diplomatic relations with the Soviet Union, which had been broken in 1947, and then bestowed Brazil's highest decoration, the Order of the Southern Cross, on Cuba's Ernesto "Che" Guevara. Some Brazilians interpreted this last gesture as merely a device to frighten the United States into more economic aid (blackmail is not beyond any Latin-American country); others saw in it nothing more than an assertion of Brazil's right to conduct external relations in its own interests. If conservatives, among them militarists, were disturbed, Quadros had the sympathy of the man in the street.

Despite the reports of mounting pressures, it was an unprepared and shocked nation that awoke on the morning of August 25 to learn that Quadros, after barely seven months in office, had resigned. Those who had opposed him discovered, all at once, that he was the only man who could keep the country together, the only one who offered hope and the necessary drive to build social and economic institutions. At least this was the way they sounded. The incredible thing in the following weeks and months is that the men and women with whom I spoke—the bankers, the trade unionists, the intellectuals—were virtually unanimous in Quadros' favor. Almost as incredible was the fact that the full story, setting out the reasons for the resignation, was unknown. Quadros himself said only, ambiguously, that he had been "smashed by the forces" working against him. The inference was that the United States had exerted pressure because of his "neutralist" policy, and that the military heads were equally uneasy. But none of this interpretation was borne out by evidence. On the contrary, the United States, fearful of the dangers of social and economic problems in Latin America's biggest and most populous country, had extended to Quadros hundreds of millions of dollars in grants and loans during his brief presidency. As for the military side, Quadros told a close aide the morning of his decision that he intended to pull out, and there was a quick meeting of the three defense ministers urging him to stay on.

The most plausible explanation, I believe, is one that combines two factors: Quadros' temperament was undoubtedly erratic and unpredictable; but perhaps more compellingly he wanted the powers of France's Charles de Gaulle—to govern firmly without worrying about Congress vetoing his legislation. But, as a U.S. Embassy political officer phrased it, "he outfoxed himself." There was no rush by the military or by Congress to offer him a de Gaulle type of authoritarian deal, and Quadros set sail for England. There was, however, a shattering maneuver by the military to block the automatic succession to the presidency of vice-president João ("Jango") Goulart. And this is what nearly precipitated civil war and destroyed much of the army's image as a guardian of constitutional observance, as a custodian of legal process.

Goulart, aged forty-two, had served his political tutorship under Vargas. He was in disfavor at many levels. Intellectuals accused him of attempting to set up a distorted kind of Perón welfare state when he was minister of labor. In more recent times he had moved to merge his Labor Party with the radical Peasant Leagues in the Northeast and the underground Communist party. Businessmen and militarists were terrified by words still freshly implanted in their minds following a visit by Goulart to Red China, where he extolled the Communist experiment. But, rationally, Goulart, one of Brazil's wealthiest landowners, could hardly be called a Communist. He described himself as a "pragmatic nationalist," whatever that meant. In fact, he was a calculating and unprincipled politician, constantly in search of liaisons to strengthen his public career—no novelty in Brazil or elsewhere. But many of the critics, despite their dislike for Goulart's personality and expediency, believed in the sanctity of the constitution, which clearly held that the vice-president would have to finish the remaining four years as president.

The three cabinet ministers representing the armed services (navy, army, and air force), all military men, thought otherwise. They issued a joint declaration that Goulart's assumption of the presidency would be "inconvenient . . . for national security." One of these officers, Marshal Odilio Denys, the war minister, added a point of his own: "The time has come to choose between democracy and communism." The loose use of the word "communism" did not have the expected effect, nor did the camouflaged military ultimatum cow people as it might have in the past. Neither the whole nation nor the armed forces shared this attempt by senior officers to violate a fundamental charter. In the far South, in Goulart's home state of Rio Grande do Sul, the Third Army (a well-equipped force of 60,000 men out of total armed forces of 200,000) declared its support for the vice-president. Civilian followers in other southern states ominously began to organize popular militia battalions, armed with their own hunting rifles and weapons handed out surreptitiously by army units. When chiefs of staff in Rio de Janeiro sent signals to subordinates in Porto Alegre, the capital of Rio Grande do Sul, ordering them to shift their aircraft from the area, the local commanders instead erected barricades in the city, blocked the harbor against possible naval landings, and issued instructions on their own radio network to rally allegiance for Goulart. The few officers who tried to obey Rio headquarters found sergeants and enlisted men removing parts from planes so they could not fly.

Other soldiers, sailors, and airmen were caught in the conflict of whether to recognize regional or national instructions, or their consciences. Roughly, the lines set North against South, but mixed emotions were everywhere. In Brasília, the new capital, deputies and senators raced from one emergency meeting to another, with pistols jutting from their pockets. It was, by all accounts, a tense and dangerous period. Brazilians are individualists and pretend that life must go on despite national crises, especially a life of pleasure. It is true that the Copacabana, Rio's extensive beach, was crowded; prostitutes walked their usual beats along the sea front facing the line of fine hotels and apartments. But, as one *carioca* told me, between dips in the surf he and his friends were meeting under beach umbrellas to form maquis units; he said he knew of at least twenty-five similar conspiratorial groups in Rio, ready to act against the defense ministers if they should insist on imposing their will.

Many principles were at stake, not only a sincere pride in the constitution and a fear of a rise in military excesses. Brazilians also had a determination to discourage any foreign notions that theirs was just another preposterous and unstable "banana" republic. "Jânio or Jango—it doesn't matter who is president. We must allow nothing to stop our progress now." This is the way one businessman put it in referring to the surge of nationalistic fervor of Brazilians to find their roots in the industrial revolution that had its start under Vargas but really gained speed only in the last decade. What was needed was international respect and confidence in Brazil; and it does much to explain why Brazilians, rather than risk bloodshed and destroy faith in their country, worked day and night for a week on a compromise formula.

Finally, the military chiefs bowed to the mid-course solution worked out with Congress. Goulart took over as president, in a new parliamentary system, dividing his authority with a prime minister elected by Congress. It was a shaky and unwieldy arrangement, which no one could forecast with any certainty would work. But it at least saved the nation from imminent fratricide and demonstrated an awareness of responsibility. In January, 1963, Brazilians voted, by a margin of five to one, for an end to the parliamentary system and a return to a strong presidency. There was no doubt that military prestige was badly weakened; people took a fresh look at the supposed sentinels over sacred institutions. While I was in Rio de Janeiro, one newspaper went so far as to suggest that Brazil should have a civilian war minister: a proposition that as recently as five years ago would have brought a quiet military injunction forcing the paper to close down.

Goulart proved, at least in the first several months of presidential office, to be far milder than the military had expected—not really so surprising in the light of his history of political shuffling. The suspenseful chapter, however, held a lesson not for Latin America alone, but for the United States as well. If Brazil's Congress does degenerate into a tool of the armed forces, it is almost certain that none of the basic social and economic reforms so desperately required will be carried out by officers of conservative leanings. Besides, a military dictatorship of Latin America's biggest country would grievously embarrass Washington in its quest to convince the hemisphere that democracy and improvement can go hand in hand, especially since United States funds have heavily subsidized Brazil's military machine. Brazil is crucial to the success of the Alliance for Progress; and its pattern, rippling out in all directions, may well set the form for an entire continent suffering from many of the same conditions. What will happen then, if, as appears probable, the scale of power has shifted away from the traditional military leaders? The recent crisis was over a constitutional issue; the next might easily be over something more fundamental, bread and butter. "Quadros was a demagogue," said Ruy Mesquita, co-editor of *O Estado de São Paulo,* Brazil's most influential newspaper. "But he was also a mixture of many things. He could understand traditional Brazil—the customs, the philosophies, the mentalities of the upper class and the aristocracy—and yet feel the movement of masses everywhere. He was our last chance for democratic development."

Quadros returned to Brazil as a private citizen, to test the political climate, six months after his self-imposed exile. But by then the social and economic pressures, especially in the impoverished Northeast with its rapidly spreading and revolutionary Peasant Leagues, had pushed closer to the surface. Reflecting on the unpredictable elements Quadros' resignation had set adrift, a senior intelligence officer said he estimated Communist strength at no more than 40,000. "Because of the social unrest," he went on, "they could be tremendously significant. But the threat is not from them. It is from the people who are starving in the Northeast and elsewhere and who see no progress and no hope for progress. Once they start to move I am afraid that we (the armed forces) will not have the strength to stop them."

The point, of course, is that if the armies were divided once, with at least one third refusing to heed orders from a central command, they could separate again, this time on social and economic issues rather than political or technical ones. If Brazil's chiefs of staff are of the oligarchy, most officers and their men come from middle and lower groups and might be expected, in any showdown, to align themselves with their own classes. Troops in Rio Grande do Sul supported Goulart partly because he came from their region. How would troops from Rio Grande do Norte and other Northeast states react to instructions to march against kinfolk struggling for social and economic betterment? In other words, it is no longer safe to assume that Brazil's armed forces will maintain traditions or provide a calm bulwark against extreme changes as they have in the past.

It is one of the contradictions of South America that within the period of half a year the two most important countries, Argentina and Brazil, saw martial mutations: in the one a return to old-style militarism, in the other a lessening of the high-command hold. This seesawing is not uncommon historically, but in recent years a new and uncertain factor has been added: the example of Cuba and the influence of its social changes. I heard some officers say they would defend their establishment against any incursions of Fidelismo if for no other than the understandable reason of self-interest, the knowledge that existing officer castes would be replaced in any successful revolution. But there were also men in Colombia, Brazil, Venezuela, and other countries who said, as one young officer said in Bogotá, "We must have major reforms. Up to now everything has failed except force."

The same was said in the 1940's and 1950's by young officers who pitted themselves against generals whose mentalities they considered rigid. Mostly, however, the incentive was not altruism but greed and personal gain. (Perón escaped from Argentina with an estimated $700 million, Pérez Jiménez from Venezuela with $250 million, Fulgencio Batista from Cuba with $200 million.) Whether the young marine officers who attempted insurrection in Venezuela in

1962 or the troops who fought Castro-style in the hills of Guatemala would be content with mere financial gain was debatable. Their motives today are just as likely to be genuinely social and revolutionary in line with Bolivia, Cuba, and an earlier Mexico.

One would think that the armed forces, commanded by supposed realists, would be universally concerned with social reforms, if only to contain the obvious "enemies": hunger and discontent that can lead to uncontrollable explosions. But on balance, right-wing traditions of the military still prevail through most of the hemisphere. Army regimes that really promote reforms are the exceptions; mostly their political intervention is a conservative holding action, going even so far as to dissolve popular parties by the threat or use of force. In Peru it was the army that declared the winner of the presidential election in June of 1962 even before the final vote was tallied; not content with this move, it threw aside all civilian political figures, and a general, Ricardo Pérez Godoy, was proclaimed provisional president. Ironically, in the process of the coup the outgoing president, Manuel Prado, a conservative banker, was deposed just ten days short of completing his term of office and exiled because he stood for constitutional process, which would have given the APRA party of Haya de la Torre a major say in government. APRA and the army had been in conflict, sometimes with a heavy cost in lives, for thirty years; but more to the point, the generals regarded it as too extremist (in reality APRA, at one time leftist, latterly was a moderate party). General Pérez, on behalf of his military *junta,* promised a new election for June, 1963, and said righteously: "We of the armed forces are middle class . . . there will be land, houses, work and food . . . we will decrease the cost of living . . . we will do all this in twelve months, not one day more." The words, in South America's third largest country, had a familiarly hollow ring and presented a new problem to a shocked United States administration desperately trying to keep alive a year-old Alliance for Progress with promises of strengthening democratic institutions. If militarism at one time could be shrugged aside by North Americans as simply another quaint Latin-American trait, its upsurge in the last year was of more serious dimensions, politically, economically, emotionally, and the basis for review in the concluding section of this book.

Meanwhile, one judgment appears valid: the atmosphere and conditions of Latin America, political immaturity (caused largely by militarism itself), decadence of old institutions, the lack of cohesive civilian alternatives, all combine to foster military rule. "If there is no agreement on the right to command or the duty to obey, either because of ethnic heterogeneity or in consequence of an internal schism," says one analyst of militarism generally, "naked force must remain the argument of last resort, and the distribution of military might must then be the principal determinant of the social structure." [7] The big imponderable for the future is whether the social structure of much of Latin America will be of a right- or left-wing nature, implemented, at least initially, by men in uniform. In view of the social forces operating, a middle road seems unlikely.

[7] *Military Organization and Society,* by Stanislaw Andrzejewski, Routledge and K. Paul, London, 1954.

7

Brasília: Symbol in the Wilderness

Some international airlines recruit attentive stewardesses who lavish on their passengers foie gras, caviar, and other delicacies. But Varig, the Brazilian airline, goes a step further. In addition to the usual crew, it carries on its main routes a hostess ("executive hostess" is the official title) whose function is to make you feel you are attending a private party. She introduces guests, suggests a liqueur after the elaborate meal, and stimulates conversation in a half-dozen languages. On the trip from New York to Rio de Janeiro, my hostess was a countess, attired in black dinner gown with just the right accessories, including a long strand of pearls. Now, on the way from Rio to Brasília, the hostess was Princess Mafalda de Bragança Chanler, great-granddaughter of Dom Pedro II, the last monarch of Brazil.

The man sitting beside me, Alberto Borges, a building contractor, pointed out that there was something quite appropriate about the royal touch on a jet doing nearly six hundred miles an hour. "Brasília," he said, almost tenderly, "was a dream back in the days of the emperors, and it came into reality only in the modern age." If Brasília is the world's newest city, born only a few years ago, it is also the most controversial capital.

It is eight hundred miles from Rio, and you fly endlessly over forests, glimpsing only occasionally a freshly cut road through the trees. You wonder what kind of civilization can exist in this forbidding territory, and then, suddenly, Brasília springs into view: dramatic, haughty, with its green and blue skyscrapers in the midst of red flatland. For miles around, the soil is ruddy, betraying its clay surface and making the city look ludicrously misplaced, as though someone had dropped it casually from the sky not caring where it would settle. "Why," I asked Borges, "did they ever pick a site like this?"

Borges methodically quoted a team of international experts who had studied many regions and made their selection on the basis of an ample watershed and other technical factors. Brasília itself might be planted on red clay, but not far away there was good farm acreage to feed its people. "Besides," said Borges, "we had to conquer the interior."

It was a simple statement, told with pride, and the key to Brasília. For beyond the fact that Brasília was hacked out of the wilderness—a great tribute to man's daring, energy, and ingenuity—it stands as a symbol. Brasília, at least potentially, wrests open a continent not only for Brazilians but for all South Americans.[1] However, how did Borges find it as a place in which to live? Could any brand-new city have a friendly character? Borges, a hearty man of about fifty, gave a wry smile. "It is," he confessed, "a trifle arid and antiseptic." Borges, who has made a fortune putting up some of the buildings, also admitted that he spends only two days a week in Brasília. The rest of the time he enjoys the beaches, the bustle, and the familiar luxury of Rio.

[1] It also arouses comparisons. While I was in Bogotá it sometimes took ten minutes to cross from the main door of the Hotel Tequendama to the other side of the street; sidewalks were up, and traffic was snarled because an underpass was under construction. Colombians commented drily that work on the incompleted underpass began before Brasília.

Before long, I understood Borges' mixed reaction; on the one hand, Brasília is a tremendous mechanical feat, on the other it lacks heart and soul. Driving through the main thoroughfares, I felt immediately this was a city of anonymity, built for the future and almost contemptuous of the present, with huge functional blocks of glass and steel dominating the human beings who are supposed to inhabit them. Children are reared in fine new apartments, but one apartment is precisely the same as the next. Men go out for drinks after work, but each bar comes from the same mold as its neighbor. One road is wide, but so is another. Brasília boasts that it is the only city in the world without crossroads, and indeed you can drive from one end of town to the other without pause, turning through tunnels or mounting overpasses. But after a while you almost wish for the nuisance of traffic lights so you might catch sight of a pedestrian at a corner. Instead, you are aware only of mammoth and pitiless concrete, or of such formations as the cathedral, which resembles a haunched and fearsome steel centipede.

Brasília has been described as a "Daliesque tableau," a conception of things to come. Certainly it is unlike any other capital I have seen. Paris has warmth and beauty, London an ingrained dignity. Peking had centuries in which to grow in gentle, curved lines; there you feel the tranquility of another age; no tower and no wall that dates back to the Chinese emperors is higher than ninety feet, in order to give devils, which fly at one hundred feet, a substantial clearance. St. Petersburg (now Leningrad) commands the stateliness and grace of a carefully plotted eighteenth-century European center of culture; Peter the Great built it from the bottom up as a gracious capital of the czars and a monument to himself.

Some of Brasília's critics say that Juscelino Kubitschek conceived the new capital in a mood of self-glory, at a cost so far of more than $600 million. There is ample evidence that Kubitschek intended his name to be enshrined; plaques on government buildings eulogize him, quoting at length his supposedly visionary statements. "We have turned our back to the sea and penetrated to the heartland of the nation," proclaimed Kubitschek. "Now the people of Brazil realize their own power and strength."

Whatever the motives of ego, the bare facts are these: For two centuries Brazilians mused about an inland capital to replace Rio de Janeiro; Kubitschek, who was president of Brazil from 1955 to 1960, devoted his vigor to its fulfilment. Brasília is only one quarter finished, but its outline and principal structures were completed in the incredibly short period of forty-three months. To get the project going, Kubitschek had to cram legislation through Congress, bulldoze five thousand miles of roads to other cities, and mastermind an airlift that put a supply plane down in the wilderness every two minutes.

In some ways Brasília gives the impression of being a frontier town of the Old West or the present North of Canada. Three "satellite" districts, twelve miles from the city center, are intended to supply it with all its food and materials, so the capital will be free from any commercial industry and devoted exclusively to government offices and residences. The "satellites" at the moment are shantytowns, haphazardly thrown together. Unpaved roads, aswirl with red dust, lead to a hodgepodge of frame huts or stores with wooden fronts. Signs scrawled impatiently on rough planks point to dentists, shoe repair shops, garages, and the pioneer bars that at the peak catered to sixty thousand construction workers. There is a lusty atmosphere to these shantytowns, for Brasília has bred new types of tin-hatted builders who proudly call themselves *candangos,* a term once given by slaves to the Portuguese. Many of these men, of African origin, spent a week in open, bouncing trucks to come down from their hovels in the Northeast. They earned enough in six months to fly home in splendor.

Two chief architects were entrusted with the creation of Brasília. Lúcio Costa drew up the master city plan; broadly he shaped Brasília like a giant airplane, with the Plaza of the Three Powers (parliament buildings, administrative offices, courts) as the nosepiece. Oscar Niemeyer, one of the world's most renowned architects, was given an ideal assignment: a completely free hand to design all Brasília's buildings. As Niemeyer recalls it, Kubitschek simply said: "I want you to build a city for 500,000 people." With this *carte blanche* Niemeyer suffered no interference of any kind. The only pressures were those of time. He had, for instance, just fifteen days in which to prepare blueprints for the opera house. "It was just as well," he recalled. "With more time I would have discovered all kinds of problems."

Speed marked every stage of Brasília's development. Fifteen hundred hastily mobilized contractors brought in armies of workers by planes and buses; ten-story ministries rose in a month, twenty-story office buildings in three months. Today, cracked plaster and chipped walls testify to somewhat hasty workmanship, but visiting architects from North America and Europe ignore these details and generally rate Brasília as superb in concept and form. A guide book states: "Brasília will be a city living under the sign of discipline, order, and logic." This ties in with Niemeyer's philosophy, which holds that intensive social planning leaves no room for individuality.

Whether one agrees or disagrees with this extreme belief, the result, as illustrated by Brasília, can be almost coldly inhuman. You work all day in an ultramodern ministry that is uniform with a half dozen other ministries in a row; at night you retire to a utilitarian—but hardly beautiful—apartment block, shared with the same office workers you saw all day at the ministry. Your block is part of a complex of eleven blocks, and there are several of these complexes, and they are identical. Each has the same shopping center, cinema, school, playground. I found the conformity depressing, a foretaste of a Brave New World starved of ardor or personality. Nevertheless, some natural spirit is creeping through the rectangular lumps of construction. An address reads: "Square 108, Block 62, Apartment 203." But instead of giving these automaton directions, people are apt to add a note: "There is a little bookstore in the middle of the square. We are in the second building to the right." Niemeyer's intended universality has not succeeded in the ultimate.

Yet none of this criticism alters the point that Brasília is a noble experiment, conducted in unorthodox fashion, in haste, but with an eye to the future. If I felt uncomfortable or depressed standing in what struck me as a coldly gleaming commune, I also remembered that men had to carry every nail, every bit of wire into the uninviting backwoods to set up Brasília; other men may be inspired by the example and tame other parts of a still largely wild continent. South America is huge. This is the first thing you grasp as a visitor. The second thing is that it is immensely rich in resources that have hardly been touched because people have not bothered or have been unable to penetrate the jungles and mountains. Flying from capital to capital—Montevideo, Buenos Aires, Santiago, La Paz, Lima, Quito, Bogotá, Caracas—you are constantly aware of the vast unpopulated areas in between. And, more strikingly, you realize the bulk of South America's inhabitants are clustered close to the sea.

There is a historic reason for South America's lopsided distribution. The early settlers from Portugal and Spain preferred the coastal towns, which had pleasant weather and few of the dangers of the unexplored hinterland or the horrors of tropical diseases. The first slaves from Africa were landed in these ports, and gradually, too, the Indians from the interior began to drift down in search of employment. Huge areas inside Brazil are still unknown: unmapped because scanty demand has provided a livelihood for no more than a half-dozen expert cartographers. At the present rate, it will take at least a hundred years to complete the mapping of the country.

But some men have always talked of the riches that lay inside the continent. In recent years another and urgent motive has been added to exploration: the grave social unrest among workers in the overcrowded centers along the Atlantic and Pacific. Governments are impelled to peer beyond the ravines and forests for more living space. In Chile I met planners who predicted great population shifts to new oil fields on the southernmost tip of the continent. In Peru, which is endowed with every natural gift for a plentiful life, they say they will move people across the Andes and into the fertile subtropical lands awaiting man's touch. In most instances it is still talk, and not much more. Brasília, however, stands out as a practical translation of pioneering spirit. Before construction began, Kubitschek has recalled, "there was only solitude and a jaguar screaming in the night."

Brasília was officially inaugurated as Brazil's capital on April 21, 1960. Since then, work on government buildings has slackened (Kubitschek, in his enthusiasm, nearly drove the nation into bankruptcy). There has also been resistance by government officials against quitting the warm comforts of Rio; some senior men still make only token visits, referring disdainfully to Brasília as "Kubitschek's folly," or to the presidential Palace of Dawn as "Niemeyer's cardiogram," because of its jutting concrete pillars. In effect, Brazil still possesses two capitals. Skeleton staffs inhabit the monumental ministries of Brasília while the ministers themselves cling to the old colonial mansions of Rio.

But Brasília even in 1962 could count a population of

185,000, and there is continuing pressure for a final move within the next few years. Congress meets there now; embassies, still located in Rio, have drawn up their plans for inclusion in Brasília's Embassy Row. The feeling is that Brasília will indeed become the working capital. It has already proved itself in an unforeseen way. When Jânio Quadros, Kubitschek's successor, quit the presidency, Rio was thrown into turmoil, with students roaring through the streets in protest against a threatened military takeover. But deputies and senators in Brasília, far from the pressures and passions of the big coastal city, were able to meet with relative calmness and reach a rational solution, which saved the nation from civil war.

Kubitschek proclaimed a "great leap forward" for Brazil even before the slogan became synonymous with Communist China. Not much later, borrowing a phrase once used by Napoleon in reference to China, he proudly declared, "I have awakened the sleeping giant." The comparison with China cannot, of course, be carried too far. Brazil still speaks of private enterprise as its guidepost. But in broad, sweeping strokes it is the China of Latin America. It is the largest political unit, taking in nearly half of continental South America's territory and population; it is also the fastest moving, the most dynamic of the republics.

But if Brazil should follow the example of relatively puny little Cuba, would the rest of Latin America be far behind? The question is not academic, but a practical possibility, as Washington indicates in its outpouring of Alliance for Progress funds to the country.

"When God was making the world," Brazilians like to say, "He gave Brazil everything." Indeed, Brazil has almost everything: fertile land, which makes it the world's leading producer of coffee, bananas, and beans; Brazil is second in the world in oranges and hog production, third in corn, fourth in cotton; it boasts of gold and silver and precious stones, plus the world's greatest reserves of iron ore; its steel plants, turning out 4 million tons a year, comprise Latin America's greatest single industrial complex. Brazil grows, economically, at the impressive rate of 6 per cent a year. Then why the concern? The trouble with Brazil is that, despite its virility, it is chronically sick, in need of massive transfusions of money and a nourishing diet that might spread a little fat more evenly over the body. Brazil is like an ungainly, uncoordinated animal, its head—bursting with brainpower—too small for its stomach, its spindly legs reaching out convulsively for firm ground. São Paulo is the head; the legs fall uncomfortably in the Northeast and other underdeveloped areas where most of the 70 million people live in misery.

I arrived in São Paulo from Brasília, filled not only with respect for Brazil's technical accomplishment but with admiration for the way its people often can laugh at themselves and misfortune. How can you be impatient with or irritated at the flagrant display of undisciplined wealth along with heartbreaking poverty when the nation still has verve and daring in whatever it does? For example, a plane, carrying the governor of the state of Rio Grande do Sul and other officials, was coming into Brasília, with a large welcoming committee on hand at the airport. The plane touched down, lurched suddenly, and burst into flames. There were no casualties; but the passengers were badly shaken and frightened; they also lost their belongings. Still, a reception was planned. The official party ran, rather hastily, from the burning aircraft toward the social committee at the other end of the field. Festivities went on as scheduled, including a fireworks display, which blended with the glow of the fuselage and the roar of fire engines.

A highly talented British journalist, James Morris, expressed his feelings about Brazil in *The Guardian:* "Perhaps she lacks some niggling virtues of common sense, but she glories in the grandest of national qualities, style. Whatever she does is big, whatever she thinks is generous. Great God! I will swap you a dozen prim and thrifty principalities for one such sprawling greatheart." I read this appraisal while I was in São Paulo, and if anything it only heightened my feeling of finding, on the one hand, exciting facts and tempo, and, on the other, gloomy contradictions. Morris was right when he talked about the style. It is everywhere manifest in São Paulo, the incredibly vibrant city that counted only 25,000 inhabitants in 1875, and today, with a population of more than 4 million, is growing four times as fast as Los Angeles. But São Paulo, contrasted with the starving Northeast, only points up the grave and dangerous condition Brazil finds herself in, an imbalance of economy and values that could lead to violent upheaval.

São Paulo is usually called "the Chicago of Latin America." The comparison is not ill taken. It looks a bit like it, and if Chicago built its strength as a slaughterhouse, so, too, did São Paulo lay its foundation on one commodity: coffee. But coffee exporting is no longer São Paulo's only source of wealth. Today motor cars, textiles, electrical equipment, and virtually all kinds of manufactured products roll from its factories. A forest of forty- and fifty-story skyscrapers is added to by new homes going up at the rate of one every hour and new factories at the rate of one a week. The number of factories has doubled in the last decade to nearly 60,000, and now the booming city—the biggest industrial beehive in Latin America—sprawls over six hundred square miles, spilling alongside the six-lane superhighways that join it to the port city of Santos, thirty miles away. Santos itself has grown into Latin America's busiest port.

The superlatives are everywhere. Brazilians treat air travel almost like bus transportation, and seventy shuttle-service flights a day link São Paulo with Rio de Janeiro. Rio may be the soul of Brazil, but São Paulo is its vital artery and in some ways a relief from the coastal playground. If *cariocas,* attired in trunks and sandals, like to wander through the streets toward the beach at midday, Paulistas, well-dressed and business-like, prefer to walk briskly in search of challenges. One reason for São Paulo's hustle and stir is its 3,000-foot elevation, making for a somewhat cooler and more invigorating climate than Rio's. But beyond this is the influence of what economists like to call "high-grade" immigrants: the million Italians, the quarter-million Germans, the Japanese, the Lebanese, and other enterprising foreigners who have made São Paulo their home. Israel Klabin emigrated from Latvia, to peddle cigarettes and then to sell costume jewelry from a pushcart; his next step was the purchase of a horse and wagon; from collecting rags for paper mills, he graduated to ownership of Latin America's biggest pulp and paper combine, worth today more than $600 million. Paulistas, without prodding, can match this theme with at least a hundred other immigrant-to-millionaire stories.

Sixty per cent of Brazil's industry is concentrated in and around São Paulo. In 1955 Brazil produced almost no appliances. In 1961, the nation turned out 80,000 washing machines, 150,000 television sets, 300,000 refrigerators, 350,000 sewing machines. In 1957, São Paulo opened its first integrated auto plant, Willys-Overland do Brasil. Today, Willys and four other United States and European car manufacturers have an investment of $500 million [2]; inside of four years they created a major automotive industry, producing 145,000 cars, trucks, and buses annually. São Paulo received its big spurt under Kubitschek, who drew in auto manu-

[2] Foreign capital investments in Brazil in 1961 totalled $3.5 billion, of which 37.5 per cent was from the United States. Canada, mainly through Brazilian Traction, was next in line with 17.7 per cent. West Germany was third was 9.3 per cent. Other countries included Britain, France, Italy, and Japan.

facturers, among others, by offering attractive tax concessions. But here the record begins to show flaws. "How economical is it," a banker said to me, "to produce a Simca for $4,000 when the same car can be brought in from France at half that price?" Kubitschek approached Brazil's industrialization with the frank use of inflation as an economic tool. He increased Brazil's supply of money simply by printing it. To keep down the cost of living, or so he claimed, he subsidized such items as newsprint and petroleum, allowing in imports at an unrealistic *cruzeiro* rate. Again he did this by printing more money, thus causing values to drop and prices to rise, so that the public paid for the favors he gave big business.

While Kubitschek promised to achieve fifty years of progress in five, some economists say he managed to achieve forty years of inflation in four. Under his administration the cost of living doubled in two years. Corruption and blatant favoritism, not unknown to Brazil in the past, also were accelerated. Congressmen even voted themselves the privilege of importing, duty-free, an expensive foreign car apiece, which they could then sell at a profit ranging from $5,000 to $10,000. "What makes Brazil different from countries abroad," mused a North American businessman, "is that at home you can expect one official in ten to be involved in graft or corruption, but here it is eight out of ten."

In the process of pushing for industrial development (and the construction of prestigious Brasília), Kubitschek wantonly neglected agriculture, on which the nation is still basically dependent. Little has been done in succeeding years to correct the imbalance. Less than 10 per cent of the cultivable soil is under crops, and the printing presses continue going at top speed. One hundred billion *cruzeiros* were churned out in 1961 alone, increasing the paper money in circulation by 50 per cent. In 1956 the *cruzeiro* stood at 60 to the dollar; five years later it was 350 to the dollar; by the end of 1962,

825. Partly the drop in value was due to a flight of capital; while Brazilian officials welcomed foreign investors, their own businessmen, fearful of the uncertain political atmosphere, were shipping some of their own funds abroad, through illegal channels. I was told that if I had $100,000 I could easily get 20 per cent more *cruzeiros* to the dollar, because large transactions were preferable to small ones.

The impact on ordinary Paulistas was mixed. Despite the spiraling inflation, many were still able to put as little as fifty cents down on a $500 refrigerator. Half could afford to own television sets. The average Paulista worker, living on at least double the scale of other Brazilians, was content to pick up his wage packet, go home, and keep out of politics or arguments about reform. If anything, he was tired of hearing that he ought to do more to help his starving compatriots in the Northeast, which, as far as he was concerned, could be just another backward African land.

The State of São Paulo, with relatively fine roads and public services, stands apart from the rest of the country. Some 10 million people, numbering among them not only millionaires but a growing middle class made up of shop clerks and industrial workers, can be said to have passed the subsistence level. But they account for scarcely one seventh of the over-all population. A São Paulo newspaperman put it this way: "They have fought their revolution, and won. But it was an industrial, not a social, revolution." At the same time, the extravagant population increase has another side to it: rural workers, drawn to the big city, find that housing—despite the pace of construction—cannot keep up with their demands. Thus, many live in *favelas,* or shantytowns. Frustrated, these unskilled migrants are able to see, but not necessarily to share, the wealth of their better-off neighbors. In the slums of São Paulo, as well as in other urban centers, the quick rise in the price of eggs by 50 per cent can make for an explosive situation.

The real drama, however, is to be found away from the boom towns. Eight out of ten of Brazil's farm workers own no land. At least half of all Brazilians never see money, no matter how fast the printing presses operate. They suffer from continual, gnawing hunger; they are depressed, miserable, unable to read or write, or to look to the future with any hope. Those who are in contact with reality find it wearisome listening to references to Brazil as the "land of the future"; they ask what is wrong with the present. The growth figures of São Paulo, cited by foreign travelers who do not venture beyond the cities, often conceal the grim fact that other major regions are stagnant.

If the heart of Brazil beats fast in São Paulo, it almost ceases functioning a mere 1,200 miles away, in the Northeast. The awakened giant referred to by Kubitschek has yet to show in which direction its steps will take it.

"I have a General on my side—Hunger." The man who made this statement—rather bland, forty-five-year-old Francisco Julião—is South America's most important revolutionary, built up, oddly enough, not by his own press but by North American newspapers and magazines, which have labeled him sensationally and superficially as a "Communist" or "another Fidel Castro." Whether Julião is a Communist is entirely academic as far as Brazil is concerned. A small-town lawyer, he gives no real impression of profundity or power. Julião, organizer and leader of the "*Ligas Camponesas*," or Peasant Leagues, in Brazil's Northeast, is significant not because he preaches violent overthrow of government (in fact, he doesn't even do this), but because he has managed to channel the passive mood of the impoverished into an effective instrument: they now take over land simply by squatting. The fashion he has generated has spread beyond the Northeast into other sections of the country, sometimes to the accompaniment of bloodshed.

"I do not exist simply as a person," Julião says. "I represent an idea. The landowners may try to kill me at any moment—and they have already tried to do so—but the idea will remain and will create a much greater penetration force." Julião has established an aura of mystique partly by lavish quotations from the Bible, which he calls "the most revolutionary book of all."

Brazil's Northeast area, comprising nine states, is fertile ground for revolutionaries. It is big—twice as big as France and Germany combined—and it holds one third of Brazil's inhabitants. If the Northeast were a separate nation, it would qualify as second in population and third in area in South America. At any rate, it is eternally hungry. Its 25 million people, mostly peasant Negroes and mulattoes, the descendants of slaves brought over from Africa by the Portuguese, subsist on a median income of $84 a year. This is an economic level lower even than in parts of India.

The other statistics are equally cold and frightening. Nearly five hundred of every thousand babies perish in their first year; the rest go on to a diet of molasses and manioc-root flour, with no milk; as they grow older they eat black beans, with perhaps meat a few times a year. Meanwhile, denied hospital care, the adults must fight tuberculosis and gastric diseases brought about by malnutrition, as well as intestinal hookworms that afflict one out of three, and an ailment called *schistosomiasis* that is spread by snails in polluted waters and causes debilitating belly-swelling in every fifth person.

By the age of thirty-two, the average Brazilian in the Northeast is dead, carried to his grave in a paper shroud because a wooden coffin is prohibitively costly. The survivors struggle on as cane-cutters in sugar plantations, for lodgings in mud huts and wages that usually run to sixty-five cents a week but can go as high as fifteen cents a day. They do not see the actual cash; it is doled out at plantation stores in the form of supplies (a pound of beans is twelve cents). The luckier ones toil as sharecroppers for the few feudal landlords who own almost all the land; in lieu of rent, they pay back about 50 per cent of their produce, keep a bit for family needs, and must sell the rest to the *patrão* at prices one third to one half below market values.

Nature has put a curse on the Northeast, giving it little rainfall and covering most of its soil with cactus. But man, in his greed, has compounded the felony by extracting all he can for quick gain, without thought to adequate conservation or irrigation or diversification. For this a handful of men are responsible. I met one of them on the flight from Rio de Janeiro to Recife, the Northeast's main city. He was the absentee owner of four plantations and sugar mills in Pernambuco state, and now he was making one of his three annual tours of inspection.

I had in my briefcase an official report prepared for the government by Celso Furtado, an idealistic economist-reformer, who claimed that such states as Pernambuco and Rio Grande do Norte were forced to import food (as much as 60 per cent of their requirements) at inflated prices because regional landowners preferred to grow industrial crops, cotton and sugar, which brought higher profits. When I quoted this report, my fellow passenger commented: "Everyone knows that Furtado is a Communist." I switched to the question of education (the rate of illiteracy in the Northeast is 90 per cent). "Well," he said, "some of my friends and I have tried to start some sort of schooling for the *camponeses*. But do you know, they wouldn't go; and they wouldn't send their children? They are lazy creatures, more like animals than humans." He would not listen to any argument—based again on the findings of Furtado and social scientists—that an undernourished person is physically unable to walk the several miles to and from a rural school.

Night had barely fallen when we touched down, and the moonlit scene on the drive from the airport into the center of Recife took my mind back to Calcutta. Men, women, and children stretched out for sleep on the bare pavement; some, however, were fortunate enough to enjoy sacks as mattresses. Occasionally I caught sight of legless men on carts, their stumps a few inches from the ground, propelling themselves by hand pushes among the reclining figures. Outside my hotel a dozen ragged beggars stood by to jostle one another for the right to carry my luggage and earn a few *cruzeiros*. If such a pathetic spectacle was to be deplored in Asia, it was even more difficult to accept in the Western Hemisphere, where affluence and Fidel Castro were only short distances apart.

The next morning, by prior arrangement through the airline, a man from a city office knocked on my door. He was to act as my guide and Portuguese interpreter, and he introduced himself as Octavio Calogeras. A slight man, of almost frightened visage, Calogeras said within five minutes of our meeting, "Things are going to have to change. People are hungry here, plain hungry." Calogeras, aged thirty, was obviously better off as a "white-collar" clerk than any peasant; he earned $45 a month. But his wife was expecting a baby, and previous deliveries had been difficult, and he said he was sick with worry about expenses. There was a doctor attached to his syndicate, or union; but the waiting list meant weeks of delay for any attention; and so he had decided to use a private physician and arrange admission for his wife to a maternity hospital. The total bill would consume two months' wages. "This is bad enough," he said, "but I must pay the hospital in advance, otherwise they will not take my wife."

The Calogeras family, including two children, ate meat twice a week; the rest of the time, using black beans as a staple, they were hardly more elevated than the *camponeses*.

"Will the Northeast ever change?" I asked Calogeras. He replied: "Only if there is a miracle. Only if God helps us." Otherwise, would nothing happen? "Yes," said Calogeras slowly. "We will have Fidelismo soon, unless we see a miracle." And he repeated: "The people are very hungry."

Calogeras was far better informed than the people about whom he was speaking. He had read quite a bit about Cuba, and had heard radio discussions on Fidelismo. He said he was not yet ready to accept it as the ideal solution, but any form of revolution would be preferable to the present existence. Julião? "Perhaps someone like Fidel, perhaps Julião, who can tell?" was the way he answered with a weary shrug of the shoulders.

I could never really be sure of what Calogeras was thinking; I had the feeling he might have expressed himself more pungently in the confines of an intimate circle. As I discovered in the next few days, there was a suspicion of strangers among the people here. Was I a government man, an agent? Walking away one afternoon from a *favela,* where I had been met by sullen hostility from the residents, Calogeras remarked: "They have heard stories about the government sending men to spy on them. They want to avoid trouble, so they do not speak frankly." This was an unjustified attitude on their part, he admitted, and was attributable partly to ignorance and illiteracy.

Nevertheless, some men said they had heard that Julião was doing a good job and perhaps they should join one of the urban Leagues now being established. "Julião thinks of the poor people," was the way one man expressed it. He, along with half of Recife's 800,000 inhabitants, lives in such squalid *favela* surroundings that, by comparison, Shanghai's slums are almost opulent. Sea water seeps through the ground, making it perennially mucky and smelly. It sometimes rises to the edge of the cardboard and tin shacks, so that barefoot children plunge through it ankle-deep. The compensation is that rats have forsaken these damp habitations for higher ground. The only life sustained is that of the human being, who also, when driven by hunger, moves farther into the city to forage through sewers for edible crabs. Drinking water is sold by commercial vendors, and if money is lacking so is this essential.

Some of the *favelas* are in more favorable positions, alongside the garbage dumps filled with refuse from the homes of the ninety or so sugar planters who dominate the coastal strip. One hundred thousand of Recife's people are totally unemployed and spend their time scavenging; another 300,000 work a day or two a week, at the docks or the sugar mills, and fill in by hawking coconut milk or combs at street corners. In Rio de Janeiro the *favelas* at least show occasional television and radio antennas, and *cariocas* can find a further outlet in the pleasures of the public Copacabana beach. In Recife there are no television antennas over the *favelas,* there are no escapist playgrounds; there are no signs of hope.

It is the same in the Northeast's countryside. Wherever I went, I saw children with the marks of malnutrition—swollen bellies, spindly legs—working in the fields as cane-cutters at six cents a day. These were the relatively blessed ones, because so far they had survived to the ages of seven or eight. Or should they be classed as the unlucky ones who must struggle on for another few years? In some villages not a single newborn lasts to its first birthday. For the most part the *camponeses* merely stumble at dawn from palm-thatched huts to the fields, and back again at dusk, hacking away in between at the sugar cane or the parched earth, which yields cactus and not much else. These are the sharecroppers who submit to the system known as *cambão;* in Portuguese the literal meaning is "yoke"; in everyday translation it means that the peasant, in addition to paying with half his produce, must also provide the landowner with his personal services for ninety-nine days a year. For this labor he is rewarded with *cachaça,* a potent drink made from sugar cane and similar to harsh rum. If he is sick during the *cambão* period, he must compensate the owner with a cash settlement; otherwise he and his family are thrown off the land.

The *camponeses* lead an isolated existence shorn of contact with the outside world. Castro? Julião? To some with whom I spoke the names implied nothing; to a few there was a vague suggestion of remote individuals beyond the *sertão,* the rolling hinterland. But for others, mention of Julião evoked a quick flash of recognition in dark brown eyes. "Yes," said one man, "he stands up for the *camponeses.*" But, significant though it might be, that was about the extent of his worldly knowledge. When I asked if he knew of the United States, he said, "It is a place past Recife." Another man said he believed that Russia was a country, but he had no idea of its whereabouts. Communism? Fidelismo? Again, as in other parts of South America, the terms drew blank responses. There were venomous snakes in the fields, and a certain hazard to the shoeless peasants. I asked, "Is there serum or medicine?" They had never heard of such things. "What do you do if you are bitten?" "Pray," was a typically submissive answer, and it told a good deal about the resignation of the people.

Francisco Julião sprang up among them as an alternative to defeatism. For years he was just another moderately successful lawyer of Recife. He had achieved a small measure of public attention by writing a slim volume of short stories describing, in rugged language, the pernicious custom of *cachaça* payment and drinking. Appropriately, it was called *Cachaça* and was endorsed by the eminent sociologist Gilberto Freyre, a fellow resident of Recife, who wrote the foreword. For a while Julião was content to be admitted to the restricted literary community of Recife; he was not expected to go much further. But his ambition centered more on politics than on authorship or a law practice. A member of the Brazilian Socialist Party, he competed unsuccessfully in town-council elections. On his next effort, however, he ran for the Pernambuco state legislature and was elected as a deputy. Just about the same time, an obscure sharecropper named João Firmino, on a plantation known as Galiléia, was about to make local history, unwittingly catapult Julião into prominence, and let loose a movement that may change the face of Brazil—and with it all of South America.

Firmino, tired of seeing friends evicted because they could not meet the payments and demands of the *cambão* system, decided to contest centuries of tradition; he set up the *Sociedade Agrícola e Pecuária dos Plantadores de Pernambuco* (Agricultural and Cattle-Breeding Society of the Pernambuco Planters). As fancy as it sounded, it was nothing more than a meagerly endowed mutual-aid organization of about two hundred sharecroppers. Each contributed a small sum every month so that members could have an emergency fund to fall back on in case of desperate need. Though the motive was modest to the extreme, it was almost ridiculous to think of peasants, who had been brought up to be tractable and unimaginative and resigned to fate, banding together even in mild form. Firmino prudently invited the owner of the plantation, Oscar Beltrão, to become honorary president of the *Sociedade Agrícola.* ("It was a humble gesture," dryly remarked the Brazilian journalist who recounted this part of the story. "Like that of a dog licking the hand of the master who beats it.")

Surprisingly, Beltrão accepted the invitation. Possibly he thought he was being charitable; he even gave the *Sociedade Agrícola* permission to use some of the timber on his property to build a small chapel. But then doubts began to set in, and Beltrão feared that Firmino and the others had really devised a "union" so they could insist on handling over a smaller share of their crops as rent. He instructed Firmino to disband the *Sociedade Agrícola.* Firmino, backed by the other *camponeses,* refused. Beltrão started to eject some of the sharecroppers from Galiléia; their mates retaliated by setting fire to the plantation's cane fields. Meanwhile, Firmino looked around for someone who might help them with legal advice; but one lawyer after another demanded a fee far beyond their reach. Finally, after a sixty-kilometer ride by horse and cart to Recife, he came across Julião. As Firmino recalled it, Julião said: "I will defend you. I am a deputy. I am well paid by the state, and you do not need to pay me anything." Thus in 1955, when Francisco Julião was aged thirty-seven, commenced a new career with far-reaching results.

Julião went to court and argued that *cambão* had no legal basis, that every man has the right to live on the land he works, or at least to be treated as a human being. He lost the case of Galiléia, but he won far more. For the first time, someone not only had spoken openly about the evils of *cambão* but had questioned its validity. Other *camponeses* appealed to Julião for guidance. When laborers at a plantation petitioned their *patrão* for a school for their children, and were turned down, Julião advised them to form a group similar to Galiléia's *Sociedade Agrícola.* And so was born the first Peasant League, a loose federation of several hundred men who squatted on the plantation with such tenacity that a frightened state government finally bought it from the owner and turned it over to the *camponeses.* Noting the success of this tactic, Julião then gave counsel to other peasants to seize land simply by sitting on it. In one instance the *camponeses* were driven off, with a loss of life, by hired gunmen called in by the omnipotent *patrão.* In another, the state, fearing violence, repeated itself by buying the title in the names of the sharecroppers. Word soon traveled, and two or three more Leagues came into spontaneous existence.

If the peasants were beginning to understand the effect of collective action, they were also spurred on by the vindictive and unreflecting reprisals of landowners. ("What is wrong with these creatures?" cried a *patrão*. "I have been paying for their funerals. Now I will stop paying.") The tragic case of Antônio Vincente—which at one time would have been considered inevitable and unanswerable—became a rallying issue in his neighborhood. Vincente had held land under the same owner for twenty-one years, and now was heard to say that perhaps a League would have some virtue. To teach him—and other potential "rebels"—a lesson, the *patrão* doubled Vincente's rent, leaving him virtually no crops for sale or for family necessities. Then one of the *patrão's* sons, a youth of nineteen, accompanied by three hunting playmates, turned one of Vincente's sons into a "fox." That is, they gave him a head start and chased him through the woods, later abandoning his body riddled with bullets.

Afterwards, a police sergeant appeared at Vincente's *adobe,* to arrest him for failure to meet the *patrão's* terms. Another son, Manuel, intervened. Manuel was shackled to the rear of a police car and dragged six kilometers to jail in the nearest town. There, according to word reaching reporters in Recife, he was subjected to a treatment consisting of a "bath" in Creolin, a disinfectant, and lashings three times a day. Released, and half-maddened, the twenty-six-year Manuel Vincente committed suicide by cutting his throat at a street corner before horrified passersby could stop him. The next morning two more Leagues were founded in the vicinity, and the *patrão's* cane fields were put to the torch.

In such a climate, and with the seeds already implanted, the Peasant Leagues had no difficulty in spreading. There was no central office, no masterful brain directing clutching tentacles. Julião himself had little more to do than meet visiting *camponeses* informally in his home, or conduct occasional open-air rallies. He advocated sit-down strikes, and, more forcefully, sabotage of plantations when necessary. By the end of 1960 there were forty-nine Leagues in the Northeast with 40,000 members; by 1962 the numbers had risen to more than one hundred Leagues, with 80,000 active followers who had taken over 25,000 acres of land. The figures themselves are meaningless. What is salient is the way in which a message, in a backwoods area with practically no communications, could be passed from one person to another, from one Northeast state to the next, so that eventually it filtered through one million square miles. A spark can flash by means other than telegraphy.

United States newspapers and news magazines were not the first to note this phenomenon. A distinguished Rio journalist, Antônio Callado, published the initial articles about Julião and his disciples in *Correio da Manhã*. But Julião remained for the most part unknown until a few American reporters began to quote him. He became an international figure even before he was a national one. Callado, who is now editor of the Brazilian edition of *Encyclopaedia Britannica,* feels that the foreign press jumped into action with the wrong incentive, seeking to make Julião out as a "Communist" or "Castroite." Elaborating on this point for me, Callado said:

> Julião is a member of the Socialist Party and therefore a Marxist, but this is far from the same as a Communist as we understand it. He has been to China and to Cuba, but so have many non-Communists. Really, Julião is an ambitious politician with ideals. You must remember that the illiterates in Brazil have no vote, which means that almost all the peasants in the Northeast are disenfranchised. Julião is their voice. I doubt if he has read to this day a book on Lenin, or even Marx. He is no fool, of course. He reads papers and knows what is going on in Russia and Cuba. But I am sure it doesn't bother him if a North American newspaperman

pays a visit and rushes away labeling him a "Communist." The publicity only builds him up. After all, previously he was completely unknown.

There is no doubt that Julião has attained the ideal desired by politicians. He is a famous and controversial figure, spoken about, commented on, the object of considerable debate. Officials, landowners, congressmen, and other members of "The Establishment" despise him and loudly call him an agent of Fidel Castro, forgetting, of course, that he arrived on the open scene four years before Castro. Intellectuals and students, not to mention the peasants, support him. Now he is taken seriously by Brazilian newspapers and periodicals, most of which see in him something much more subtle than communism and quote his simple, straightforward manner of speech: "Hunger cannot be postponed or transferred; either one kills hunger or dies from it." *O Cruzeiro,* Brazil's largest picture magazine, has devoted increasing space to Julião and his activities, and argued: "The people who are contributing in the greatest degree to the potential social revolutions in the Northeast are the owners of the lands and the governments—the landowners through feudal and inhuman action, the governments by sins of omission. . . . The great landowners and the bad governments are today emulating the old Roman Emperor; they are lighting the fires of subversion and watching the fire, entranced by the music of guitars in night clubs and by the frivolity of so-called society life." The highly respected *Jornal do Brasil* had a similar observation: "The agents of subversion are the big landowners who refuse to admit times have changed."

Julião lives in a moderately sized, eighteenth-century house on the outskirts of Recife. The cement walls, painted a faded yellow, are woefully chipped, adding to the generally decrepit surroundings; a couple of geese wander through the thick brush of weeds in the yard, their honking sometimes cutting through the murmur of voices on the balcony. Here, every night, are gathered from a dozen to a score of *camponeses,* waiting for a handout of food (Julião supposedly inherited a little money from his father, a prosperous farmer), or for guidance. When you ask them, as I did, what the Peasant Leagues stand for, you are apt to hear this kind of reply: "The Leagues will give us land." Some of these men, in relative proximity to the city, are better informed than most peasants; but they profess to know little about land reform as it has been carried out in practice in Cuba or China. "Dr. Julião tells us it is good for the *camponeses,*" says one. "It is enough for us to hear Dr. Julião say this." Julião, in the confines of his library—filled with books on law and philosophy—is cordial and cooperative, but he gives the appearance of being a rather wan and colorless individual. Physically, he is not terribly prepossessing; of medium stature, his shoulders fall forward to form a slight hollow; his bushy black hair, streaked only in one or two spots with gray, is unkempt; his wide mouth droops at the corners, implying almost perpetual sadness. But if his ideas seem only roughly sorted out, and at times he contradicts himself, he makes his key points with masterful simplicity.

"The Cuban method would not be suitable for all of Brazil," he says. "But it would be right for the Northeast. I am in favor of collectivization of the land, of establishing cooperatives. Everybody would benefit. The peasant no longer would be isolated, without security. He could have the advantage of medical attention and send his children to school. And with his greater prosperity he could purchase, through cooperatives, equipment and help industry. There is no reason in my mind why such a system could not work in a capitalist country."

"But do you think the Brazilian peasant can adjust, psychologically, to life in a cooperative?"

"Perhaps not immediately. But he can be educated to understand what cooperation means. We are already making the peasants aware that they have the means to protest against exploitation. They are individualists. We are teaching them to work together."

"How can you see your goal being reached?"

"I think Brazil is in a position to make reforms without revolution. When I chose as a slogan, 'Agrarian reform or revolution,' I put the responsibility on the government. What I want is to agitate the country: to arouse consciences, to alert public opinion, to make peasants, who are now half asleep, wake up and participate in politics. I demand for illiterates the right to vote, so there will not be a dictatorship by one class, the big landowners. Once there is a vote for everyone, the rest will follow."

But since it is unlikely that the vote will be extended beyond the Northeast's 10 per cent who can read and write, what then? Armed revolution?

Julião smiles and shrugs his shoulders. "I admire," he says, "the method of Gandhi, but his was a period of the past. The Leagues are symptomatic of a phase of transition. If the government, the Church, the landowners do not move quickly to solve the most pressing problems, then the peasants themselves will make a violent revolution."

In general, Julião prefers to play down the possibility of an armed struggle, saying instead that the momentum of the Leagues will carry them not only through rural areas but the cities of the Northeast. "The movement," he says, "has grown in a disorderly manner. It is only now that we are endeavoring to set up some kind of records. We are not even certain of the exact number of members. There is the field worker who is openly and fearlessly affiliated with the League, and there is the other type who is afraid of joining but remains underground as a latent force. Potentially, you might say, everyone in the Northeast belongs to the Leagues."

And here is where arises a contradiction. Julião rejects any suggestion that he is preparing peasants for guerrilla warfare: "General Hunger does not train his soldiers." But then he claims that, if the Quadros crisis had led to civil war, he would have had men ready to invade forty cities and towns: five hundred men for each city. "Civil war," he adds, "would have brought in its womb agrarian reform." But what could a few hundred unarmed men have done in the big centers? "They would have compelled the armed forces to disperse their normal bases, brought about confusion, and made it easier to find a solution by means of a struggle." If this is rather weird logic, Julião, who denies that arms have been smuggled into the Northeast from Cuba, appends a somber footnote: "Weapons will never be lacking, as they have never been lacking in any country in a time of need. In the event of any civil war, the army in the Northeast would be divided and we should have weapons on the spot. Furthermore, weapons would shower in from Cuba and Czechoslovakia and other countries."

"You would, then, accept help from Communists?"

"I am ready to accept the help of anyone who will free my country from the big landowners."

Is Julião really a Communist? He has claimed Castro as "a close friend" and described the Cuban revolution as "a miracle performed through the unity of the peasants." He returned from Red China "immensely impressed." But I could quote a dozen similar phrases from other Latin Americans who visited these countries and were no more than reformers out to improve, without extremism, conditions in their own countries. Brazilian Communists actually call Julião "an opportunist," and have set out among the *camponeses* to undermine his prestige. This is no mere camouflage; Julião's style of socialism is a threat to communism since it is aimed at eliminating the set of conditions on which communism blossoms. My own appraisal of Julião is that he stands part-way between the obstinate right and the other terminal. "Incredible as this may sound," says *O Cruzeiro,* "Julião has been a *moderating* influence in the Northeast . . . a brake on armed revolution." The argument is that he has been using the warning of revolution as a device to hasten peaceful reforms.

Whether *O Cruzeiro*'s estimate is exaggerated is inconsequential. The immediate peril could spring from any one of several directions. What would happen, for example, if Julião, failing to make headway by other means, was pushed into an alliance with the Communists? He is shunned by his own government; the only recognition he has received has been from such governments as the Cuban and Chinese, which have shown him their experiments, praised and encouraged him, and sent him off with promises of help. In this sensitive age of personal contact, it is ironic, and possibly tragic, that the United States—at least up to the date of this writing—has not found it appropriate to invite Julião to take a firsthand look at the people ("United States money-grabbers who exploit us") he occasionally includes in his denunciatory speeches about landowners and other oligarchs.

Meanwhile, despite their policy of opposing him, Brazil's Communists are watching and waiting while Julião unbolts the hidden frustrations of the masses; he could, of course, be destroyed by the landowners who need only issue orders to hired assassins. Equally, he might be destroyed by the same people he has been trying to help. These are unsophisticated men, their hands calloused from wielding long knives in the cane fields. They have heard from Julião the example of Cuba, and a few have even made the journey there to see for themselves how the "big owners of land" have been driven off. It is not inconceivable that Julião, the sorcerer, whose organization is loosely knit and undisciplined, will be unable to contain the flood he has released and will himself be swept away.

But Julião's personal fate, as he often boasts, no longer counts. He has encouraged a movement, it has caught on, and no matter what becomes of him there are others already talking his language. In Julião's hometown of Recife the mayor, Miguel Arraes, has formed a National Liberation Front along with the governors of two states. Their motive is to incite different factions in all political parties to push for radical social reform. "Brazil is marching toward something new, consciously, with eyes open," Arraes says. "It happened when we abolished slavery. It happened again when we became a republic—always bloodless, without physical battle. Ours will be humane solutions to the present problems." And if bloodletting is necessary? Arraes, after a long, hard stare, says simply: "That would be unfortunate." Farther south, a scant sixty miles from the big city of Rio de Janeiro, a twenty-four-year-old man named Mariano Beser has established branches of the Northeast's Peasant Leagues and trained followers in military methods. When a quartet of land speculators attempted to drive *camponeses* off fields they claimed as their own, Beser summoned together a band of armed peasants. One of the speculators was shot, and the other three were about to be executed when police intervened.

Other Peasant Leagues, or their counterparts, now exist in several states in Brazil. In a few instances, wary state governors have tried their own techniques to divert frustration. In Rio Grande do Sul, for instance, Governor Leonel Brizola encouraged *gauchos* to invade a large, privately owned ranch; then he signed a state decree expropriating the ranch "in the social interest of the community." In Rio Grande do Norte, Governor Aluizio Alves expropriated 47,000 acres of idle land held by the federal Bank of Brazil, and distributed it among the *camponeses*. But these have been isolated cases, on a local rather than a national level; if anything, they have only sharpened peasant appetites for more of the same. During one period alone, in May, 1962, peasants marched through a half-dozen Northeast towns and villages, crying out their hunger and looting food stores. Some were armed with shotguns; in an exchange of fire with police, one was killed and two were wounded.

That violent revolution is more than a possibility is confirmed by military authorities. In Recife, an army general, examining the situation for the press, said: "Julião will be one of the first to go before a firing squad." The general betrayed his anxiety by using the phrase, "when the revolution comes," only later catching himself and adding, almost in an undertone, "if it should come." A colonel said bluntly: "The people have nothing to lose." Almost the same words were employed by the man who accidentally touched off the vast surge of peasant feeling, João Firmino of the plantation Galiléia. Told that the army was prepared to crush any attempted upheaval, Firmino said: "If they kill us we shall lose nothing. They will lose the people who work for them." Some of the intellectuals of Recife say that the right man to lead a revolt has not yet emerged, that Julião lacks dynamism and a conception of firm authority. But, they add, one day a Brazilian Castro will emerge from the hills, or a *favela,* from a valley of the Amazon or the *sertão*. And from that day the Northeast will be witness to the most bloody uprising in the history of underdeveloped areas.

In the meanwhile, Julião has his worshipers. ("Below God there is only Dr. Julião," said one peasant.) He makes use of language and images readily understood by the people. "We must eliminate the feudal landlord as one would kill a dog with rabies," he tells them. Julião has confounded the landowners who, in self-delusion, like to categorize their tenants and laborers as patient and placid, incapable of responding to political incitement. The *camponeses* now attend Julião's outdoor rallies in the thousands, and the small-town lawyer, who in private appears so ineffectual, suddenly becomes converted into an impassioned orator. "I believe in agrarian reform," he declares, "as surely as I know the sun will rise tomorrow. In our prayer for reform let us use the words of the Bible. Yes, because the Bible is a revolutionary book." As he builds up the drama, he says: "We are not concerned with anyone's ideology or religion. We see no enemy in the soldier, the priest, the student, the industrialist, the Communist. Let them all come forward. Our only enemy is the feudal landlord. We must put an end to the society of the cunning."

At one moment he says: "Pope John was the first pope to come from a farm origin. The encyclical that he has issued is proof that the Pope supports our Leagues." The next instant he pours ridicule on priests who promise that the poor will go to heaven. At one rally, an emaciated peasant, dressed in sackcloth, called out: "Dr. Julião, may I say a word?" And then, inspiring a kind of tragic laugh from the audience, the peasant said: "I have no wish to go to this heaven with an empty stomach."

8

Fidelismo: The Protagonist

THE NAME given by Chileans to the slums of Santiago is *poblaciones callampas,* "mushroom villages," because they spread so quickly. These shantytowns are not much different from similar districts in the other principal cities of Latin America. The inhabitants are mostly migrants from the countryside who have asserted squatters' rights over unoccupied pieces of city property while they look to better themselves in industrial jobs. About 400,000 of Santiago's 1,600,000 people live in the hovels and tumbledown shacks of a score of *callampas,* and one of them, *Población la Victoria,* is particularly worth noting. It is called "Victory Village" in evidence of how an organized group can fight for and obtain minimum demands. In this instance, the group consisted of socialists in coalition with Communists. The Communists provided the main drive.

The case history began on October 30, 1957, in San Miguelo, a suburb on the southern outskirts of Santiago, when 15,000 men, women and children, living without water, sewage, or electricity, decided to move closer to the sources of these facilities. That night they descended in a mass on a site, an unused field inside Santiago itself, that was to become *Población la Victoria.* By dawn the first huts were up, crudely fashioned of packed mud walls and straw roofs, bits of tin, and wooden cartons. Hours later the police arrived to push the squatters back to San Miguelo. But a committee, elected by all the men and led by Communist Party members, was ready with its strategy. It ordered the women and children out in front, to form a human perimeter around the *callampa.*

Thus confronted, the police did not open fire or use strong-arm methods. Instead, they cordoned off the site, and for twenty days there was a siege. No one went to work, and the only persons permitted to enter or leave were those on missions of mercy, carrying food and drinking water. Mario Pallesclo, the socialist mayor of San Miguelo, defended his former neighbors in the press and recruited several engineers, all leftists, to help them with rudimentary sewage disposal and sanitation. A couple of doctors, who proclaimed themselves as Communists, set up an emergency health clinic. Finally, the government relented; *Población la Victoria* was allowed to remain.

By the time of my visit, more than four years later, the population had risen to 35,000, and *Población la Victoria* had its Carlos Marx Street and "Red Square," a rather dusty corner flanked on each side by mud huts. Most of the members of the local "central committee," or Soviet, as they preferred to term it, lived around "Red Square." Until a few months previously, the majority of the committee members were socialists; but now, after a new election, there were six Communists, three socialists, and one Trotskyite, who believed, as did some of the other "Trotskyites" with whom I spoke, that the Communists were not sufficiently revolutionary. Julio Cesar Solis, one of the Communists on the central committee, said: "We don't believe in revolution, because if we inform the people about necessary changes, and they get a vote, we will automatically have power." He was, of course, referring to power beyond *Población la Victoria,* but if in the meanwhile the example of his community would spread by word of mouth he would be quite content.

Población la Victoria holds some lessons and warnings not only for Chile but for the rest of the continent. There is no doubt that the Communists have shown a remarkable sense of dedication and organization in improving the physical standards of *callampa* dwellers. Compared with Santiago's other shantytowns, *Población la Victoria* is almost a model town. A hygiene committee teaches women fundamentals of child care, so that the infant mortality rate is appreciably lower than elsewhere. The clinic has been expanded to include three volunteer doctors, a pathetic ratio of less than one for every 10,000 persons, but again better than neighboring *callampas,* which never see a physician. Disciplined planning extends even to nonessential levels; a group, for instance, has set up an exchange shop for old magazines and books: in effect, what passes as a lending library, another rarity in a slum area. It is not by coincidence that the group is headed by a Communist, and Communist literature finds its way onto the shop table stacked with nonpolitical reading matter.

The Communists also started *Victoria's* first school, erected by the residents themselves from mud bricks; this effort pushed the government into building another school, a frame building, which at least cares for eight hundred of the four thousand children of primary age. When the socialists were in office they began a concentrated campaign, partly with the help of socialist newspapers, to get the government to install water tanks, so that today, unlike the squatters of other *callampas,* who must purchase or carry water in buckets, each family in *Victoria* can boast its own tap. The Communist Soviet later used the same badgering techniques to have electric lines extended to their site, employing a communal system of payment; the cost of electricity is pooled according to the number of light bulbs, on the average two, in each hovel.

But the most impressive feature is not the physical side of *Población la Victoria,* for, despite its advantages over other *callampas,* this is still an impoverished and primitive collection of mud huts with mud floors and mud streets. What is striking is the genuine community spirit, illustrated in tiny ways; people water down the lanes to keep the dust from rising; they plant flowers, so that children, barefoot as in other slums, will experience a splash of color in otherwise drab surroundings. "There is a sense of pride here," commented my guide, Luis Ratinoff, a prominent sociologist. "It denotes a true victory of people over a system in which they have no place."

Ratinoff is not a Communist, but his words were almost echoed a few minutes later when I had a separate conversation with Julio Cesar Solis. "We are nobody in the city of Santiago," said Cesar Solis, "and we have no hope of ever becoming anybody under the present system. But here we belong, here we are somebody." A mate of his, another Communist, added: "We really have much more dignity than the people outside, because we created this, and fought for it ourselves. The class to which the President of Chile belongs doesn't consider that we are human beings. But here we are human beings."

Sociologist Ratinoff analyzed this attitude: "They want to replace a complex outside world with something of their own, which they can manage by themselves. Moreover, Marxist ideology gives them an identity with at least part of the outside world." Peculiarly enough, when the government put up a nearby low-rental housing development, complete with modern amenities, the response from *callampa* dwellers was far from overwhelming. Most of them preferred to remain in *Victoria,* where they felt a strong, determined committee would protect their future interests. In other

words, comparatively fine brick buildings, which do not always take into account the herding instinct or need for broad security, are not the whole answer.

Julio Cesar Solis is as close to being a devout Communist as I found in Latin America. So is the rather naïve woman who said: "In such countries as the Soviet Union there are no prisons because there are no murders or crimes." But the majority of *Victoria's* people have no conception of the meaning of communism, nor are they particularly interested in finding out. They are not even concerned about the fiery competition between moderate socialists and extreme Communists to win their favor. Simply told, they will support anyone who promises, and delivers, a better break in a life that pays one dollar a day, if a man is lucky enough to find work, and demands one dollar for a kilo of meat. Sandoval Gonzáles once had a job as a bricklayer; but, when I saw him, he was unemployed and trying to make enough to feed his wife and two children by peddling coal and wood. How much did he earn, how much did it cost him to live? He was too proud to say. Well, then, with how much would he be content? He quoted the equivalent of forty dollars a month. But he wants to gain this without socialism or communism.

Gonzáles is essentially a free enterpriser; he opposes the method of paying for electricity on the basis of the number of light bulbs in his shack and not the quantity of electricity he actually uses. "This is too much like communism," he says. "It would be better if we had meters, like other people in Santiago." Gonzáles is a man of forty, and in an uneducated but profound way he has respect for individuality. However, the clue to his thinking, and the drama of communism's draw, is contained in the next statement: "The socialists and Communists have made *Victoria*. It is better than any other *callampa* I have lived in."

As in *Población la Victoria,* the popular socialists and

the closely knit Communists in Chile on a whole are collaborating—in a joint effort to gain political control of the nation. Chile's Communist Party is the oldest in Latin America, and the strongest, with the exception, of course, of Cuba's.[1] It claims 60,000 paid-up members, and in the 1961 elections polled 11.5 per cent of the votes, putting a sizable bloc of twenty-eight senators and deputies into the 195-seat Congress. Chilean Communists, in common with their comrades in a few other Latin-American republics, do not preach—at least openly—violent revolution. They work on the assumption that if living conditions continue to deteriorate they will be able to take over quite lawfully. Chile's urban population is bigger than its rural, and contains the larger proportion of enfranchised voters, of whom 10 per cent are chronically unemployed and another 10 per cent only partially employed. The dismay with life, or discontent, is quite accurately reflected in the eyes of men such as Sandoval Gonzáles.

This having been said, however, the peasantry form at least an equal target for the Communists, if for no other reason than that so-called "proletarian" areas—*Población la Victoria* as an example—are made up largely of farm people fresh from the countryside. "The lust for land is strong now," said Orlando Millas, secretary of Chile's Communist Party. "Our biggest advances are among the peasants, and I must say that we are cautious with them. Peasants are conservative. They want a gradual approach, and it would be fatal for us to tell them they can achieve goals by picking up weapons."

This brought up a couple of obvious questions. Was Millas, a forty-three-year-old journalist, member of Con-

[1] In Chile the Communists form a legal party; they are also recognized officially in Uruguay, Bolivia, and Ecuador, in addition to Cuba. Venezuela outlawed the Communists in 1962; but here, as in other countries where they are technically disqualified from holding office, they remain active.

gress, and his party's most influential spokesman, suggesting that this was to be a peasant movement, a break from classical Marxism? Millas responded heatedly: "I believe this is a limited view on the matter. Marxism has not changed at all. Reforms must also be made in the industrial society." But in the hinterland, Communist Party men from Santiago are holding an increasing number of rallies and have succeeded in organizing the Peasants' Federation, affiliated with the largest trade union federation in Chile, which, in turn, is a center of Communist activity.

On the second question—had Chile's Communists dissociated themselves from any armed uprising to bring about social changes?—Millas was quite adamant. "We do not need violence," he said. "We will double our seats by a normal vote in the next election, and we will help form the government." This was not simply an idle boast, nor even a remote possibility—a point to be delved into shortly. Meanwhile, I believe Millas was quite honest in arguing that he and his party have discarded old notions of bloody upheaval in order to attain communism. Chile's Communists follow the current philosophy of Moscow: that wars and violent revolutions are unnecessary because the power of example, of economic advances of the Soviet Union, will diminish support of capitalism where it still exists. This line is not followed by Communist parties in all Latin-American countries. On the contrary, some adhere to Mao Tse-tung's dictum: "On the debris [of war and revolution] we shall build a new civilization a thousand times higher than the old." The Ecuadorian Communist Party, having a very small membership and little support among the electorate, endorsed at a convention in March of 1962 the Chinese principle of achieving power through violence. Almost its entire concentration, unlike that of the Chilean Communist Party, is on the peasantry.

If lack of a unified strategy (sometimes dictated by domestic conditions) exists among the separate Communist parties in Latin America, it can also be found within national groups themselves. In Brazil, for instance, I talked with Communists who clearly were of the "Chinese" variety, and with others who could be identified as "Russian." In Venezuela I heard glowing forecasts of how Khrushchev's policy would bear fruit; I also saw on the wall of a remote country restaurant the scribbling: *"Viva Meo"* (Long live Mao). In sum, the ideological clash between Russia and China stands revealed in this hemisphere. Communist parties in Latin America are far from cohesive and are generally small in numbers.[2] Paradoxically, their indirect influence today, and future potential, constitutes the most serious issue in Latin America, but not because of Russia or China. Any maneuvers or attempts at infiltration by the two Communist giants have met with relatively little success. With the possible exception of Chile, where the Communist movement has long been strong in its own right, the real boost for communism has come from the Cuban revolution.

This is not to suggest that the Russians and Chinese are quiescent in Latin America. Uruguay, which prides itself in a Swiss approach to "neutrality," recently took the unprecedented step of instructing the Russians to cut down the size of their embassy. In a country of only 2.5 million people the Soviet Union maintained a huge establishment, with thirty-seven members on diplomatic passports. Four thousand pounds of literature entered Uruguay each week in diplomatic bags, free from customs inspection. It was clear that Montevideo was headquarters for a propaganda network spreading into southern Brazil, Chile, and Argentina.

In Argentina itself a North American diplomat told me

[2] Argentina has an estimated party membership of 60,000; Brazil, 40,000; Venezuela, 30,000; Peru, 10,000; Colombia, 5,000; Mexico, 5,000; Bolivia, 3,000; Ecuador, 1,000.

how shocked he was, on attending a wine festival in an isolated area eight hundred miles from Buenos Aires, to witness the warmth with which local school teachers greeted on a personal basis envoys from Soviet-bloc countries. The Communist diplomats had obviously been in contact with the teachers on previous occasions. In the Peruvian Andes the few Indians who possess radios can tune into Moscow broadcasts in their Quechua language, while other Latin Americans have their regular choice of Spanish or Portuguese programs from the Soviet Union.

The Chinese, at the same time, are also beaming their own variety of radio propaganda: in 1961 twenty-eight hours a week in Spanish, ten hours a week in Portuguese, compared with a total of only seven hours in 1957. China's interest in Latin America has developed steadily since 1949, when Mao Tse-tung declared that he knew "the peoples of Latin America are not slaves obedient to United States imperialism." Few tangible signs of this interest existed, however, until the Chinese decided to hold a "Peace Conference of Asian and Pacific Regions" in Peking in 1952. To this conference came observers and Communist delegates from all the eleven Latin-American countries bordering on the Pacific; in addition, special guests arrived from Brazil. From then on, the flow of visits, in both directions, increased in measured strides. In 1956 the Peking Opera company toured Chile, Uruguay, Brazil, and Argentina, followed in the next couple of years by teams of acrobats, scientists, and cultural experts who set up exhibitions of Chinese paintings, photographs, and so on.

In some of the countries, notably Mexico and Brazil, newspapers made pained references to the fact that the visitors spent much effort in contacting local Chinese. The 100,000 overseas Chinese scattered through Latin America are also the recipients of broadcasts in Cantonese and other dialects. Peking obviously intends that its brand of communism be recognized as possessing greater application to Latin-American conditions than that of the Russians. "The Soviet Union is too advanced as a society, from our point of view," said a Brazilian intellectual shortly after his return from a visit to Russia and China. "The Chinese are closer to us, in that they have had to lift up masses of landless peasants from feudalism. Their experience is much fresher than the Russians'."

If the Russians were upset by Chinese intrigues in Latin America, they gave no indication of this during the first few years of Peking's activities. By 1960 Peking was outdrawing Moscow as an attraction; in that year alone 168 delegations from Latin America visited China, compared with slightly more than a score to the Soviet Union; indeed, Latin-American groups (not all of them necessarily Communist) outnumbered the delegations from any other continent and accounted for nearly one quarter of all the foreign visitors to Red China. In turn, the total of Chinese delegations visiting Latin America leaped from four in 1958 to twenty in 1960; one direct result was the establishment of bureaus of the official *New China News Agency* in Chile and Brazil, offices which not only send back reports to Peking but offer a free service to any Latin-American paper that wishes to take it.

Since the Chinese had diplomatic representation only in Cuba, they relied on the Russians in other countries to make some of the technical arrangements for them. In 1961 only a few Chinese delegations went to Latin America. The interpretation may well be that the Russians, acutely jealous of the advances of their rivals, were withdrawing diplomatic facilities. But at the same time another situation developed: a tightening up on the part of Latin-American governments. Ecuador, for instance, deported after an eight-day stay in May of 1961 a Chinese youth delegation for "trying to intervene in the country's internal affairs." It may also be that the Chinese were now content to allow Cuba to carry the ball.

In the final analysis, both the Chinese and Soviet attempts to win friends by propaganda and other means were fairly standard practices, engaged in all over the world by other nations, including the United States. What made the Latin American situation so interesting was that the internal Communist parties themselves had few active followers, and in effect any inroads of a foreign ideology were fairly slight. Then along came the Cuban overthrow of Batista, followed by Fidelismo, an ideology that could be publicized as Latin American. The Chinese still assert that Cuba's reformation is based on the successful application of the Chinese pattern. However, they have taken great pains to ensure that this claim is transmitted in Cuban, not Chinese, words. For this reason much attention was given by *New China News Agency* to remarks made by Ernesto "Che" Guevara during his visit to Peking, especially when he said he "knew China had fought for twenty-two years and had attained liberation under the leadership of one of the greatest leaders of the world today, Mao Tse-tung," and that "the agreements concluded between Cuba and China reflect the best that a socialist country can do for a small nation which is fighting for its independence and have set an example for many countries in the Americas. . . ."

Chinese policy today is summed up by a message from Chou En-lai to Fidel Castro on February 3, 1962: "The Cuban revolution represents the genuine interests of the Cuban people and the hope of all Latin-American peoples. . . . The heroic Cuban people and the united Latin-American peoples will certainly win final victory in their struggles against United States imperialism." Though the Russians may not have been quite as ready as the Chinese to accept the Cuban revolution at face value (a fascinatingly debatable mystery that will be touched on in a chapter on Cuba itself), they, too, saw the "priceless value" of Fidelismo. A highly important Soviet guidance pamphlet, from which the foregoing phrase is quoted,[3] confirms that present Russian tactics toward Latin America are built around three fundamentals: first, exploitation of the Cuban revolutionary example; second, offers of Soviet bloc aid; third, encouragement of local Communist parties. The emphasis again, it will be noted, is on the image of Cuba.

Just what is this image? "A window of hope has been opened with Fidelismo," said a Bolivian cabinet minister. "It is not that Latin-American people know what is going on in Cuba. It is that they are tired, and have no hope, and so will turn to anything that offers hope, even the unknown. For humble people, democracy is meaningless if it is not accompanied by prosperity." This was a fair and realistic appraisal. Wherever I traveled I found basically the same story: those people who are thoughtfully aware of the abuses and the executions and the excesses that have taken place in Cuba have lost their enthusiasm for Castro as a person; but their support for the Cuban revolution remains unabridged. For Fidelismo is an image with a variety of characteristics. At its most elementary, it represents for millions of vaguely attuned Latin Americans a sister country that has managed to take land from the wealthy and give it to the poor, and at the same time put a big country, the United States, in its place. Cuba has the rare magic that belongs only to a smaller power that somehow seems to elevate itself to an equal political footing with a great power. If part of the image is uglier, the face of a ruthless revolution determined to export itself, it haunts only a minority: those government leaders and Latin Americans

[3] *The Situation and Struggle of the Workers in the Countries of Latin America,* published by the Soviet Society for the Dissemination of Political Knowledge, Moscow, November, 1960.

who believe that even if Fidelismo is acceptable to Cubans it should be confined to the Caribbean island.

"All Latin Americans are brothers. Two hundred million Latin Americans look to Cuba, and Cuba looks to them." This was the recurrent theme I heard in Havana whenever I found Latin-American visitors: intellectuals, students, peasant or labor leaders, politicians, foregathering. The Cubans sang it to them, the Latin Americans—at least most of them—echoed it back. These were *invitados,* official guests, and while not all were involved in left-wing organizations the effect of what they saw and heard was generally deep. Not for a moment could they forget that they were witnesses to a *Cuban* phenomenon, a revolution in all forms, political, social, economic, brought about by fellow Latin Americans, instead of by academic revolutionaries with strangely foreign accents and ideas. This was not China or Russia, thousands of miles away. This was American soil, measured in mere hundreds of miles and in common history and the same language. Almost the first sign the *invitados* read on stepping off an aircraft was the Spanish for: "Welcome to Cuba, Free Territory of America."

They came from the nearby Dominican Republic and Haiti, from Guatemala, Venezuela, Brazil, Chile, Bolivia, from virtually every part of the continent. Some were avowed members of Communist parties; but again, it must be emphasized, many were not. One young man, a trade unionist from Ecuador, told me: "I studied Marx, Lenin, Stalin, and the writings of other Communists—even Chou En-lai and Mao Tse-tung. But I could never make much sense of them. A Latin revolution is much more attractive." Particularly, he might have added, a revolution that embarrasses the mighty United States. The Ecuadorian, incidentally, had arrived in Cuba by an indirect route. To avoid any possible complications with his government, he pretended he was off on a holiday in Mexico, and actually flew there. But once in Mexico City a quick transfer was made to a Cubana Airlines flight to Havana, where solicitous immigration officers left his passport unstamped. The same device is employed as camouflage for other *invitados,* including occasional United States citizens.

The *invitados,* of course, are taken on impressive sightseeing tours, lasting from two to three weeks, with all expenses paid. They see some of the undoubtedly dramatic and favorable imprints of planned economy: the replacement, for example, of miserable *bohios,* or peasant huts, by clean and functional housing developments. They talk to *campesinos* and hear firsthand accounts (and there are many genuinely enthusiastic ones) of lives improved almost in fairy-tale fashion. They attend rallies and experience the spine-tingling sensation (terrifying to a nonsupporter, inspiring to a believer) of twenty thousand voices in a frenzied and rhythmic chant: "Fidel, Fidel, Fidel." And then they return to the air-conditioned comforts of the Havana Libre or the Riviera Hotel, which at one time rented rooms to North American tourists at $30 a day, without meals. If the fare is now austere (black coffee, dry toast, and nothing more, for breakfast) the *invitados* shrug this off as the result of the iniquitous *yanqui* embargo and say conditions will get better once "socialism" is really under way. If a delegate stands up at a youth conference—as one did during my first visit—and questions even mildly the lack of civil rights in Cuba, he is shouted down as a "Trotskyite."

The majority of *invitados* are young, in their impressionable late teens or early twenties. Some break away from the set routine and move about by themselves, hearing another side of the story: the disenchantment of Cubans who initially applauded Castro but now are awaiting only what they call "liberation," the everyday problems of mothers trying to locate enough milk for their children, the exodus not only of "capitalists" but of ordinary workers who find the atmosphere oppressive, the economic chaos created by factors greater than a United States embargo alone. A few *invitados* return to their homes in other countries themselves disenchanted, disturbed, and troubled, filled with doubts about whether Fidelismo is the answer after all. But a greater number are impressed; any qualifications that might arise are quickly attributed to growing pains, inevitable adjuncts to any revolution. At least most of the ones I spoke to appeared unconcerned about the things that bothered me, including the enforced conformity and rule by gun rather than by law, the betrayal of what started out as liberal principles, the trading of one "master," the United States, for reliance on another power.

On balance, the youngsters who flock to Havana from sister republics go home with adulation for Fidelismo that will last with or without the man himself. They speak of the brave new anti-Yankee world, of the new homes and schools, and brush aside the shocked and worried liberals as malcontents. "As the Cuban revolution was born in the University of Havana, so the Peruvian revolution will grow out of the University of San Marcos," said a student from Lima. If this was an oversimplified historical reference, it also carried a perilous warning. The student, along with other *invitados,* had attended a series of lectures given by Sierra Maestra veterans. These experts in guerrilla warfare related personal experiences in their fight with Batista troops, and, after enamoring their young audiences, went on to broad lessons: first, revolution is possible without violence if enough people agitate at one time, but if force should become necessary the best strategy is to bypass the cities until the last and to concentrate on the countryside (leaves from a handbook once written by Mao Tse-tung and supplemented by Guevara on the basis of trial in the Cuban hills).

The extent of Cuba's physical subversion in neighboring states is unknown. Venezuela, when it broke with Castro, complained that arms were being smuggled into the country from Cuba. I asked Venezuela's minister of defense, General Briceño Linares, if there was much evidence of such trafficking, and he answered frankly: "No, we have no evidence, only suspicion." Then he ran his hand over a map of the Caribbean and singled out the long coastline, saying it would be reasonably simple for any vessel to unload in an unpatrolled strip at night. Whether or not Cuban-based weapons were actually reaching Venezuela, there is little doubt that President Rómulo Betancourt had some justification for announcing on November 10, 1961, that there was no other possible answer to the insults from Castro than a severance of diplomatic relations: the first such move by an important Latin-American country. Venezuela had been a prime target of Cuba because it was both strategically and psychologically important, oil-rich and held up by the United States as a hopeful example for the rest of the hemisphere. Much Cuban radio and written propaganda was aimed at the oligarchy and more of it at Betancourt in person.[4]

Betancourt claimed that the intrusion went further, that a series of riots was led by left-wingers financed from Cuba. It may also be, as some of his domestic critics argued, that Betancourt, as a self-styled "socialist," was sensitive that Castro was stealing headlines as the first real Caribbean reformer and the answer to Latin America's problems. When I put a question to Betancourt along these lines, he responded with some irritation, pointing out that he was elected to the presidency of Venezuela while Castro was still isolated in the Sierra Maestra; he conveyed the impression that he felt that he, Betancourt, had come first, while Castro was an upstart. Regardless of this possibly personal aspect,

[4] A considerable part of Cuba's propaganda effort in Latin America is conducted through its official news agency, *Prensa Latina*. Funds for regional bureaus of *Prensa Latina* are transferred from Havana by way of the Royal Bank of Canada's headquarters in Montreal.

he was convinced that the only recourse was to be firm in dealing with Castro's influence, even to the extent of imprisoning socialists and students, as well as Communists, and suspending some constitutional rights. "To be frank," Betancourt told me, "I haven't my heart in some of the measures we have taken, but on the other hand I have done some of these things out of a conviction that democracy has to be sustained even through controls. I know all too well that democracies have been lost because too much reliance was placed on persuasion. I have just been reading Shirer's *The Rise and Fall of the Third Reich*, and it is obvious how the Weimar Republic was lost because it was unable to control the situation."

There have also been reports, unconfirmed, that Francisco Julião, in Brazil's Northeast, is furnished with propaganda literature and other supplies from Cuba. Even if this active intrusion is not so, there is no uncertainty about Castro's aim to spread revolution. At the height of the Brazilian crisis over Jânio Quadros' resignation, Castro broadcast: "If the Brazilian people make use of Cuba's experience and take arms and throw themselves into the fight in the mountains, jungles, and forests, the reactionaries will never be able to succeed. If workers, peasants, students, and progressive people, and honest military men take up arms and organize not one front but a thousand fronts, never will the military reactionaries be able to defeat them." Provoked as it might have been, Brazil nevertheless did not break relations with Cuba. San Thiago Dantas, Brazil's foreign minister at the time, explained it to me thus: "The Cuban phenomenon is symptomatic of the realities that exist everywhere in Latin America. The real therapy for this disease is economic development and strengthening of governments."

In blunter words the Brazilian attitude was aptly described by Antônio Callado, the first journalist to draw attention to Julião. Callado, chatting informally, confessed how astonished he was every time he discussed Cuba with Americans. "We simply don't see red the way the United States does with every mention of Castro's name—maybe because Brazilians better understand the conditions that led to the Cuban revolution," he said. "The other day, at lunch with a New York publisher, I was asked: 'But aren't you afraid of Castro and his infiltration?' 'What infiltration?' I replied. Castro hasn't the resources or the strength to infiltrate us. If anything happens in Brazil it will be because of a Brazilian version of Castro and Brazil's own problems—not because of Fidel's influence."

This, I believe, is an intelligent and realistic summation of Fidelismo's impact on Latin America. The Communists are obviously determined to take full advantage of any mood generated by Castro—to exploit flaws in the social structure—and their appearance has been given luster and allure by the model of Cuba. Where the Communist parties of Latin America may be considered weak numerically, and historically of little consequence, their influence today is heightened, but again, only by indirection. In Brazil, the Communists scrawl slogans on walls and win prominent positions in trade unions; most people do not cry out in horror or panic. Does this mean that Brazilians are being duped? Not, I think, in the way that North Americans usually like to reckon.

While I was in Brazil a bank strike in Rio de Janeiro tied up normal trade and commerce for a week, and spread to eight other cities. Clerks and tellers, bearing placards, marched up and down Rio's Avenida Rio Branco, shouting: "We cannot live with hunger." Earning $75 a month, they wanted a wage increase of nearly 70 per cent, to keep up with spiraling food costs that consumed a proportion greater than half of the average man's income. Clerks with whom I talked said they had knowingly elected Communist leaders of their syndicate, even though they themselves were strongly opposed to communism. "The Communists know how to fight for our interests," said one man while his mates nodded in agreement. What about the built-in, long-range danger of such leadership? "We'll worry about that another time. At the moment our worry is hunger." And so, stated simply, the issue was not Red but Bread.

Going a step further, Communist members themselves present what they consider a compelling argument in favor of communism or Fidelismo. "My great objection to capitalism," said a Peruvian, Genaro Carnero, "is that it never really developed in most of Latin America." Carnero, the fifty-one-year-old editor of a weekly magazine of small circulation, went on to talk about feudalism and the fact that between 40 and 50 per cent of his compatriots in Peru live outside the monetary economy. To put over his ideas he does not speak officially as a Communist, since the party has been outlawed in Peru since 1933. Instead he belongs to what is known as the *Frente de Liberación Nacional,* a loose alliance of extreme left-wingers, which he defines as "the new army of emancipation for Peru." I pointed out that in a country such as Chile the Communists talked, and seemed to mean it, of changes within the framework of elections. Carnero had a ready answer: "In Chile the Communist Party will be able to achieve a victory through democratic means, and once it has reached power it will start reforms. The Communist Party in Chile is legal, and so there is no reason why it shouldn't try democratic process. But here in Peru we have an oligarchy completely impervious to any suggestion of change, an oligarchy which takes measures against anyone who has ideas of change. Our only hope is physical and violent revolution."

Carnero was obviously unperturbed by my comparison of Chilean and Peruvian Communist tactics. In Venezuela, however, I encountered marked objection to any attempt to lump together, deliberately or unconsciously, the Venezuelan Communist Party with counterparts in other Latin-American countries, some of which are inspired by Moscow thinking, others by Peking's philosophy. "The Communist Party of Venezuela," declared Gustavo Machado with some vehemence, "is completely guided here. Naturally we study other experiences, but only we—in Caracas—make the decisions. Our problem is to relate Marxism to everyday conditions as they exist here." He declined even to discuss the Chilean situation.

Machado, the leader of Venezuela's Communist Party, is a big, hearty man of sixty-four, whose straight, silver-gray hair adds to a look of distinction. His case history is interesting—and not only because of his obvious breeding, high culture, and good taste in clothes. (Few of the leading Communists I met in Latin America would fit the old caricature of unshaven and uncouth bomb-throwers.) Machado's story is noteworthy because he is, in his own words, "a black sheep," the scion of one of Venezuela's oldest and wealthiest families, with assets accumulated from industry and land. It is related that Machado, when asked once how much money he himself had, admitted to seven million bolivares. "Right," said the questioner, "if you're a Communist you must share your wealth." Machado agreed, pointed out that the population of Venezuela was seven million, and handed the questioner his share, one bolivar.

In more serious vein, Machado told me he rebelled against a conservative background when he "decided that social changes were necessary." One of his brothers, Eduardo, joined him, and together they were banished by the government in 1925. They moved to Cuba, helped to organize the Communist Party there, and fought a namesake, Gerardo Machado, the Cuban dictator. On and off, Gustavo spent thirty-one years in exile, mostly in Mexico, with some time in Paris. On two returns to Caracas, in 1936 and 1942, he was jailed. He came back in 1958, after the downfall of

Pérez Jiménez, to run in the election campaign later that year. Gustavo and brother Eduardo were among seven Communist deputies elected to Congress.

The Venezuelan Communists are considered to have excellent leadership under Machado. When I saw him, in the members' smoking room at the legislative buildings, he was concerned about his immediate future, and for practical reasons. Several prominent Communists had just been arrested (the main ones untouched were those with parliamentary immunity) and there was considerable talk that the government was about to declare the Communist Party illegal, part of the measures to curb violence cropping up with greater frequency throughout the country. Machado denied that his party had started trouble. "Violence is the order of the day," he said. "The government accuses us of committing it, we accuse the government. There have been killings on both sides." The future? Machado, who made a point of mentioning that his party had gone along with the declarations of the 22d Congress of the Communist Party in Moscow in 1961, calling for Khrushchev's "soft" approach to revolution, said: "There will be legal or revolutionary changes. When all legal roads are closed, then we will resort to full violence."

The legal possibility of communism in Venezuela was not far-fetched. In 1958 the Communists—despite a party membership of scarcely 30,000—polled 160,000 votes, 70,000 of them in working-class districts of Caracas. They came second only to the socialists in the city vote and got more urban support than *Acción Democrática,* Betancourt's party, which counts its principal appeal in rural areas. The Communists, along with other left-wing groups, including breakaways from *Acción Democrática* and the socialists, were forming a "national front" that could be of considerable strength in the coming 1963 elections. But now the forecast, if Machado's implicit warning holds true, is one of greater violence; for, on May 10, 1962, the government issued a decree outlawing the Communists. The Machado brothers continued to sit in Congress, since they had been legally elected, but at the end of their terms any parliamentary immunity or political rights would expire.

The account of communism's legality returns, therefore, to Chile, where, in any event, the movement has had the longest and now the most significant success in Latin America, short of Cuba. Chilean Communists are in active coalition with the Socialist Party, whose leader, Senator Salvador Allende lost the last presidential election, in 1958, by scarcely 2 per cent of the votes. A third political group, the National Democrats, complete the coalition that goes by the initials FRAP (*Frente Acción Popular*). According to trends at this writing, there is a better than even chance that Allende will be the next President of Chile in 1964. The Communists would then have a major say in the affairs of one of the continent's most highly developed and influential nations.

Prominently displayed in the vestibule of Allende's office in Congress is a poster of Fidel Castro. The poster, issued in Havana during the abortive invasion of 1961, is addressed to "*pueblos de América y del Mundo*" and calls on all Latin Americans to resist "the aggressors." Allende is an open and frank admirer of Castro, and has been four times to Cuba. He started out, however, as a physician and not a politician. The son of a wealthy senator and the grandson of Chile's highest-ranking Freemason (33d degree), Allende attained a good reputation as a practicing doctor, and then, at the age of twenty-seven, decided to run in congressional elections. He was elected a deputy, and from that moment on his interest in medicine was in the public field. Appointed minister of health, he put through—at least on paper—a comprehensive national health service. By the time he was thirty-five, and chosen for the senate, Allende had achieved wide fame as the author of some two hundred articles and books on Chile's deep and growing social problems.

Now, at the age of fifty-four, he is the champion of the landless poor, and even in isolated villages I found his picture hanging from the mud walls of peasant huts. Allende is a dedicated socialist, sincerely so, and not merely personally ambitious. His program calls not only for agrarian reform but for state ownership of all public utilities and resources, including copper mines owned by United States companies. He defines it as "escape from foreign capitalist imperialism," and he talks convincingly of his chances of achieving a radical and bloodless social revolution. With each day of added despair among the masses, hardly alleviated by the conservative government of President Jorge Allesandri, Allende's bid for his country's leadership grows firmer. "Chile, from the political point of view, is the only country in the world where the popular forces are united, to include Marxists and non-Marxists (National Democrats)," Allende said. "This fact is important, because it indicates a political maturity in the country. The process of getting together is now seven years old. FRAP's program is not the result of a committee decision but of a national convention, attended by all the parties of FRAP as well as by such public agencies as trade unions."

I asked the obvious question: Looking at the history of "Popular Fronts" in Europe, wasn't Allende afraid of the Communists simply taking over? He shook his head and said: "The Communists are a serious and responsible party and they wouldn't dare create dissension that could lead to civil war. Their aim, like ours, is to reform society step by step." But I thought I detected hesitation in this remark; and it was confirmed later by some of Allende's close confidantes, who said that of course he knew his history and was nervous of the alliance with Communists; but what was the alternative?

If we in North America recognize in communism a grievous challenge to individuality or liberty, Chileans see it as an aid to attainment of the material essentials taken for granted in North America. They cite just one or two facts to make a point: every fourth child dies in infancy; a half million dwelling units are needed immediately to provide minimal housing facilities. They argue that if they use communism, or at least some of its forms, they can later abandon it when a reasonable level of material welfare has been reached. We may look upon this as misguided optimism, but we fail to take into account the real desperation of Chileans. Ironically, many of the socialists are more demonstrative than the Communists themselves and call for general strikes and even violent overthrow of the present government. The Communists, on the other hand, appear supremely confident of reaching their goals quite by legal process.

FRAP is joined in many key congressional issues by the Christian Democratic Party, the third highest vote-getter in 1958. The Christian Democrats are anti-Communists who blend Christian morality and liberalism but are not, curiously enough, swayed by the emphasis of their European forerunners. At a recent world congress of Christian Democratic Parties in Santiago, European delegates were mainly concerned with communism and its advances. But Venezuelan, Peruvian, and Chilean Christian Democrats said that communism was not the main problem; instead, the problems were poverty, social justice, and economic development. Between FRAP and the Christian Democrats lie 47 per cent of Chile's votes, based on the last election; they are likely to do even better in the next round.

But what about the fundamental question, the fear of Communist power in any coalition? Socialists, National Democrats, and Christian Democrats with whom I spoke said they were frankly terrified that through internal maneuverings the Communists might indeed run Chile's government. But, like the bank clerks of Brazil, they said it was a gamble they must take in order to change conditions.

What is the best way to offset the rise in appeal of communism or Fidelismo in Latin America? A group of businessmen and industrialists in Bogotá believe they have the answer. They have formed "The Society for Social and Economic Development of Colombia." It is, however, more commonly tagged by the public as *mano negra*—"black hand." Intellectuals and foreign diplomats speak of it and its organizers with scorn and impatience; for, as the name implies, *mano negra* is thoroughly negative in its approach. It conducts smear campaigns by identifying any would-be reformer as a "Communist." It petitions its members to withhold advertising from any newspaper that condemns its methods. When such tactics fail, as they did in the case of *La Semana,* the group fall back on their economic reserves. *La Semana* was a progressive political weekly, one of the best in Latin America, continually calling for sensible reforms and drawing attention to the frightening and short-sighted attitude of *mano negra.* Then *mano negra* men quietly bought up a controlling number of shares and converted *La Semana* into a fatuous, shrilly reactionary publication.

"I think it is true to say," commented a discouraged diplomat, "that in countries with a strong, well-developed democratic left it is more difficult for the Communists to make headway. Such a force is at present lacking in Colombia. The Colombian ruling classes have yet to realize the unpleasant fact that only by offering policies designed to steal the Communists' thunder can they avoid in the long run a Castro-oriented government. The methods adopted by *mano negra* will merely serve to intensify the explosion when it comes."

Colombia's *mano negra* has its equivalents, in one form or another, in every Latin-American country. In Brazil, a self-styled "citizens' committee" took to painting in tar a slogan on the exterior walls of Rio de Janeiro houses and office buildings: "Keep the city clean by killing one Communist daily." Fortunately, this ugly and foolish kind of technique did not go unchallenged. The thoughtful *Jornal do Brasil,* in an editorial on the tarpainting, said:

> It sounds brutal, but it is tragic—because it reveals the desperate and absurd impotence of those who try to combat an ideology without knowing how to do it. Communism gives sleepless nights to many leading people in Brazil who are paralyzed by fear of it, as birds are fascinated by a snake. They consequently leave the door open to professional anti-Communists who propose to save Brazil on the basis of suspicion. These anti-Communists lose all restraint and make hysterical appeals. . . . In their propaganda they paint Communists as a minority of supermen responsible for all strikes, capable of organizing all plots and of infiltrating all sectors of military and civilian administration. Through attributing to the Communists the leadership in all moves for higher wages or social improvements these anti-Communists insinuate to the masses of the people that only the Communists defend their rights and interests. These anti-Communists render inestimable service to the Communists. . . . The task is not to preach anti-communism but to establish true democracy. Anti-communism is negative and empty. . . . It is essential to recall what a Brazilian leader said recently: "No regime survives starvation." . . . The Communist specter will fade if our problems are approached efficiently.

I found some of the anti-Communist perplexity to which *Jornal do Brasil* alluded in a man named Ivan Hasslocher, a Rio advertising-agency owner. Hasslocher, in his early forties, is an intense, sensitive, and articulate patriot. In his spare time he publishes a monthly magazine, *Acão Democratica,* on behalf of a group of upper- and middle-income people who feel the way he does: that unless some major reforms are instituted, Brazil will follow Fidelismo. It is difficult to place Hasslocher in a political category. He calls himself a "democrat," but so even do Brazilians of the extreme right. The simplest definition might be: anti-Communist reformer.

The only trouble is that Hasslocher sees a Communist behind every pillar and typewriter. Anyone, in fact, who thinks vaguely of socialism or advancement that runs counter to his philosophy, is "a Red." For instance, in his words, "a coalition between Reds and rightists has prevented agrarian reform up to now." How is that? "Blocking by the extreme right is obvious, since the rich, especially absentee landlords, would suffer from any land redistribution." But the Communists? "Every time an agrarian reform bill is introduced in Congress the Reds, through the press, say it is inadequate. Naturally they want to prevent advances since they thrive on poverty conditions." But how can this accusation against the press make sense when almost all the big papers are owned by members of the aristocracy or wealthy political parties? "There are fourteen dailies in Rio and at least nine are Red-dominated, because 70 per cent of the reporters and editors are of the left. The publishers are their unsuspecting puppets." According to Hasslocher's rule book, the editor who wrote *Jornal do Brasil*'s editorial was a "Red."

In the final analysis, of course, talk of who is a Red and who is not a Red has no meaning. The only rebuttal to communism's promise is practical action. A thousand organizations of the breed of *mano negra* can fire ten thousand slogans and reach nowhere near the required target: the hungry and despondent *campesino* or slum dweller. There are, however, a few individuals who have shown enlightenment, awareness, and courage, at personal financial loss. Jorge Lavadero, for example, belongs, by his own interpretation, to "one of the two hundred and forty families who control 48 per cent of Chile's wealth." His father is a right-wing senator; but Jorge, at the age of thirty-two, is leader of the National Democratic Party, the non-Marxist but reformist group in the FRAP coalition. The elder Lavadero owns 15,000 acres of rich farmland; while, according to Jorge, his father agrees that agrarian reform is essential, he has done nothing about it. Jorge, in contrast, has distributed free his own land holdings among seven hundred *inquilinos,* farm laborers. His family virtually disowned him for his antioligarchy stand; in one bitter reprisal alone, he lost $50,000 when he was cut out from his grandmother's will. Jorge has no regrets. "Chile is like a river dammed up," he says. "We are ready to run smoothly if only given the chance."

Jorge Lavadero may be considered unreasonably altruistic, making self-sacrifices he can hardly expect other *ricos* to emulate. He is, obviously, an unusual example. More balanced—and hard-headed—is another Chilean, Manuel Ibáñez, a forty-year-old businessman and farm owner. Ibáñez parlayed a relatively small inheritance into a big enterprise; he operates a chain of supermarkets in Santiago, a food-processing plant and a distribution agency for a sugar combine, and manufactures restaurant equipment under licence from a United States firm. Part of his inheritance was the family *fundo,* run down and unproductive when he took it over but now a thriving estate with seven hundred acres under cultivation. Ibáñez approaches farming with the same modern and scientific acumen as he does his business interests. While Chile has to spend vast sums it can ill afford to import food, largely because much land lies fallow or is otherwise neglected by owners, Ibáñez gets a high yield and even exports some of his produce; about 25 per cent of the crop from his sixty thousand peach trees goes to the United States as fresh fruit; the rest is packed in tins in his own cannery.

The day-to-day affairs of the *fundo* are left in the hands of a salaried manager, a graduate of an agricultural college, who runs it as efficiently as any similar property I have seen in North America. Ibáñez is an absentee landlord. He lives in a large and expensive home in Santiago, belongs to country clubs, and visits his *fundo* perhaps once every couple of weeks. But here the stereotype ends. Ibáñez is content to earn 6 per cent on his investment, while other landowners cry that farming does not pay because they cannot net more than 24 per cent. More to the point, however, he is aware that peasants or *inquilinos* are restless and that influences from the outer world, particularly Cuba, are catching up with South America's social and economic inequalities. Even before there was talk of the need for land reform Ibáñez began to do something about it. He gave his *fundo* workers a chance to buy a piece of land each, on extremely easy terms, and to build their own homes. His philosophy is simple: "The sense of possession—of land, of a house—is in all of us. A man is restless unless he is satisfied." At the same time he admits candidly that his motivation is not entirely unselfish; as a shrewd businessman he wants to hang on to as many of his profitable holdings as possible; he knows that without some sharing now he may lose everything later. "The Communists," he says, "have been active in the valley."

The Ibáñez *fundo* is located in the Aconcagua Valley, about one hundred kilometers northwest of Santiago. The approach, for scores of miles, is through bleak and hilly semiarid countryside but the valley itself is green and beautiful. A sharply inclined stone face of a mountain dominates the setting and gives the *fundo* its Indian name, *Colunquen,* "Place of the Precipice." Ibáñez says he loves taking a break here (his wife and four children do not share the same feeling), and it is quite apparent that Ibáñez, a short, handsome, and friendly man, does enjoy, even for brief periods, the traditional role of *patrón* in its fine and benevolent old meaning.

During the week end I accompanied him, however, there was a touch of sadness. Two weeks previously, while Ibáñez was on a business trip to Buenos Aires, one of the farm hands was thrown by a horse and killed. Now, as we drove up to the *fundo,* Ibáñez stopped to ask a group of *inquilinos* how they felt. "All right," said one, "*más o menos* . . . more or less." There were no smiles that day, because people were still upset by the tragedy. Ibáñez went around to make a condolence call on the widow. An attractive, sturdy woman, she was meanwhile being supported by her parents, who also work on the farm. Ibáñez pointed out that undoubtedly she would be remarried within a year, but in any case there was a job waiting for her in the cannery. Then, to eliminate the *inquilinos'* superstition, he deliberately mounted the "killer" horse, left untouched in the fields these past two weeks, and rode among them for a few hours, inspecting the peach orchards and thousands of rows of asparagus plants. In the evening he settled back in the immense living room of his *fundo* home, the walls lined with oil portraits of ancestors, sipped a brandy, and reminisced.

There was paternalism here without doubt, he said, though not nearly so marked as he remembered from his father's day, when the grand *patrón* really dominated everyone. His father had known personally every worker on the estate, while he, Manuel, knew some of the hundred odd men and their families, but not all; today when they had personal problems they leaned on his manager, a rather aloof sort. Still, a few years ago, when he got to thinking about what was wrong with the system of peonage, Ibáñez realized that in his city companies he offered shares to older employees, to give them a sense of participation and security in retirement. Why not try the same principle on the *fundo*? And so he hit upon the idea of buying an adjacent piece of land, which he divided into lots of three or four hectares each; these he offered to his *inquilinos* at cost and with no interest charges, to be paid for gradually out of their average earnings of a dollar a day. They could farm their own land while they still worked for the *fundo*.

Ibáñez admits to two reasons for the scheme: first, to keep his men tantalizingly indebted so they would not desert the countryside in quest of higher wages in the city, and second to give them a measure of independence and security from want in old age. And he reiterated his belief: "I think there is no greater thrill than the possession of land. I first felt it when the *fundo* became mine to operate. I know how the others here must feel."

Vestigial signs of paternalism are still evident on the Ibáñez *fundo*: a mess hall and free lunch for field workers (chowder and a plate of beans) provided by the Ibáñez family; a school room provided by the Ibáñez family; adobe huts provided by the Ibáñez family. These facilities dated back generations, and so did the *inquilinos* who previously had felt in bondage to the Ibáñez family. But now I detected in them contentment because, unlike peasants on neighboring *fundos,* they had for the first time an opportunity to shape their own lives. Miguel Valdez' father, for example, toiled for the Ibáñez family and seldom saw more than a few cents a day. But now Miguel himself owns eight acres of land; he grows a bit of wheat and maize, some grapes, and can afford to keep a hired hand while continuing on the *fundo*; I watched as Miguel and his "employee" piled up mud bricks to build a proper house in replacement of the old *adobe*. About one quarter of the men so far have been able to take advantage of the Ibáñez financial arrangement and can look forward to decent retirement. As small landowners they have also been transformed into capitalists. Miguel says he once heard some men, who had arrived in the valley from Santiago, promise land to everyone. He recalls saying, rather wisely, to a friend: "They promise land, but where are they going to get it? The owners won't give it up." Still, he confesses, the appeal to listen to the men was great. Now Miguel owns a radio in addition to land, listens to broadcasts, and says: "Fidel Castro is a crazy man."

How many Latin-American *ricos* are there like Manuel Ibáñez, sensitive to current moods and willing to think and act in constructive ways? In every major city I visited I made an effort to ask this question, with appalling results. North Americans, confronted with a similar question about local "enlightened capitalists," would have difficulty selecting arbitrarily a few names from the multitude that flash immediately to mind. In Latin America the few are the exceptions, so rare that often I left an area without hearing of a really positive case of a landowner or industrialist who would fit the Ibáñez category. In Caracas several Venezuelans independently singled out for me Eugenio Mendoza; his was the name that kept recurring; others never arose.

Mendoza, fifty-six and distinguished-looking, runs an industrial network that includes three cement plants, three quarries, a lumber mill, and a paper converter mill. He stands out among his fellows because his sense of social responsibility can be traced back long before there was any portent of Fidelismo. Since 1926 he has paid his employees good wages, and, more tellingly, bonuses based on profits. "In Venezuela," he says, "we have been working hard to develop industries that provide jobs for the people, but we have neglected the social side, the human side. In the same way that we give dividends to shareholders we should give what I like to call 'spontaneous dividends' in some amount that can make employees realize that the capitalist system is good, that enterprises belong not only to the people who own them but to the people who work in them." In 1961

Mendoza distributed among his 5,000 employees dividends totaling $5 million, or an average of $1,000 each.

There are other generous features. An autonomous social service department, composed of thirty social workers and psychologists, is available to any Mendoza man or woman with marital, home, or health problems; free medical services are provided for all; for the last fifteen years a nonprofit subsidiary has been building houses for employees, who can get financing through a cooperative bank. Aside from the employer-employee relations, tremendously impressive by Latin-American standards, Mendoza's work as a public benefactor is unusual and notable. He devotes one third of his working hours to commerce, the remainder of the time to the three foundations he has established. One, a polio foundation, organized in 1940 and the only one of its kind in South America, cares for 3,000 children a year, partly in its own 175-bed city hospital and country convalescent home; it operates on an annual budget of $1,200,000. Last year Mendoza raised $300,000 in a public campaign; the rest of the bill he paid himself.

Another Mendoza foundation, with capitalization of close to $3 million, offers day nurseries for Caracas working mothers, playgrounds in collaboration with the Y.M.C.A., and free text books for school children. The most recent foundation, set up with $5 million of Mendoza's money, is the *Fundación de la Vivienda Popular,* a building society that delivers low-priced homes at cost, for a down payment of 20 per cent. The first batch of three hundred homes was constructed in Valencia in 1961; the next year 1,500 were built. Now Mendoza has a pilot scheme to turn out prefabricated houses, at $1,000 each, to replace the *rancho* hovels in which 400,000 of the people of Caracas live in subhuman conditions. "The government," Mendoza said, "is attempting to provide some new homes, but in view of the magnitude of the problem it cannot be solved by government action alone. I consider this as part of my duty."

But has Mendoza made any headway in putting over his ideas among members of the oligarchy? "I have tried to tell business friends that they must be logical, that they must understand the social needs of the community," he said. "Some react well, but most are indifferent." In any public demonstrations, Venezuelan Communists usually throw bricks through the plate glass windows of the handsome downtown building in which Mendoza's foundations are grouped. The excuse is that Mendoza is a capitalist, but obviously it is his kind of benefaction that is the most dangerous to them. I asked Mendoza: "Is there time?" Wearily he said, "There is time only if we work fast." When I drew a comparison between him, as a rarity, and North American industrialists as a galaxy, Mendoza said: "In the United States and Canada democracy is a success because people understand the meaning of public duty and responsibility, and, moreover, they are willing to work at it. In Latin America everyone criticizes the government because the government is expected to do everything, without anyone else doing his share."

The point, of course, can be turned. Since there are not enough individuals of the caliber of Mendoza and Ibáñez, then the salvation—or, stated more bluntly, the prevention of communism—must rest with governments. But here the record, too, is depressing. In one of Latin America's most vulnerable areas, the Northeast of Brazil, a government-appointed economist-reformer, Celso Furtado, has been attempting, with great frustration, to translate the constructive examples of the Ibáñez *fundo* and the Mendoza industries on a massive scale. His battle is against the government itself, insincere politicians, and blindly greedy landowners. Furtado is one of the most inspiring and exciting men I have ever met, a dedicated yet shrewd idealist who stands out in contrast to those Latin Americans who say cynically that nothing can change or, worse, who do nothing to bring about change. At the age of forty-two he is in charge of a crucial program to revitalize the Northeast and give hope to 25 million people. In a way, it is a pathetically sized army he has: 260 Brazilian experts, a score of United Nations personnel, and even fewer Americans, to help all these people. But it is, at least, a beginning. Furtado says at times that he is hopeful; at other times he confesses a fear that he is too late.

What makes Furtado so outstanding is that he is a fighter; he has outmaneuvered the politicians who thought of him only as "a theoretician" and thus a safe man in the job because he would be unable to upset the established routine of graft and corruption. Brazil's Northeast is in the main arid, marked by huge expanses of erosion and blight. Its depressed people often resort to cactus for food or plant seeds in a river bed that has dried up; they pray for just enough rain to water the crops but not so much that it will fill the river bed and destroy the crops. For more than fifty years the various state and federal governments had gone through motions of pretending to solve the key problems, by starting irrigation schemes or building roads to move peasants from the merciless interior to the more fertile coastal regions. Though dams and reservoirs were built, most of them were useless since they were not part of any coordinated program but were designed rather for local patronage reasons. In a territory bigger than Texas, California, Montana, New Mexico, and Arizona combined, the web of hard-surface roads covered fewer than two thousand miles; many of the roads began at remote villages and ended blankly in the desert, while politicians filled their pockets with the proceeds from contracts. More charitably, Furtado expressed it to me this way: "After a half century what we had was a drought industry—people living on schemes designed to get other people to live."

In 1958 a tremendous drought, bringing with it widespread starvation and death, aroused the conscience of Brazil. This was just about the period, too, when revolutionary Francisco Julião was beginning to make an impact through the Peasant Leagues. In any case, federal relief amounted to 14 million *cruzeiros;* of this sum, according to Furtado, about 65 per cent went into the bank accounts of corrupt politicians and local officials. President Juscelino Kubitschek was too busy trying to industrialize the southern part of the nation and to build his glorified capital, Brasília, to pay much attention to the Northeast. But public pressure at least compelled him to invite a few economists to examine the problems there. A report by Furtado was accepted as the basis for the establishment of a government agency, known as Sudene, to undertake fundamental economic reform and development of the Northeast.

Furtado had splendid qualifications to become Sudene's director. He was born on a ranch in Paraíba, one of the Northeast's semiarid states. He studied economics in Brazilian universities and at Cambridge, took his Ph.D. at the Sorbonne in Paris, and served as an infantry lieutenant with Brazilian forces in Italy during World War II ("the army was a good experience; it taught me that if you want to get things done you must work like a machine that cannot wait"). For nine years he was with the United Nations Economic Committee for Latin America as head of the development division. Stationed in Santiago, he traveled extensively through Latin America and reported on conditions in textbooks that have become standard university references. His dedication and honesty were unquestioned.

One of the prime conditions Furtado laid down when he took on his new post was that Sudene would be the sole arbiter of how and where government funds should be spent;

no politician would be in a position to grant contracts. Since Furtado was looked upon as an ivory-tower type anyway, and harmless, Congress passed the Sudene bill and even agreed that the agency should receive 2 per cent of the national budget for its work of rehabilitation: not an extravagant proportion when one remembers that one third of all Brazilians live in the Northeast. Furtado was satisfied. The only small flaw was that Congress, having gone through the grandstand gestures, typically failed to deliver the money. In effect, Furtado was bankrupt before he was even in business. Or so the politicians thought.

What they did not anticipate was Furtado's resourcefulness. Furtado has friends at the Brazilian Development Bank, another official agency. On the strength of Congress' promise of money, he borrowed enough to organize a staff and set up headquarters in Recife, the Northeast's center, pledging to repay when Congress would come through with the 2 per cent. What it meant, of course, was that the government owed the government. Sudene (it stands for Superintendency for the Economic Development of the Northeast) was formally established in January, 1960. In April, 1962, two years and three months later, Furtado was finally able to announce that Sudene had received its first instalment from the national treasury, the equivalent of $9.5 million, and could now start letting contracts for electric power plants and other key projects. The government also promised to make regular monthly deposits to the agency's financing fund.

The belated action did not denote a sudden change in political hearts. It resulted from two sharp points of pressure: one the growing unrest of peasants, the other the growing impatience of Washington. If Brazil expected to be eligible for grants under the Alliance for Progress, it would have to show a little faith itself. Once domestic funds began to appear in Sudene, the United States pitched in with $181 million specifically designated for housing, education, and sanitation in the Northeast. Together with other Alliance allocations and credits from the Inter-American Development Bank, Furtado could now count on close to $300 million for his program over the next five years.

There is nothing radical about Furtado's intended reforms, but the battle is far from won. His strategy calls for two parallel and orthodox principles: the establishment of diversified industry and the creation of a vibrant agriculture. Between these twin pillars he hopes to see the Northeast rise as a reasonably self-sufficient economic unit. Even before the existence of Sudene, the area had the nucleus of industry: some textile mills, a couple of cement plants, and a few chemical factories. In planning new industries, Furtado got the government to offer attractive credit terms, tax reductions, and other incentives. By mid-1962 forty-two fresh enterprises were in operation. They gave work to 30,000 men, a minuscule number in an unemployed body of millions. But at any rate it was a start.

A start—but a terribly slow one—has also been made in agriculture. Furtado does not believe in grabbing land and merely distributing it. His first aim is to move indigent peasants from the arid zones, where they can do little more than grow cotton or raise a few head of cattle, to the humid coast with its sugar belt and potentially rich fields. What he offers the big plantation owners is scientific and free Sudene irrigation, which he guarantees would double their present sugar yields. The planters could then get by with half their present acreage, permitting Sudene to subdivide the liberated land among smallholders; simultaneously these peasants would be free to work when required on the big plantations, thus providing a stable labor force. Furtado's thinking is not entirely academic. This is also his defense against the mushrooming Peasant Leagues. "If we don't succeed," he cautions, "the solution will be much more violent."

Furtado has managed to convince a few planters of the wisdom of his words. However, the majority refuse to budge. They call him a "Communist" (despite the fact that in one of his books Furtado tears to shreds the Marxist theory of production, arguing it makes no sense economically) and say that, like Francisco Julião, he is prejudiced against the sugar interests. Julião has actually defended Furtado and offered to form a common front against the planters. Furtado considers Julião a reformer of the extreme left, but "certainly not an international agent." However, any link with Julião, in Furtado's mind, would really ruin chances for a *rapprochement* with landowners, and so he tells the revolutionary that as a civil servant he is not permitted an alliance. But Julião's agitation helps; Furtado continues to bandy his name among planters as a warning of what will happen if they refuse to cooperate with Sudene.

Is there any danger, I asked Furtado, that the politicians and planters might try to get rid of him? To answer, Furtado reached for a sheaf of newspaper clippings, a few dozen just from that day's culling of the national press and all describing glowingly the work and possibilities of Sudene. "Public opinion," he said confidently, "would not permit the politicians to do anything drastic." But what did trouble him was the urgent matter of time. He was not even certain that massive United States dollar aid would be effective "without a little more idealism on our part." And since voluntary effort by landowners was almost nonexistent, the only hope was a firm agrarian reform law that would oblige planters to use land economically or forfeit it to the government.

"The peasant is drawn toward Fidelismo because he believes that society is an enemy," Furtado said. "Our job is to give the peasant a positive alternative to revolution." The question, again, is whether this can be done in time.

9

The "Little" Republics

I spent thirty-three years and four months in active service as a member of our country's most agile military force—the Marine Corps. I served in all commissioned ranks from a second lieutenant to major general. . . . I helped make Mexico and especially Tampico safe for American oil interests in 1914. I helped make Haiti and Cuba a decent place for the National City Bank boys to collect revenues in. . . . I helped purify Nicaragua for the international banking house of Brown Brothers in 1909-1912. I brought light to the Dominican Republic for American sugar interests in 1916. I helped make Honduras "right" for American fruit companies in 1903. . . . Looking back on it, I feel I might have given Al Capone a few hints. The best *he* could do was to operate his racket in three city districts. We Marines operated in three *continents*.

If the above quotation had been fabricated by a writer from *Pravda* it would be put down as typically distorted Russian propaganda. It was, however, written by Major General Smedley D. Butler of the U.S. Marine Corps. Butler fought in every Marine Corps campaign from the Spanish-American War to World War I, and was twice awarded the Congressional Medal of Honor—for his part in the capture of Vera Cruz, Mexico (1914) and of Fort Rivière, Haiti (1917). After his retirement in 1931, he expounded his views in an autobiography, *War Is a Racket.* His life story mirrors, in a way, the history of United States policy in the Caribbean and Central America, and helps to explain, as Paul Johnson expresses it in Britain's *New Statesman,* "why Washington now faces the most serious crisis which has ever confronted a United States government in its own hemisphere."

Specifically, it is the crisis of Cuba, but in broader terms it can also be called the crisis of neo-colonialism. Johnson, as a Briton, speaks with a sharp knowledge of his own country's record: "We have already learned, in the Middle East, that the most dangerous type of colonialism is neo-colonialism. Britain moved into Egypt in the 1880's on a strictly 'temporary' basis; we finally moved out early in 1957 in an atmosphere of shame and anger which nearly precipitated a world war, and which still leaves a sediment of rancour on both sides."

For the average United States citizen it is shocking, even ludicrous, to be told that his country and Cuba are trapped in the same kind of emotional equation as Britain and Egypt. How, an American asks indignantly, can British-style imperialism be used even as a remote basis of comparison with United States ideals and intentions? After all, he asks further, did not the United States liberate Cuba from oppressive Spanish rule? And did not Cuba, with complete ingratitude, turn about years later and slap the United States in the face?

The average United States citizen has just enough knowledge of the Caribbean to feel a vague sense of pride; to him, Americans have always behaved as older brothers, nobly and unselfishly introducing the highest principles of democracy, honest administration, and fair play for everyone. But this knowledge is not necessarily complete, at least from the point of view of people living in the Caribbean islands or the tiny republics of Central America. To many of these people, United States motives and actions have not been as altruistic or generous as they may appear at home. "Neo-colonialism" is a flexible phrase in terms of time. Nicaraguans accuse the United States of it to the present day; Dominicans softened their condemnation after the fall of Trujillo in 1961. But the main point is that a fear of it lingers in every part of the Caribbean. It is essential for Americans to understand this sensitivity, no matter how unpalatable the accusations may be. Without this understanding, it will be impossible to grasp the mood of Cuba or to realize why all Central Americans and Caribbean islanders do not share the United States indignation over Cuban "ingratitude."

If one can forget for a moment that Cuba has turned communist—a development that will be traced a couple of chapters from now—the larger picture, sweeping into its neighboring states, will become more comprehensible. In 1898, when President McKinley sent a message to Congress, leading to a declaration of war against Spain, the consideration was pure in the extreme. Since the 1870's, the Cubans had been in almost permanent revolt against the Spanish, but now the reprisals were so harsh that the American public demanded action. The volunteers who rushed into what was to become known as "The Splendid Little War" were motivated only by the desire to rescue Cubans from the cruel grasp of the Spaniards. No further imputation could be made; but as it turned out, the United States emerged with three valuable territories: the Philippines, Guam, and Puerto Rico. If the Americans regarded themselves as the liberators of Cuba, disclaiming any intention to exercise sovereignty over the island, the Cubans in turn were only calmly grateful. To them, the loss of American life was small in comparison with their own losses against the

Spaniards in the previous twenty years. Moreover, they argued, eventually they would have driven the Spaniards out anyway. In any event, the United States was abundantly rewarded with the acquisition of the new territories.

This argument—as unreasonable as it must seem to Americans—is not exclusively a part of Castro propaganda, although it is heard constantly in Havana today. It also permeated Cuban writings after the turn of the century, for any hopes that Cubans would be appreciative of the Rough Riders were minimized by subsequent United States conduct. Despite early United States recognition of Cuban independence, American troops remained in occupation until 1902. Under the Platt Amendment the United States reserved the right to intervene "for the preservation of Cuban independence, the maintenance of a government adequate for the protection of life, property, and individual liberty." It also kept the right to maintain military and naval bases, and to create an intricate trading structure favorable to United States businessmen, who took over especially the sugar estates. And so, a half century later, when Washington canceled the Cuban sugar quota, which the United States public had assumed was an example of American benevolence, Cubans had another version; they regarded sugar as an instrument of "Yankee imperialism" with which the United States gouged a greater profit than it left in Cuba.

In the years, too, between 1902 and Fidel Castro, there were other events that had an impact on Cubans different from that on United States citizens. Invoking the Platt Amendment, Washington shipped troops back to Havana from 1906 to 1909, virtually running the country. To Americans, this was humanitarianism; to many Cubans it was neo-colonialism. Doubts about United States nobility were heightened later when Washington sponsored one conservative Cuban president after another, in a series of fraudulent elections that brought in such men as the infamous José Miguel Gómez and the corrupt and tyrannical Gerardo Machado. The last appearance of U.S. Marines was in 1933, setting—at least the way Cubans view it—the scene for a takeover by a greedy dictator, Fulgencio Batista. Batista boasted of United States support and approval almost until the eve of Castro's arrival; he operated Cuba in profitable collaboration with United States sugar companies, banks, and utilities, in addition to gambling and vice syndicates.

There may have been strategic and economic reasons for Washington to encourage "reliable" presidents in Cuba, but these reasons were evaluated from United States needs. The facts of intervention have another, distinctive interpretation in Latin-American minds. For instance, when President Theodore Roosevelt enunciated his famous corollary to the Monroe Doctrine ("in the Western Hemisphere... the Monroe Doctrine may force the United States... to the exercise of an international police power") it was hardly appreciated by the people of Colombia. Panama's revolt against Colombia was clearly promoted by Roosevelt so the United States could step in and ensure American sovereignty over the militarily important Canal Zone; and so, to Colombians, Roosevelt's "big stick" policy was selfish and unjust. One step led inevitably to the next. In 1913, the United States Secretary of State, Philander C. Knox, stated: "Our tremendous national interest created by the Panama Canal makes the safety, the peace of Central America and the Caribbean of paramount interest to the government of the United States"; therefore, the United States must "apply a remedy in these regions where the malady of revolution and financial collapse is most acute."

By the time of Woodrow Wilson's inauguration as president, the United States had reduced four Caribbean and Central American republics to the status of quasi protectorates (Cuba, Panama, the Dominican Republic, and Nicaragua). Curiously enough, Wilson, the opponent of imperialism as practiced by other powers, added Haiti to the list; and under his Administration, United States proconsuls ran the biggest empire in American history. Wilson's sincere desire was to ensure democracies in these areas, and also to protect the United States from the danger of any foreign military incursions. But Latin Americans could think only that Washington intended to create a hemispheric protectorate to suit United States interests, mainly business ones.

In his radically new "good neighbor" stand, Franklin D. Roosevelt abrogated many of the policies of his predecessors, and established, at least in theory, the principle of nonintervention in the Americas. But in practice, intervention took on other, more subtle forms, and left in the region a strong distaste for the United States for having installed unpopular and ruthless governments. It left also a grave suspicion of any current programs, such as the Alliance for Progress, which may be honorable, well-intentioned, and selfless. Contemporary Latin American moods, therefore, can only be interpreted in the perspective of history. If the United States citizen feels disturbed and dismayed because Latin Americans do not always seem to respond to an American hand with complete enthusiasm, the following reports may help explain the reasons.

"Our Boys"—the Somozas

In Managua, the capital of Nicaragua, I sat one evening at a sidewalk café with a local newspaperman who pointed to the fine-looking building across the road where a neon sign proclaimed: General Hospital. "Do you wonder why there are no lights inside?" he asked. I had been struck by something strange about the appearance of the hospital, and now that my companion mentioned it, it was obvious that, aside from the bright red neon letters, the building was in darkness. Were the windows deliberately shaded, or was the glass treated in a special way for the comfort of the patients? The Nicaraguan laughed at what turned out to be a naïve question.

"It is nothing so scientific or noble as comfort for the patients," he said. "The building has stood there, much as you see it, with its name illuminated, for the last six years. There is an administrator, and a staff of doctors, all drawing salaries—but there are no patients. We paid a special welfare tax for the hospital's construction, but somehow the contractors and 'advisers' can never quite finish it. The hospital is really a showpiece and an annuity for some of Somoza's medical friends and a continual source of direct income to him through more taxes. Only the other day it was decided that before the hospital could be opened, a new wing would have to be added. Four thousand bricks were delivered, but the next morning they were gone. As far as we were able to make out, the bricks were transferred to the site of a home for one of Somoza's lieutenants."

This was an odd bit of manipulation, since Somoza had a monopoly on all the brick-producing plants in Nicaragua, as well as other structural material companies. The bricks could simply have been dropped directly at the lieutenant's lot and saved the wear and cost of transportation. However, this probably did not matter too much, since Somoza owned the principal trucking firms. Besides, it was much better, from a propaganda point of view, to make delivery first at the hospital, so people could see where their tax money was going—not that many Nicaraguans would be deceived by the blatant maneuver. In a continent of cynicism, Nicaragua is outstanding for its brand of thievery, corruption, and extortion.

I had my first taste of this only that morning at the shabby airport, where, in order to get by the four men in passport control, I had to fill out six forms and pay $1.50. When I protested that I had already paid $5 for a visa to the Nicaraguan consul in San José, one of the immigration officers shrugged his shoulders and said he did not know what the additional charge was for, but it was a fresh regulation. As it developed, a new airport chief had just been appointed, and this was his personal take, which, no doubt, he would share with Somoza. An American businessman, standing next to me, paid $50 for a permit to bring in the slender sample case which he carried under his arm. He glanced at me and said with a weary smile: "You'll get used to it. This is old stuff. I make the trip three times a year. Fifty dollars to get my samples in, fifty dollars to get them out."

Driving into town, I commented to the taxi driver about the high fare he was charging. The taxi driver angrily shot back: "This is not my money. It is Somoza's money. Somoza, *mucho malo, bandido.*" Then, with a flourish of one hand, he said, "How much do you pay for a tire for your car? Ten dollars, fifteen dollars? Here we pay five hundred cordobas—seventy dollars. All for Somoza, *bandido.*"

Who was Luis A. Somoza? Aside from the fact that, in 1962, he was one of Latin America's few remaining dictators and owned, along with members of his family, one third of Nicaragua's best land and its major industries, and ruled through torture and execution, he was the embodiment of a United States policy that has led to the particularly virulent anti-Americanism of Central America. Within forty-eight hours of my stay I found myself making these notes:

> This is one of the most shocking places in Latin America and I curse the United States for letting it happen.... Fully half the people are either unemployed or underemployed, selling soft drinks at street corners, shining shoes for two cents, or just begging. Lord knows how they live, but they can get rice and beans reasonably cheaply....Passed at noon the

International Club, where Somoza's brother Tachito, "The General," was throwing a lunch. Troops everywhere, surrounding the club; tough-looking men with submachine guns, armored cars at intersections. . . . U.S. Embassy estimates that 96 per cent of the 1,500,000 Nicaraguans are "lower class," 3 per cent "middle class," 1 per cent "upper class." . . . The shanties are grim, and I stopped outside one to talk with a man, sitting on a crate, holding a baby in his arms and rocking it gently. The baby, with eyes unblinking and just staring ahead, seemed abnormally still, almost lifeless. I asked the man, the father, if the child was sick. "Not sick," he said, "dying." He said it with Indian fatalism, and kept on rocking the baby. A half-dozen other children scampered in the dust, shoeless, without a sideward glance. . . . Had drinks with a Nicaraguan who was forced to cut the session short, to catch a plane to New York. It was a business trip, and he said he was annoyed because a friend, a Somoza cabinet minister, wants him to drag back from New York a pair of black Florsheim shoes. "I know his habits," he said as he was leaving. "He's already got five hundred pairs, and he'll wear the new ones just once, and they'll stay in the cupboard." . . . Told my driver to take me past Somoza's presidential palace, an immense, ornate place on a hilltop, adjacent to a slightly smaller palace occupied by Tachito. Surroundings are beautiful tropical gardens with a private zoo; sometimes, I've heard, Somoza throws his political prisoners into cages next to the animals so his children can look at them. . . . Told the driver to stop the car because I wanted to take some pictures. He refused, saying it was dangerous. The entire area, about half the city center, is considered a "military zone" and photographs are not permitted. I did not press my request. With armed patrols everywhere, I did not relish the prospect of ending in a Nicaraguan jail, even though I would surely not be subjected to the beatings and electric shocks which are standard procedures here. . . . Bordering the palace grounds, and included in the "military zone," are the fine homes of army officers, with exclusive little parks for their children; built largely with United States military aid funds, the men themselves trained in United States camps in Panama and the States. . . . It is part of the indictment of a terrible heritage left by the U.S. . . .

These notes, I must admit, were written at white heat, late at night, after I had spent several evening hours speaking with a group of Nicaraguans, numbering among them editors, intellectuals, and would-be reformers. My observations, and their comments, added to a gloomy record of American intervention at its worst, tactics sufficient to enflame any genuine patriot and leave bitterness in the heart. In looking at the jottings in less emotional moments I would amend them only to this point: the present Administration of President Kennedy has been attempting to make some constructive changes in its relations with the regime, to push reforms in the proper direction. But one fears again that it is too late, that Nicaragua inevitably will swing from one form of extremism to the other. Here is a brief modern history of Nicaragua, at least as critics of the United States—and they include most of the non-Somoza elements, both liberal and conservative—see it:

Private United States business interests marched through Nicaragua as early as 1849, when Cornelius Vanderbilt secured a contract that gave his newly organized transport corporation—Accessory Transit Company—the right to transfer gold-hungry East Coast "49ers" across the isthmus on their way to California. Soon Vanderbilt was running Nicaragua, and its conservative political leaders, for the benefit of his company; though he was supposed to pay the state a share of the profits each year, he piously reported that there were none to divide. Soon, too, shipping rivals in New York were financing military expeditions by the famous American "land pirate," William Walker, to knock out Vanderbilt's lucrative concession. Walker, who had been unsuccessful in earlier careers in law, medicine, and journalism, was by now a frustrated adventurer, having failed to establish his own republic in Lower California. His reward for leading three hundred mercenaries into Nicaragua was to be glory, wealth, and land.

Thus began what Central Americans still refer to, with distaste, as the "National War." Walker and his mercenaries quickly gained control of southern Nicaragua, but then found themselves opposed by an allied army recruited partly by Vanderbilt but largely by Costa Rica, Guatemala, El Salvador, and Honduras. It was a unique moment in Central American history, with so many states and factions for once united in purpose; but the motive was a simple one, to drive a Yankee invader from their soil. Walker, wounded and isolated, eventually gave himself up to the British in Honduras and was executed by a Honduran firing squad in 1860. His exploits created great debate in the United States, some people applauding him for what they remotely took to be his efforts to keep the British confined to British Honduras, others condemning him for a violation of existing American neutrality laws. President James Buchanan said that North Americans had the mission to "civilize" Central America, but perhaps the government ought to restrain the sanguinary Walker types.

Over the next few decades more and more United States firms, among them the United Fruit Company, moved into the area. The United States government itself felt impelled to move whenever it considered the affairs of American companies and citizens in jeopardy. A new factor was added, contributing to intervention on a government level. European as well as New York bankers were advancing loans to Central American governments, which, feckless and transitory, constantly threatened to default on their debts. This, in turn, aroused threats of invasion by the great European powers to collect the money by force. Washington began its operations of a military nature in what it considered a defense of the Monroe Doctrine: to keep out the European powers. But in the process it left itself open to the accusation of neo-colonialism and economic imperialism, an accusation that echoes as loudly today as it did a half century ago.

Nicaragua was an almost classic case. At the turn of the century it was under the rule of a strong man, José Santos Zelaya, who not only fell behind on his payments to European bankers but spoke glibly of selling exclusive canal rights through Nicaragua to Japan or Britain. The United States had just decided on a canal through Panama, and, with a growing strategic interest in the isthmus, could not tolerate Zelaya's threats. Accordingly it embarked on what was to become a pattern for the area; it backed, with material support, the opponents of Zelaya, who was overthrown in 1908. There followed a succession of puppet rulers, maintained in office by the grace of the United States, which ensured its control with the mobilization of Marines. For a short while the implied threat of a Marine invasion was enough to keep any political opponents in line. But in 1912, when a "dependable" Conservative president was in danger of being overthrown by "irresponsible" Liberals, the U.S. Marines landed.

From that time on, except for a few months in 1925, the Marines were in occupation of Nicaragua until 1933. They ran customs collections, doling out revenues for interest payments to American and foreign creditors, and supervised sham elections that invariably returned Conservatives as presidents. This blatant United States military government rule was more refined than it sounds. The Marines were stationed in Nicaragua as "legation guards." In turn, they trained a Nicaraguan *guardia,* constabulary, which would preserve safe and subservient regimes, in preparation for an eventual United States withdrawal. The Marine evacuation of Nicaragua took place under mounting and loud charges of imperialism from all corners of Latin America.

If Nicaragua had once been run as a private United States domain, it now became what Nicaraguans bitterly call *la finca de Somoza*: Somoza's personal estate. General Anastasio Somoza, a former shopkeeper and mechanic who had risen under Marine tutelage to become chief of the *guardia*, simply moved in as president in 1936, establishing, with the help of his troops, a family dynasty unusual even for Latin America: in effect, the first hereditary dictatorship of modern times. When Somoza was assassinated in 1956 by a youthful and idealistic poet, the succession fell automatically, with the blessing of the *guardia*, to his two sons, Luis and Anastasio, Jr. In the meantime, Somoza, while amassing his own fortune by graft or simply by seizing the properties of political enemies after executing or banishing them, had preserved United States ties and interests, had been entertained at the White House, had sent his younger son (who preferred to be known as Tachito rather than Anastasio, Jr.) to West Point. On Tachito's graduation, his father presented him with a general's uniform and command of the *guardia*, which by now, with United States financing, was Nicaragua's full-fledged army.

A similar build-up was going on across the Caribbean in Batista's Cuba, with hardly a demur from the American public or press. After all, Batista kept law and order, and was a "friend" of the United States because he permitted United States companies and investors to operate without hindrance. The tragic and myopic attitude toward Somoza's Nicaragua was fashionable even in the so-called "good neighbor" days of Franklin D. Roosevelt. Speaking of the dictator, Roosevelt once said: "He's an s.o.b., but he's *our* s.o.b." [1] A latter-day American, Ambassador Thomas Whelan, carried forward this philosophy with unfeigned

[1] Quoted by Lester Velie in *Reader's Digest,* January 1962.

enthusiasm for ten full years, from 1951 to 1961, referring affectionately to Somoza and later to his heirs as "my boys." Whelan, a political appointee, had no background in diplomacy, no sensitivity, and, above all, no understanding of the ferments and needs of the Nicaraguan people. He was as much hated by Nicaraguans as the Somozas themselves. Whelan spent his social time with the clan, even to the extent of attending military banquets (the only foreign envoy to do so), and neglected to meet or talk with opponents of the dictatorship.

His successor, Aaron Brown, a career State Department man, was far more acceptable to the articulate public: that is, the professional people, the intellectuals, the small merchant class who have waited, with increasing fury and dismay, twenty-six years for the end of the Somoza dynasty. Brown, a reticent, slow-speaking individual, at least got out into the countryside, saw for himself the deplorable conditions under which the peasants lived, talked with anti-Somoza elements, and had an understanding grasp of their problems and aspirations. But no amount of enlightenment at this stage could be expected to alter a resentment against the United States that began several generations ago and found fuel even in current United States practices. Nicaraguans who have been attacked, beaten, arrested, and tortured by the *guardia*—and the victims include, for example, one third of all the lawyers—are quick to point out that these Somoza goon squads were prepared by American military men. At least 3,500 of the 5,000-man *guardia* have spent training periods at Fort Gulick in the Panama Canal Zone; others have been taken to the United States itself.

It is hardly any wonder that bitterness against the United States is so ingrained that even if U.S. Marines have officially pulled out, the memory of them—and of the power the United States handed their successors—still translates itself in small but ugly incidents. Shortly before my arrival, a U.S. Marine attached to the Embassy (this Marine was legitimately a security guard, as Marines are in all U.S. embassies around the world) married a Nicaraguan girl. Two thousand students marched through the streets of Managua, shouting anti-American slogans and hurling stones at the church in which the ceremony was taking place.

With some belated recognition of the situation, and an awareness that Fidelismo had a made-to-order set of grievances in Nicaragua, the United States, through Brown, last year finally began to exert pressure on the Somoza brothers to amend their ways. The Somozas were reminded that since 1956 the United States had supplied them with $70 million in aid, and the Alliance for Progress now called for reforms. The Somozas eased up on press censorship—not as dramatic a gesture as it might appear on the surface, since 65 per cent of Nicaraguans cannot read (but the brothers still prohibited radio broadcasts of a "subversive character," adverse criticism that could reach the ears of the public). Luis, the president, also promised an election for early in 1963. He even went so far, again with United States prodding, to decree that no Somoza could run for the office of president. "I am looking forward to giving up the presidency just as a farmer looks forward to the rains of May," said the portly, forty-year-old Luis. "There is nothing I would rather do than go to the United States and rest."

But there were few informed men and women who believed that an election could be anything but farcical. Luis Somoza may indeed have sniffed the wind of change. After all, not far away a fellow dictator, Trujillo, had recently been assassinated; and not far away, too, a dictator of the other extreme, Castro, was making his influence felt. But too much was involved in Nicaragua for any reasonable expectation of an honest election. The exact size of the Somoza fortune is unknown, but Luis once boasted openly that he and his brother owned 20 per cent of Nicaragua's wealth, including the only shipping line bringing supplies to and from the country, the only internal airline, the only sugar mills, the only brewery, the only slaughter house, plus about one hundred other strategic and monopolistic concerns, and about five hundred plantations.

The family fortune, however, goes beyond this, for in an environment of nepotism some fifty cousins and uncles occupy key positions and control much of the remaining industry and agriculture. While the brothers are believed to have a fair amount of cash—running to millions of dollars—safely entombed in United States banks, three quarters of their holdings are directly tied in with Nicaragua itself. In addition, there are some ten thousand "government" families, plus the *guardia,* who would be uprooted in any genuine change of administration. In other words, the Somozas and their military dictatorship are too deeply engaged to give up the private *finca* voluntarily. And so the assumption was that a Somoza-appointed aide would become figurehead president, duly "elected" in a ballot carefully scrutinized by the *guardia* under the command of thirty-six-year-old "General" Tachito Somoza. This, in fact, is what happened on February 3, 1963, when a Somoza nominee, René Schick, was declared president, the cynical announcement of his "victory" being made after returns were known from only three of the country's 1,386 precincts.

The parallel with Batista's Cuba is remarkable and disturbing. Like Batista, who collaborated for a while with the Communists by allowing them to take over the Cuban labor unions, the Somozas have supplied campaign funds enabling the Communists to run the Nicaraguan trade federation. This, supposedly, was a means of containing labor unrest while the Communists themselves were under scrutiny. And yet, inevitably and with some good reception, the Communists have been active in the countryside, among the *campesinos,* among the unemployed. One of the foes of the Somozas, and the leading opposition politician, moderate Dr. Fernando Agüero, told me: "I believe every month we lose is a loss for democracy. The situation here is exactly the same as in Cuba before Castro, with the United States arming and supporting an unpopular dictatorship."

Agüero, an ophthalmologist who before his fortieth birthday had been in and out of Nicaraguan prisons three times and exiled twice, risked further banishment by holding rallies among peasants while I was in the country. He called for basic agrarian reform (to divide the Somoza land holdings which run anywhere from 500,000 to one million acres), universal education (not a single school was built in Nicaragua in 1962, even though only three out of ten children go beyond Grade 2), adequate public health (50 per cent of the children die before the age of five), housing and proper nutrition (many Managuans sleep on the streets, and eat nothing but rice and beans), and free expression (an estimated 2,000 political prisoners were still in jail last year).

"At least 25 per cent of the people here are active Fidelistas," said Agüero. "If we did not offer an alternative the figure would be much higher."

If the United States was showing delayed uneasiness about the Somozas and the discontent of Nicaraguans, it had itself to blame for the state of affairs; any "intervention" in elections would not now be so easy to manage in a country controlled by a military machine built up with United States guidance. And yet Agüero posed the dilemma for the United States: "Without an honest election this country will simply end in violent revolution, and we know the outcome in Cuba. Nicaragua receives Point Four technical assistance; we receive military training from the United States. So why should we not get technical assistance—supervision—in an election? We must have moral support of the United States to give people faith."

The complexities of such a request will be examined more fully at another point, but in the meanwhile I still have before my eyes the parting scene at Managua's airport. Hordes of barefoot children scampered among the waiting passengers, while a group of festive Nicaraguans were waved with ease through passport formalities. Among the group was the editor of *Novedades,* the Somoza newspaper, a non-professional "journalist" leaving for a regional meeting in Puerto Rico of the Inter-American Press Association. With him, boarding the plane, were his wife and two young children, his secretary and her husband, and a personal friend and his wife as "advisers": a total party of eight. "And who pays?" said a knowledgeable Nicaraguan standing beside me. "The people! Disgusting, isn't it?"

But even more disheartening was the sight and sound of a rumba band, and the flow of champagne among *guardia* officers bestowing farewell celebration at the exit gate for a Nicaraguan major about to take off on a military course in the United States.

A Geographic Scar

The issues of Panama, in a way, are rather clear cut, though far from simple in solution. On one hand, the United States has spent more than one and a half billion dollars to build and improve the Panama Canal: a feat involving finances and skills beyond the capacity of Panamanians. On the other hand, Panamanians complain of an infringement of their sovereignty, since, under the terms of a treaty, control of the seaway remains in United States hands "in perpetuity." Nationalist-minded men and women say that their land is carved in two by an alien presence, a geographic scar that has done little to establish internal stability. In little more than fifty years, Panama has had twenty-nine presidents, only five of whom have served their full terms.

Administration by the United States of the ten-mile-wide Panama Canal Zone touches off, regularly, riots by Panamanians who have a varied set of motives. At one extreme are those who insist on complete withdrawal of United States civilians and military personnel, and end to United States sovereignty over the Zone. The milder anti-American demonstrations have called for the flying of the Panamanian flag alongside the Stars and Stripes (ordered by President Eisenhower, September 17, 1960). And, in between, almost all critics are united in one demand: a higher rental for the use of the Zone (the United States pays a flat sum of $1,930,000 a year, which Panamanians claim is a woeful price for the total tolls collected in the canal).

If these grievances are symptoms of a nationalist spirit, they have also taken on the tone of social unrest. This unrest was always present; Panamanians have long been aware of the contrast between the fine homes of United States residents of the Zone and the huge slums inhabited by their own children. But the unrest is now channeled by Fidelistas, who are vocal and active, and who make a point of emphasizing that Panama's oligarchs, living on an even more lavish scale than Americans, exist largely with the support of United States arms.

Trouble in Guatemala

In 1954, when Guatemala's president, Jacobo Arbenz, was overthrown in a military revolt, the United States government and press lauded this as a defeat for "communism." Up to a point there was some truth in the allegation that Communists were active in the Arbenz regime, but, to many Guatemalans and Latin Americans generally, only up to a point. The real truth, as they see it, involves intervention by Washington to protect the United Fruit Company, which was undergoing nationalization. Ironically, the land reform introduced by Arbenz ten years ago was, by present standards suggested by United States experts for Latin America, moderate indeed.

Guatemala had had a long string of presidents and dictators subservient to United States wishes. But the end of an era came in 1944, when an army coup brought in a *junta* determined to introduce long-needed social and economic reforms. Disputes between conservative and liberal factions held up the program until, in 1950, the defense minister, Colonel Arbenz, won a presidential election with a large majority. Arbenz was a reformer of the left, and he set about to alter the land tenure and farm labor situations, which were among the worst in Latin America. "For all the furor it produced, Decree 900, which had its roots in the constitution of 1945, (was) a remarkably mild and a fairly sound piece of legislation." [2] Decree 900 provided for the expropriation and redistribution of uncultivated or fallow land above a basic limit, with compensation for the large landowners in the form of bonds. Despite an inexperienced administrative machine, the program made considerable progress in little more than a year. One million acres (much of this land had been taken over by the state from Germans during World War II) were divided among small farmers; some cooperatives were established. About 100,000 *campesino* families felt for the first time the dignity of working their own soil.

There was, of course, strenuous opposition from right-wing groups who saw in this "socialism," or, worse still, "communism." But the most controversial move of the Arbenz government was the expropriation of 400,000 acres of uncultivated land from the United Fruit Company. The United States company argued that it needed this territory as a reserve for its banana-growing operation; the government contended that the remaining reserves alone totaled

[2] Thomas F. Carroll, *Latin American Issues*.

twenty times as much acreage as the company actually had under banana cultivation. In 1954 anti-Arbenz exiles invaded Guatemala from Honduras, with arms supplied by the United States. It was the end of Arbenz, and—so the United States claimed—the end of a Communist threat. It was also the end of land reform, for Decree 900 was promptly revoked and replaced by other bills that carried no effective provisions for changes in the agrarian structure. Rightly or wrongly, Latin Americans saw the invasion not as an internal clash over an "ism" but as old-style United States intervention to safeguard American business investments.

Colonel Castillo Armas, the leader of the invasion, became president and virtual dictator of Guatemala. He was later assassinated by a member of his palace guard, to be succeeded by an equally conservative officer, Miguel Ydígoras, who also enjoyed the protection and aid of Washington. Ydígoras has been accused by a former Mexican president of paranoia. Certainly he has a habit of seeing Communists behind every reform demand in his country. The plain fact is that Ydígoras ran in 1962, if not precisely a dictatorship, a semidictatorship with the aid of secret police and an army trained and built up by the United States. His main visible support came from just those elements: the army, the police, and, tragically, the U.S. government. His opponents, in the majority of the population, included not only left-wing elements but professional men from the center: doctors, lawyers, engineers.

When students became angry over what they considered fraudulent congressional elections (the Ydígoras machine took the bulk of the seats), and paraded through the streets of Guatemala City, demanding the resignation of Ydígoras, he called it a "Castro-Communist plot." When, after three days of riots, the students were joined by adults, including railway workers, bank clerks, government employees, and the National Liberation Movement founded by the late

Colonel Castillo Armas, Ydígoras still blamed "Communists and Castroites," and had his troops open fire with machine guns. The demonstrations were a compound of many grievances: incredible corruption of the Ydígoras government, poverty, lack of social advances, and a continued rankling that Ydígoras, bowing to the United States, had permitted anti-Castro Cubans to train on Guatemalan soil for the 1961 invasion attempt, thereby making Guatemala a legitimate target for Castro ire. At the end of a week's riots, some forty Guatemalans were dead, more than six hundred were wounded, and a thousand were in jail.

One of the men picked up by the police after the manifestations was Francisco Villagrán, who was interrogated by Ydígoras personally and accused of inspiring the students to riot. Villagrán, possibly the outstanding opposition politician in Guatemala, denied any connection and was later released. Villagrán is a socialist, with, as he defined it for me, the leaning of a Mendès-France. He believes in a mixed economy, saying: "We should not think of full nationalization. Perhaps basic utilities should be under state direction, but even here, where an enterprise is productive, we should not touch it."

He cites a practical illustration: The main railway in Guatemala was built with United States capital and controlled by Americans. From 1944 to 1954 socialists demanded its takeover, and the government went so far as to build a competing truck route alongside the tracks. The government even encouraged strikes among railroaders, so the state would have an excuse to move in. As a result, the frightened railway company invested no further money and allowed maintenance to slip so badly that today no one wants the line. "We realize our mistakes now," says Villagrán. "The railway is not helping the economy any more, and so in some cases nationalization can defeat itself."

This having been said, Villagrán is also against the state

managing farms. Rather, he wants the division of uncultivated estates into small holdings and cooperatives: much the same kind of reform attempted by Arbenz. He concedes that by 1954 the Communists had gained some influence over Arbenz, but by comparison with the Cuban revolution later, Guatemala's "was a social revolution in baby-pants." He goes on: "The United States simply didn't understand it, and therefore overthrew Arbenz. Now the terrible contradiction is that while the United States would welcome similar reforms today, peaceful changes will be difficult because of the entrenchment of the oligarchy under Ydígoras."

All of which leads up to a rather grim conclusion: the likelihood of one form of extremism being replaced by another, in which reasonable men such as Villagrán would have no say. For the past two years guerrilla bands have been gaining in strength in the northern hills of Guatemala. Ironically, these bands were being led by former army officers who took their training in guerrilla warfare in United States camps in Panama. Their motives for resisting Ydígoras were varied; in some cases, the grievances were personal; in others, men defected from the army because of allegedly slow promotion. But still others, according to leaflets they distributed among the peasants, talked of "restoring the dignity of the nation."

Some of the early battles between government forces and the guerrillas took on comic war aspects. Since, for example, the rebels wore regular army uniforms, government troops were never certain at whom they were shooting, and sometimes, in error, fired at their own numbers. For a while there was talk of issuing armbands to government troops, changeable every day so the guerrillas could not copy them. But if these were lighter sidelights, no one in Guatemala dismissed the guerrillas, well trained and well commanded, with levity. Memories were still sensitive about the origin of Fidel Castro and his movement in the hills of Cuba.

10

In the Wake of Trujillo

AT 10:30 P.M. on a moonlit Tuesday night, May 30, 1961, on a highway outside Ciudad Trujillo, a car carrying Generalissimo Rafael Trujillo was ambushed and one of the most cruel dictators of modern times, who ruled the Dominican Republic for nearly a third of a century, was assassinated. Four miles away a well-known public figure, Dr. Viriato Fiallo, was at home, preparing to retire. As usual his house, at the corner of El Conde and Espillat Streets, was under the scrutiny of three members of the secret police, the dreaded S.I.M. (Military Intelligence Service). For Dr. Fiallo, aside from being a prominent physician, was suspected of leading a clandestine political group, the Popular Revolutionary Union.

Dr. Fiallo had indeed been active in the underground, though his group, which had vague hopes of getting rid of Trujillo, never organized itself effectively. But on five occasions Dr. Fiallo went to jail. The first time was in 1942, when he wrote a magazine article for a New York publication expressing his thoughts about fighting for freedom in Europe and depicting what life must be like under a dictatorship. There was, of course, no mention of the Dominican Republic or Trujillo, but the allusion was obvious. Dr. Fiallo was thrown into a cell so small for his frame—six feet, two inches—that he had to remain in a half-kneeling, "natal," position for thirty days.

In later arrests he was never told the charge, except once, when an officer said: "Wherever you go, subversion flowers in the air." This was told him during his longest imprisonment, seven months of solitary confinement. Still, a solitary cell was preferable to incarceration in *La Cuarenta* (The Forty), an S.I.M. torture house so-named because it was in the heart of Ciudad Trujillo, on 40th Street. In *La Cuarenta* Trujillo's men slowly exterminated political foes by subjecting them to the *pulpo* (octopus), an electrical device with several arms that were attached to the skull by screws. The shocks came in gradual doses. An electrified rod was also used to shock the genitals, and then later came castration, nail extractions and other methods of inducing confession and slow death. The agony was known to be slow, because survivors could hear the victims' screams over an amplifying system deliberately hooked up to the cell blocks.

Dr. Fiallo, in 1962, when the immediate danger from Trujilloism had subsided somewhat, visited *La Cuarenta,* as did several other aghast citizens and representatives from O.A.S. But on the night of May 30, 1961, he was in no mood to take chances. Shortly before midnight, and unaware of the incident on the highway, he heard his doorbell ring. As he recalled it for me: "I did not answer the door. All I could think about was the presence of the three S.I.M. men outside. Either they wanted to take me in again, or if this was a friend, the S.I.M. might think a political meeting was going on." Dr. Fiallo peered through the window and saw that it was indeed a friend, a political ally, and his wife. (Such is the fear, even today, of the long arm of exiled Trujillo kin that Dr. Fiallo would not identify his friend, since he was in on the plot and might be the target for vengeance;

Dr. Fiallo would label him only as "E.") He heard E. cry out: "If we don't get another doctor, the woman will die." And so the hovering S.I.M. men were misled into believing the caller, who sensed why the door remained unopened and who promptly left, was not someone in search of a political conference.

A half hour later the bedside phone rang. When Dr. Fiallo picked it up, the voice at the other end said: "The man is dead." Dr. Fiallo leaped from bed, quite in a stupor, and said, "What? What?" E. now repeated the news in the classical French phrase: "Il est mort." Dr. Fiallo: "I knew, of course, to whom he was referring, but I was afraid to believe it. I went out on the balcony and saw the three police watchers and everything seemed normal. The street was quiet and peaceful, not filled with tanks and military cars, as one would expect if the dictator was dead. I couldn't sleep, and so I stayed up all night and discussed with my wife whether such an act had really happened, whether Trujillo was really dead, and if so what would be the results. . . ."

For the end of Generalissimo Trujillo would not necessarily mean the end of a reign of terror. There were still Trujillo's son, Rafael ("Ramfis") Trujillo, Jr., the thirty-two-year-old heir apparent, and other beneficiaries of the large Trujillo clan—including the generalissimo's two brothers, Héctor and Arismendi—plus the military, with whom Dominicans would have to contend. Would the nation now be subjected to greater agony and reprisal than ever before? And what would the United States do? As a young student, Viriato Fiallo had spoken loudly against the kind of United States intervention, complete with Marine landings, that had set the stage for a takeover by Trujillo. But now would the United States know how to save the Dominican people and support them in their quest for freedom? And how could a people, after thirty-one years of one-man rule, manage to govern themselves? From where would come the skills, the intimate knowledge of democratic process, the essential discipline and experience needed for stability?

While Dr. Fiallo, now sixty-six years of age, was pondering these questions, a present-day student, Armando Hoepelman, a lean intense young man, was walking down El Conde, Ciudad Trujillo's principal street, around nine A.M., when a group of other students pulled up in a car. One whispered: *"Arreglaron al hombre*... the man has been fixed." Again there was no mention of a name, but Hoepelman's instinctive, hopeful reaction was to say: "Are you sure?" One of the students explained that troops were searching for Trujillo and couldn't find him, but the story was all over town that he had been shot and killed. Another added: "I hear they found his body at dawn."

Hoepelman still was not sure whether to trust this information, but he did notice now an "expectant kind of excitement" in the streets; heavily armed guards stood in front of the cable office, a usual first sign that the authorities were anticipating trouble. "I began to think something serious had happened," he said. But he could not feel a sense of relief until the official news of Trujillo's death was announced over the radio at four in the afternoon. Victor Sallent, a twenty-seven-year-old bank messenger, also listened for broadcasts, and later recounted: "In one way I was happy that *hechivo* (the goat)... we never mentioned his name in public, and it is still hard to get used to the idea ... that *he* was dead. But in other ways I was scared. I thought there would be a bloody revolution."

Actually, no one rejoiced openly—not even Germán Ornes, who at least was physically out of danger, a few hundred miles away, in Puerto Rico. Ornes, a burly journalist in his early forties, with black bushy hair and warm, troubled brown eyes, had gone into voluntary exile in the United States in 1955, there to write a book of exposure, *Trujillo:*

Little Caesar of the Caribbean. Ornes had been compelled to serve for a while as editor of Trujillo's paper, *El Caribe*. As he explained it: "I was under police surveillance. I had two kids, my brothers were in exile, my father had been kicked out of a judgeship for releasing political prisoners. The government jailed me four or five times for a day or two." Now, if jail was far behind, memories were still bitter. And yet Ornes could not celebrate. He saw the news flash of Trujillo's assassination as cable editor of *El Mundo* in San Juan. "In my job," he said, "practically everything fell on my shoulders that afternoon. I even wrote an interpretive piece. There was no time to be emotional." Later, when the impact and significance of the event struck him fully, Ornes still could not go back, because the Trujillo image had not yet been erased.

Some women in the capital wept when they heard about Trujillo, because to some he was *El Benefactor,* the man who occasionally gave food parcels to the poor, or even radio sets. Others wept because of the uncertainty of the future, the horrible fear that everyone would be swept up in an undisciplined series of purges and revenge killings. In this sense there was a parallel with the death of Josef Stalin, whose terrible figure had, in a weird way, made life orderly and clear-cut and secure, at least for men and women who were not involved in politics; when Stalin died many tremulous Russian women, like their Dominican counterparts eight years later, cried too. But three Dominican women were beyond tears, for they had only recently been buried. These were the three Mirabal sisters—Minerva, Patria, and Marie Teresa—who, to judge from photographs and word descriptions, were exquisite creatures. The daughters of a wealthy landowner, they were all well educated—and revolutionary. Minerva married Manuel Tavarez Justo, a lawyer of leftist leanings; Patria married Leandro Guzman, an engineer; Marie Teresa married Pedro Gonzales, a liberal landowner.

Manuel Tavarez Justo is quiet spoken, with certain qualities of idealism and dedication that sound almost youthful. Tavarez Justo is relatively young—thirty-one years old, to be precise. However, with graying black hair and a gaunt face, physical characteristics made understandable by occurrences, he looks more like forty-five years of age. He even talks of recent history as though it were long past. For him, a highlight of the Dominican Republic's record was the attempt to overthrow Trujillo, by invasion, on June 14, 1959.

The invasion was launched from Cuba by Dominicans armed and trained by Castro's army. There was no air support, and of the 225 men who landed, half were killed in battle; almost all the rest were tortured to death in prison. An unknown number of Dominican civilians, but estimated in the thousands, were also rounded up and executed on suspicion of complicity. Still, in Tavarez Justo's words: "It was the spark for resistance on a national scale." Manuel, his wife, his in-laws, and a few friends decided it was time to act; and so was formed the underground 14th of June Movement, in memory of the ill-fated invasion, with Tavarez Justo as the leader. But his role was known only to a few people, for the movement was built on a pyramid structure, each man having no more than two or three immediate contacts.

By January of 1960 there were some eight hundred members, mostly students and professors, doctors and lawyers. Unfortunately for the movement, one of the late joiners turned out to be an S.I.M. informer; the pyramid structure collapsed. Men put to the *pulpo,* or to leather-thonged whips, nail extractors and scalpels, talked about their immediate contacts, and these men in turn talked about theirs. Within three weeks half of the band, four hundred persons, were in prison, among them Manuel and his brothers-in-law.

The trio were kept alive and tortured (Tavarez Justo's body bears the scars of burnings by blow-torch) on the assumption that they would betray others, including their wives. They kept silent.

But Trujillo's military police were far from defeated. After several months, Manuel, Leandro, and Pedro were transferred from *La Victoria,* an old jail in Ciudad Trujillo, to Salcedo, a small village on the Atlantic coast. This, as it turned out, was part of a cunning S.I.M. plot, because it was obvious that the sisters would travel to visit their menfolk. And so they did, the three of them together, in a car, on November 25. As they approached Salcedo they were ambushed by secret police and taken away, but not before they managed to scream out their names so nearby peasants could hear them. The Mirabel sisters were prominent in the Dominican Republic, and popular. Any mishap would have to be prudently camouflaged.

Manuel, of course, knew nothing of the incident until, as he recalls it now—quietly and without rancor—a prison captain came into his cell on December 4 and said that though it was against the rules he was going to show him the morning's edition of *El Caribe.* He flung the paper at him, and Manuel read a front-page story saying that the well-known Mirabal girls had died "tragically in a car accident." A half hour later the captain reappeared, laughed and said: "This is the story for the paper, but I want you to know that we tortured your wife and then killed her, and we did the same to her sisters—and this is what we are going to do to you." Manuel now says: "I was on the verge of going crazy." Among other things, he did not know what was happening to his two young children.

From Salcedo the three brothers-in-law were moved back to Ciudad Trujillo, this time to *La Cuarenta.* They were herded together, naked, in a cell which was six feet wide and six feet long. High up on the wall was a ten-inch slit, just big enough for them to see a piece of the sky and a flag on the roof of a neighboring public building. "One morning, earlier than usual, we were awakened by the screams of prisoners being tortured," Manuel recounts. "Leandro said, 'Look, the flag is not flying today.' Nobody said anything else for a few moments, and then Leandro said, 'Something might have happened.' " This "something," to men obsessed with hatred for Trujillo, could have meant only one thing. But Manuel remembers shaking his head and saying, "If something has happened to *him,* we would all be killed by now." Still, the gnawing thought lingered back of his mind, especially since the screams from tortured prisoners were louder that day than ever before.

A week later the three men were given clothing, and taken, handcuffed, into the prison yard along with about sixty other men. For the first time Manuel saw that guards were wearing black arm bands, "and now I really dared hope that Trujillo was dead, but I could not be absolutely sure." The men were being shifted to more civilized quarters in *La Victoria,* because an O.A.S. commission of enquiry was due to arrive at any day. In his new cell in *La Victoria,* Manuel Tavarez Justo learned the confirmation he had sought. On the wall was a scribbling left by a previous inmate: "Trujillo is dead, but terror is still with us."

"There can be no land to compare with it in richness and beauty," wrote Christopher Columbus after he discovered the mountainous but fertile green Caribbean island which he named *La Isla Española.* And indeed, Hispaniola, the island that is now divided between the Dominican Republic and Haiti, has the physical attributes of a paradise. Endowed with a soil that yields almost any tropical crop, surrounded by rich fishing grounds, the islanders should be the "lovable, tractable, peaceable people" described by Columbus in 1492. But the original Indians have long since gone, wiped out by disease and slavery imported by the Spaniards. The Spanish legacy, as in other sections of the hemisphere, included tyranny, corruption, ignorance, and poverty. In this century, the totality of control enjoyed by Trujillo was also compounded in part by an earlier United States policy of intervention—*the Dollar Diplomacy* so searingly written about by Scott Nearing and Joseph Freeman in 1928 ("a policy worse than a crime; it was a blunder").

In 1904, in order to ensure payment of debts, President Theodore Roosevelt took over the customs houses of the Dominican Republic, practically the only source of revenue. This led to even greater United States financial influence, and in 1916 to outright occupation of the island by the U.S. Navy. For the next eight years the Dominican Republic was under direct United States military rule; in the instability that followed United States withdrawal, Trujillo, in 1930, was able to seize power. By now United States business investments were considered safe, for *El Benefactor's* tight command guaranteed against expropriation or revolution. The investors who were entertained by the dictator could not hear the cries of his tormented political prisoners.[1]

Trujillo, in the meanwhile, was busy accumulating his own fortune and spending $4 million a year on public relations, most of it in the United States, where he took out full-page newspaper advertisements reassuring investors: "No Time for Communism." By 1960 it was estimated that his personal hoard in overseas banks was $300 million; in addition, he and his family controlled about two thirds of the nation's best cattle and sugar land. But megalomania was also driving him into dangerous foreign directions, principally a vendetta against Venezuela's president, Rómulo

[1] "Relatively few Americans, unless they were readers of *The Nation* and other 'radical' journals, knew what was going on at their back door," complained *The Nation* recently. "This era, however, is better known to many Latin Americans than the good intentions of the United States which followed it."

Betancourt, who openly proclaimed his distaste for the dictator. In June, 1960, Trujillo assigned four hatchetmen to fly to Caracas to kill Betancourt. The would-be assassins were foiled only because an intricate dynamite device did not contain enough explosive; Betancourt escaped with minor burns. But the evidence was clear enough for the Organization of American States, at a meeting in Costa Rica, to accuse Trujillo of "acts of aggression and intervention" against Venezuela and to impose a diplomatic boycott and limited economic sanctions. Trujillo lost a United States income of over $30 million in sugar sales alone.

When the dictator met the fate he had once plotted for Betancourt, son Ramfis Trujillo flew back from Paris, where he had been engaged in a polo game with another Dominican playboy, Porfirio Rubirosa. He assumed his country's leadership along with Joaquín Balaguer, the puppet president he inherited from his father. Then he promptly invited a team of O.A.S. representatives (from Panama, Colombia, Uruguay, and the United States) to prove for themselves that the Dominican Republic was in for a new look, a process of "democratization." His motive, of course, was to regain favor with the United States, whose relations with the Trujillos had cooled considerably even in the last days of the Eisenhower Administration, and to win a lifting of the costly O.A.S. embargo.

By now the Kennedy Administration was evolving a new policy toward the Dominican Republic that might include "intervention," but this time to assist peaceful transition from dictatorship to democratic government. Six months would elapse before such United States action would take place. And in the meanwhile the embargo would remain as a warning to young Trujillo to mend his family's ways.

The rest of this narrative is intended to illustrate that democracy does not come easily to a people who for generations have known autocratic rule only—a trial all the more important to understand because it has yet to be experienced by the peoples of Nicaragua, Haiti, and elsewhere.

In the days immediately preceding the arrival of the O.A.S. mission the S.I.M. secret agents were active, rounding up hundreds of men and women who might have had anything to do with the death of *El Benefactor*. Actually, two groups of men, totaling thirty, were engaged in the assassination plot. In a way it resembled the old German plot against Hitler's life, because many of the men were former collaborators of the dictator, and others were generals who had become disenchanted with the oppressive trends in their country and filled with a gloomy foreboding for the future. Through mutual contacts, the two groups united in January, 1961, but had to wait for an opportune moment in May, when Trujillo, accompanied only by his chauffeur, was driving out from the capital to visit his mistress. In the exchange of fire, when the car was attacked, the chauffeur wounded one of the conspirators, who was promptly picked up by the S.I.M. and tortured for information. The blood bath then was turned on in earnest. Literally scores of people, including distant relatives of the plotters, were mutilated and slaughtered, some under the sadistic and vengeful eye of Ramfis himself.

"The month of June," said Dr. Viriato Fiallo, "was the most horrible month of our lives." Even Victor Sallent, the bank messenger who was remote from active politics, dreaded walking the streets, for fear of being swept up by indiscriminate goon squads. The end of a dictator did not establish the beginning of freedom; the old order, made up of Ramfis, his kinfolk, the army, the police, was not going to relinquish ingrained habits and privileges. But with the landing of O.A.S. observers and dozens of foreign newspapermen who could shape world opinion, some outward relaxation was necessary. Ramfis even said he would permit the formation of political parties and promised an "election" for 1962. But Dr. Fiallo and others experienced in Trujillo tactics remained wary and silent for a while.

The students, as might be expected, were the first to hold a public meeting, early in July. Armando Hoepelman received a phone call from a classmate who passed on word that an informal group was going to gather on the campus of University of Santo Domingo at four P.M. "I didn't even know the purpose of the meeting," confesses Hoepelman, though he assumed that it was to discuss ways of requesting autonomy for the university, a sacred right common in Latin America but denied by the late dictator. In their whole lifetime, in fact, students had not been permitted to hold any open meetings, nor even to form fraternal associations which might be hazardous to the regime. Now about four hundred brave souls (of a total enrollment of four thousand) collected on the grounds, just outside the office of the rector, José Machado, a Trujillo appointee. Hoepelman felt ill at ease as he looked up at the huge statue of *El Benefactor* which continued to dominate the setting. No one seemed to know what to do or to say, and the group just stood there awkwardly in their first taste of public assembly, the students talking in whispers among themselves.

Someone shouted: "The police are coming!" And indeed Hoepelman and the others could see in the distance two rapidly approaching police buses. The crowd began to move off, until someone else, a student named Rojas Fernandez, climbed onto the pedestal of the Trujillo statue and cried out: "There's nothing to fear. This isn't a political meeting." Fernandez went on to say that all they wanted to do was regain the sanctity of the university, but before he could say more the police had dismounted from their buses, formed a ring around the crowd, and set up machine guns.

Two officers ordered Fernandez to come down from the

statue, and when he did they led him away in custody. A student bellowed, "Let's defend ourselves." But Hoepelman, seeing the helmeted men crouch behind their machine guns, had the presence of mind to warn: "No one move." And so ended, bloodlessly, the meeting. But the students were not yet through. Three days later, with Fernandez still in jail, a quickly summoned committee chose Hoepelman as provisional president of the Dominican Students Federation, and another rally was called on the campus to demand the release of Fernandez. By now, with foreign newsmen onto the story, Ramfis Trujillo was prepared to show some leniency. Fernandez was deported from the country. But at least a slight dent had been made in the Trujillo armor by public pressure.

The next big move came from Dr. Fiallo and the other members of the onetime underground Popular Revolutionary Union, now named, in the flush of political "liberty" pledged by Ramfis, the National Civic Union (U.C.N.). This was, rather than a mere shadowy movement, now an ostensibly active and legal party, with Dr. Fiallo as its leader. Still, caution dominated the actions of men unfamiliar with and uncertain of free assembly. In proclaiming the Dominican Republic's first massive public rally in thirty-one years (aside from those that used to be held to pay homage to *El Benefactor*), the U.C.N. placed notices in the press saying nothing about politics. Instead, tribute would be paid to fallen Dominicans, with the highly respected Dr. Fiallo as principal speaker. Thus, on July 29, 1961, there congregated in Independencia Square some eight thousand men, women, and children, most of whom were curiously quiet. The opening words from the gray-haired, dignified doctor were: "It has been a long time since I have wanted to speak to you."

What was his feeling? "A kind of emotion hard to describe," Dr. Fiallo recalls softly. "And then, after these few words, there was tremendous cheering and applause, and I knew the people had the same emotion." With the Trujillo machine still functioning, it was dangerous to say much, and so Dr. Fiallo confined his early remarks to a plea for "a halt to torture and persecution." But then, emboldened by the sight of O.A.S. representatives and United States reporters close by, he went on to say: "It is necessary to finish with the political power, the economic power, the military power of the Trujillos." There were no military bayonet charges, no reprisals. Victor Sallent, who was in the audience, says, "Liberty was intoxicating." People at last walked down the streets uttering, *"Libertad, libertad,"* as though it was a newly discovered phrase.

This, however, is not to suggest wild exuberance; there was no singing or dancing in the streets, because people still remembered the pernicious kind of Trujillo oppression, probably the most methodical in history. If you applied for a job in a government agency or one of the Trujillo enterprises—and these included six out of ten in the country—you had to list all relatives, even cousins twice removed, with the understanding that if you stepped out of line not only you but all your kinfolk might be punished, sometimes with torture and death. The memory of this alone was inhibiting, for the lists still existed in the files of the S.I.M. Nevertheless, *libertad* was a fine expression.

For Manuel Tavarez Justo *libertad* was a fact. Just before the O.A.S. investigators arrived he was so weak from a loss of fifty-four pounds (he is a slight man, anyway), and last-minute beatings, that he could not stand; he had to lie on the stone floor of his cell. But his jailers shaved him, and propped him up so he could answer questions from the O.A.S. (with guards in the background, he said he had not been maltreated). He was released almost the same hour the U.C.N. rally was taking place, after nineteen months of imprisonment. His home had been wrecked by Trujillo marauders, but at least he found his two children—a daughter, five, and a son, three—safely in the care of his mother-in-law. Of his wife there was only a photograph shrouded in black.

Four days later Tavarez Justo called a meeting of his 14th of June friends, and again what had been an underground movement became an official party, for by now Ramfis Trujillo was saying there would be amnesty for all former political prisoners and even exiles could return in safety. He even—as a sign of good faith—shipped out of the country Juan Abbes García, the hated chief of the secret police. García went to Tokyo as first secretary of the Dominican Embassy; but the S.I.M. itself remained intact with its 10,000 agents. Some exiles risked a return, though others, like journalist Germán Ornes, who thought it more prudent to remain in Puerto Rico, decided to wait until it really looked as if Trujilloism had vanished.

In the meanwhile, the first cracks in the fledgling parties were appearing. Some people, for instance, deserted the 14th of June Movement, claiming that its leader, Tavarez Justo, was too far left. They joined the more moderate U.C.N. But at the same time some U.C.N. members were grumbling that Dr. Fiallo was "oligarchic," and they defected to the 14th of June Movement or to a Fidelist outfit whose leader was still in hiding.

For a period, while everyone learned to catch his breath and sort out his political allegiance, the nation was quiescent. One feature, after the cruel repression in the wake of the assassination, was that Ramfis himself had no real desire for the exacting life of a dictator. His main interest was to preserve his wealth (much of it, anyway, in banks abroad), so he could pursue his more appealing career as a playboy. The O.A.S. commission, after a month's investigation, decided that the regime was indeed attempting to "democratize" affairs and to restrain the more bloodthirsty of *El Benefactor's* lieutenants who had, of course, everything to lose in any substantial relaxation. The figurehead president, Joaquín Balaguer, even invited Dr. Fiallo and other opposition political leaders to join a coalition government. They refused, unless a set of conditions would first be met, one of them being the immediate banishment of the twelve most dangerous military leaders, including the late dictator's brothers, Generalissimo Héctor Trujillo and General Arismendi Trujillo. Balaguer said he would discuss the terms —with his boss, Ramfis. Ramfis vetoed them and publicly accused Balaguer of exceeding the limits of his office. In a brief statement, Ramfis said it was "clearly understood" that any discussion about exile "would be contradictory and unacceptable to the position of the armed forces." Ramfis, who happened to be chief of the armed forces, obviously, and despite a growing distaste for the tribulations of leadership, was not yet prepared to jeopardize a regime made possible by the support of the generals.

But if Trujilloism could not be erased, at least the symbol of the man who had started it all could be wrecked. The next event was a major turning point.

On October 17—as student leader Armando Hoepelman recounts it—undergraduates at the University of Santo Domingo began to march, first to protest the retention of the Trujillo holdover, José Machado, as rector; then to destroy all images of *El Benefactor*. Machado, they felt, was simply a collaborator of the S.I.M., betraying professors who were trying to express what were still bold ideas. And Trujillo's own presence could still be seen in the scores of statues, portraits, and photographs dotting the campus buildings. Engineering students broke into their dean's office and ripped a huge framed picture of *El Benefactor* from the wall. Other students, hearing the commotion, raced from classrooms and forgot all restraints of the past few months. Soon *El Benefactor* was exterminated in a thousand bits of smashed plaster busts and shredded canvases. Balaguer instructed Machado to close the university. It was a foolish move, because now the students had nothing else to do but wander the streets and set off a wave of demonstrations.

High school students joined in, and so did many adults, parading down El Conde Street, invading restaurants and public buildings, and smashing every Trujillo image in sight. Police attacked with rifle butts, but the crowd roared a cry they now tried for the first time: *"Viva la revolución!"* It was contagious, and soon thousands of people were milling through the streets shouting it. Some students set up barricades in the heart of Ciudad Trujillo and proclaimed it *"territorio libre."* Police, they said, could enter this "free territory" only at their own peril. As the police did, they found themselves bashed on the heads by students leaning from windows with heavy bats and rocks. Riot squads used tear gas, and the students climbed to rooftops, from there to hurl gasoline bombs. For a while it looked as though the mobs would simply take over, but then, after four days of disorders, the police opened up with machine guns.

It was the end of the rioting, and, oddly enough, the end of Trujilloism—or so it seemed. For by now Ramfis was becoming really tired of the game, especially under prodding from Washington. If the United States could be blamed for a lack of sensitivity in the past about the Dominican Republic, it was now clearly determined to hasten liberalization. And it handled the situation skilfully, working out a plan of "disengagement" for Ramfis. Sanctions would be lifted, and Ramfis could stay on, provided he fulfilled two conditions: first, hand over genuine authority to a civilian government, and second, get Uncles Héctor and Arismendi Trujillo out of the country before their presence incited more trouble. Otherwise, it was implied, if disturbances broke out again, the United States might have to step in.

None of this, of course, was said publicly. Armed intervention, even against a loathed dictatorship, is a highly sensitive point among Latin Americans dedicated to the inter-American principle of nonintervention. But Ramfis managed to get his uncles out of the way; Héctor took to sea in a private yacht, bound for Bermuda; Arismendi, posted to Spain as ambassador, sailed in leisurely style aboard a Dominican frigate, pausing to relax at Nassau. Ramfis even announced that he would retire once sanctions were eased. These were encouraging signs, although Dr. Fiallo and other opposition leaders feared a double-cross; they pointed out that Héctor and Arismendi were really not far off and could return in a matter of two or three days if they so chose; moreover, they said, let Ramfis quit *before* the ending of sanctions, otherwise the O.A.S. would be giving away its strongest weapon. But the United States, as a measure of good faith, declared that it would recommend the ending of the boycott.

The plan fell apart in the middle of November when Héctor and Arismendi did in fact land again in the Dominican Republic. Technically, Ramfis had already written his resignation as chief of the armed forces, though this news was not made public for a few days. In the meantime, the uncles hastily set about to line up old Trujillo generals in an effort to restore the firm grip of Trujilloism as it had existed before *El Benefactor*'s death. The United States withdrew its recommendation to O.A.S.; Ramfis, thoroughly weary of the shuffling affairs of state, embarked for Paris, where part of his estimated cache of $400 million was located. There was no cheering with his departure, for the uncles, known as cruel and determined men, were far more dreaded than the pleasure-seeking Ramfis. Again a paralysis of fear swept the country. Anti-Trujillo leaders suspected their names were on a liquidation list. Dr. Fiallo and Tavarez Justo fled to Puerto Rico; others went into hiding. Their suspicions were not exaggerated. As it turned out later, the Trujillo brothers, with the aid of loyal S.I.M. agents, had marked for execution all the opposition politicians and resistance men who had emerged into the open; it would have been the greatest single massacre in the nation's history.

But there was no time for them to carry the coup to its completion. Two things happened almost simultaneously. An anti-Trujillo air force general, Pedro Rodríguez Echavarría, succeeded in withdrawing most of the serviceable military aircraft to his own base in the North; and at dawn United States warships appeared on the horizon. At first there were only three of them, but as they came closer, and then lay offshore, just beyond the three-mile limit, they were in plain view of the capital and their number had grown to fourteen. Among the vessels were two aircraft carriers with Marines prepared to land, if necessary, on Dominican soil by helicopter. Three squadrons of United States fighter jets roared across the waterfront, and, in the words of bank messenger Victor Sallent, "We cheered. It was a thrilling sight." If any Dominican, aside from a Trujillo, had any views on "intervention" he was not bothering to discuss them that day.

On that fateful Sunday, November 19, some of Rodríguez Echavarría's planes also approached the capital, to drop leaflets declaring air force support for the civilian government of Balaguer. Radio stations broadcast message after message, with a background of martial music, announcing at first the names of individuals, and then whole groups—such as associations of doctors and lawyers—who were pledging their lives against the attempted coup. Meanwhile, the Trujillo brothers were busy at the presidential National Palace trying to push Balaguer into their support. In a series of meetings, pro- and anti-Trujillo generals came and left, and at one point the United States consul-general dropped by—with a suggestion that the *Trujillos* had better leave. With an American fleet looming at one flank and Rodríguez Echavarría and his forces at the other, Héctor and Arismendi finally packed up. They took off shortly before midnight, along with a planeload of two dozen leading members of the Trujillo family.

It was the end of the Trujillo dynasty, but this fact hardly sank in. For at least a day, people such as Victor Sallent wandered the streets feeling "numb and puzzled" by the sudden release of tension. But by Tuesday the capital was wild with celebration. Dr. Fiallo and Tavarez Justo flew in from San Juan (on the same flight was journalist Germán Ornes returning home for the first time in six years), to find tens of thousands of uninhibited Dominicans clogging the road from the airport to town, weeping, cheering, throwing flowers. The last of the Trujillo statues and street signs were torn down, and President Balaguer decreed that henceforth Ciudad Trujillo would again be known by the name Columbus gave it, Santo Domingo.

It would be comforting to conclude with the above and say that they all lived happily ever after. Unfortunately, this is a true story about human beings, some groping and trying to adjust to light after darkness, others fearful of losing their superior positions. Within a week of the exodus of the Trujillo hierarchy, the Dominican Republic discovered itself caught in a power struggle that verged on civil war. On the one side were the newly emancipated politicians, such as Dr. Fiallo, backed by a restless populace; on the other were President Balaguer and General Rodríguez Echavarría, who had become the new chief of the armed forces. Balaguer and Rodríguez Echavarría, the people said, displayed courage in resisting the comeback attempt of the

Trujillo brothers but now they themselves were guilty of two-man rule.

Dr. Fiallo and other opposition leaders demanded that the president and the general resign in favor of a seven-man council whose task would be to prepare the nation for an election within a year. When this demand was rejected, the U.C.N. called a strike. Steel shutters banged shut on shops in El Conde Street, factories closed down, buses stopped running. The strike spread everywhere, quickly, and for eleven days mobs of rioters and demonstrators roamed through Santo Domingo shouting, "Down with Balaguer," and "Liberty! Liberty!" Victor Sallent was among them, and he remembers that he marched as much to experience the novelty as to protest against Balaguer and Rodríguez Echavarría. "We had never had a strike before in the Dominican Republic—at least in my memory—and so I suppose we were getting rid of some of the old Trujillo frustrations," he says with some accuracy. The U.C.N. raised funds to help those who had no money, and grocery stores opened their back doors for an hour or two a day to sell emergency food supplies. "It was good," says Sallent, "the way one helped the other."

But the atmosphere also became ominous. General Rodríguez Echavarría had to call out his troops to throw tear gas bombs at a mass of one thousand housewives who formed a parade; tanks engaged in clashes with other civilians who took to looting old Trujillo property. At stake, of course, was something fundamental. Backing President Balaguer and General Rodríguez Echavarría were Trujillo holdovers: businessmen, government officials and others who stood to lose money, power, and possibly their lives in any thorough purging of Trujilloism. One of the complaints against Balaguer was that many S.I.M. men were still in posts of authority. The armed forces, too, had to consider their own interests (Balaguer, to keep them appeased, raised servicemen's basic pay by $20 a month).

Even as Balaguer and Dr. Fiallo looked for a compromise to end the strike, a stipulation laid down by Rodríguez Echavarría was that no military man would ever be punished for actions committed under Trujillo. Finally, the idea of a seven-man council was accepted by Balaguer, but on terms more favorable to him than U.C.N. had wished: Balaguer would remain as president, to be replaced in any emergency by Rodríguez Echavarría. Meanwhile, in an ironic aside, United States warships still hovered just beyond the three-mile limit but were now accused—by the same politicians who had cheered them only a week or two previously—of propping up the Balaguer regime. It was a delicate situation for the United States. Having helped to get rid of the Trujillos, Washington could hardly act against Balaguer and Rodríguez Echavarría without risking the complaint that it was violating Dominican sovereignty. But kept in reserve were the economic sanctions, which were not yet lifted, as reminders to the two men to behave themselves.

On January 1, 1962 the Council of State took office, and the Dominican Republic looked, at last, as though it was on the proper road. The Organization of American States voted to remove diplomatic and trade restrictions, and Washington announced it would send a mission to see how the Alliance for Progress could help build up economic stability (in the disruptions following events of the previous six months, almost half of all Dominicans were thrown out of work). The University of Santo Domingo, closed since the middle of October, was reopened on January 9; and now the much-resented Trujillo appointee, José Machado, was replaced as rector by a man elected by students and the faculty in a popular vote: the first election in more than a quarter of a century. The campus was also declared inviolate territory; no armed body could gain admission without a permit from the rector.

There was, as Hoepelman recalls it, much rejoicing. This lasted precisely one week. On January 16 Hoepelman and other students heard machine-gun fire in the distance. The army was attacking a crowd of people who had gathered outside U.C.N. headquarters to hear over loudspeakers a fresh outburst of criticism against Balaguer and Rodríguez Echavarría. Six Dominicans lay dead, with a score wounded. Students promptly began a parade of protest to the National Palace, to demand the resignations of Balaguer and Rodríguez Echavarría, but, finding their way blocked by tanks, they returned to the campus. There, three hundred of them decided to go on a hunger strike.

But at ten o'clock that night they heard some unexpected news: Rodríguez Echavarría and one hundred soldiers had descended on the Council, the general saying that the Council was not functioning properly and he was taking over personally. The students, by now six hundred strong, and led by Hoepelman, decided that a hunger strike was no longer enough; and so they set about fabricating Molotov cocktails, by draining gasoline from parked cars, then throwing bottles of the volatile liquid at police and army patrols. And so once again "democracy" in the Dominican Republic was short-lived. But now the general, the former champion of the people, was in for a shock. The United States said it would not recognize his *junta,* and, moreover, it would call off the Alliance aid it had planned.

In the meantime, after a brief taste of press freedom, Germán Ornes was having his problems. Now, as editor once more of *El Caribe,* he sampled under Rodríguez Echavarría the same restrictions he had known under Trujillo. Censors moved in, and pulled out of type some of the stories that Ornes planned to publish; among the stories was a strong condemnation of the coup, and the crucial news that Washington was refusing to support the military regime. However, instead of filling the blank spaces with innocuous material, as he would have done under Trujillo, Ornes defiantly left them blank. The next morning *El Caribe* came out with gaping white columns, over which were printed in bold letters *Bajo Censure,* "under censorship."

Actually, Ornes did not have long to wait before printing the suppressed columns, because the general's coup collapsed after a brief forty-eight hours. A group of fellow officers marched in on him, and Rodríguez Echavarría now found himself under arrest. There were two main reasons for the turnabout: first, the threat of renewed economic pressures from the United States; second, the armed forces were beginning to feel the need, as Dr. Viallo explains it, "to be on the people's side." President Balaguer, sniffing the atmosphere, prudently took refuge in the residence of the papal nuncio. Mobs spilled out again in El Conde Street, singing "*Libertad, libertad.*"

The seven-man Council of State reconvened with a new president, Rafael Bonnelly, a leading figure in the U.C.N. The idea now was firmly implanted that the Council would rule as a caretaker government while the nation prepared for a general election. Dr. Fiallo was not eligible for the Council if he was to run as a presidential candidate. Eventually, both Balaguer and Rodríguez Echavarría were flown off to exile, with visas to Puerto Rico shrewdly arranged by Washington to get them out of the way. Was this, finally, the happy end to the tale? Not at all. Now the United States was the object of scorn by left-wing Dominicans who said Balaguer and Rodríguez Echavarría should not have been granted visas but should have been kept in Santo Domingo to face punishment. Anti-Yankee rioters burned the official car of the newly appointed United States ambassador, and, as a further token, looted the offices of Pan American Airways. Hoepelman disclaimed any student participation, saying the demonstration was organized by a new party known as the Dominican Popular Movement, led by a Castroite named Máximo López Molina. It was plain, early on, that Castro could be expected to make life as awkward as possible for the Dominican Republic's fresh government; it was as vital to him that a solution backed by Washington should fail as it was to Washington that it should succeed.

It was also clear that the birth of democracy could be painful and unsettling. At least, under Trujillo, the opposition was reasonably united; now the political parties showed the fragmentation characteristic of Latin America. Tavarez Justo explained it this way: "Previously, we were all preoccupied with a consuming hatred for Trujillo, the need to get rid of him. In effect, it was a negative force. Now for the first time we—all the parties—are faced with the realities of building a program." But such was the irony in a country learning to breathe politically that Tavarez Justo's 14th of June Movement was already weakened by internal rebellion; even the main party, U.C.N., had its disturbing splinter groups, one of them led by a Marxist politician, Jimenez Grullon, who had just returned after twenty-six years in exile to accuse Dr. Fiallo of possessing a "mentality of the oligarchy." Dr. Fiallo, in turn, said that Jimenez Grullon "has been away so long he has lost touch with the people and their needs." Another long-time exile, Juan Bosch, was directing the moderately leftist Dominican Revolutionary Party and busily condemning his rivals for being either radical or reactionary.

I arrived in Santo Domingo just as people were preparing to celebrate the first anniversary of *El Benefactor*'s downfall. The mood was a pathetic mixture of fear for the present and hope for the future. Trujilloism was far from ended, in the sense that few men in leading positions were completely free from charges of past collaboration with the dictator; this was almost inevitable in a state operated by one man who controlled almost all essential services and industries. Even the head of the Council of State, President Bonnelly, had at one time been Trujillo's minister of education. If the others on the Council—two physicians, a priest, two businessmen and a lawyer—had a "clean" record, they also lacked, as a result, experience in government administration. And so there was a vicious circle: in order to function with any degree of efficiency, the government still had to rely on men who had helped build up Trujillo's power.

On a visit to the National Palace I passed through several rings of heavily armed guards: a sign, President Bonnelly assured me, of the Council's determination to prevent further attempts at a coup. This, however, was a rather lame explanation, because it was obvious that the Council was able to operate only with the approval of the still powerful military leftovers from Trujillo's time. Any future government would also have to reckon with a military grip, despite soldiers' pleas that they preferred to stay "on the people's side." A few of the main Trujillo officers had been retired, but there was no massive purge of the old guard. Any attempt to clean house thoroughly would lead automatically to armed conflict. Civilian politicians even had to tread warily in dealing with the loathed S.I.M. secret police; a year after Trujillo, only a handful were under arrest, and not one S.I.M. officer had yet gone on trial. Curiously enough, this shaky truce with the military prevented massive bloodletting. Thousands of Dominican families were waiting to settle scores with the men who had oppressed them, but there was, by necessity, restraint. When one considers revolutions in other countries, the Dominican case was indeed remarkable; not more than forty persons died in the several riots and demonstrations that took place in the turbulent months following Trujillo's assassination.

"But you really can't call it a revolution, like Mexico's or Cuba's," said Germán Ornes, sitting in a frame of dejection in his *El Caribe* office. "It is a transformation, not a revolution." Ornes' prime concern was that too little was being done to start basic social and economic reforms. The Dominican Republic, he pointed out, was in a unique position. Since most of the land had been owned by the Trujillos, and now was confiscated in the name of the state, it was a perfect chance to introduce land distribution without the obstacles that exist in other Latin-American countries that have strongly entrenched landowning classes. "We must set up cooperatives, or in some other ways let the people feel they are participating in national life and helping themselves," Ornes said. "I thought Trujillo had destroyed the old oligarchy, and I even wrote this in my book. But I was wrong. The same men are active again, and we are drifting backwards." In essence, he feared that eventually much of the former Trujillo property would be sold privately to individuals "who have the same mentality as the oligarchs in Peru."

Editor Ornes was not alone in this thinking. Student Hoepelman said, too, that he did not believe there would be substantial social changes "because the ones in power do not seem to have a clear vision of the changes necessary. If changes are not made—if land goes back into private hands—we will be compelled to make more Molotov cocktails." Dr. Fiallo told me that he would not like to see the Trujillo estates publicly administered; rather, he said, they should be sold to private individuals or organizations "who would do a better job of running the land than any government." But to the far left of the scale, Tavarez Justo said land must be divided among peasants working in cooperatives, with larger sugar plantations remaining in state hands for efficient production. Dr. Fiallo calls Tavarez Justo a "Communist." If he is a Communist, he does not sound like one. He argues that Castro has done some good things, and many bad things, and he defines his 14th of June Movement as being close in sentiment to Britain's Labor Party.

The name-calling, the uncertain loyalties, the plain political shufflings, might be expected in any society reaching out for a new way of life. But some odd sidelights also accompanied the Dominicans' plunge toward democracy. Victor Sallent, for example, welcomed the freedom from fear and the chance to strike (bank messengers got a raise of ten pesos a month after a three-day walkout) but he disliked it when others went on strike and tied up services or supplies; at least under Trujillo's cold machine there was efficiency. When I last saw Sallent he complained: "We haven't been able to get cooking oil for a week" (because of a strike at the bottling plant), and "milk for our children is scarce" (because of faulty administration of the confiscated Trujillo farms and dairies).

Germán Ornes was having a task trying to educate people to the unfamiliar luxury of a free press. He printed on the front page of *El Caribe* a letter from the ex-president, in which Balaguer, writing from Puerto Rico, warned that the Dominican Republic was in danger of falling once again under a one-party system. Balaguer generously offered advice on how to avoid this peril. As soon as the letter appeared, Ornes received threatening phone calls from members of the various political parties. "It was not what Balaguer said that bothered them," the editor recounted, "but the fact that we had given him a public forum. They simply couldn't understand that people should have a chance to hear all sides of a story. Under Trujillo there was only one side."

Confusion also existed regarding the United States "intervention," which had been slow to start under Trujillo but was effectively and intelligently applied as time went on. Hoepelman, in remembering the approach of the United States fleet to speed the exit of the two uncles, said: "At first I didn't like it, but then I realized the pressure was for *our* good. It would have been better if it had ended there. But it seems to me that Washington's influence went too far, that the Council of State was set up as a convenience for the United States. The United States got rid of Balaguer only because it discovered he was not trustworthy." Such is the irrational talk one hears among a people who deplore intervention in principle but accept it if it conforms to what they consider a proper course.

Even the acting president, Bonnelly, rationalized about the United States warships: "Since the action did not go further than the presence of vessels *outside* territorial waters, no discussion is necessary. A discussion would be possible if a landing of Marines had taken place." Ornes, too, was clearly at conflict with himself over this issue. He said flatly: "There must be no intervention in Latin America." And then he contradicted himself by adding: "The only good example of intervention that I know of was here in the Dominican Republic." This statement, in turn, was qualified by still another, for he condemned the United States for making possible Trujillo's takeover in 1930, then for backing him until only a year or so before his fall. "But," Ornes said after a bit more reflection, "I suppose we are to be blamed, too. After all, we put up with him for nearly thirty-two years."

"What else could you have done?" I asked.

"Well," said Ornes, "we finally killed him, didn't we?"

Again this should be the place to write a firm "finis" to the story, but in many ways the story of the Dominican Republic is only beginning. The Trujillo clan looted the national treasury before their flight, weakening still further the economic structure. To help revive the economy, Washington pushed through large sums of Alliance for Progress aid; it also recruited Puerto Rico farm experts and industrial advisers who arrived in Santo Domingo speaking the same language as the Dominicans and minimizing any possible criticism of "Yankee neo-colonialism." The United States was openly committed to convert the Dominican Republic into a showcase of democracy and prosperity for other Latin Americans to compare with Cuba next door. Only the passage of time would answer the question whether the military and the politicians would pitch in to give their country stability.

Meanwhile, there were some encouraging signs. The first freely conducted election in decades took place in December. The fact that it was carried out peacefully, without major violence, was in itself almost a political miracle. Dominicans thus demonstrated a capacity and desire for democratic process. The results of the election were of far more than domestic interest, for they reflected a mood for reform, of a liberal or "left" variety, that is pressing from below the surface throughout Latin America. Juan Bosch, the moderate leftist, defeated Dr. Fiallo for the presidency. Although Dr. Fiallo was highly respected, and during the campaign proposed substantial economic and social reform, he was still identified with conservatism. Dominicans obviously preferred the "radicalism" of Bosch, who had no inner conflict about basic land reform for the benefit of the republic's predominantly rural population.

Most of the forecasts had said Dr. Fiallo would win, largely because he had remained inside the Dominican Republic to fight Trujilloism, while Bosch, a novelist and political science professor, had spent a quarter of a century in exile and security abroad. What the forecasts obviously failed to take into account was the temper of an impoverished, restless people more concerned about hope for the future than politics of the past. Fidel Castro had no hand in Bosch's election. There was no evidence of foreign "infiltration." On the contrary, O.A.S. had its observers present to ensure that Dominicans were neither tricked nor coerced in their selection of a leader. They chose a man of the distinct left, though, happily, non-Communist. However, the extent to which President-elect Bosch would be able to pursue his objective of wholesale reform remained to be seen, for he was far from popular with conservative elements and powerful Trujillo military holdovers.

11

"The Stars Are Low Tonight"

On my first visit to the Cuba of Castro, in August of 1960, I was greeted, along with other passengers at Havana airport, by a trio of guitarists who gallantly tried to compete with the drone of engines all around. As I stepped from the plane, the musicians broke into a cheerful smile, struck a happy tune and made me feel that perhaps Havana was still the gay place the old travel folders extolled. It was true that the waiting rooms were crowded with uneasy Cubans about to board the aircraft that had brought me over from Miami and was now going back. But these were the same kind of people who had begun the exodus shortly after the *barbudos,* the bearded ones, had roared triumphantly into Havana in January of 1959 to the ecstatic acclaim of at least 95 per cent of the populace. Among them were former Batista supporters or members of the *haute bourgeoisie,* disgruntled shopkeepers, and landowners who could hardly be expected to understand the mood of the revolution.

It was equally true that a slightly discordant note was reached on the radio of the taxi transporting me to the center of town; now another trio was at work, broadcasting a jingle, "Fidel Castro our pa-pa, Eisenhower ha-haha." Still, this could be put down to expected, if unsophisticated, exuberance of a small nation feeling new confidence in the shadow of a mighty nation it had long accused of domination. Other things were going pretty well. The "humanism" referred to by Castro may have smacked a little of communism, but not more than a little. Fewer than 10 per cent of Cuba's homes and farms had been "intervened"—that is, taken over by the state—and most of these had belonged anyway to Batista men and were now suitably used by Batista victims. There was plenty of food, and if gambling casinos, once frequented by American tourists, were temporarily closed in a surge of puritanism, the restaurants and night clubs offered enough scintillating diversity. At least 70 per cent of the people continued to give Castro their enthusiastic support.

On my second look at the country, in February, 1961, the demarcation had sharpened. Cuba unquestionably had gone "socialist"; 80 per cent of property had now been nationalized, and Castro's following had declined, though it still embraced better than half of the 7 million Cubans. However, the surface changes in six months were not overly distressing; food shelves remained stocked—if not with United States hams, at least with Polish hams. And the slogans were not much more devastating than the familiar *Cuba si, yanquí no*. It was on my third round, in March, 1962, that I found a shocking contrast. Instead of the strumming of guitars, I was greeted by the blasting from amplifiers of the *Internacionale*. The Cubans who now stood by to depart on my plane were no longer exclusively of the wealthy or aristocratic classes; they included artisans and truck drivers and other wage-earners. They were leaving behind them, on the other side of the glass barricades of José Marti airport, simply clad and tearful relatives. They were also leaving freshly introduced ration books, hunger, and disenchantment.

If the United States break in diplomatic relations and the trade embargo had had such quick effect, were not the Russians and other Communist-bloc nations supposed to be filling the gap, to be feeding the Cubans and helping to revitalize their industries? What had gone wrong, from Castro's point of view? *Venceremos,* the banners across Havana buildings proclaimed: "We will win." But the banners had said the same only a year previously; and now, at least to the eye, Havana had the frightening appearance of a person dying of cancer. Who was really winning? The Americans, the Russians, or the Cubans? What did Castro mean by "Libre" in the huge signs that confront every visitor? *Cuba: Territorio Libre de América.* For Cuba was unmistakably a police state.

And yet the ones who still supported him, perhaps half, perhaps fewer than half the population, kept repeating many times over the word *dignidad.* "We have attained dignity, the rest will follow," said a youthful Cuban, and he, possibly, in this simple language, was telling why the Cuban example, despite its setbacks or even horrors, was so meaningful to so many Latin Americans. Fidel Castro had a cynical but valid claim when he boasted to fellow Latin Americans, after the United States started a new and different aid program, "You have got to thank me for all that *yanquí* money." But was this the only reason why Cuba was so important in the Latin-American mind? If the Cuban revolution itself was inevitable, did the revolution inevitably have to take a Communist direction?

In the whirlpool of questions that occur today, and in the rigid bitterness of the United States toward the Cuban regime, what is sometimes lacking is perspective. It is convenient to talk in terms of black and white, of right and wrong, and to forget that at no time in the early stages of the Cuban revolution was there evidence of a Communist-Castro plot. On the contrary, the Communists in Cuba initially opposed Castro; moreover, it took the Russians almost two years after Castro's entry into Havana to decide that he was worth a tangible investment. The popular misconception today in North America is of an ordained, carefully calculated Communist course long before the world had heard of Fidel Castro. The lessons of history are important to relearn: essential, in fact, if we are to understand the atmosphere of the rest of Latin America and know how to accept the future Castros who are bound to arise, whether or not the prototype himself survives very long.

The story of Cuba's drift toward communism breaks into two parts. The first part is relatively easy to sort out with some certainty; for it involves history and statistics, and, to a degree, a short-sighted United States policy: a compound of government and business practices. This first part need not have ended disastrously. The second part, beginning with Castro's ill-fated visit to Washington three months after his takeover, is more complex in its sequence; and one cannot be so dogmatic about the causes and effects. Nevertheless, there is again indication that Washington, had it understood the mood of Cuba, might conceivably have avoided what it now calls a threat to hemisphere security. In citing the record, I am not so much reflecting my own appraisal as I am the estimate of responsible Latin Americans who, unlike North Americans, tend to regard Cuba in a whole frame and not merely in convenient compartments that portray Castro as all-villain. This broad view does much to explain why Latin-American intellectuals and many political figures sympathize with the Cuban revolution in its essentials, even though deploring the excesses of Castroism.

Cuba enjoyed a higher standard of living than most Latin-American countries; but income was unevenly distributed, especially in farming, which dominated the economy. Although people in Havana benefited from proximity to the

United States, the life of *campesinos* was characterized by extremely poor utilization of land and human resources. Only about half of the soil was cultivated. Of this territory, fully 75 per cent was turned to sugar plantations, building up one crop that accounted for the bulk of revenues. One of the richest agricultural states in the world, Cuba could not feed herself; she imported an enormous amount of food, about $100 million worth annually. Meanwhile, one third of the arable land was in American hands, and one third was owned by Cuban landlords, many of them absentees who disported themselves in the luxury of Havana or Miami and paid more allegiance to United States interests than they did to their own nation's needs.

Here was a set of circumstances crying for change, especially since American planters saw little compulsion, either, to involve themselves in the welfare of their employees. Three out of four *campesinos* worked as hired hands in the sugar plantations, usually for peak periods totaling four months of the year. The rest of the time they were idle and unpaid, reduced to subsistence living in dingy *bohios,* huts. Including city workers, almost one quarter of Cubans were constantly unemployed, a greater proportion even than in Canada or the United States at the height of the depression of the 1930's. Ernesto "Che" Guevara, one of the masterminds of the revolution, was not far off the mark when he outlined the old extremes of wealth and poverty. Cuba's cities, with the aid of United States technocracy, had five television channels and scores of radio stations. But when a group of ignorant rural children saw for the first time electric lights, burning in a Castro-built schoolhouse, they exclaimed: "The stars are low tonight."

Castro's movement against the Batista regime started in the hills of the Sierra Maestra, largely with the blessing of the peasants. He spoke of land reform as an inducement. His officers were from the intellectual and middle classes, but at least three quarters of his fighting men were of farm ancestry. In those early days the Communists dismissed Castro as an ineffectual "adventurer," in other words an amateur, and called him, according to their literature, "a romantic petit bourgeois." Basically, they disliked the fact that he had been able, where they had failed, to gain strength from the peasantry; such limited success as the Communists could claim was in the cities, among factory workers, a hangover from an old Batista deal to keep labor in line. But as Castro grew in stature, and when it appeared in mid-1958 that his revolt might succeed, the Communists sent an emissary, Carlos Rafael Rodríguez, into the hills to meet him and pledge their support. Castro may have had some woolly Marxist ideas; but, as he confessed years later, he had never been patient enough to get beyond page 370 in Marx's three-volume *Das Kapital*. His was to be a Cuban reformation geared to Cuban conditions.

In January, 1959, as Castro arrived in glory in Havana, his main pronouncements were pro-Cuban and not anti-American. He spoke of the urgency of agrarian reform, in a land dominated by individual United States and absentee landowners, and sensible social changes that even some officers at the U.S. Embassy, with whom I later spoke, had considered essential and had said so in their reports to the State Department. This enlightened American feeling, however, was not shared by the ambassador at the time, Earl E. T. Smith, a businessman and political appointee. Smith, in the Cuban view, was the archdisciple of "economic imperialism"; his sole interest was to protect United States investments that had been consolidated under Batista. These investments, of course, would be affected in any nationalization program. A month after Batista's departure, Smith was replaced by Philip Bonsal, an ambassador of rare stature and knowledge: a career diplomat who spoke Spanish and understood Cubans. When Bonsal arrived, relations between the United States and Cuba, though becoming strained, were still correct and hopeful. The slogan, "Cuba yes, Yankee no," had not yet been developed; instead, it was, "Revolution as Cuban as the palm trees."

The real, visible turning point came in April. Castro, on an invitation to speak to the American Society of Newspaper Editors, went to Washington accompanied by economic advisers. Publicly he announced: "We did not come here to get money. Many men come here to sell their souls. We are not that kind of people; we want only an understanding of the deep Cuban revolution." However, aside from an obvious desire to build sympathy, the motive undoubtedly was to obtain a United States loan that would help Cuba carry out agrarian reform (this has been reported by advisers who were with Castro and have since broken with him). Castro was not seen by President Eisenhower.

Technically, it was not necessary for the President of the United States to meet with the new leader of Cuba, since this was not an official state visit. But many months following this event, I encountered bitterness among informed Cubans, men who were disillusioned not only with their own regime but with the United States government; sadly, they recalled that Eisenhower had been busy playing golf. Whether the golf game was exaggerated out of proportion, it at least pointed up the sensitivity of Cubans groping for some recognition of their importance status. One wonders how Nikita Khrushchev would have behaved under similar circumstances; the Russians do not stand on protocol when there is a chance to win friends.

Castro was well received by the public, and the Acting Secretary of State, Christian A. Herter, gave a luncheon in his honor. He also had a session with the Vice President, Richard Nixon. According to some Cuban and United States reporters, Nixon, instead of talking of land reform—a priority stressed by Embassy officials but not, apparently, deemed advisable at the State Department level—spent most of his time warning Castro not to touch United States property in Cuba. Cubans argue that Nixon, characterizing American thinking, could not visualize the necessity for drastic economic and social changes, since these conjured up the horrible prospect of "socialism," a word abhorrent to the United States. Moreover, any state move against United States property in Cuba could set up a chain reaction throughout Latin America, where the United States had substantial holdings. There are some people, on the other hand, who claim that the Administration would have welcomed a request for a loan to get agrarian reform underway and pay American investors for any nationalization of the sugar estates. But, still according to this version, the United States did not want to make the first overtures lest Castro would accuse it of attempting bribery (the same kind of bribery Cubans said had gone on during the Batista era). Castro, for his part, was too proud to ask directly for a loan or financial assistance that would have been interpreted as a handout.

The foregoing part of the story is muffled in contradictions and counterclaims, and will long be debated. Whatever the truth, the known facts are these: the highest financial authorities approached by Castro aides during his trip to Washington were those of the World Bank and the International Monetary Fund; at no time were there negotiations on the level of the United States Administration. On reflection, some State Department officials have admitted to me that feelers could have been made indirectly, through second parties, thus saving face on both sides, a device commonly used by European statesmen. But the tragic sum total was that Castro left the United States empty-handed and indignant. From New York he flew to Buenos Aires to attend a meeting of the "Committee of Twenty-One," a new economic unit of the Organization of American States. There he astonished everyone by proposing what later was to become the basis of the Alliance for Progress; he suggested that the United States should advance to Latin-American countries fifty billion dollars over a ten-year period to finance the economic and social development of the continent.

The proposal got nowhere. But it enhanced Castro's reputation among at least some Latin Americans: the ones who even today attempt to place in focus the sequence of happenings so that failures and betrayals would be blamed not only on Cuba but on the United States as well. In Caracas, for example, Ignacio Luis Arcaya, who is the Number Two man in the Republican Democratic Union (U.R.D.), the second strongest party in Venezuela, spoke to me for a concentrated two hours on this subject. When U.R.D. was still in coalition with Betancourt's Acción Democrática Party, Arcaya served as foreign minister; he resigned in 1960, refusing to follow Betancourt's instructions to sign a resolution at a San José conference of O.A.S. obliquely chastizing Cuba for accepting Soviet aid.

But, returning to the Buenos Aires meeting of 1959, Arcaya, who was there, said: "The United States in its craziness faced too late the problem of Castro. Castro in many ways has a child's mind, and in Buenos Aires he sounded as though he was talking to a doll. However, after he proposed that the United States should solve Latin America's problems by lending a lot of money, I remember talking with Thomas C. Mann (Assistant Secretary of State for Economic Affairs) and saying that this particular idea of Castro's was a good one. Mann said, 'Impossible. How can we expect the American taxpayer to go for it?' I said, 'Do it now, while there is still time—not four or five years from now.' Instead, the United States delegation got Nicaragua and Haiti to say that Castro was insulting the dignity of Latin-American countries by begging for money. That was the end of that. Now Washington says that the Alliance for Progress is the salvation of Latin America."

If Arcaya was demonstrating remarkable hindsight, he was expressing at the same time a commonly heard (though nongovernmental) dilemma in Venezuela as in other republics: "The trouble today is that there is a fight between the United States and Cuba: the big fish trying to swallow the small one. We have to be on the side of Fidel Castro because he is a symbol for all Latin America."

The open, no-holds-barred fight built up swiftly, and the violent hate campaigns began on both sides, with Castro in July, 1959, accusing the United States of "interfering" in Cuban affairs; there is little doubt that he plunged into an unjust and vitriolic campaign of distortions and half-truths against the United States government ("imperialist, terrorist, aggressive"). Even the well-disposed Ambassador Bonsal received personal insults. Gradually, heartsick and gloomy, Bonsal felt impelled to talk to other diplomats about the "cynical" attitude of the Castro regime.

There are some who say that the United States showed great patience and forbearance, striving to avoid countercharges that would impair disastrously United States-Cuban relations. There are others, however, who argue that the United States, as a big and mighty power, should have shown even more restraint, should have understood—as hard as it might have been—the unpleasant truth that a small Latin-American state was letting off steam and was acting like a petulant child that had just told Big Daddy where to get off. The British, in their history of gunboat diplomacy, have heard much language of abuse, but over the centuries have learned to cope with it. When Ghana achieved independence, Kwame Nkrumah continued to shout about Britain's "evil colonialism." Such newspapers as London's conservative *Daily Express* urged that Ghana be taught a lesson and expelled from the Commonwealth.

But Prime Minister Macmillan and the British government, aware that in any revolution someone has to be the whipping boy, kept silent and ignored the jibes; Ghana and Britain today are on friendly terms. It was not the United States press alone that reacted against Castro's abusive language. The State Department itself joined in the battle of words, giving Castro a chance to goad his people into still more anti-Americanism and warn them to beware of "counter-revolutionaries."

There is no doubt that some of the leaders of the revolution, Guevara among them, had at least flirted at one time with communism. And it may well be that they were happily awaiting this turn in order to introduce with greater ease a Communist pattern in Cuba. Whatever the reasons, the Communists undoubtedly came into their own rather early on, when two Communist trade unionists volunteered to go to Prague and, through channels there, got the Russians to offer trade on barter, an appealing prospect to Castro confronted by a growing shortage of cash. This was followed, in February, 1960, by a visit to Havana of Anastas Mikoyan and a trade agreement between Cuba and the Soviet Union, an agreement to which the United States took exception.

The Partido Socialista Popular (Communist Party), as a reward for starting the ball rolling in Prague, was given the status of an open, legal party: the only political party, in fact, in Cuba, since Castro's 26th of July Movement was not a political entity, even in those days. Communists resumed full leadership of the trade unions, and through them developed a foolproof device for confiscation of Cuban property as well as United States holdings. Union workers had simply to complain that the management of a company was "counterrevolutionary" and the government "intervened." Action by Cuba was followed by quick reaction by the United States. When Castro took over American oil firms, claiming they had violated Cuban law by refusing to refine Soviet oil, Washington promptly cut the quantity of Cuban sugar it had been buying. The Russians and Chinese picked up much of the slack, throwing the Cubans into greater economic dependency on them.

Cubans quote the record and say they were compelled to deal with Communist countries in order to save their economy. Some European and Latin-American commentators hold that Castro was doing nothing more than Nasser did during the Egyptian revolution: playing off the East against the West in order to attract the best of two worlds. This argument, of course, loses some of its force when one remembers that Nasser, in dealing with the Russians, had no truck with any internal Communist group. Nevertheless, the broad, big issue must still be kept in mind. Patrick O'Donovan, the British journalist who won major United States awards for his sympathetic accounts of the American scene over a number of years for *The Observer* of London, found himself reporting from Havana as late as February 19, 1961: "I do not believe that the revolution was a Communist conspiracy.... It has been bending further and further in the direction of communism, because its leaders are opportunists and have got almost all they asked from the Soviets, because they have been utterly rejected by the West. Even to make the sort of revolution they planned in the hills ... the breaking of the economic and political power of the foreign companies, the redistribution of land, the total destruction of the old pro-American regime, this would have meant the same degree of furious not-wanting-to-understand rejection. The American fear of communism so close to her shores, the intransigence of her interested business leaders, and of their natural representatives in Congress has gone far to create and plant communism in Cuba."

Harsh though this appraisal might seem to United States citizens, it does represent dispassionate foreign opinion. More specifically, it is an accurate mirror on much Latin-

American thinking. "Even if Fidel had Donald Duck as his symbol, American business circles would still try to destroy him," commented a Brazilian congressman, Wilmar Orlando Dias. "His crime had nothing to do with doctrine: it is the fact that he has ended the dominance of the big United States corporations. We are all, in varying degrees, in the same cage, and even if we plan to use different methods from Castro's, our object is the same: to free ourselves from the political and economic grip of the United States."

Thus, the main point produced by Latin Americans is that Castro probably would not have been considered such a knave if United States business interests had not been aroused. Much of the public indignation in the United States undoubtedly came from the fact that the regime seized the property of United States concerns without paying a cent as compensation. This bitter resentment only contributed to a breakdown in contact and a refusal even to attempt to fathom the nature of Cuba's revolution and the reasons behind it. But lost in the uproar was a barely publicized note. For more than twelve years the United States government had made available to United States investors going into foreign countries an inexpensive insurance policy. The policy, underwritten by the American taxpayer, guaranteed against outright seizure, nationalization of assets, sudden restrictions on the export of profits, or other unforeseeable developments. Ironically, not a single American enterprise confiscated in Cuba had ever bothered to take out the insurance. Here was a touch of arrogance, myopia, or shocking unawareness of the real mood of Cubans. Today, of course, in the aftermath of the Cuban experience, United States investors in Latin America are more realistic and are willing to apply for the policy.

In this speedy world of emerging nations, of former colonies, political or economic, the story of Cuba is crucial. I mention "political" as distinct from "economic" colonies, because this is a differentiation that even anti-Castro Cubans make in an effort to trace the background of the revolution. The British, at the height of their empire days, may have had a profit motive in establishing colonies; but they also had a sense of responsibility toward the people they directed. They built hospitals and schools; and generally they showed an obligation, even if paternalistic, toward the welfare of their subjects. The same instinct may have applied in the cases of individual United States firms setting up business in Cuba; and, in fact, it can be said that Cubans, under American economic paternalism, enjoyed a better material scale than all but one or two other Latin-American countries. But by the very nature of the American system of free enterprise there could be no control from Washington to ensure that *all* firms would take into account the interests and needs of the Cuban people.

Many of these firms, in self-defense, pleaded that they could do business only by bribing the old regimes, latterly the Batista government. It is true, in turn, that Batista did build some schools, but again for a profit motive. Some of the schools, once fat construction contracts had been padded in a series of kickbacks, never opened their doors. In others, teachers were hired at relatively high salaries and permitted to subcontract their jobs to less qualified teachers at lesser salaries; they themselves lived off the profit margin. This kind of corruption only added fuel to the fire of nationalism among a people who saw much of the benefit of American enterprise going into a few pockets and not their own.

I am not at all sure that the U.S. State Department was wrong when it assumed early on that Castro's revolution was turning Communist; I am not even sure that much could have been saved if the United States had acted in a different fashion. These are now academic debates because Cuba, as of 1962, was plainly Communist. I am merely throwing out a few observations most commonly heard among Latin Americans who plead for a better understanding of the Cuban transition and who fear the same pattern in their own countries, if the same set of conditions continue to prevail.

Much of the atmosphere of Cuba on my last visit had turned, from a formerly hopeful and colorful one, to grimness and grayness, even in small ways. Gone were the picturesque characters who had made Havana, when the inflow of tourists ceased, an intriguing Hong Kong or Tangier of the Americas. What, for instance, had happened to the counterparts of Paul Wilson, an Americano I met, as he sat in dejection in Sloppy Joe's bar, one hot August afternoon in 1960? Wilson, thirty years old, thin-faced and highly strung, was by his own admission a former convict. He claimed he had worked as a "spy" for the U.S. Air Force in Germany, and was "unjustly" accused of going AWOL into East Germany, when, all along—he insisted—he was over the border in pursuit of his trade, espionage. Anyway, one irrefutable fact was that Wilson was convicted of grand larceny and forging military orders, and he even grandly produced for my benefit papers to prove it. Wilson spent three years in prison and was then released on parole, on the condition that he remain in Miami with his mother.

But now, as we sat drinking a daiquiri, he said that he had been unable to land any job short of ditch-digging, and so he had decided to break parole and skip to Cuba. This was a fairly shrewd maneuver, since Castro, in his anti-Washington temper, was hardly likely to honor any demands for Wilson's return. Wilson, on arriving at Havana airport, confessed all to immigration officers and said he wanted to work for the revolution, either in the secret police or as a propagandist. Cuban officials, not knowing what to do with him, bundled him off to the Sevilla-Biltmore Hotel and said the government would pick up the tab. But now, a week later and with no word from anyone about a job, Wilson was afraid he would be stuck with the hotel bill and deported. He had cabled friends in the United States, asking for some money so he could move on to Brazil, far from the reach of the F.B.I.

He was also planning to contact William Morgan, the American adventurer who had fought alongside Fidel Castro in the Sierra Maestra and had rounded up some counter-insurgents making a landing from the Dominican Republic. Wilson hoped his fellow countryman was sufficiently well in with Castro to ring up and say, "Fidel, I want you to help my friend." Wilson was somewhat downhearted when I suggested that Morgan, sharing the same fate as other Americans who had once served a purpose, was no longer a man of influence; he had just been put in charge of a frog farm some forty miles from Havana (and subsequently, on March 11, 1961, was executed as a "counterrevolutionary").

The last I saw of Wilson was when he slipped out for the third time in two hours to see if any money had arrived at the cable office. On my next visit, six months later, there was no sign of Wilson, and I never did discover his fate. Sloppy Joe's, however, was still a hangout, though with a diminished number of Americans—only a few reporters. Sloppy Joe's bar was famous long before it became a backdrop for the film *Our Man in Havana.* Dario, the chief bartender, remembered how the bar, sixty feet in length, was once so crowded with tourists that it took in $6,000 a day; now it averaged $30 to $40 a day. It was while sipping a daiquiri here that Alec Guinness was recruited by Noel Coward for the British Secret Service. Dario, who earned $20 for appearing in the brief movie scene at the bar, also recalled that part of the fee was eaten up, because Guinness and Coward neglected to pay for their drinks.

If the fictional flavor had vanished, some real-life drama still remained in February, 1961, when I sat beside a Cuban newsman, listening to his quiet but bitter denunciation of Castro. A man came in from the darkened streets, clutching a leaflet that he slipped to the Cuban newsman. The leaflet had just been dropped from a plane that had cut its engine to swoop, undetected by antiaircraft batteries, over Havana's rooftops. The leaflet, one of thousands dropped that night, urged students to go out on strike *"contra la tirania."* "What time," asked the Cuban newsman of his friend, "did the plane arrive?" Ten minutes ago, he was told. The Cuban newsman glanced at his watch and said, softly, "It was five minutes late."

Alas, on the third visit, a year later, the Cuban newsman had gone—luckily escaping, I learned, the massive roundup of suspected saboteurs that took place immediately after the ill-fated invasion attempt of April, 1961. Sloppy Joe's was bereft of all "characters"; the only tipplers were a few hardy Cuban workmen who seemed uncomfortably out of place. Also missing were the sounds of explosions—the small plastic bombs—that had occurred with regularity every night in Old Havana. The only outward signs of resistance to Castro were scribblings on the walls of rest rooms in bars and restaurants (and sometimes, with more effect, the firing of cane fields to hamper the economy). The crushing of the invasion, and the sweeping in of 50,000 suspects, among whom there were many innocents—but also, just by the sheer weight of chance, key saboteurs—had had its effect, at least at that point.

Now the hangout was the bar of the Capri Hotel, a rather sad letdown, because "characters" included only a couple of Canadian pilots ferrying stuff back and forth between Cuba and Canada, one or two visiting British journalists, and a small assortment of Britons who posed as reporters but whose actual occupations were in doubt (there was still trade to be done). Among the legitimate fulltime correspondents were one man from Reuters,[1] one from Agence France-Presse, and an Argentine citizen heading up the Associated Press bureau; United Press International was staffed entirely by Cubans, working for a Yankee outfit at some risk to themselves.

Since the invasion, there had been active censorship of outgoing stories, with a member of the union of telegraphers sitting in judgment in every cable office. Nothing was said to correspondents about what was cut or killed, unlike the old practice of censorship days in Moscow when foreigners at least could see the slashings before copy was transmitted. In some instances words were even added to alter meaning. When Guevara, for example, said in a speech that in some sectors production had faltered, and there must be improvement, a zealous censor changed a dispatch to read that production had not slumped and that advances had been substantial. In a log kept by Reuters over a ninety-day period of 207 cables written, 31 failed to arrive at their destination, 44 lost some words, and 10 gained words. The hazards to life and limb were equally unpredictable. A British free-lance photographer, in Havana two years, had been arrested nineteen times, mostly in the past few months. Speaking of his last confinement, he said dryly, "Six days in, twenty-four hours out."

The tightened security was only one manifestation of the marked changes that had taken place in a year. I was struck instantly by the incredible physical deterioration, even to the extent of the few cars on the roads of Havana. But the main changes were in attitudes, the open grumbling, brought about largely by the shortages of food and other essential materials. Cuba never had a shortage of government critics; these had even existed in 1960 and 1961. I remember hearing

[1] The Reuters man, John Bland, was expelled in September, 1962. British, European, and Canadian newspapermen, who up to then could enter Cuba freely, simply by showing their passports, were now required, as in the case of United States reporters, to obtain visas.

a typical example of the sarcastic humor: a double play on G2, the secret police organization, and a favorite Cuban song, "We'll Pass a Thousand Years—And a Little More." Castro, the story went, dropped into a cafe and was promptly besieged by admirers. "Say, Fidel," one man finally said, "when are we going to have those elections you promised so long ago?" Castro motioned toward a jukebox and told his questioner to press button G2. Out came the favorite song.

But this was the kind of story spread at the time largely by the wealthy Cubans who still remained, and by some of the professional groups—doctors, lawyers, and journalists—who had hoped for liberal social reforms and a stable government but feared that Castro was converting the revolution into the classical egalitarian lines of class hatred. The stories I heard in 1962 were of a much more embittered nature, and, more significantly, were told by humble folk who were important to the revolution. So long as the big flexible mass of people ate sufficiently well, there was reasonable contentment; and the remarks were restrained. But now privation had brought about openly resentful comments. One man, a dock worker, tried on me what I later discovered was a prevalent routine. "I want some boots," he said.

"Boots?" I said. "How many pairs? One, two?"

"No, seventy thousand pairs."

"Seventy thousand?" I echoed. "Don't you know you can be put in jail for black marketeering?"

"Bring them back filled with Marines."

This was not entirely facetious humor. Anti-Castro Cubans realized that the United States would hesitate itself to participate in an active invasion without at least a technical excuse. But what would happen, they asked, if desperate housewives started rioting and looting, and a whole series of contagious mob scenes took place? What would happen if one outburst after another had to be suppressed by gunfire and the killing of women? And then if a clandestine radio appealed, "in the name of the Cuban people," for active intervention? The mere fact that these hypothetical questions were thrown at me was in itself startling, for only a year previously I had noted (and reported in news dispatches) that any invasion attempt, even by Cuban exiles acting in the name of Cuba, would be highly hazardous, because the regime still could count on considerable support. But now there was a new factor, severe rationing, with women creating disturbances in market places when rations were not forthcoming.

In 1961 there were some minor shortages, of foodstuffs and household items such as soap; but these were nothing more than petty irritants. In 1962 the shortages had grown to ominous proportions. Women lined up outside grocery stores and markets at midnight, waiting for the doors to open at seven in the morning. When I visited shops at eight o'clock, entire supplies had vanished; and the women walked away clutching parcels of three or four onions, two or three bananas and—if they were there early enough—three quarters of a pound of meat to last a person a week. The only remaining foodstuffs I saw were tomato purée and bottles of ketchup. On ration were twenty-two basic commodities, including milk for young children. In my hotel, the Riviera, I had to make do with breakfast of dry toast and black coffee; in eight days I had one egg. On nightly tours of the best restaurants I was lucky occasionally to find two or three bits of stewed beef in a platter; otherwise my meals consisted of macaroni or black beans, with occasional fruit salads as the main course. "If this is the Russian shop window for Latin America," said a non-Communist diplomat, "it is a pretty empty one."

Why had Russia and other Communist powers not done more for Cuba? Why had Russia not shipped over masses of food and goods to make Cuba in fact the shop window for Latin America, to consolidate what would appear to be a heaven-sent opportunity? The glib answer was that Russia and China, both with harvests below expectation, could not afford to feed extra mouths. But this theory was weakened when one considered that only six or seven million additional mouths would not be an overwhelming burden, especially since the prize was so valuable. Cuba's food shortage became critical only around January and February, 1962. It is possible that the Russians were misled by earlier optimistic forecasts of Castro and his colleagues about the Cuban capacity to swing from a primarily sugar economy to diversified agriculture; it is likely also that the Cubans themselves miscalculated what the Soviet bloc could do for them. But more probably—and this is a theory shared by Western and some Eastern diplomats with whom I spoke in Havana—the Russians made a slow start in Cuba because they were never entirely certain of the stability of the regime or the direction in which it was heading. What follows has a bearing on this fascinating aspect of the Cuban revolution.

In August, 1960, I stayed at the Havana Libre Hotel. Until a few months previously, though owned by the Cuban union of gastronomic workers, it had been managed by the Hilton chain. And then it was "intervened." An eighteen-year-old youth named Rancano was named as "interventor," which meant that he was now the director. His qualification for the job was that he had once worked as a bus boy in the employees' cafeteria (other staff people commented sourly that he had never been efficient enough to qualify even for the guests' coffee shop). Now, resplendent in militia uniform, an automatic and holster prominently in view, Rancano cut a dashing figure as he wandered through the lobby. There was considerable informality about the way the hotel was run, almost symbolic of the island's erratic economy. Six elevators were lined up in a double bank, but only two functioned at any given moment, usually rising or descending together.

Despite the poor service I found the Havana Libre exciting, especially since I lived for five days in what amounted to the Soviet Embassy. This arrangement came about by accident, and it struck a reassuring note: Russian and Cuban security is far from perfect. When I checked into the hotel, I was given Room 1825, and I was alone on the vast floor for almost two weeks (tourists by now had stopped coming). But gradually some Russians began to appear. They were, I learned, the vanguard for Sergei Koudriavtzev, who was about to establish the first Soviet Embassy in Cuba since 1952. Koudriavtzev, I recalled, had been a secretary in the Soviet Embassy in Ottawa back in the 1940's, and was named by a cipher clerk, Igor Gouzenko, as the organizer of the spy ring that shook Canada, and the West generally, shortly after World War II.

I was not aware of it at the start, but the eighteenth floor of the hotel was to be Ambassador Koudriavtzev's new embassy until permanent quarters could be found. My room, at the end of the long corridor, was part of a three-room suite, and the next thing I knew was that Koudriavtzev himself, in Rooms 1821-23, was my suite-mate. The inner doors were locked; but once in a while, I could hear the ambassador gargling or engaged in conversation. This small Western island in a Red Sea was obviously an oversight, and some poor Cuban and Russian security officers were going to have to do a lot of explaining. Aside from the point that I could easily have planted a microphone on Koudriavtzev, I received phone calls intended for the Embassy. Once, an amused hotel switchboard operator said, "What are *you* doing in that den?"

Finally, after a few days, I decided it was time to exploit my luck, and I slipped a visiting card under Ambassador Koudriavtzev's door suggesting a neighborly drink. The next morning I had a phone call from someone who said he was the ambassador's secretary, saying that while Mr. Koudriavtzev would like very much to meet me—especially since I was a Canadian and he had fond (!) memories of Canada—he was terribly busy, and could I wait until next week? Ten minutes later the phone rang again. It was, not surprisingly, the chief room clerk, filled with apologies. He had not realized, when I was assigned my room weeks previously, that it had been booked by someone else, and could I conveniently move down one floor?

"When?" I asked.

"Right away," he said firmly. Later, my switchboard operator consoled me by saying I was much safer in my new quarters. Only the night before, two small bombs were exploded outside the Havana Libre in Ambassador Koudriavtzev's honor.

I never did get to see him. But Koudriavtzev told some envoys that he was bewildered by the so-called Marxism he found in Cuba. Old-line Communists were more orthodox than the Russians, while younger ones had a Cuban flamboyance irritating to the dour diplomat. Possibly, Koudriavtzev was saying these things to confuse westerners. But at that stage another analysis made sense: Koudriavtzev was not at all sure that Castro had the stability to stay in power, and he was reluctant to take a gamble that might prove as much a slap in the face as did the eviction of Soviet diplomats from the Congo only a few months previously. Certainly there was no great rush on the part of the Russians to ship in huge quantities of supplies. Some Czech arms began to appear in the fall of 1960, but no substantial program of assistance was arrived at until the Communist summit conference in Moscow in November-December of that year.

One theory is that the Chinese got the Russians to agree that activities should be stepped up in Latin America, starting with the natural investment ground of Cuba. Another is that Guevara, who in December traveled first to Moscow, then to Peking, then back again to Moscow, skilfully played the Chinese against the Russians in extracting the greatest aid any country outside the Soviet bloc had ever been promised. Between them, the Russians and Chinese were now committed to take most of Cuba's sugar crop in exchange for goods. In addition, Russia extended an initial interest-free credit of $200 million; China $60 million; Czechoslovakia $40 million; East Germany $10 million—to be spread over the next few years in the construction of Cuban factories.

But still the story was hazy. I had an interview with Guevara two months after his return, and he spoke glowingly and optimistically of the future, thanks to the barter and credit arrangements he had just completed. He cited the introduction of 180 factories to make substitutes for the United States equipment and supplies on which Cuba had been reliant. These factories were in various stages of development, he said. Some were merely being "studied," but thirty-four had already been contracted for, and "several" would be completed by the end of the year 1961. Just as examples, he singled out a Czech-designed plant that would be turning out building tools in three months, and another Czech plant that would be manufacturing spark plugs ("for any kind of car, including American") in December. This was by way of refuting the American claim that Cuba would collapse without United States replacements for its existing machinery.

"You say," I pointed out, "that your move has been against what you call American economic colonialism. Isn't there now the danger that you will become totally dependent on the Soviet Union and its allies? In other words, they will want a reward at Cuba's expense, and you will be back where you started."

Guevara replied by recounting his meeting with China's Premier Chou En-lai: "When we were writing the final communiqué, in which was mentioned China's 'disinterested' help to Cuba, I insisted on clarification—until Chou said again and again, and we accepted it, that China was not disinterested in helping Cuba. On the contrary, China was offering quite selfish help, because in helping Cuba the Chinese were maintaining the front against United States imperialism. And so we were on common ground. Besides, it is precisely forbidden for a factory built here to be owned, say, by the Chinese. Personally, I do not fear the kind of colonialism you speak of. We are giving back as much as we receive."

My interview with Guevara took place in his office at the National Bank, of which he was president, shortly before he became minister for industry. If Castro was the inspirational chief of the revolution, Guevara was its brains, the acknowledged strategist who applied ability, coolness, and competence, in contrast to Castro's bombast and instability. A handsome man in his early thirties, the Argentine-born physician exuded charm, dedication, and single purpose, to make, in his words, "Cuba a fully socialist state." There have been suggestions that Guevara was long a Moscow-oriented Communist, subject to orders from higher authority. This allegation has never been substantiated. The truth, I believe, is that he was motivated by a deep dislike for the United States and a genuine belief in Marxism as an answer to problems of impoverishment and illiteracy, but on Latin-American terms. Any doubts about Guevara's faith in Marxism can be dispelled even in the simplest dialogue. Midway through the interview, my ballpoint pen ran dry. Guevara reached for two fountain pens in the breast pocket of his olive-green battle tunic. One was American, the other Russian. "Coexistence?" I asked. "Coexistence," he said with a grin.

I tried first the Russian pen, but the nib was rough and the ink flow erratic. Then I picked up the American pen; it was smooth and efficient. I pointed out how much better it was than the Soviet product. "Yes," admitted Guevara. "The Russian pen is not very good. But in China I found a pen even better than the American one, and it was made by the Chinese." I said I had been to China just a couple of years before him and had not found any pen very satisfactory. "Two years ago?" said Guevara lightheartedly. "It just proves that socialist progress is very rapid."

But the whole of the interview was not in this easy-going vein. At times Guevara was reflective, in admitting to shortages and betraying second thoughts about attitudes toward the United States. "Maybe we made mistakes; maybe we have not guided ourselves in the best way, the way some people with diplomatic experience would have done," he confessed, and then went on: "We are honest and simple revolutionaries. You should remember the moment when actions were taken. We never really planned; we reacted. When someone is kicked, he tries to kick back as strongly as he can, without thinking whether he will be kicked again." But what could be done now to achieve some sort of harmony with the United States? "We could look," he said, "to a new formula." But he could not spell out further what such a formula might consist of, short of emphasizing the sensitivity of Cubans: "Any new formula would be arrived at on equal terms." He added: "If American firms whose property was confiscated would like to send representatives to Cuba to discuss ways of settling differences, they would be well received." But all this, it was evident, would be within the framework of Cuba's economy, which he defined as not yet "socialist" (Communist) but swiftly coming near it. In sum, Guevara wanted a restoration of trade and diplomatic relations with the United States, but on a "coexistence" basis.

I did not detect, at that time, any sense of desperation. On the contrary, there was supreme confidence that the Cuban economy would be built up with Soviet assistance. Shortages? (Salt and soap were absent from the shelves.) "These will be remedied very soon, with supplies due in by ship," Guevara said. Future shortages? "We are still not able to see exactly the next shortage," he said. "If we could, we would have the perfectly planned economy, and this has not yet been reached." When did he expect such an ideal state? "With the right effort, next year."

But in the next year, as I saw, the economy of Cuba had reached the proportions of chaos and disaster. Where were the factories Guevara had forecast with such confidence? Where was the foundation of the Soviet-designed steel rolling mill, with a capacity of 1.2 million tons, which he said would be abuilding in 1962? Where, even, were the Czech factories for simple farm tools, or spark plugs, or any of the other thirty-four industries for which contracts had been let? The only establishments so far built by the Eastern partners were four insignificant ones: a tomato cannery (Hungarian), a cotton mill (Chinese), a biscuit bakery (East German), and a pencil factory (Czech). A few Czech and East German plants, for household goods, were under construction in the interior, but none would be in production before 1963 or 1964. What had gone wrong? In a remarkably candid public speech, Guevara denounced "absurd plans, totally unreal dreams about targets or quotas," and heavy-handed bureaucracy.

"We find ourselves in a paradoxical situation," he said. "The revolution is one year older, has dealt with an enormous number of difficulties, but we are further behind than last year. Why? Because we put into action a series of bureaucratic brakes, and we have diluted responsibility and dynamism . . . we have lost our altitude, dropped into an air pocket." In essence, Guevara blamed a slump in revolutionary ardor, which was true up to a point, but hardly the whole explanation. The story, painfully, was that neither the Russians, who started slowly, nor the Cubans, who overestimated their own ability, ever anticipated the crisis of 1962.

First there was sheer inefficiency on the part of Cubans, who, having lost their skilled managerial people, simply could not cope with the practical side of planning. For a while, when transport broke down, they had an excuse that United States replacement parts were unavailable; Czech and Soviet trucks (aside from military vehicles) had not yet arrived in quantity; besides, it would be prohibitively expensive to scrap a United States truck just because of a worn-out generator—and Canadian-made spare parts, contrary to United States belief, never filled the gap. Canada's trade with Cuba dwindled by 1962 to virtually nothing, because Canadian exporters, refusing Cuban barter offers, demanded cash payments; Cuba did not have the dollars to spend.[2] The automotive side was illustrative of the broader picture involving all forms of mechanical objects. The Cubans, in their pride, had declared that they would be able to patch up and make do with old equipment until Soviet-bloc factories were in operation. But what happened in practice was something else. If, for example, the telephone in your hotel room broke down, you were simply moved to another room. But the biggest fault was in the lack of coordination. Thousands of feet of aluminum irrigation pipes were landed at Havana docks, there to remain uselessly for months, because a Cuban had forgotten or neglected to order the essential couplings. "We've got fifty thousand East German voltmeters on hand," lamented a member of the Central Board of Planning. "But we haven't the plants to put them in.

[2] Canadian exports to Cuba in 1962 fell to $10,875,000, compared with $31,100,000 in 1961. Most of the sales were in pharmaceutical products and livestock for breeding purposes.

What are we supposed to use them for?" Similarly, he said, warehouses all over the island were stocked with bits and pieces that ultimately would make sense, but in the meanwhile served no purpose; he estimated that at least a year would be required, after factories were erected, to sort out the backlog of miscellaneous equipment.

This failure of distribution was translated in small, and yet—from a public point of view—alarming ways. One night at La Roca, once one of Havana's finest restaurants, after dining on a barely edible concoction of macaroni and a few shreds of nondescript meat, I was confronted by an apologetic headwaiter who said some fresh lobster and shrimp had just arrived (it was 10:30 P.M. and the restaurant was about to close because it had finished even the macaroni). The public ran into worse problems in state markets and shops while waiting the arrival of essential foodstuffs. Tied in with sloppy distribution was the overwhelming bureaucracy to which Guevara admitted. Overcentralization stifled initiative and slowed down the normal working process. In Havana, as a tiny example, I had to make two trips to a government office in order to obtain an exit permit; the formality could have been handled in five minutes, but it involved a loss of five hours of time.

Such distortion of effort was matched by an imbalance in purchases. Castro used up, early on, at least $100 million of his Soviet credits to buy jet fighters, heavy tanks, antiaircraft guns, automatic rifles, and other assorted arms, claiming the need for self-defense. Whether or not there was justification for the claim, Cuba, by 1962, was maintaining a militia force of between 200,000 and 350,000 men and women, and a regular army of 70,000, adding up to a military machine second in size in the Americas only to that of the United States. Still, this heavy financial drain did not explain the main puzzle: Why the Russians did not saturate the country with food and goods, propping up the economy and making Cuba a physically appealing lure for the rest of Latin America. To get at some of the answers I spoke with eastern Europeans—East Germans, principally—who were amazingly outspoken in their disgust at what had happened. The summation was this:

The Russians, once they had overcome their initial suspicion and mistrust of the Cuban revolution, advocated a go-easy course. They urged the Cubans to benefit from their own experience after the 1917 Bolshevik upheaval, warning them against alienating the middle and technical sectors of the population, the men with the skills and experience. But what the Russians did not reckon with—as Koudriavtzev learned to his dismay—was the tempestuous, headstrong character of Castro and the revolutionaries around him. They had a disdainful word for the malcontents, *gusanos,* about which more will be said shortly, and simply did not care if they offended them. The result was an exodus reaching a proportion of some two thousand a week. Less than three years after Castro's entry into Havana, more than 200,000 Cubans had departed, and not all were of the *haute bourgeoisie*; latterly, in fact, the bulk were of the so-called proletariat, or were men with technical and managerial knowledge. It was only when the flight of doctors, for instance, reached a critical proportion, with about half of them gone, that the regime began to take notice. It kept back the rest of the physicians by making exit permits difficult to obtain, and, in a more positive way, offered attractive bonuses, subsidized housing, and other state gifts.

The Russians, moreover, advised the Cubans against rushing headlong into collective or state farming; instead, they told them, farmers must be given incentive by being permitted to produce privately; so, too, should the means of food distribution be left in private hands. But again these words went unheeded. An East German told me: "We have been at this business sixteen years, and we have more private enterprise today than the Cubans have after only three years. They're green and ignorant." As recently as July, 1961, the wholesale food market in Havana was controlled by individuals, mostly Cuban Chinese, who, because of contacts and insight, managed to get supplies into the city daily, despite transport breakdowns and other disadvantages. Then one day the government accused the wholesalers of inflating their prices, and "intervened" the market place. The next morning Havana had no fresh supplies. Unqualified young "interventors" took months to restore food distribution to any semblance of order.

Some of the East Germans with whom I spoke went so far as to say, in the words of one engineer, "This revolution is a failure. It should be written off." He was an electronics engineer, in Havana to fit equipment to a Cuban freighter. Every time he required nuts or bolts, he said, he had to go through endless paper work with the Cubans, who thought they knew more about his field than he. "And," he said in disgust, "they expect us to take sugar for our efforts. There is a limit to the amount of sugar Germany requires. We would like some money, instead." The East Germans, however, need not have worried too much last year about oversaturation of sugar. After 1961's record sugar crop of 6.8 million tons, Cuba's 1962 output was not much more than 4.8 million tons, owing partly to drought, partly to sabotage of the cane fields, and largely to unscientific cutting; because of agricultural dislocations the *campesinos* had their ranks augmented at harvest time by amateur city volunteers who often did more harm than good.

If the Russians were distressed by Cuban blunders, they trod warily at the start. Koudriavtzev's policy was to avoid irritating Castro and his colleagues with rigid demands, knowing they were independent-minded and, since their break from the United States, more sensitive than ever about possible "overlords." Like the East Germans, the

Russians sampled the Cubans' fanatic insistence to stumble through by themselves. The first Soviet technicians, moreover, were astounded when they caught sight of Havana, a city with far greater comforts and a higher standard of living than most Russians had experienced at home. A Yugoslav told me that initial Russian reaction was to inform the Cubans: "You'll have to learn you don't build socialism by shouting slogans. You must work for it." The Russians, in other words, were not going to throw everything in, without extracting a little sweat in advance. Another point raised by Yugoslavs, whose criticism, incidentally, was directed at Castro because he did not strike a "neutralist" stance, was this: The Russians at any time could have shipped in massive food supplies with relative ease, but they were waiting for the precise psychological moment, when hunger was really acute, to win gratitude from those Cubans who were hostile. More to the point, one Eastern envoy said flatly: "This place is near collapse, and I am not talking about food alone. Food could be brought in overnight, if necessary. The industrial picture is more serious, because factories have used up all their raw materials (remnants from pre-Castro days), and there are no replacements." The same man estimated that Castro had put his country back, materially, by twenty years.

On this basis, the United States strategy of an economic embargo appeared an unqualified success. How long could any nation carry on in the fashion of Cuba without total disintegration? But now the picture must be viewed through Russian eyes. The Cubans were wholly dependent on the Soviet bloc. Once having committed themselves, the Russians believed in their approach to Cuban affairs as much as did the Americans in theirs. By March, 1962, Koudriavtzev succeeded in getting Cuban leaders to swallow their pride and to accept increased Soviet direction. Guevara announced that all previous plans for an industrialization program were scrapped, and now Soviet experts would set up work norms for Cubans based on Russian experiences. Plainly, the Russians were not going to let Cuba slip away by default.

In talking of the island's shortages, ordinary Cubans—especially the youth—did not put the blame on their own leaders' faulty planning or on Soviet slowness to pitch in. The United States embargo, they said, was responsible for Cuba's distress, but they would disappoint the Americans and muddle through. More analytical Cubans, however, understood that this glib reaction was far from realistic. Among them were men who showed a desire to renew relations with the United States, and behind this feeling was much soul-searching. Roberto Retamar, a young, well-known poet, and secretary of the Cuban Writers and Artists Union, argued that Cuba had not deliberately provoked its big neighbor. "This," he said, "would have been silly. But, since the economic position of Cuba was so dependent on the United States, it was inevitable that the revolution would turn against it, just as the American revolution was against the British." And then, rather sadly, he talked about the invasion attempt of 1961 and the food crisis which followed in 1962: "Cuba won the first round. The United States has won the second round."

Was there a possibility of Cuba and the United States coming together? Even more sadly, he said: "It is the only hope." What would be the first step? Retamar pondered for a moment, and then, his voice trailing into uncertainty, he said, "the United States would have to be the weaker...." The inference, of course, was that Castro would require a face-saving device in order to climb down from his anti-United States stand, and that the United States could provide it, if it wanted to make the overtures. Retamar did not pursue this point; instead, he shrugged his shoulders, as though conceding that the present mood of the United

States ruled out such a possibility. Neither did he blame the Soviet Union for Cuba's deficiencies. "The real fault was in Cuban planning itself, and the mistake we made in assuming that everything would be handed to us," he said. "We have never really learned to work for ourselves. Cuba today, in its austerity, is not, say, like Britain during the war. British patriotism never wavered, but here we have upper and middle class Cubans divided in their loyalties between their own country and the United States. This can never do." He went on to claim that the only true patriots were those who understood the revolution and accepted it, not necessarily blindly—because even Castro had doubts about some of its aspects—but at the same time not deserting Cuba by running away. When I pointed out that many fine and idealistic Cubans, aside from obvious Batista types, were in Miami and regarded themselves as patriots in trying to overthrow Castro, Retamar nodded, again sadly. He said: "Perhaps it comes down to semantics. But basically I do not believe you can call a man a patriot when he plots against his country."

But had not Castro plotted against Batista? Retamar's answer was that Castro's movement was a popular one against a man who thought more of the United States than he did his own country. Well, since we were going in circles, I returned to my main question: What was the solution, how could the impasse between Washington and Havana be ended? Retamar made an obvious reference to Yugoslavia, saying that Cuba had not signed the Warsaw Pact and was not officially a part of the Soviet bloc, that on this basis the United States did business with Tito. But then, in the next moment, he admitted that even this kind of proposition would hardly be acceptable to Washington, because Yugoslavia had not seized American sugar plantations or other property; he also recognized that any effort to establish a *modus vivendi* would be accompanied by a United States demand for free elections in Cuba, and "so I suppose it is all rather hopeless." Retamar's final words were a reiteration of the belief that Cuba had been pushed into its dangerous position, had not intended to go so far into Marxism, that Castro had no choice but to hand over the revolution—on a platter—to the P.S.P. (Communist Party). "This was different from other revolutions, such as the Chinese or Russian," said Retamar aptly. "It did not start as a Communist revolution. But it became one, stumbling on its own mistakes."

Retamar's views were not confined to sensitive and intelligent Cubans. I heard somewhat the same reasoning from Western diplomats in Havana (among the countries with continuing relations were Britain, Canada, Israel, France, and several other European states). The commonly held opinion was that Castro had to turn more and more to Cuban Communists, just as he had to lean on the Soviet bloc for economic aid when he was rejected by the United States, because many of his original July 26th Movement people were deserting him, and only the P.S.P. had the organization and determination to administer the country. It was, tragically, a vicious circle. Cubans were quitting because of a betrayal of liberal principles; Castro was getting deeper and deeper in the mesh of the men who were violating those principles. But before long, Castro made it plain that the Marxism he would wear would be Marxism with a difference.

His first major move, however, was alarming. In the summer of 1961 Castro announced the formation of the Integrated Revolutionary Organization (O.R.I.), melding the P.S.P. and the 26th of July Movement in a monolithic Marxist-Leninist party. Thus were mixed together the "Old Communists," who had faithfully followed Moscow's line during the old early Batista days and then jumped on the victorious Castro bandwagon at the last minute, and the "New Communists" who had done the fighting in the Sierra

Maestra. The "Old Communists" possessed the trained and disciplined minds Castro needed to push the revolution. But what he had failed to take into account was the standard method of skilled and cunning Communist practitioners; while pushing the revolution, they also pushed loyal 26th of July men out of strategic positions in order to increase their own strength.

The veterans of the hills were understandably and openly resentful, and Castro himself finally showed misgivings about the liaison. For, in March, 1962, less than a year after setting up O.R.I., he made a series of announcements calculated to demonstrate that he was still the master. In a particularly fiery public speech of denunciation, he ostracized an "Old Communist" stalwart, Aníbal Escalante, for the crime of "sectarianism." Escalante, according to Castro, had employed his important position in O.R.I. to wiggle into key administrative posts more P.S.P. protégés than had ever been intended. Men such as Escalante, Castro went on, had vilified the 26th of July heroes who had faced death in the battle against Batista while they, the Communists, were hiding "under the bed."

The words, obviously, were not intended for Escalante's ears alone. Castro hit out at all "Old Communists" for thinking they had "won the revolution in a raffle," and he set up a new six-man secretariat to lead the O.R.I. Only one of the six, Blas Roca, was an old-line Communist; the others, including brother Raúl Castro and "Che" Guevara, were trusted devotees of Fidel. Moreover, said Castro, the role of a Marxist party should be to "orient" and not to dominate the affairs of state. And he added that militant Communists had been guilty of "criminal errors" and "idiocies" in attempting to impose their control while ignoring the "masses" who had a right to representation in any revolutionary development. He restored many of his 26th of July followers to their former posts, reviving their faith in him. In the essential analysis, it was Castro striving to recapture popular support, which was fast dwindling, and to set the course again in the direction of what he believed to be a Cuban type of Marxism.[3]

Thus, more than three years after the fall of Batista, Castro was still the prime figure of Cuba, ruling through personality and sheer magnetism. The "Old Communists" at no time in their history, even when given latitude by Batista, had been able to claim more than 150,000 followers. But in 1962 Castro's disciples—whether or not they called themselves Marxists—numbered in the millions. Forced to comply with this reality were such artful hands as Blas Roca, by now the editor of the Communist newspaper *Hoy*, and Carlos Rodríguez, the Communist who had first contacted Castro in the Sierra Maestra and was now president of the highly important National Agrarian Reform Institute (INRA), the main instrument for Cuba's economic reformation.

It was obvious that a major split between the P.S.P. and the 26th of July Movement was avoided because such men as Blas Roca and Rodríguez realized they needed Castro as much as he needed them. If they were proceeding with caution, it was because Castro warned that there were at least "five hundred other Escalantes" on the island, and implied that other purges would take place unless the Old Guard behaved itself. Roca and Rodríguez must have known of Escalante's activities, and indeed probably gave him his instructions, but they joined in the general condemnation, Roca saying: "He used his position in a thrust for personal

[3] When Castro gave a now famous speech on December 1, 1961, he did not declare that he had "always been a Marxist-Leninist." This was widely misquoted in the North American press, which relied on a garbled news agency account. He made the fine distinction of saying that he *now* believed in Marxism-Leninism. I was in Lima at the time, and editors there interpreted Castro's motive as twofold: first, to irritate the United States; second, to make himself more presentable to the Russians so he could obtain greater aid.

power." Escalante found himself alone in his defense against Castro's wrath, and left for Moscow to contemplate how he had been used as a scapegoat by old comrades.

The Russians appear to have accepted Escalante's dismissal calmly, realizing, too, that it was better to lose one Escalante than to alienate Castro. It worked both ways: Castro had to avoid a complete break with the "Old Communists" on whom he continued to rely for administrative skills, and he had to avoid offending the Russians on whom he now relied for economic survival. For their part, the Russians, with money and prestige invested in Cuba, were content to think of Castro as an image for the rest of Latin America. From what diplomats could gather, Koudriavtzev even urged Roca, Rodríguez, and other lieutenants to "welcome" the new O.R.I. secretariat that gave fresh authority to the 26th of July men at Old Guard expense. After all, what did it really mean? The ship might have erratic helmsmen, but it was heading for the proper port.

From my 1962 notebook:

A word that was not in the revolutionary lexicon last year is now widely used. It is *gusano* (worm), and it is tossed with contempt by Fidelistas at any malcontent. It came into prominence immediately after a speech made by Castro when he was cleaning up bands of insurgents in the Escambray in 1961. "We will shake the rotten trees," said Castro, "and the *gusanos* will drop out." The *gusanos* exist in a variety of shades and complexions, some more outspoken than others, and while in theory they do not frighten the regime they have caused some second thinking. Castro, when he announced the start of food rationing, conceded a point the Russians had long been stressing: the flight of technicians and other craftsmen could be extremely damaging to the nation's economy. "We made mistakes," Castro confessed. "There was a lack of intelligent treatment here, which meant that some people, instead of being conquered by the revolution, were frightened into leaving." But even after this remarkable admission, an official with whom I spoke said: "Sure we need them, but I am sick and tired of hearing people in my own department complaining and talking about the 'old days, the good old days.' If they don't like it here, let them get out. They are all *gusanos.*"

Talkative "worms" are seldom arrested or maltreated. The regime seems to make a practice of letting them blow off steam, as though this will provide adequate therapy. They can be found in most bars, especially on Saturday nights out, advancing themselves upon the rare foreign visitors and speaking with great and sometimes alarming frankness. For instance, one night at the bar of the Embers, I was engaged in conversation by a young man, an engineer, and his wife. There was a little caution at the start, while we traded in generalities, but soon the young man was recounting a fairly typical story of disenchantment. As recently as six months ago, he said, he still supported Castro, even though there were clear indications that the revolution had turned completely toward the Soviet bloc. "I didn't think it would matter," he said. "At least we could feel we were free of the Americans." But now the food shortage disgusted and upset him: "It was all lies we heard—the promises that the Russians would help." Now he was intensely opposed to the regime, and awaiting only a chance to get out of Cuba. He was, by his own definition, a *gusano*.

I made a point of visiting a doctor I had met on my previous trips. His transformation is interesting. Like other intellectuals, he originally supported Castro because he believed Fidel would restore the civil liberties absent under Batista, and would introduce social and economic reforms. The second time I saw him, six months later, he had the beginning of doubt; the reforms were taking shape, but civil liberties were farther away than ever; still, he was not prepared to concede fully that Castro had distorted the revolution. Now there is no hesitation, no doubt in his mind. With tremendous vehemence, he said: "I am staying because I don't want to miss the last act." In his inflamed vision the last act will consist of the body of Castro being dragged through the streets.

The doctor is a relatively violent *gusano*. Most of the critics do not hate Castro personally; they rather pity him, almost with the feeling that he is a sick man. They talk simply of "something" going wrong when onetime devout Fidelistas quit the country, to be replaced by Czech and Russian technicians. In their view, this is no longer a "Cuban" revolution, no matter how strongly Castro might make such a claim. A shop clerk told me: "Now we are being taught that Lenin, not Columbus, discovered the islands." Another man said: "When the Spaniards ran Cuba it was fashionable to name our daughters Juanita or Maria. Then the Americans came along and we picked such names as Alice and Mary. Soon we will be calling them Nadja and Olga." An older resident of Havana made the cynical but representative observation: "If we must be a colony of either the United States or the U.S.S.R., we might as well pick the one that gives us the comforts and luxuries."

In defiance, some of the *gusanos* have taken to singing in the bars a ditty, to the tune of the "patriotic" hymn, *We Are Socialists:* "We are little *gusanos*/Tomorrow, butterflies./Watch out, *milicianos.*/Things will materialize." Children at street corners try to annoy marching militia men and women by wiggling their fingers at them—the way a worm wiggles. But the opposition, at the present stage, is not much more open than that. Canefields are sometimes set afire by saboteurs, yet the organized and active underground, which flourished before the invasion roundup, appears to have disintegrated. Instead, a passive kind of resistance has developed. A Havana physician recounted how he had agreed to give physical examinations to a group of young farm girls brought in from the countryside for a course in motor mechanics. "When they show up in the morning," he told his nurse, "I will not be here. Their leader will fume and rant, and say I am a *gusano*. Simply tell the girls that I could not come to the office because I had to go to the market to line up for my family's meat ration."

This technique adapts itself to various forms of undermining the regime. As soon as rationing began, anonymous callers telephoned Havana homes at random to say: "My children are hungry, they need food.... Pass on this message." Recipients of the call multiplied its impact by quickly picking up the cry. Also making the rounds was a joke about the yellow envelopes in which ration books were issued: "Don't throw away the envelope. You'll need it to carry home your rations."

Such verbal effort, of course, is sporadic and unscientific: a poor match for the vast propaganda and indoctrination machine that has been built up by the regime. Here the Communists have proved their worth to Castro, drawing from a background of long experimentation in the field, even from the street committees developed in China. The Chinese committees are pervasive, and serve three main purposes: to carry out such practical tasks as seeing that children are inoculated when required, to spread the gospel of communism through pep rallies, and to act as extra eyes and ears for security police. The combination, from the regime's point of view, is extremely effective, for every Chinese *hutung* or alley has its own committee with an intimate knowledge of all residents in the immediate area.

Almost every street in Havana also has its "Committee for the Defense of the Revolution," fulfilling an assignment useful to the government. In February, for instance, women made a house-to-house canvas to ask neighbors how much milk their families consumed daily; this was an obvious prelude to rationing which started shortly afterward. The committee women, in fact, distributed the ration books, making sure to collect first the rent of tenants who had fallen in arrears to the state landlord. On the less tangible but equally vital point of security, the organizers automatically include in their committees the janitors of every apartment block. The janitors are supposed to scrutinize callers and make a note of mail that appears suspicious, informing, if necessary, the G2 secret police. In China, where the system has had more than a decade to dig its roots, the routine is more or less blindly followed. But Cubans are not Chinese; they are not as submissive or pliable, partly because of Latin temperament, partly because of remaining influences from next-door United States. Therefore, many of the janitors ignore the dictum to be vigilant and diligent. But there are some who do work with zeal, for it must be remembered that the Cuban revolution is geared to the wants and susceptibilities of the former "have-nots," among whom janitors would be included, and the present-day youth. The emphasis, in the style of China and Russia of a former day, is on the young people. If older generations are beyond remolding, who can tell what can be done with young minds?

The bigger question, of course, is whether repression and Marxist-Leninist orientation will prove sufficiently thorough to offset the unrest created by disenchantment and economic depression. In the meanwhile, the indoctrination is pushed in subtle as well as blatant ways. Even the annual carnival I witnessed had its political flavor. There was the usual dancing in the streets until two or three o'clock in the morning; and there were the usual parades of *samba* bands in colorful costumes, and amusing floats of a nonpolitical nature. But interspersed among them were other floats with a message: for example, the Sanitation Department's coffin-on-wheels and the huge sign, "O.A.S. Rubbish." Teen-agers, in militia uniforms, wandered through the crowd, displaying their rifles and submachine guns with great glee, for guns have become as much a part of the setting as the gay costumes.

The power reflected in the eyes of the youth is quite frightening and disturbing, for although there is the rationale that weapons are essential today for defense, there is also the danger that a distorted philosophy will set in: the belief that only might can serve the purpose of Cubans. In the coffee shop of the Havana Libre Hotel, the day after the carnival, I sat at the counter next to an attractive young woman and her three-year-old girl. It might have been an idyllic mother-daughter scene, except that the young woman was dressed in the blue shirt and khaki skirt of the militia, and wore on her hip a holster and pearl-handled pistol. Instead of a purse she carried a Czech automatic rifle. Briskly she removed the ammunition clip and laid it on the counter. The child reached for the clip and fondled it like a toy. The mother then rested the rifle across her knees, causing a man who sat in direct line nearby, but had not seen the unloading, to gulp his coffee and move hastily away. The depressing image of the three-year-old playing with ammunition stayed with me for several days.

The militant attitude is attended by hero worship. I remember in my first visit talking with a sixteen-year-old girl who said: "We have waited a long time for Fidel. He is our father. To get at him, they will have to cut our throats—mine included."

"Who?" I asked, "are *they*?"

The answer was sharp: "The counterrevolutionaries and the Americans." On my next tour, before Castro had officially declared himself a Marxist, though the direction in which he was moving was apparent, another youth told me: "If Fidel is a Communist, then sign me up, too." This was said in defiance of the United States allegations of a Communist plot to control Cuba, but also with the righteous feeling that Cuba was *not* Marxist. But now, in 1962, the definition was more precise, and so was the outspoken support of the youngsters.

The youth are undoubtedly the mainstay of the revolution. One day while I was in Havana there arrived a trainload of a thousand country girls, brought to the big city to learn nursing. They had left behind them shacks and oil lanterns, and now were esconced in the Havana Libre and other glamorous hotels, complete with dining rooms and swimming pools. For them Fidel, naturally, was the idol, the great emancipator. For them there would be no problem or conflict in echoing the new school primer that was a feature of 1961's "Year of Education." Instead of "A for Apple" the book preached "A for Agrarian Reform." "A" also stood for the Associated Press, "the counterrevolutionary mouthpiece of the imperialist United States."

A Western diplomat, predicting the imminent collapse of Castro, agreed with me that Cubans are not like the Chinese; they do not respond to discipline, they have always preferred a disorganized, carefree life. "They are not ants," said the diplomat. "They are grasshoppers." But again one is forced to wonder. While there is no doubt that many adults are dissatisfied and resentful, the youth show an inclination not only toward hero worship but toward acceptance of the regime's diet of propaganda and indoctrination. In this sense there is a similarity with the youth of China, and for some of the same reasons: a sudden awareness that the rest of the world is taking their nation seriously, a spirit of nationalism and what passes for patriotism, as distinct from, or in addition to, Marxism. The operative word is *dignidad* with its elusive but essential ingredients of self-respect and pride.

In one of Havana's finer residential districts I dropped around, unannounced, to a home with the freshly painted letters "A.J.C." on the walk. Until a few days previously, the letters had been "A.J.R.," standing for *Asociación Jóvenes Rebeldes,* the original 26th of July youth movement. But Fidel had just delivered a speech at the university, in which he said that while Cuba was still building communism, and could only be called at the moment a "socialist" state, the youth should think of themselves in phrases of the future. Therefore, the name should be *Asociación Jóvenes Comunistas.* The youngsters quickly repainted the letters. If it was not exactly a command from Fidel, it was a suggestion, and good enough for the disciples.

There were forty-two young men in the house I visited. It had once been the home of a wealthy merchant, and it was big and spacious and ornate. The present occupants slept in double-deckers in the eight bedrooms that had been converted into dormitories; two house-mothers did the cleaning and cooking for them. They were from all parts of the island, and now were enrolled in nearby technical schools, in welding, carpentry, plumbing, and a variety of other crafts. A group of a dozen or so, from teen-age to mid-twenties, gathered around me in the reading-room. I asked how it was that only a few days ago they had not thought in terms of communism, but now, as indicated by the fresh paint outside, they proclaimed themselves "Communist Youth." "Before, we did not understand the meaning," said one. "Now we do." The others nodded. They were friendly, cheerful, and extremely eager to explain their position.

To help them understand the nuance of change in Cuba, Fernando Escot was available. Escot, aged twenty-three, said he was in charge of "political education." Every evening, for an hour or two, they all reclined in the comfortable living room, listening to Escot discourse on Marxism. Escot had been a printer's apprentice. Where had he learned his Marxism? "From books," he said. The chances are, however, that Escot had gone to one of the sixty branches of the

National School for Revolutionary Instruction, the highest institute for the training of cadres, with texts provided by the Academy of Sciences of the U.S.S.R. If he had not been considered important enough for a National School, he at least must have gone to one of the 330 lower-level schools for basic revolutionary instruction. In any event, he was now commissioned to pass the message on to others, of the type of Melquiades Iznagas, a mulatto farm boy who could claim a little schooling but intended to move eventually into civil engineering, "the way young people in the Soviet Union have a chance for engineering."

"Why haven't the Russians sent you more food?" I asked. Iznagas replied with seeming conviction: "There is a difference between the food habits of the Russians and the Cubans. What could they send us?" Was there a possibility, I asked, of Cuba and the United States becoming friends again? Iznagas shook his head, while his mates made a similar motion, and said: "The Americans work only for dollars. We are a socialist country. Our friends are in other socialist countries."

Lest it be considered that Iznagas was an atypical sample, I found basically the same talk among many other young people with whom I spoke. At the time, there were some 60,000 *becados*—scholarship winners—in Havana, undergoing similar courses of instruction and indoctrination. They had aided in the Alphabetization Program, by spending months with children in remote villages or by teaching basic reading and writing to elder *campesinos* who had never before met any kind of instruction. If they were hardly qualified to act as teachers, they were now themselves pupils in higher education, the prizes for their work of the previous "Year of Education." Aside from the Havana Libre and other hotels, the *becados* were established in confiscated homes in the Miramar and Country Club districts, with all expenses paid, and, to crown the glory, a spending allowance of fifteen pesos a month: more luxury and money than any had ever dreamed of seeing. The *becados* formed only a core, and if you multiplied their number by youth groups throughout the nation you could sense the cumulative effect that will be felt in a few years.

I saw a massive display of youth enthusiasm at the Chaplin Theatre in Havana, where Castro received his Lenin Peace Prize. There was a difference from the rallies I had attended in past visits, when audiences consisted of middle-aged people as well as youths; now the older ones were conspicuously absent, bored or tired with the constant idolatry. But the youngsters still chanted, "Fidel, Fidel," singing and roaring in chilling adoration. Castro just stood there, once or twice running his hand inside the open neck of his army shirt, looking humble and ethereal. It was no accident that while others of the original *barbudos* had long since shaved their beards, Castro retained his, trimming it slightly to present a saintly appearance. Nor was it a coincidence that one of the rallying slogans was: "He who is for the revolution is for Christ, and he who is for Christ is for Fidel Castro." Undoubtedly, the intention was to create a lingering image of the Messiah of Latin America.

If there was near-hysteria while young men and women cried "Fidel" and "Venceremos," the mood was also telling in calmer, more fundamental fashion. An elderly Cuban, whose hatred for Castro and the regime was mirrored in his eyes, told me disconcertedly how he had just come from a grocery store where he stood in line waiting for his ration of butter. Ahead of him was a woman with her young daughter, perhaps twelve years old. When the grocer, obviously an old friend, tried to slip the woman an extra lump of butter, the girl called out for all to hear: "No—it will hurt the revolution. We must have the same as everyone else." The touch of the mystique is not confined to youth. It exists also among some of the older men and women. Printed proclamations in bars say that no liquor may be served to uniformed men, and the edict is taken seriously, and not necessarily because of fear of punishment. In one of my visits to a rural area, a *campesino* offered me a tot of rum, and said with some pride that twice a week he never drinks even at home—the days he goes on militia drill.

As I write this, in 1962, it is impossible to know for certain the support Castro could command at any moment. Instead of guessing in percentages, it is more practical to think of three broad groups: first, the very hard nucleus of dedicated youth and Communists who see the regime, right or wrong, as the salvation of Cuba; second, at the other end, the convinced antiregime Cubans, the "*gusanos*," the liberals, the men and women who intellectually feel and know that exposure to the Soviet bloc is not the answer to Cuba's problems. And, in between, are the huge, flexible middle group who really want only a good life, are not interested in ideology in any form, yet nevertheless approved of Castro, became disturbed when he allowed the P.S.P. to monopolize important administrative posts, were a little relieved when he reacted against the Old Guard Communists, but whose hunger pains still created dissension. In this group I met women who literally changed feelings from day to day, depending on how successful or unsuccessful they were in collecting rations.

No account of life in Castro's Cuba could possibly be complete without this aspect of the story: the ones who, on balance, do support him, the women who do queue up with patience and without grumbling, the ones who do hang Castro's picture in their houses alongside cards saying, "Thank you, Fidel," or "This is your house, Fidel." For there is no question that many, especially workers and *campesinos,* have benefited from material advances. If there is mediocrity for many Cubans, a decline in their standards, the same mediocrity implies for others a move upward. A factory hand, speaking ecstatically of the New Order, told me: "My rent used to cost sixty pesos a month. Fidel cut it in half. There were never any public beaches in Havana; all the beaches were private and owned by the rich. Now there are six beaches I can take my family to. It is a good life." If Castro alienated some by confiscating the luxury resorts and clubs, he pleased others by converting them into working men's paradises. If he copied the hideous security techniques of totalitarian states, he also proved that such things as illiteracy and primitive housing, fatalistically taken for granted in most parts of Latin America, could be changed.

In 1961 I passed through a village with an unpaved road. Children without shoes played in a cloud of dust. A derelict tram car served as the lone, improvised schoolhouse. A year later the main road was paved, and the children had footwear. The tram car lay on its side, the windows smashed by villagers when they celebrated the opening of the first brick school building. Seemingly content, the adults, 40 per cent of whom had been illiterate, were themselves taking night courses, a continuation of 1961's "Year of Education," and learning the new A.B.C.'s as defined by the regime. It was awfully difficult to expect these *campesinos* to see any evil in a cunningly plotted primer, where, before, there had been no primer.

If they now worked in cooperative or state farms, it was at least work for the year round, instead of work for only one third of the time. If city dwellers were complaining about the meagerness of their diet, and the lack of Kleenex or other familiar United States items, the *campesinos* had no such complaints. Kleenex was always unknown, and, despite the chaos of distribution and production, some food was available. Once there had been automatic rationing by poverty; now there was rationing by the state, and, for most *campesinos,* it was more equitable than in the past. In many areas I saw advances in general living conditions, with the *bohios,* the pathetic shacks made of palm tree scraps, no longer the essential habitations. In the province of Pinar del Rio I was proudly shown new and neatly landscaped four-room dwellings. "Two months ago," said a local peasant, "we had nothing here. Fidel gave us the material, and we built everything ourselves." This was not merely a show-place for visitors; it represented similar developments throughout the island.

Castro and other Cuban leaders have understood a point that other Latin-American leaders have failed to grasp: widespread slum clearance and housing programs are not only humane but are politically rewarding. The appeal, however, is not solely on economic grounds; it is also based in that word *dignidad,* and this involves Americans; for, to young Cubans especially, dignity and self-respect were lost in direct proportion to United States investments in their country. The debate ended long ago about whether Cuba has gone Communist; plainly it has. Nor is there any doubt about Castro's objective to export the revolution to the rest of Latin America. He boasts openly of the creation in Latin America of a "single, great nation, free and independent." Castro's Cuba is the only Communist state outside of Europe and Asia, but North Americans have yet to accept that it is "communism with a difference." An astute Western diplomat gave me his own definition, which is as good as any I have heard: "Communism in Cuba is Martism plus Marxism." José Marti, the great Cuban patriot and the outstanding figure in the emancipation movement against the Spaniards in the late nineteenth century, spent many years in the United States. He wrote with clarity and sympathy and beauty about American institutions. But he also declared: "The nations of South America are free to the degree in which they are isolated from the United States." This belief, validly or illogically, still persists in many parts of the continent.

Fidelistas genuinely believe that they are blazing a trail, that others will eventually take Cuba's direction. This does not imply, despite the Soviet attempt last autumn to establish missile bases in Cuba, that Castro intends to start a military crusade of "liberation." Even before the United States retaliated with a blockade, and there was the danger of a nuclear showdown, it could be assumed that both Castro and the Russians were aware that President Kennedy meant it when he warned that any armed intervention in the rest of the hemisphere would be met by United States might. What they were counting on was the power of example, the kind of subversion that comes from *internal* forces encouraged, obviously, by propaganda and guidance from Cuba, but using Cuba as a model rather than a formidable machine. I was reminded time and again in Latin-American republics that any "threat" is from within each country: the set of conditions that arouses a revolutionary cry.

Precisely why Nikita Khrushchev embarked on his missile adventure will long be a matter for debate. One theory is that he was anxious to redress his inferiority in intercontinental striking power by confronting the United States with a *fait accompli* of emplaced intermediate-range missiles within easy range of three quarters of the United States. Another theory is that the Cubans, fearing a United States invasion, appealed to Khrushchev for the missiles, as visible and conspicuous tokens of Soviet readiness to deter such American action. In making this appraisal, Isaac Deutscher, one of the world's foremost authorities on communism, believes that Khrushchev accepted Castro's request and deliberately decided that sites should not be camouflaged, but on the contrary, should be constructed openly so as to catch the American eye, and to catch it as soon as possible. The Soviet estimate was that Washington would react with an outburst of indignation, leading to temporary strain in relations but nothing worse; and that in the process the

United States would have to accept the fact that nuclear arms existed in Cuba. "This," Deutscher says in attempting to represent Soviet mentality, "would free Castro from the threat of invasion, give the U.S.S.R. an enormous gain in prestige and propaganda, and weaken Washington's influence, and so stimulate the 'anti-imperialist revolution,' throughout Latin America." [4]

The miscalculation was as "incredibly and monumentally" simple as this: Neither Khrushchev nor Castro foresaw that the missile sites, instead of deterring an American invasion, would make the likelihood of an invasion real and imminent. In the face of obvious United States determination to eliminate the bases, Russia quickly retreated from its grossly clumsy military move. Khrushchev agreed with President Kennedy over the dismantling of the sites and inspection in return for a lifting of the United States blockade and a pledge not to invade Cuba. Castro was not consulted over the terms, which could only be a blow to his pride. Soviet Deputy Premier Mikoyan went to Havana, ostensibly to get him in line. During the first couple of days of Mikoyan's visit, Havana radio beamed eulogistic broadcasts about the undying friendship of the Soviet Union, and then there was silence. Hardly a reference was made to the presence of the Soviet Union's leading troubleshooter.

This in a way was surprising, for Mikoyan, to judge from previous experiences, had a habit of getting things done in a hurry. But in another sense there should have been no surprise over the silence, for Mikoyan was not dealing with Hungarian or Czech puppets under his thumb. He was confronted by the distinctive personality of a Castro with the flamboyance of a Latin American. When finally he did speak publicly, in a meeting with a group of Havana students, Mikoyan recalled that he had devoted forty-five years to revolutionary studies, and added: "I am glad that my last

[4] *The Montreal Star,* Nov. 20, 1962.

ten days of studies have been in Cuba." One can imagine the sheer bewilderment that underlay that statement.[5]

If Castro was striving to redesign his relationship with Moscow, after being so blatantly overlooked in the Kennedy-Khrushchev exchanges, he was forced to bear in mind two key points: Economic life depended entirely on the good graces of the Soviet camp, but this did not mean that he had to accept with docility any dictates on the political front. Mr. Khrushchev may have made substantial agreements with Mr. Kennedy involving Cuba, but Dr. Castro had made no commitments—and, in fact, had not even been consulted. Castro could not afford to be regarded as the forgotten man, and this was one reason for the long negotiations between him and Mikoyan. Mikoyan left Havana only after a three-week stay, with some of the main issues still unresolved.

There was obviously some feeling among partisans of the Cuban revolution that they had been let down by the Russians. Correspondent Jan Carew, reporting in *The Observer* from Havana, quoted a neutralist diplomat as summing up the underlying realities: The Cubans, obsessed with their quarrel with the United States, had put themselves in a position where they had no room to maneuver; they wanted an absolute commitment from the Russians on their terms, and this the wily Khrushchev would not give them.

There was, too, a cautious glance on the part of neighboring Latin Americans at the fate that can befall a small state that becomes too closely identified with the Soviet Union: ignored and tossed aside in the major contest. Nevertheless, articulate Latin Americans continued to make a distinction between Cuba and such countries as Poland, Hungary, and Czechoslovakia, which had communism thrust on them by

[5] Herblock, the political cartoonist of *The Washington Post,* caught the mood superbly. He depicted Mikoyan, on his return to Moscow, reporting to Khrushchev: "Well, to start with, of course you know he's a nut."

Soviet armies. If the Russians showed early hesitation to go along with Castro, and if in the 1962 crisis they ignored him temporarily, they were now, nonetheless, committed to the revolution. As technicians were withdrawn from missile sites, technicians in other fields—agriculture and industry—continued to arrive in the island.

Just as Washington had confidence in its strategy—the economic isolation of Cuba—so the Russians were convinced that the United States approach was doomed to failure. They looked back on recent history and recalled that so far, in a forty-five-year span, no Communist regime had ever been brought down by economic devices. In 1921, when one gold ruble was worth 27,000 paper rubles, Russia was near collapse. Factory output dropped by more than two thirds, and there was widespread discontent; Lenin retreated and introtroduced what was called "state capitalism" in place of "socialism." The point, of course, is that the Soviet Union survived, no matter what the system was called and despite the fact that it stood alone in the world, without any allies. It survived initially through massive repression and terror. A strong police apparatus is available to Castro. But, more tellingly, Cuba is not isolated as Communist Russia was during its formative years. It now has "socialist" friends.

Cuba is neither a satellite of the Soviet Union, like East Germany, nor an uncommitted country, like Yugoslavia. The basic questions, short of invasion or internal uprising, are whether the regime will blend its dogma with more liberal ideas adopted from the West and whether, internationally, some sort of neutralism can be achieved. Under present circumstances, Cuba certainly cannot be looked on as a "victory" for the Soviet Union. Nor, conversely, can the Soviet recoil in the confrontation with American firmness, a "triumph" for the United States, be regarded as solving the Cuban question. In purely Cuban terms, the revolution assumed its present form because of neglect, misunderstanding, connivance, intrigue. One can argue the fine points indefinitely. But basically the revolution came from within.

Cuba's potential impact on the rest of Latin America can be confined to the island's shores, provided Latin-American governments themselves are prepared to accept the lesson. The present United States administration, in proposing the Alliance for Progress, has demonstrated its wisdom and awareness of the real problems that transcend Castro himself. That the United States will also have to reexamine its loyalties and values is indicated in the next chapter.

12

Alliance for Progress?

On March 13, 1961, President Kennedy proposed the formation of the Alliance for Progress in which he invited Latin-American nations to join in a crusade "to build a hemisphere where all men can hope for the same high standard of living—and all men can live out their lives in dignity and freedom." The president's objective was "to transform the American continent into a vast crucible of revolutionary ideas and efforts . . . an example to all the world that liberty and progress walk hand in hand." Five months later, on August 17, representatives of all Latin-American republics, except Cuba, gathered at Punta del Este, Uruguay, to make formal this lofty doctrine and to subscribe to the Alliance.

It was a solemn occasion, marked by Latin-American pledges to introduce an ambitious program of betterment for their peoples. Delegates signed an 8,000-word document in which the key sections committed their governments to two basic structural changes. One was agrarian reform, altering the system of large landholdings that were in the hands of a tiny minority; the other was tax reform, "redistributing the national income in order to benefit those who are most in need." In return, the United States promised the most generous rewards ever known in Latin America: enormous sums to eradicate illiteracy among children of school age, establish farms and homes on a wide scale, cut disease, raise life expectancy by at least six years, and generally translate *Alianza para el Progreso* into human terms. All these things would be accomplished by 1970.

Considerable publicity was given to the official introduction of the Alliance; it was to be the dramatic answer to threats from Fidelismo, and, more positively, to offer encouragement, along with *dignidad,* to scores of millions of Latin Americans paying the penalty for their own leaders' past selfishness and, to a degree, former United States indifference to Latin-American sensitivities. A year after Punta del Este, the coordinator of the Alliance, idealistic Teodoro Moscoso, wrote a memorandum to his staff: "On August 17 we mark the first anniversary of the Alliance. We 'mark' it. We do not celebrate it. There will be time enough to celebrate it when we have achieved a working alliance and an extensive progress. As yet I am not satisfied that we have either."

These were honest words, and, in many a view, words of understatement. To some Latin Americans, the Alliance was doomed to failure from the start; for it neglected to take into account the diehard attitude of oligarchs and politicians, who simply would not support legislation designed to cut their personal profit margins; to others, its measures, involving both private enterprise and state planning, were inadequate: on one hand, it was argued, because more socialism was required, on the other because socialism was implied. To some North Americans, talking anyway of curtailment of foreign aid, it was too costly a venture; to others, the Alliance betrayed the principles of capitalism, or, conversely, it played too much into the hands of capitalists. To some foreigners, the Alliance was, in the words of Sir

John Lomax, former British ambassador to Bolivia, an "old remedy in a new wrapper." To José Figueres, former president of Costa Rica and one of Latin America's most astute statesmen, the Alliance was too late because it "is already one minute to midnight in Latin America." To Dr. Salvador Allende, a physician by training and leader of Chile's Socialist Party by conviction, it was "like putting on a mustard plaster to cure pneumonia in this era of antibiotics."

From the point of view of a perceptive United States authority on Latin America, Peter R. Nehemkis, Jr., Washington counsel for Whirlpool Corporation, the problem was expressed thus: "I have disturbing doubts as to whether we [Americans] possess sufficient understanding of what makes a social revolution tick. I have a gnawing anxiety as to whether we have really made a commitment of the heart to rescue Latin America from a peril, which, as in the Greek tragedy, is proceeding inexorably towards its inevitable doom." Seen from the other direction, from a Latin-American viewpoint, the responsibility rested on Latin-American shoulders. "The basic defect," said Dr. Raúl Saez, a distinguished Chilean economist, "is that national opinion has not been won over to the Alliance for Progress, and this is a phenomenon in practically all Latin America. Excepting perhaps Colombia, where the president-elect made the Alliance for Progress the banner of his campaign, there is no country in Latin America where the Alliance has been considered an internal responsibility and been given all the importance it deserves."

Which of these two comments, in an apparent vortex of contradictions, was true? The irony is that both were true. By the first anniversary, only three nations, Bolivia, Chile, and Colombia, had submitted ten-year master plans demanded under Alliance terms. Only a few had enacted agrarian reform laws, and of these Colombia's was the only fresh one; Bolivia and Mexico, and to lesser degree Venezuela, had gone through the motions of agrarian reform before the Alliance was even formulated. On the question of financing, the figures were far from heartening. Boiled down to essentials, United States loans and aid to Latin America, under the Alliance, totaled hardly more than in previous years of other schemes.

But the Alliance, despite the carping of critics, did wear a new cloak. It was based on the principle of self-help; that is, for every United States dollar going in, Latin Americans, governments and businessmen, would have to show sincerity by putting in at least four of their own dollars, much the same way that the Marshall Plan after World War II called for massive European participation. In other words, the Alliance was not to be construed as a "handout" program; its value would come from the degree of Latin-American participation. Yet, by the end of 1962, the flight of Latin-American capital, headed for the safety of bank vaults abroad, was greater than the inflow; for each United States dollar that arrived in Latin America, approximately $1.50 was sent out by Latin Americans.

"For too long, my country, the wealthiest nation on a poor continent," said President Kennedy, "failed to carry out its full responsibilities to its sister republics. . . . We have now accepted the responsibility."

In the final analysis the question is whether Latin America has accepted its responsibility.

Income-tax dodging, next to making money, is the most popular pastime of Latin America's *ricos*. The wealthy look upon tax requirements, such as they are, with cynical contempt. In Brazil, Peru, and Ecuador, among other countries in 1962, fewer than half of the eligible taxpayers filed returns. This kind of situation, of course, results in serious and resented inequalities. Wage and salary earners suffer from deductions at the source. But industrialists and professionals find it easy to maneuver through loopholes deliberately designed for their benefit, or to bribe assessors. In no country in all Latin America is a jail sentence a threat; the only punishment for evasion is a mild fine; and this, too, exists mainly on paper; when a court case does occur, as we shall see, it creates a sensation.

"Self-help! That is the key to much of our common concern," Adlai Stevenson has said. "If it were lacking, no amount of money in outside aid would do much good." Stevenson was addressing a meeting of the Inter-American Press Association, a group made up largely of influential Latin-American publishers. He indicated that, aside from redistribution of land, no reform is more urgently needed than in taxation: "reforming tax systems to relieve the low- and middle-income groups, ending the tax evasion that costs Latin-American governments billions of dollars every year." According to United Nations tax experts with whom I spoke, if all Latin Americans started to pay up as they should, their governments would take in an additional two to three billion dollars a year: a sum that would go far toward eliminating poverty and social unrest, and more than the amount the United States has planned to funnel annually from its own coffers into the Alliance for Progress.

On an official level all Latin-American nations say the Alliance is a splendid idea. "If the United States held back its money, the results would be disastrous," Alex Zarak, Peru's minister of finance, told me. "We could not think of developing the country, and we would fall into chaos."

"What is Peru doing about the Alliance's prime stipulations, such as tax reform?"

"We are installing electronic computers," Zarak said.

"What good is electronic machinery," I asked, "if there isn't legal machinery to make evasion a criminal offense?"

"We have sent two bills to Congress to impose criminal sanctions if taxes are not paid."

"The government has sent the bills?"

"Yes."

"And what has happened to them?"

"They have not yet been passed," said Zarak.

"How long has Congress had the bills?"

"For some time," said Zarak.

In fact, Congress had been sitting on these bills since November, 1959.

A key question is: Does the will exist on the part of the governments, most of which are oligarchic, to make changes and set the foundation for the Alliance? A leading opposition senator in Chile commented: "Putting a landowner in charge of agrarian reform is like putting a fox in charge of a poultry farm." A businessman in Peru, astute enough to understand not only the impatience of Washington but also the attitude of his own class, said: "It is unreasonable to count on miracles in tax reform. You really can't expect us to enact laws that would go against us."

Most Latin-American *ricos* simply are not accustomed to paying income taxes. Guatemala and Paraguay, both badly in need of development funds, have never known income taxes of any kind; in Nicaragua, only 7 per cent of government revenue has come from personal income tax; Mexico, until it put into force new regulations in 1962, collected only one third of its total revenue from direct taxation (compared with the United States figure of 70 per cent). In lieu of effective tax receipts, most governments have been forced to finance themselves through heavy export-import duties and levies on manufactured goods, a pernicious ritual that often deflates the industrialization the Alliance is trying to encourage and keeps down living standards.

In response to Alliance demands, governments send representatives to international meetings, guided by United Nations and United States tax authorities, with the avowed purpose of studying ways and means of improving their collection systems. Some claim, as a result of this prodding, that they have instituted reform measures. But in most instances the steps are not much more significant than the Peruvian gesture of installing computers to verify returns and, in theory, to prowl electronically for errant taxpayers. In Mexico, for instance, the old lists contained the names of only 700,000 taxpayers; with modern devices introduced last year, it was said, the new registry would reach several millions. But what will happen in reality?

Brazilian tax experts reckon that merchants in Rio de Janeiro alone cheat the government out of more than one billion dollars a year. "Do you really expect them—or the Mexicans, or anyone else in Latin America brought up to honor greed—to mend their ways?" said a Brazilian journalist rhetorically. The common practice on the continent is to keep two sets of books. When an assessor drops around, to say that returns are out of order, an industrialist is likely to look at his inquisitor, who earns under $200 a month, and say that a good position is open at double that salary. "You might as well take it," the industrialist tells the civil servant, "because the government is likely to change soon and you will be out of a job in the usual reshuffle." The other principal device calls for a flat settlement of 10 per cent of the assessed taxation, with the collector pocketing a portion and handing over the rest to higher officials.

Many doctors, lawyers, and other professional men do not bother with records of any kind. An Ecuadorian, presently assigned to the United Nations, told me what happened when he worked for his country's finance department. He would call on a doctor, living on a scale of $50,000 a year and paying only a couple of hundred dollars in tax, and say: "Your declared income is very low, considering the size of your home and the two cars you operate." The doctor would reply: "Ah, my practice does not pay very well, but I have other income—from my *fundo*. The harvest this year was very good." In Ecuador there was, at that point, no tax whatever on farm income; in most countries it is still so small as to be negligible. In Colombia, which recently passed a new tax law, I asked a professor for his forecast. He said: "It looks good on paper, but, like agrarian reform, it has yet to be put to the test. When you are wealthy, and have connections, you can get away with what you want. What is the use of laws when they are not observed?" In Chile last year a businessman was brought before the courts for income-tax evasion. The story made headlines throughout the continent, because it was the first case of its kind ever to occur in Latin America!

Teodoro Moscoso cites the Chilean example as an encouraging sign that Latin-American governments at least are trying to alter the old pattern. But he does not delude himself into thinking that the battle is won; he knows that the real test is not in formal legislation but in Latin-American mentality. "I remember a few weeks ago talking with a group of rich planters in one unnamed country to the south," he relates. "After the formal speeches, they began crowding around me and complaining that the newly increased taxes their government was forcing them to pay were wrecking their business. One of my principal aides from Washington was standing beside me. Finally, I turned to him. 'What is your salary?' I asked him.

"The aide, somewhat embarrassed, replied: Fifteen thousand, two hundred dollars."

Moscoso addressed the group: "If anybody here makes less than that, my next question doesn't interest him." Then, he asked his aide: "How much do you pay in taxes?"

"Approximately four thousand dollars on my last return," he said. "My Federal return."

"That is more than one quarter of his earnings," Moscoso pointed out to his audience. "And that's only income tax—

Federal income tax. We also have state income taxes and indirect taxes."

Moscoso sums up: "I'm not sure I changed the way of life of those planters or made them line up outside their revenue bureaus the next day to pay their taxes. But I do know that the amount of the tax staggered them."

If North Americans find much about Latin Americans to irritate them, the reciprocal feeling is also important to note. Latin Americans in general condemn the United States for what they consider foolhardy years of neglect and misunderstanding that Washington hopes will be forgotten in a short time. Liberal Latin Americans, in particular, castigate the United States for such policies as supporting military machines with heavy financial aid, while overlooking—until now—social reforms, and for being more concerned with preserving the established order than in facing the realities of change. Both points relate directly to the Alliance for Progress and form part of the suspicion, and in some instances outright hostility, toward the current United States policy of enlightenment.

"We are completely aware," said Salvador Allende in Santiago, "that the United States has this new policy because of Cuba. It is pitiful that the United States has discovered Latin America after its failure in Cuba."

Perez Salinas, a trade-union leader in Caracas, said: "The economic development of countries should go together with democracy. In the case of the *Alianza,* it aims to help countries which have dictatorships—Paraguay and Nicaragua, for example. Dictatorships should not be included. Instead of being an Alliance for Progress, it is an alliance for regress."

I heard opposite opinions from businessmen such as Alvaro C. Alsogaray, Argentina's former trade minister, who said: "The thing to do is to work with governments which are responsible governments. You cannot work with socialistic or nationalistic countries. You must proceed as bankers, not as benefactors."

But far more typical were the first two views, summed up by a student in Guatemala: "Progress for whom? We are a bit tired of slogans. At one time, 'good neighbor' meant something, but Eisenhower changed all that. We have faith in President Kennedy, and the plan itself, but we doubt if it will be applied by our present government."

Underlying the pessimism is a knowledge of history, which, no matter how deep the sincerity of the current United States administration, no matter how hard Washington tries to bury the past, induces Latin Americans to remain wary and unconvinced. "Exhortations from Washington lustily call upon the Latin-American leaders to root up their social disorders," observes *The Economist*. "But only a few years ago, the same men, or their predecessors, were being admonished from the same quarter to lay no hand on the ownership of land, and to put their trust in the seminal virtue of private enterprise." Scarcely a year before the Alliance was enunciated, two sociologists from Notre Dame University, Fredrick B. Pike and Donald W. Bray, in Chile on Fulbright scholarships, described with considerable bitterness the "false optimism" fostered by leading North Americans. Writing in *The Review of Politics,* they noted how President Eisenhower, on a visit to a Chilean housing project, decided "by looking into the eyes of the occupants that he was viewing a happy people (these happy-eyed people gave the majority of their votes in the last presidential elections to the Marxist ticket)."

And then, almost overnight, came this statement from Douglas Dillon, United States Secretary of the Treasury: "Since World War II, we have been preoccupied with the problems of other areas—first Europe, then Asia, then Africa. We were deaf to Latin Americans when they asked for help. . . . We were accused of neglecting Latin America because we were concentrating on problems in other parts of the world. This accusation, unfortunately, was justified. The urgent need to help reconstruct Europe after the war could not have been ignored. Neither could the needs of the newly emerging nations of Africa and Asia. Nevertheless, until recent years, our response to the crying needs of our two hundred million Latin-American neighbors was clearly inadequate."

If words alone could alter history, then surely these words by a man of responsibility, reiterating similar utterances by the President of the United States, would set out a fresh slate. If deeds—unselfish ones such as visualized by the Alliance—could be trusted, then would not all be made right? United States taxpayers are understandably resentful when their motives are questioned, for are not they, the taxpayers, making sacrifices to help their neighbors? And after all, what right have Latin Americans to complain if, between 1945 and 1960, they received scarcely 2 per cent of the billions of dollars the United States divided among nations of the world? Who else provided even a fraction as much?

Unfortunately, Latin Americans do not see matters in quite the same way. They suffer largely from the psychological disability of any recipient; at one moment demanding a bigger slice of the pie, at the next resenting the person powerful enough to bake a big pie. But, the psychology aside, a more cogent question they ask concerns the use of the money. To many Latin Americans, United States aid has meant only one thing: weapons and armaments in the grasp of governments determined to preserve the *status quo*. Though United States military assistance to Latin America has been relatively small (an average of $65 million a year since 1952), it points up, in the Latin-American mind, a negative aspect of past United States foreign policy toward the hemisphere.

This military aid is, ostensibly, for hemisphere defense; but, taken in its essentials, it is regarded as a political expediency—a means of keeping Latin-American regimes friendly and cooperative. During World War II, when Lend-Lease equipment was shipped southward, the intention not only was to arm states against possible enemy attack from the outside, but to enable them to maintain internal order and stability against any possible Axis attempts at subversion. The same reasoning held after the war, when Soviet aggression became the concern. From what I could gather, however, this military aspect of United States policy has been appreciated and supported by few Latin Americans, aside from those in the armed forces. The more common attitude is that United States assistance has encouraged militarism and coddled dictatorships, since the mere provision of such aid by the hemisphere's leading power gives a propaganda lift that sustains a regime. The price for the United States, if not high in finances, has been arduous on nerves. For reasons of prestige or fear, if one republic is given or buys a certain type of jet aircraft, its neighbor demands one precisely like it, and the United States has to comply to keep friends. Obviously, even without United States aid or training programs, Latin-American armies would not wither away; national pride and innate suspicion of one state for the other would ensure their survival by one means or another. But the point raised by Latin Americans is that in cases of civilian and military elements competing for power, United States aid has unwittingly tipped the balance in favor of the militarists.

The question, therefore, is this: Has the United States, in the effort to gain cooperation of the armed forces, been losing the support of the rest of the population? The answer, broadly, is: Yes. Another question is this: Does the military or political return make such alienation worthwhile? Edwin Lieuwen, Chairman of the Department of History at the

University of New Mexico, provides one answer in his remarkably informative, well-documented book, *Arms and Politics in Latin America.*[1] "Judged by United States standards," writes Lieuwen, "Latin-American armies are ill equipped and badly trained, despite the work of military missions and the aid programs. No Latin-American state has a significant air force; only [a few] have even marginal navies. United States military strategists are well aware of these facts; consequently they do not count on Latin-American forces to provide any significant assistance in operations outside the hemisphere, either in a general or in a limited war." (Only Brazil put a force in the European field during World War II; Mexico had a token air squadron in the Philippines. Of the twenty republics, only Colombia contributed troops to the United Nations fighting in Korea.)

Lieuwen goes on: "Even for military tasks closely related to hemisphere defense, such as keeping the Atlantic, Pacific, and Caribbean sea lanes open and defending the Panama Canal, all but the most peripheral must be assumed by the United States.... Since in fact neither the United States nor the Latin-American countries are convinced that the latter have any real role to play in meeting the external Communist threat, the only practical military justification for providing them with military training and aid is to enable them to combat the internal Communist menace. ... It seems that if the United States military planners are primarily concerned about the internal Communist threat, they should channel aid to the police rather than to the armies." Lieuwen's conclusion is that the thwarting of Communist subversion depends far more on the attitudes of the Latin-American governments than on the level of their armaments, and "insofar as the military aid programs have

[1] Published for the Council on Foreign Relations by Frederick A. Praeger, New York, 1961.

increased the political influence of the armed forces, the prospects for democracy have suffered."

Both points have been echoed time and again by prominent Latin-American civilians. Opposition to United States military aid existed even before World War II. In 1937, when Washington proposed lending warships to some hemisphere republics, Eduardo Santos, leader of the Liberal Party in Colombia, pleaded: "Don't do this evil to us. The use of armaments is like the vice of morphine. Once begun, the cure is almost impossible. You will ruin us with cruisers and create for us new problems, because there is always someone with the desire to try out the armaments and obtain from them some advantage." Santos accurately forecast what would happen in his own country when military men took to leading suicidal war parties among Colombians. The next time he spoke for United States ears it was as a tragic figure in exile in 1955: "If in Latin America, the dictators prevail, if they continue to discredit freedom and law, a fertile field for Communist harvest will be provided. Why? Because our resistance will be gone. We are poor nations who have no investments or great fortunes to defend. What we would defend against communism would be our freedoms; but if we have already been stripped of them, we have nothing left to defend. It is thus that the gateway for the Communist invasion is thrown open by the anti-Communists."

More recently, in August, 1962, another Colombian repeated the worries of liberal politicians. In the midst of a fresh military crisis at home, Germán Arciniegas, Colombia's ambassador to Italy, said: "It is an unpardonable error for the United States to stimulate the growth of Latin-American armies.... It threatens to turn Latin-American nations into countries occupied by their own armies." The admonition received a more thoughtful response than it might have in previous years, when the concept of an

Alliance for Progress, with its underlying philosophy of democratic social transformation, was unknown. Speaking in United States congressional debate, several senators and representatives questioned the wisdom of military assistance for Latin America. Representative Thomas M. Pelly of Washington virtually followed line by line the argument of Arciniegas: "It [military assistance] strengthens dictators and would-be dictators. It sometimes forces a population to live under its own military occupation." Senator Ernest Gruening of Alaska called for "an end to this unsuitable and fruitless" program. Several others demanded a re-appraisal of the whole policy of military aid.

The immediate stimulus was the ominous trend of just the past few months, beginning with the overthrow in Argentina of Frondizi's civilian government by an armed forces *junta,* which then threatened civil war because of a personal fight for power among the generals, and coming to a climax in a military take-over in Peru. The latter event was particularly disturbing to the United States; the symbol of militarism was a United States Sherman tank that Peruvian soldiers used to ram down the gates of the presidential palace. Though the bitter reaction from Washington was quick and clear, the end result, as we shall examine shortly, was that the United States still had to conduct business with a distasteful military regime.

There is a widely held belief in Latin America that the United States has two policies for Latin America: the State Department's, which favors civilian rule, and the Pentagon's, which encourages military rule. This is not so. There may be contradictions between the tactics of the two agencies, but both have been struggling for the same objective: to attain political cohesion in the hemisphere. The dilemma is not one of hemisphere defense; no one placed much faith in the few gunboats that Peru or Venezuela or Guatemala offered to provide during the Cuban blockade. The dilemma is that, in making the offer, Peru, Venezuela, and Guatemala were demonstrating a solidarity that was a prime objective of United States policy.

Nevertheless, an opinion written two years ago by Edwin Lieuwen may have more application today than ever before. "The time has now come," said Lieuwen, "for the United States government to promote vigorously [the] suggestion that Latin America curtail its military expenditures. A program of arms limitation in Latin America, sponsored by the United States and by some Latin-American governments, would provide a simple method by which some of the inconsistencies in our current foreign policy could be removed. It would be welcomed by the Latin-American public, relieve the United States of much of the onus of supporting unpopular governments, and allow the savings on arms to be plowed into economically productive endeavors."

"I am astonished by the lack of common emotional language between Latin America and the United States." The man who made this remark to me, José Figueres, has an appropriate reputation for being peppery and incisive. He led a revolution that brought democracy to Costa Rica, and, as president for five years, introduced middle-of-the-road measures that helped to make the tiny republic an oasis of hope in an otherwise restive Central America. Figueres studied and worked in the United States as an economist, and has a deep grasp of the realities of United States moods and political necessities. He stands as a keen interpreter midway, physically and spiritually, between North and South America. "The advanced business community of the United States and many congressmen," he says, "have an unavoidable tendency to consider the oligarchs as their counterparts. When they visit Latin America they talk to businessmen and senators only, and fail to understand the real forces at work here. To them, communism is a thing that starts and ends with Fidel Castro."

Interestingly enough, Figueres, as leader of Costa Rica's big National Liberation Party, denounced Castro for fostering tyranny in Cuba long before his nation made an official break with the Cuban regime. This, however, does not alter his belief in nonintervention. He states a philosophy that, to many North Americans, may appear contradictory, but to Latin Americans is perfectly logical: "From the Cuban people's point of view, the present dictatorship is a catastrophe, but I do not share the view that the presence of Castro makes our position more difficult. There is a great vacuum in Latin America and a great urge to fill it. If the Cuban government were overthrown tonight, our internal situation would not improve one bit. Poverty and agitation would continue."

And so, here is the dilemma of a Latin American who went along with his government's decision to sever links with Cuba but questions the meaning in terms of essential problems. Two thousand miles away, in La Paz, Victor Paz Estenssoro, the president of Bolivia, sat quietly puffing a pipe while he explained why he would not support sanctions against Cuba: "We are attached to the principle of self-determination and nonintervention." Bolivia, as a landlocked country, could feel relatively secure from direct Cuban influence, in contrast to Costa Rica, which was separated from Castro by a few hundred miles of open Caribbean waters. But was this the whole reason for Bolivia's stand? Bolivia's social revolution, barely ten years old, was faltering, partly because of chronic economic ailments, partly because of a government inability to set priorities that would satisfy all factions. Paz Estenssoro's desk in the presidential palace was but a few feet from the same window through which a recent predecessor was flung into the hands of an irate mob, to be strung up to die on a lamppost.

Bolivians, putting it as an understatement, combine passion with politics. "The greatest danger," Paz Estenssoro said, "is still from the left." Thus, he was saying implicity, he could make no move that would alienate the disciples of Fidelismo.

But the quandary was not even that simple. Bolivia had been offered substantial credits from the Soviet Union to build a tin-smelting plant and other required industrial projects. Paz Estenssoro would dearly like to accept the Soviet offer, but then what would happen to United States funds promised under the Alliance for Progress? Bolivia could hardly complain about previous United States assistance, which happened to be particularly lavish in her case; but there was an attitude, shared by other republics, that it was the responsibility, even the duty, of the United States to pay the major cost of any development program. At the same time, Bolivia felt its economy would be boosted if it could accept Russian loans or grants and expand trade with the Soviet bloc. Any move in that direction, however, would have to be waived to cater to United States susceptibilities about external communism, the United States fear of encroachment that could begin with major trade or aid.

I said to President Paz: "But this is an independent country, is it not?" My intended inference, of course, was that Bolivia could make any arrangements it saw fit. The effect of the question was as I had expected.

"Which country today," said Paz slowly, "is truly independent?" There was sadness, weariness in his voice. It told a good deal about the struggle of conscience within realistic Latin-American leaders, on one side trying to maintain what they believe to be an independent posture, on the other understanding the facts of international life: that the United States, from the point of view of its own beliefs and security, would reject outright any Latin-American country that allied itself with the Soviet Union, whether through economic or other means. And so, to Bolivia, as in the case of other republics, Alliance funds would have to be more important than Soviet funds.

This is part of the handicap under which the Alliance functions, one of the reasons why it is regarded, justly or unjustly, with doubts by many Latin Americans. Scarcely five months after the Charter for the Alliance was signed, another meeting was held at Punta del Este, this time to consider action that might be taken against Castro's Cuba. Woven darkly together in Latin-American minds were two points that many considered should have been unrelated: the need to develop the Alliance as a cooperative plan for the social and economic growth of the hemisphere, but also the need to pay the price of United States bitterness and fears over Cuba. On the main issue, the expulsion of Cuba from the Organization of American States, Latin Americans observed that Haiti, which languished under its own oppressive dictatorship, cast the deciding vote necessary for a two-thirds majority and was promptly granted more Alliance support. A waggish Brazilian journalist itemized Secretary of State Dean Rusk's expense account as follows: Breakfast, $2.85; taxis, $6.70; lunch with Haitians, $30,000,000.

That old-fashioned "dollar diplomacy" is prevalent today is, I believe, an unjust accusation. But this is not the point; the fact is that the belief persists in many quarters, especially among Latin America's students and intellectuals, with their wide influence. I do not think it is fair to assume that the outspoken Castro opponents, who voted for Cuban banishment from hemisphere affairs, did so consciously to endear themselves to the United States. From my conversations with such men as Venezuela's Betancourt and Colombia's Lleras Camargo, and with lesser personalities, it was clear that many countries took a "hard" line out of genuine conviction that Fidelismo was an external as well as internal menace. It is noteworthy that of those countries that allied themselves at Punta del Este, the majority were Caribbean neighbors (Colombia, Costa Rica, Dominican Republic, El Salvador, Guatemala, Haiti, Honduras, Nicaragua, Panama, Venezuela, Peru, Uruguay, and Paraguay). It is equally noteworthy that the number of states in itself was not terribly significant. The three major proponents of a "soft" line, Argentina, Mexico, and Brazil, accounted for two thirds of Latin America's area and three fifths of its population. Along with Bolivia, Ecuador, and Chile, they argued that most Latin-American republics had already broken diplomatic relations with Cuba anyway, and that removal of Cuba from O.A.S. agencies would simply intensify its dependence on the Soviet bloc.

The refusal of these six nations to evict Cuba from O.A.S. indicated again a deeply ingrained repugnance for any hemisphere intervention, no matter how mild its form. Partly there was a fear that such intervention might be applied one day against their own governments. But there was also the practical consideration, as in Bolivia's case, of facing home audiences sympathetic to Castro. Brazil, with a weak and divided government, strong movements in the Northeast, and leftist sentiments everywhere, could think only of "peaceful coexistence" with Cuba. Other "soft" countries were motivated by other internal considerations. Argentina was menaced more by Peronistas than by Fidelistas, and this stemmed directly from a cutback in a relatively high standard of living. Arturo Frondizi, the president at the time, made plain his feeling that the United States was too preoccupied with Central America and the Caribbean, and was not paying enough heed to the economic woes of Argentina. This, then, was his way of drawing attention to Argentina and trying to extract more cash from Washington. "Blackmail," some Americans said. Frondizi's tactics, however, did not please his own militarists; shortly after

Punta del Este, they forced him to break relations with Cuba, making Argentina the thirteenth Latin-American state to do so.

In Ecuador, I discussed the Argentine development with President Carlos Julio Arosemena. Since Ecuadorians, as well as others, were citing the "coincidence" that as soon as Argentina broke with Cuba it received a substantial United States loan, was Ecuador likely to be penalized for not doing the same? Arosemena, a huge, clear-speaking man of forty-two who impressed the visitor with his candor, said: "I have no fear that Ecuador will be left out of the Alliance. The United States needs Latin America more than we need the United States." If those, to United States readers, are galling words, they express a fairly typical sentiment even if it isn't always put so bluntly by chiefs of state. It explains in part the lack of haste of countries such as Brazil and Mexico to submit to United States pressures over Cuba.

Shortly after my talk with Arosemena, and following the example of the Argentine army, Ecuador's generals forced a reluctant president to end relations with Castro.[2] But Washington could take little comfort from the Ecuadorian gesture. Promptly, a pro-Castro revolt erupted in the hills around Quito. Even in October, 1962, after the arms buildup and the much publicized arrival of Soviet "technicians" in Cuba, there was no substantial shifting in the position of Mexico and Brazil, which between them embrace more than half the peoples of Latin America. At a Washington meeting of foreign ministers, called in a further effort to get the big powers to isolate the island, the response was hardly more united than at Punta del Este. While a general communiqué expressed unanimous condemnation of trends in Cuba, and a determination to prevent the spread of communism, in simple facts these were mild resolutions. Political

[2] Leaving only Bolivia, Brazil, Chile, Mexico, and Uruguay with missions in Havana.

or geographic factors still determined the actions of each country.

I was in Washington during that meeting, and a Chilean journalist summed up the attitude: "I suppose you can't expect Brazil or Chile or other countries that are remote physically from Cuba to feel as strongly about a 'threat' from Castro as, say, Costa Rica or Venezuela. You might say that we fear as much 'big-stick' diplomacy from Washington as we do so-called 'Moscow aggression' from Cuba." It took, just a couple of weeks later, a startling revelation by President Kennedy—about the scope of Soviet missile sites under construction in Cuba and their capacity to deliver rockets to far parts of the continent—to jolt Chile and other "soft" liners into unified action. The Council of the Organization of American States voted as a bloc in support of the President's "quarantine" measures against Cuba to halt the inflow of offensive weapons from the Soviet Union. This was an impressive and swift display of hemisphere solidarity in the face of a crisis: the greatest such display since World War II. It was rightly hailed as such by the United States press and public, caught up in the quick-changing and tense drama of United States naval vessels preparing to sink if necessary Soviet vessels, at the risk of nuclear war, in a determination to protect the continent.

But the unity was not quite as complete as it appeared initially on the surface. Three nations, Mexico, Brazil, and Bolivia, made it clear that they would not go as far as the others were prepared to go: to invade Cuba. Though, along with sister republics, they agreed to that part of the United States resolution that called for the searching of ships and the dismantling of the Cuban missile sites, they halted at a significant section. This section would have given the United States a blank check to attack Cuba whenever she decided that Cuba had become "an active threat." There was a subtle difference, but a vital one, in the views of

Bolivia, Mexico, and Brazil between blockading arms shipments and landing in a country to seize those arms. It was the same kind of distinction made previously in the case of the Dominican Republic, when United States warships hovered off the coast to compel the withdrawal of the Trujillos; because U.S. Marines had not actually landed, according to this logic, "intervention" had not taken place.

The Cuban crisis also pointed up the sharp divisions inside countries that had long taken a firm stand against Castro. In Venezuela saboteurs, identified as Fidelistas, dynamited power stations, halting temporarily one sixth of the nation's oil production. Even in Chile, one of the few countries that had refused to go along with the majority in the vote to exclude Cuba from the Organization of American States, students reacted violently when the government, shocked by the missile disclosures, reversed itself and embarked on an anti-Castro policy.

However, aside from the genuine desire to maintain the principle of nonintervention, many Latin Americans continued last year to draw a distinction between the "offensive" and "defensive" character of weapons possessed by Cuba. Thus, even in states nearest the island there were men and women who agreed with Castro that he had every reason to arm himself as best he could to protect his revolution, especially after the abortive landing in 1961 at Cochinos Bay. Not only, according to some interpretations, did the United States-inspired invasion violate the many pledges of nonintervention, reviving fears that past policies were merely dormant and not dead, but it had a curious side effect. The invasion's failure made the Russians, who up to then were unconvinced about the stability of the Castro regime, examine the allegiance he still commanded and, as a result, go all out in his support.

If this, from a United States view, appears as distorted reasoning, it nevertheless ties in with other Latin-American versions of events. When Castro announced that the Soviet Union was financing and helping to build a port for a "fishing" fleet, which the Russians would be able to draw upon, not all Latin Americans uttered the cry that here was more evidence of a "military threat" against the hemisphere. A Mexican editor, who can be described as a moderate, said: "For the last fifty years the United States has held on to its naval base at Guantánamo Bay, admittedly by legal treaty. But in that half century no effort was made by the United States to give Cubans a sense of participation. Instead, Guantánamo is regarded as sovereign United States property, isolated from the rest of Cuba by a fence and a foreign mentality. Now the Russians come along and say: 'Here is a new base. We will build it for you, and maybe use it, but it will belong to *you.*' This was more than a strategic victory for the Russians; it was a psychological victory."

Mexico's stand is one of the most interesting, for Mexico shares the sea in proximity to Cuba, and, at the same time, lives closest of all Latin-American nations to the United States. Mexico has not regarded political action against Cuba as pressing. It is better, in her opinion, to leave Cuba alone; for the Cuban people will not long tolerate the imposition of an alien system, if this, in fact, is what Fidelismo is. Underlying the Mexican argument is an instinctive opposition to "intervention" as it is commonly understood in Mexico: that is, any form of pressure by the United States to protect its interests in Latin America. It is not primarily the influence of Fidelismo, substantial though it may be, that dictates such a caution; more, it is the ever-present memory of United States influence and policy toward Mexico as it was exercised until recent times.

"To understand Mexico, ask about Cuba," commented a writer in *The Nation* a while ago. It was an apt way of putting it, for Mexico is still fired by its own old revolutionary spirit that demands sympathy for the revolution of others. But simultaneously Mexico's revolution is called "The Unfinished Revolution" or "The Three-Quarters Revolution." There has been substantial progress in land distribution and education, but there has also been frustration among millions who feel slow progress. Mexico City boasts its skyscrapers; it also has vast slums, and, not far away, *campesinos* whose material lot is not much greater than it was a generation ago. The restive ones have witnessed a new middle class grow in prosperity and conservatism, and, with a change in administration every six years, a new group of politicians riding to glory in Cadillacs.

"Our progress has been uneven," said Senator Manuel Moreno Sanchez, one of Mexico's most powerful political figures and a member of the government. "We see that great advantages have been concentrated in one part of our people in only a few geographic zones and in privileged activities. This is only serving to accentuate the contrast between those who have too much and those who lack everything and are living prostrate in misery." Moreno Sanchez could not visualize any threat from Castro, but warned instead that Mexico must step up the rhythm of its own social revolution or encounter forces "pressing up from below." His views are disputed by men who, at the other end, accuse the government of introducing too much "socialism" in economic matters.

Mexico has indeed moved sharply to "Mexicanize" foreign-backed enterprises by insisting on local participation; it has also nationalized such varied fields as motion-picture distribution and electric power and light. But these moves are part of a trend established long ago by such leaders as Lázaro Cárdenas, who, as president, was the expropriator of oil and other properties, and, to millions of Mexicans, the great emancipator. Cárdenas emerged from retirement last year to speak out loudly on the Cuban issue. "To defend the sovereignty of Cuba," he said in an obvious reference to the United States, "is to defend the sovereignty of Mexico."

And so, to many Mexicans, Cuba is placed in the context of Mexico's own history, which implies a constant struggle to prove to itself, and to the United States, that it is free of external domination; accompanying this is an intense desire to carry on the revolution without being subjected to extremes of right or left. All the while, Mexico bears in mind that it cannot afford to alienate the United States, which buys well over half its exports besides providing most of its imports and supporting the peso with special funds. Thus, the current president, Adolfo López Mateos, walked an intricate course in 1962 involving neither outright support for Castro nor subservience to the United States.

But this policy has not always been understood by North Americans, especially investors, who believed that Mexico's "soft" approach to Cuba was an open invitation to Fidelismo to take over. In 1961 the rate of industrial growth fell from 5 or 6 per cent a year to 3.5 per cent, barely enough to cope with the normal population increase. The drop was caused largely by curtailment of United States investments and an exodus of Mexican capital itself. However, a marked change took place after Punta del Este. If Mexico did not support the eviction of Cuba from O.A.S., it at least juggled adroitly to agree that "Marxism-Leninism" was "incompatible" with hemisphere conceptions of freedom. "Those few words," recounted Don Augustin Legorreta, managing director of the largest private bank in the country, "did the trick. Money began to return. Our worry was not whether we were going to have a Castro regime but how to restore the confidence of investors. There was nothing wrong with Mexican policy regarding Cuba. The only thing wrong was United States interpretation of it." Putting it another way, a foreign-office man told me: "Cuba may be the black sheep, but we consider she is still in the family."

Augustin Legorreta said he was optimistic about the future, that Mexico should be able to return to a healthy industrial expansion. Certainly by Latin-American standards, and despite some faltering aspects of the revolution, Mexico's record is impressive; as one example, steel production is expected to grow from the present 1.7 million tons a year to 4 million tons by 1965. And yet the government is cautious about predicting the effects of the Alliance for Progress. Official statements emphasize that Mexico boasts her own plans and programs for economic and social development, that she must rely chiefly on her own resources to carry out improvements, that when she requires outside assistance she prefers to borrow directly from banks, thus encountering a minimum of unsolicited advice.

What this amounts to, of course, is pride and chronic mistrust of the "giant" to the North. There was no inconsistency in the fact that President Kennedy received an enthusiastic personal welcome when he visited Mexico in 1962 at a time when press commentators were recalling past United States incursions in Mexico and warning that the Alliance for Progress might be a political weapon. Anti-gringoism dies hard in a country where every literate school child can recite the dates of a score of occasions when the United States forcibly imposed itself on Mexico or on one of the other Caribbean and Central American republics. "We Mexicans," said Dr. Mario de la Cueva, one of the nation's most noted educators, "don't think the Alliance for Progress, or any other kind of aid program, will solve our problems; what we need is a better balance in trade and better prices for Mexican raw materials. For instance, the United States pays low prices for our cotton, and in turn dumps its own cotton products on world markets at prices we cannot possibly match."

If I have gone, at some length, into the foregoing comments, it is merely to emphasize that the United States in stretching out a hand in an honorable and imaginative project, which is what I believe the Alliance to be, has not overcome any fundamental hurdles. It is erroneous, as some Latin Americans insist, that the price of Alliance membership is conformity over Cuba. President Kennedy, in his trip to Mexico, announced that Mexico, which could hardly be considered to share fully Washington's attitude over Cuba, was the recipient of a new $20 million agricultural loan. Brazil, another of the "soft" republics, received one third of all United States disbursements in the first year of the Alliance's existence.

But this did not stop Brazilians from complaining that the Alliance was a political device, or, conversely, that funds were slow in arriving. From virtually every leader with whom I spoke—men such as Paz Estenssoro and Arosemena and Betancourt—I heard the same lament: Washington is falling down on the job; United States "bureaucracy" is holding up delivery of promised aid. Harshly, in United States ears, this is ingratitude; to Latin Americans it is a just complaint based on the notion that the United States has wronged its neighbors in the past and must make amends.

If there is one lesson to be remembered, it is this: Regardless of what the United States does, regardless of how it tries to wipe out the image Latin Americans have of North Americans, it will be condemned. Whether it gives with "strings" —in this case, reasonable ones which call for reforms—or whether in desperation it overlooks theoretical stipulations in order to prime a country's economy, it will be accused of insensitivity by one faction or another. The dilemma is clearly expressed by the Alliance's Moscoso: "This attitude of criticizing us whatever we do reflects the ambivalence of Latin America's relationship with the United States. It is an ambivalence born out of a complex mixture of feelings—reliance on us, resentment of that very reliance, and the tendency to exaggerate the faults and minimize the achievements of the strong and powerful brother."

The reader will note the constant repetition in this chapter of the word "dilemma." It enters into both Latin-American and United States language. The dilemmas revolving around the Alliance are multifold, and are caused in part by confusion over some basic definitions. The President of the United States has called for "revolutionary ideas," but just how far are these revolutionary ideas supposed to go in the field of economics? For many years, the United Nations Economic Commission for Latin America (ECLA) has been trying to sell a key principle: Intensive planning by the state is necessary if priorities are to be established for the investment of domestic resources and foreign contributions. ECLA's executive director, Dr. Raúl Prebisch, has continually stressed that state planning must come first, as "the only way to utilize fully the enormous potentialities of private initiative." More conservative economists disagree with this approach, some going so far as to label Prebisch's thinking as "Marxist," and warning of the "dire" risks of government "interference."

In a sense, the Alliance stresses central planning and government-to-government assistance; but it also relies heavily on private investment, without resolving what, if any, conflict exists between the two sectors. *The Economist* states the problems squarely:

> The requests for government-to-government aid that Latin Americans regularly advanced at the inter-American economic conferences were as regularly brushed aside with the brisk rejoinder that an economic project worth its salt should be able to find a private backer. But the perplexity in Latin America, as indeed in all under-developed regions, is that the projects that are eminently desirable from a social and political point of view are not always those that are likely to be

profitable to a private investor. Washington's torpidity towards its southern neighbours has been whipped into life by the anxieties that Fidelismo has aroused. But it is still not at all clear what encroachments upon private enterprise the United States government is prepared to accept with equanimity, and even less whether North American and European business men in Latin America are prepared to accept government officials as their active partners. Moreover, it would be utterly misleading to suggest that the Latin Americans themselves are automatically responsive to the ideas that the state should play a more important part in planning and controlling their economies.

The problem, as I learned, is compounded by semantics. To many North Americans "socialism" is a bad word, implying an ideology that exists in Russia or Cuba, or, at the very least, a first step toward that kind of ideology. To many Latin Americans, however, it describes not only an acceptable but a desirable way of life; the Latin-American meaning of "socialism" is akin to that understood by Danes and Swedes and Britons and Australians under "socialist" governments. "We fear that Latin America is turning socialist and that communism may be around the corner," says Moscoso. "It may be of some consolation that, since the New Deal and even before, we have viewed with alarm what many of us thought was the same dangerous trend in our own country. Latin Americans look to their governments today for a variety of reasons. The kind of 'free enterprise' they have known has by and large been of the kind that we in the United States outlived many decades ago. In Latin America there are too many instances where private enterprise is synonymous with landholding oligarchies who keep their farm workers living at a bare subsistence level and who live in luxury. So people look to governments for solutions. They do not see the threat of 'creeping socialism.' They see the reality of hunger, disease, and hopelessness."

Moscoso concludes: "We would be ill-advised to get involved in acrimonious debates with our Latin-American neighbors on the details of where private enterprise ends and where government enterprise begins."

United States business practice in Latin America, with the notable exceptions of such areas as Cuba and to a degree Central America and the Caribbean, has been good, at least in comparison with Latin-American practice; many United States businessmen, even before President Kennedy's formal program was enunciated, were carrying out their own private little alliances for progress. In Brazil and Argentina, for instance, Kaiser Industries, after opening automobile plants, encouraged local manufacturers to produce more than 90 per cent of the components; equally telling, Kaiser has established multimillion-dollar educational programs to train technicians and to send promising young men abroad for further learning. Sears, Roebuck reinvest at least 50 per cent of their Latin-American profits in the countries in which their stores operate; this is a positive contribution to national interests that many a Latin-American industrialist, with an eye to Swiss banks, cannot claim. Even the archetype of "Yankee imperialism," the United Fruit Company, has embarked on a far-sighted scheme of selling or leasing much of its banana land in Central America to local farmers whom it calls "associate producers." There is a double purpose: to economize on operations but also, after the Cuban experience of take-overs, to satisfy the natural lust of Latin Americans striving to be masters of their own land.

José Figueres, who as president of Costa Rica negotiated a new contract with United Fruit, leading to the present trend, still talks, however, of "a large economy exploiting a small economy." He says: "It is not a deliberate or conscious effort, but it still goes on. For instance, we transport our coffee in a truck made in Detroit where a worker gets twenty dollars a day. In exchange, we send coffee, for which producers pay only $1.50 per day. This sort of situation used to happen internally, in the United States or Western Europe, at the birth of the industrial era, but gradually it equalized itself. Now, innocently but dangerously, it is happening internationally. It is not deliberate colonialism; it is an ignorance of the times. The civilized industrial world is indebted to Costa Rica at the rate of $30 million a year in what would be reasonable prices for coffee, cocoa, and bananas. No Alliance for Progress can compensate for this amount."

This murmur, repeated in every country that depends on one or two basic export commodities for survival, is an adjunct to the main debate of private versus state development. Latin Americans look with bitterness and frustration on the continuing decline in the prices of the raw products they sell to the United States and the rise in the prices of manufactured goods they buy in return. The result is that losses incurred by Latin-American countries in their trade with the United States have, in some cases, exceeded the amount of aid they have received. Coffee, the most important export of Latin America, has suffered a steady price decline since 1955; it dropped 8 per cent in 1961 and 1962 alone. Stated another way, the lowering of only one cent in a pound of coffee may amount to a loss of from forty to fifty million dollars to the chief producing countries. Colombia claimed last year that it lost nearly three times more foreign income through the slump in coffee prices than it gained in Alliance credits.

Some governments, as a consequence, argue that the United States should give priority to trade stabilization rather than outright aid. Colombia's finance minister, for example, warned that Alliance grants, "however generous," will fail unless prices for Latin-American commodities are put on a firm footing through international agreements. The United States would have preferred that Latin-American nations help themselves by controlling commodity production, diversifying products, and expanding trade with one another through their newly formed common market. In a move of major significance, however, the United States consented to subscribe to a "workable" world coffee agreement and to impose domestic import controls in order to carry it out. The agreement, which eventually may help resolve the problem of coffee, still has a long way to go to prove itself. Serious problems in other key exports of Latin America also remain.

But the most serious issue of all is still the central one, at least for Latin-American nationalists: how to escape what they regard as the complementary dominance by foreign commercial interests and internal feudal oligarchies. In other words, how to reach a "socialist" system that would distribute the wealth with greater equality and achieve the type of reforms that even Washington demands. There are pungent reasons, of course, for the widespread bias against private enterprise, both national and foreign. Ownership of domestic companies in Latin America is most often concentrated in the hands of a wealthy few. In Chile, for example, eleven banking and industrial groups, with interlocking directorships, liberally sprinkled with senators, control companies representing 71 per cent of domestic corporate investments.[3] Owners, working on profit margins of around 35 per cent on net investment in manufacturing, are reluctant to plow back funds in expansion to provide goods and jobs for more people. At the same time, Chile's main industry, copper mining, which accounts for three quarters of its exports, is almost wholly controlled by two United States companies, Anaconda and Kennecott. Chileans charge that these North American companies are "taking away our resources."

Chileans ignore the argument that without United States

[3] *Business Week,* Sept. 22, 1962.

capital and engineering the copper resources would never have been developed to their present extent. Much of the mistrust for American businessmen, throughout the hemisphere, comes from the mistrust of most Latin Americans for their own *ricos*. Guilt by association, therefore, mars the image of many United States concerns. Nevertheless, the Chileans have a strong point when they show that Anaconda and Kennecott have neglected to invite any local participation and are staffed on a senior level entirely by Americans, in contrast with United States companies in other parts of Latin America that tend today to recruit some key officers from among Latin Americans and to invite domestic stock communion. Parties of all complexions in Chile demand nationalization of the copper companies. Some offer considerable compensation. Others, such as the socialists, would make token payment only, or no payment at all. Salvador Allende says that the two companies have sent back to the United States more than three billion dollars in profits in the last decade (a figure disputed by the companies) and therefore initial investments are more than adequately covered. He told me that in any government he might head there would be immediate nationalization of the copper industry; he was not sure whether there would be compensation, but in any event it would be a fraction of the valuation set by the companies and in the form of long-term bonds. "The bonds," Allende added with a telling shrug, "would not be redeemable until long after my death."

Latin America needs heavy infusions of state planning of the European variety, democratic and socialist, to achieve social and economic change. Only by "radical" measures will greater excess, communism or Fidelismo, be avoided. It is debatable whether there is even time left to implement the calculated changes that social democracy entails. But, leaving this feature aside for the moment, three other major questions require answers: First, how much can be expected of Latin America's regimes, represented for the most part by short-sighted industrialists, landowners, and other oligarchs, to accept any argument in favor of socialism? Second, does Washington realize that, once unleashed, a reform mood of the type called for by the Alliance may not be contained at the desired level? And how far would Washington itself be prepared to accept socialism that would include the nationalization of United States property and investments, currently worth more than eight billion dollars?

The first question is relatively easy to answer. I have attempted to point out throughout this book the simple fact that most Latin-American governments have proved unwilling or incapable of making the required changes in meaningful proportions. This part of the story is reemphasized, frankly, by a Brazilian businessman who said: "Don't ask us to cut our own throats." The second and third questions cannot be answered quite as dogmatically, for they involve major rethinking not only on a United States government level but on the part of the United States business community and general public. A group of visiting Brazilian students asked President Kennedy what the reaction of the United States would be "in the event we were to socialize the means of production in our country as a way to wage more effectively the battle against underdevelopment."

President Kennedy (as quoted by *Newsweek*, Aug. 20, 1962) replied: "The decision of your country as to the means of providing progress is your decision, and if by socialization you mean ownership of the means of production or of the basic industries, that is a judgment which you must take. ...We prefer the competitive market economy here. We believe that by free competition we can satisfy the needs of our people best. Every country must make its own choice." There was obviously heartening indication that the United States administration, under Kennedy, had attained a clear-sighted vision of the currents and demands in Latin America. But would the President be free to act, or to carry out sympathetic wishes, in the face of a hostile Congress or press or public?

In the same issue of *Newsweek,* Henry Hazlitt, the commentator, delivered a stern lecture on the Presidential reply to the Brazilian students; he argued that the President would have done a greater service by extolling the virtues of private enterprise and citing life in the United States as an example of beneficial capitalism. Such an argument, with images of workers' cars parked in massive parking lots outside United States factories, with happy and prosperous middle-class families planning a day's outing at the beach, sounds ludicrous to Latin Americans, whose immediate concern is to get rid of hunger pains. Capitalism never developed in Latin America on rational lines as it did in the United States. Latin America, for the most part, still lives in the age of feudalism. Is there time for it to graduate to the phase of capitalism? In its next step, many Latin-American reformers believe, it must leapfrog to socialism, or else the jump will be utterly devastating.

Hazlitt, in his sermon to Kennedy, said the President should also have pointed to the example of Canada, whose economic growth "has been greatly accelerated by the investment of private United States capital." Again a distortion occurs. Canada has indeed benefited from United States investments, but its stages of development have always kept fairly good pace with the times. Canada escaped feudalism; its people live and think with basically the same values as those in the United States. Even so, many Canadians—though Hazlitt chooses to ignore them—fear what they consider United States economic "domination." Elections have been fought, and won, on the issue of curtailing such influence. How much greater is the mood of "nationalization" in a Latin-American country that feels that capitalism has let it down? Hazlitt suggests that the President should have told the Brazilians: "If you want to go in for socialism, it's your funeral. But don't expect us to subsidize it."

One wonders whose funeral it will be. "We will bury you," warned Nikita Khrushchev, and he was talking about burial with economic tools. Can the United States reasonably expect to maintain its present standards, determined by its capacity to trade with a friendly world, if that world shrinks in size? Has the United States—or rather its opinion-makers and businessmen—truly begun to understand that social democracy is probably the only hope against communism? There is profound doubt about this question among exponents of socialism in Latin America. Salvador Allende almost won the 1958 presidential election in Chile; now, in coalition with the Communist Party, he stands a good chance of winning in 1964. He is taking a calculated risk by linking himself with the Communists, but he believes that he can control them. He is less certain about his possible influence over the United States. Would Washington support a Chilean government such as Allende's if United States business interests were affected? "We are dubious," Allende told me, "because we see that all the so-called American principles of self-determination were broken when it came to the case of Cuba." Allende's formula calls for government-to-government assistance only, to minimize what he considers a threat from private capital and its powerful lobbying in Washington. What it amounts to is a fundamental worry that, despite the philosophic approach of President Kennedy and the objectives of social and economic reforms, United States pressures mitigate against a Latin-American country going too deeply into socialism.

One recent example of United States excitability occurred when a Brazilian state governor, Leonel Brizola of Rio Grande do Sul, expropriated the telephone subsidiary of International Telephone and Telegraph Corporation, offering as compensation 5 per cent of the value of the investment claimed by the company. United States congressmen promptly demanded a halt to all aid for Brazil; businessmen talked of investing elsewhere. It took the President of the United States to warn that nothing would be "more unwise" than to get into disagreement "with the whole Brazilian nation" because of the action of one governor. Kennedy urged vehement critics to "look at the map (and) keep a sense of proportion." This was a cool and realistic approach. But the problem is bound to recur with greater frequency than in the past. The big question, therefore, is whether the will and understanding of the President will prevail over United States pressures that are also bound to arise.

Mexico has a "mixed" economy, with government ownership or control of several basic industries. Agriculture, which permits private farming, also features a system previously repugnant to the North American mind: collective farming. Yet, because of the stability compared with other Latin-American republics, private United States capital continues to arrive in Mexico, content to go into partnership with the state or conform to government regulations that require Mexican majority stockholders. Some Mexicans preach that their brand of "revolution" is the answer for all Latin America; they add that this kind of "mixed" economy, together with an independent foreign policy, is about the best deal the United States can hope for in the hemisphere. But other Mexicans—possibly more realistic ones—point out that they have had fifty years in which to reach their present position, while time has been held back in other countries and does not allow such gradual evolution.

And so the swing of the pendulum presents perplexing issues: Would the United States be willing to deal with an Allende type of government that includes Communists? Would it consent to Chile, or any other country, receiving assistance deals from the Soviet Union? Would even assurances of "neutrality" be acceptable? This aspect of the broad picture is problematic and could easily lead to a rupture between Santiago and Washington, with the inherent danger of the same insidious spiral in which Cuba was caught: a push into dependency on the Soviet Union.

One question in the circle of intricacy, the role of private capital in Latin America, is perhaps academic at this point. With the exception of Mexico, the flow of United States investment in Latin America came to a virtual halt last year. There is a tragically ironic touch here, since the Alliance for Progress is based largely on financing from private sources. To make the plan work, one billion dollars annually (aside from United States government assistance) is counted on from private foreign sources, largely North American. But in the first quarter of 1962, only $5 million was invested by United States industry, in the second quarter almost nothing—compared with an average of $300 million annually in past years and one and a half billion dollars in the peak year of 1957. The general excuse of United States industry was that a higher yield was obtainable in Western Europe with its flourishing Common Market. But the more telling reason was the vision of Fidelismo and property seizures. North American businessmen were hardly reassured by the lack of faith of Latin-American businessmen who betrayed their own insecurity by hoarding money abroad.

In round figures the Alliance contemplates, over a ten-year period, a total of one hundred billion dollars in public and private investments in Latin America. Of this amount, 80 per cent is expected to come from Latin America itself, for, as Douglas Dillon has expressed it, "the heart of the Alliance is the concept of help for self-help." But private Latin-American money, as we have seen, has left the continent rather than remained there (anywhere from eight to eleven billion dollars is estimated to have taken flight in the last few years), and United States private investment last year was unimpressive. In the public sector, Latin-American governments have merely made token gestures of spending on basic developments. Only the United States government came through with its pledge of one billion dollars in the first year. This, incidentally, was not "hand-out" money; 87 per cent was in the form of loans, the remainder in grants. Nor was it "new money," for even before Punta del Este the commitment of public funds, through the Export-Import Bank, Food for Peace Program, Development Loan Fund, and other agencies, totaled $950 million a year. Thus a net increase of only $50 million was noted in 1962.

Was the billion dollars doing what it was supposed to be doing? More than half was used not for development but to pay off Latin-American debts and trade deficits. For instance Brazil, which is regarded as the pivot of South America, received 35 per cent of the first billion; but most of this was absorbed in balancing Brazil's international accounts instead of improving living conditions. The Brazilian government then asked for a further substantial contribution to get it out of difficulties that, in the words of *The Economist,* "are due largely to its own incompetence." No one in Washington—at least in the administration—liked the idea of employing Alliance funds to support internal budgets of inept Latin-American governments, but it is an accepted economic fact of life that development projects cannot be contemplated in the midst of economic chaos. And so, in its first year of operation, the Alliance made hardly any dent in getting through to 200 million men, women, and children.

In only one area was there anything resembling a dramatic move; the Alliance pledged $181 million to help Sudene revitalize Brazil's Northeast. But even here the money did not gush in volume; only a few millions were delivered immediately; the rest was held back until Alliance experts could evaluate Sudene's progress. "It is going to show results," an Alliance man told me in Washington. "It hasn't yet, but it will." He spoke, I sensed, with a furtive eye on the clock. Alliance people quote José Figueres' classic remark, "It is one minute to midnight," but add, "We intend to make it a long minute." In that minute the Alliance must weigh urgency with practical considerations.

Moscoso has warned the privileged classes of Latin America that they have a choice of supporting the Alliance's reform goals "or risking a Castro-type destructive revolution." But simultaneously Moscoso, aware that the U.S. Congress and public demand that their money be spent wisely, asks: What is the sense of pouring funds into, say, Bolivia when the state doesn't even possess plans on paper for such fundamental items as water supply and housing? And so, last year, Bolivia was given eight million dollars to produce plans, with the understanding that, on acceptance, more generous sums would be available. The underlying policy in these opening years of the Alliance is to use small amounts of cash to provide leverage to get long-range schemes rolling. And because of this utilitarian approach, Latin Americans sometimes condemn it as the *Alianza sin mucho Progreso* (Alliance Without Much Progress).

The United States has some outstanding ambassadors in Latin America today, in contrast with previous periods when they were not renowned for ability or perception. The New Frontiersmen I met were almost uniformly understanding and well informed. But so acute is the problem of knowing how or when to recommend Alliance aid, so grave the preoccupation with forestalling violent upheavals, that I heard two diametrically opposite points of view about solutions: one calling for absolute toughness and control in the allocation of funds, the other for wild but necessary venture. An ambassador, who confessed that he felt near desperation, told me: "If there is no immediate land reform there will be communism. So it is better to risk dictating to these governments and saying that unless they do something about land reform they won't get a penny from us. With this dictation, there's a slight chance; without it, there's no chance."

Another diplomat said: "We haven't the time to insist on prior stipulations to see how our money will be spent. We've got to pour in money without strings, and hope that some of it will be put to good use. The gamble, of course, is that much of the money will get into the wrong pockets. But the other gamble is greater. We have lost unless we show the people that we intend to help."

This arouses another major quandary for Washington. How much supervision by the United States will individual governments permit? Will the United States have the right to ensure that its billions of dollars are not squandered or thrust into the private bank accounts of Latin-American politicians? A Peruvian banker said: "As a banker I lend money only when I know the use for which it is intended. I also have the privilege of examining books to check up in fact whether the investment is sound and the money is being used properly. It should be the same procedure for the Alliance for Progress." But the banker admitted that his view is not shared by many Peruvians.

There is a natural reluctance on the part of Latin Americans to allow any control by the United States. A typical comment was made by Brazil's foreign minister, San Thiago Dantas: "We think the United States can know the destination of the money. But to know the destination is one thing. To supervise it is another." Another foreign minister, Chile's Carlos Martinez Sotomayor, also expressed a characteristic opinion. He said there was some justification for the United States to keep its eye on its expenditures "in certain instances," depending on the governments, especially in Central America with its long history of blatant corruption. "But this," he also declared, "would not apply to Chile. We have shown responsibility. We have never defaulted on loans." Much the same was said to me by Argentines in relation to Brazil, by Brazilians in relation to other republics. In each instance it was the *other* country that required a watchful eye—never the country under immediate questioning.

Apart from insular sneering, a broader consideration enters Latin-American thinking. Suspicion of United States motives is so deeply rooted, the concept of *dignidad* is so sensitive, that even reformers who oppose their own social systems are allied to their governments on the issue of United States accountants. Enrique Zileri, a young Lima author, said: "The United States should be tough and should lay down the law: no reforms, no money." Should the United States oversee the money? Zileri answered with a flat: "No. We don't want those kinds of strings."

On the surface the Alliance for Progress makes sense. But its application presents almost insoluble problems. Washington has learned not to be rigid in insisting in advance on reforms; otherwise some programs would never get off the ground. Last year, for example, Chile, despite the absence of a working agrarian reform scheme, was allocated $40 million toward road-building and other capital improvement; more, it was said, would be made available when reforms were underway. "In most cases," says Moscoso, "we have been insisting on reform, but we cannot wait for *complete* reform; the march of events is much too swift for this. We can, and must, look for evidence of good faith on the part of a particular government, but to some extent we still have to play it by ear."

Dozens of reasons have been advanced for the Alliance's less than impressive record. Among them is the criticism, expressed by *The Reporter,* that what the Alliance is seeking is to buy revolutionary change without paying the price of revolution; it wants, in a hurry, contradictory objectives:

reform, efficiency, planning, and democracy; and it wants to achieve all this while a score of nations move abreast. Another criticism is that, at least for the first year, Washington was so busy with internal bureaucracy and organization that it gave little attention to the political and psychological aspects of "selling" the Alliance to the Latin-American public, which, for the most part, remains in ignorance of its objectives. Allied with this is the belief that the Alliance, concentrating on economics, has lacked ideological content to engender the kind of mystical dedication that was awakened among Cubans in their 1959 revolution.

Latin Americans offer a variety of "solutions." Jorge Lavadero, leader of Chile's National Democratic Party, insists that what the United States should do, to prevent local corruption, is to buy up land and designate it for schools or homes, regardless of any government complaints of "interference." José Figueres says that what Costa Rica needs is a return to the system of Lend-Lease, "when London would cable Washington to say it had to have material in a hurry, and Washington would cable back, 'On the way.' " Now, Figueres argues, "there is a mentality in Washington of 'projectitis.' That is, every request has to be examined by committees and experts. Time is wasted in red tape and paper work. I feel desperate, the way Britain felt when France fell."

As many people as you speak to, as many different ideas on how the Alliance should be conducted do you hear. But fundamentally its success or failure revolves around what Moscoso calls "good faith" on the part of Latin-American governments and leaders. Tragically, the Latin-American oligarchy is unable to resolve the crisis of Latin America because it is incapable of adjusting itself to a revolutionary situation. In Washington there is a mood of urgency. In his first anniversary memo to his staff, Moscoso said:

> Honest miscalculation is better than letting the forces of inertia rot our program. . . . Taking chances on the scale in which we have to work inevitably means making mistakes. . . . Let's face it. We are not going to please everybody—either in the United States or in Latin America. Let's just please those great underprivileged masses of Latin America. That is our real job; not to placate governments or kill Castro or satisfy every last member of Congress (nobody ever did that). . . . I am expendable. The Alliance—and much less Latin America—is not.

Prominently displayed on a wall in Moscoso's office is a sign for visitors and staff: "Please be brief. We are 25 years late."

A Brazilian army colonel said: "During the last world war we had tremendous respect for the United States. We had grown up with Roosevelt's 'good-neighbor' policy, and we felt an affinity with it. When the United States went to war, we followed suit. In fact, I did my training in the States. Of a thousand Brazilian officers at that time you would not have found one who was anti-American. Today it is just the reverse; nine hundred and ninety-nine are anti-American."

"Why?" I asked.

"In 1945 our economy was in a critical state," the colonel went on, "but the United States did nothing to help. It spent billions of dollars in Europe because it was afraid of communism there. Perhaps it was aware that the third world war had already begun in Berlin. Anyway, we were neglected and overlooked. But now, when the third world war looks closer, and the United States knows it must have allies, it turns to us and offers all kinds of money. I think the Alliance for Progress is too late. The disenchantment, not only in Brazil, but in all Latin America, has grown in these fifteen, sixteen years."

"Isn't it conceivable that the United States could regain its popularity?"

The colonel, a man of about fifty, pondered a moment, and then said: "Is an old love affair the same when an attempt is made to revive it? Suspicions, mistrust have grown, and both parties are a little older, a little more cautious."

In Brazil's Northeast, the mayor of Recife, Miguel Arraes, cynically told me: "Even the much-publicized 'Food for Peace Program' was designed to solve the problems of American overproduction rather than our problems." It is of considerable significance that Arraes last October was elected governor of Pernambuco State, the locale of one of the Alliance's most urgent and ambitious undertakings. Arraes can hardly be classed as sympathetic to United States goals and intentions.

In Lima, I met with a group of university professors in a discussion about Latin America's image of the United States. One of the men, by agreement with his colleagues, said: "President Kennedy has good intentions, and he is surrounded by some people of high caliber. They may have a genuine desire to help Latin America. The trouble is that the majority of us feel the United States will follow the same pattern as in the past."

What is this pattern, as Latin Americans see it? It is a quilt-work of political and economic imperialism. Men on the left accuse the United States of supporting undemocratic regimes that return favors at their own countries' expense. Men on the right say the same thing in reverse. Mario Gutiérrez, leader of the semifascist Falange Party that opposes Bolivia's reform government, said to me: "When we were being exiled or sent into concentration camps by the revolutionaries, diplomats in the U.S. Embassy looked the other way and gave money to the government. Is this their notion of helping a country?"

The question, of course, should be put the other way: How far are Latin-American countries prepared to help themselves and one another? How much willingness are they showing in translating the principle of "self-help" in a tangible way? I asked Arturo Frondizi, while he was still president of Argentina, whether Latin America might emulate the European example under the Marshall Fund. "We cannot do the same thing," he replied, "because in Europe it was a question of working on an established economy that had to be further advanced. On the other hand, in Latin America it is a question of propelling undeveloped economies. It is up to each country to intensify its own efforts, through sacrifices of our own people and through credit from abroad." No mention, it will be noted, was made of faith or credit from the domestic business community. I heard Frondizi's remarks, in one form or another, echoed by leaders in almost every republic.

Not all Americans accept the view that Latin America is incapable, financially, of helping itself; some say that the continent has a greater capacity to pick itself up by the bootstraps than it is willing to admit. In Santiago, I sat in on a lunch meeting called by a group of Chilean editors. The guest of honor was United States Senator Hubert Humphrey, who was on a tour of South America. When I related Frondizi's statement, Senator Humphrey remarked with a trace of anger: "I suspect these people can afford more than they say." Then he confronted his hosts and said: "Americans are tired of being told they're making a mess in Latin America. Some are beginning to say, 'Let the Russians pick up the bills.'" Specifically, he pointed out, United States taxpayers are fed up contributing—through heavy taxation—toward projects in countries whose own people refuse to pitch in. "It doesn't go over too well," he added, "when men who vote for me say they need a new bridge in their town, and I tell them they can't have a bridge in their town because we've got to build a bridge in Santiago. Half the time they've never even heard of Santiago. But they have heard the accusation that we are slow in spending, that we deal with the wrong people, that we're insensitive to the needs of Latin America."

After the luncheon, Senator Humphrey was asked by Luis Rubén Azócar, editor of the influential satirical weekly *Topaze,* how the Alliance was supposed to work. Humphrey said the way to think of the Alliance was in terms of an airplane: the main fuel tanks to be filled by Latin America, with the reserve tanks filled by the United States. Later, Azócar observed, wryly: "It is a typical North American analogy. What Mr. Humphrey does not realize is that Latin America has *always* gone on its reserve tanks."

The senator's reference to the Russians was, of course, a biting one, because the Alliance is expressly designed to elevate the standards of Latin Americans and thus discourage any possible alignment with the Soviet bloc. And yet my impression in talking with Humphrey, one of the more liberal and enlightened of United States senators, was of pessimism on his part. "We're at the end of the road," he said. "If the Alliance doesn't work, the United States public won't waste any more time." And so, in the vicious spiral of cause and effect, the twist is first in the direction of Latin America and then back again to the United States. A vital question, therefore, is this: What will happen if the U.S. Congress, mirroring the frustrations of the public, holds back in voting funds for aid? The suicidal attitude of Latin-American oligarchies, which refuse to face facts and to introduce reforms, would then have become contagious, infecting the United States with equally suicidal isolationism.

At the height of last year's congressional debate over the foreign aid program, *The New York Times* observed that "neither nuclear weapons nor space ships affect the poverty which is the chief source of world instability and the chief breeding ground of communism. It is incomprehensible that this nation can afford what it is spending for arms and space research purposes and cannot afford the modest foreign aid request." Despite such pleas, the administration had to accept a drastic 20 per cent cut in the amount it considered minimum for foreign assistance programs; $75 million was cut from the Alliance for Progress. In an unwittingly ironic touch, President Kennedy signed the foreign aid bill during the Cuban blockade crisis: a crisis attributable, at least in part, to previous myopia over the needs for social revolution.

What can the United States now do? In the face of inaction by Latin-American regimes, how can the United States counter the rise in nationalism, cut down on anti-Americanism, and gain enough time so the Alliance can dig its roots and prevent Fidelismo from developing at its present disturbing rate? Several steps can be taken. Former Senator William Benton, in his book, *The Voice of Latin America,* suggests that tensions between Latin America and the United States would be diminished if the headquarters of the Organization of American States were shifted from Washington to a Latin-American republic. Latin Americans feel that O.A.S., in its present location, is a captive of Washington; psychologically, then, it would be sound to remove it by geography. Senator Benton recommends Panama as the ideal site; also on the subject of Panama he urges that the United States should consider a plan to internationalize the Canal Zone. He points out: "This scar . . . that bisects Panama rankles in the hearts of Panamanians and provides tinder for their political wars."

Another recent author, D. H. Radler, believes that United States business enterprises in Latin America would win more favor if they took on Spanish names; in addition, he prescribes that United States personnel, who tend to remain aloof from Latin Americans, should become more integrated in their local communities. Edward M. Kennedy, in a series for North American Newspaper Alliance, regrets that the United States Information Agency spends only a tiny fraction of the huge sum the Communists devote to the distribution of inexpensive books and manuals in Latin America. "It is not surprising," he notes, "that so many of Latin America's students have an intellectual list to port." The obvious answer is more money for more books to raise "the voices of freedom and democracy in the Latin-American battleground."

These are sensible and positive recommendations, and they do not pretend to be panaceas. They offer only partial solutions to enormously complex problems. Latin Americans have others to offer. In Brazil it is pointed out that Francisco Julião, the leader of the Peasant Leagues, is courted by Russian and Chinese Communists, but has yet to be invited to visit the United States. Julião's impression of the United States, as reflected in his talks with rebellious peasants, is far from friendly. In Guatemala, Francisco Villagrán, who studied at the University of Iowa and has a genuine understanding of the United States, speaks with mixed feelings of affection and frustration. Villagrán, a socialist, is one of Guatemala's outstanding young politicians. In 1961, along with another socialist congressman and a half-dozen intellectuals, he accepted an invitation to tour Communist China and the Soviet Union. He approached the U.S. Embassy suggesting a similar invitation to the United States, so that Guatemalan intellectuals, whose influence is considerable, would have a chance to absorb at first hand another point of view. But, as Villagrán related it to me, his suggestion was rejected, on the grounds that the State Department does not encourage dealings with men who are in opposition to the local government; otherwise, Washington would be accused of meddling in internal affairs. "But Washington has always meddled in Guatemala's affairs," Villagrán commented unhappily.

Ever since the Russia-China trip his position has been peculiar. He has been ostracized from official U.S. Embassy receptions, but he is accepted on a personal basis in the homes of members of the embassy. The tragedy, in simple terms, is that Guatemala's socialists, who early on went on record condemning Castro for his methods in Cuba, offer Guatemala a reasonable and democratic alternative to Fidelismo.

In the foregoing pages I have attempted to describe the problems as I have seen them, as objectively as I know how. There is, obviously, a grave situation: a kind of helplessness dictated on the one side by the feeling that Latin-American rulers are unprepared for major changes, on the other by a United States reluctance to act too drastically for fear of arousing antagonistic accusations of "intervention." But it is precisely because of the gravity of the situation that a desperate, almost ruthless, gamble on the part of the United States is required to alter a course that, if it continues unchecked, will lead inevitably to extremism. I am saying, in other words, that radical surgery, with all its obvious risks, is essential. This surgery involves United States intervention in every form; hidden if possible, overt or active if necessary.

The objections of Latin Americans to intervention are well known; but what makes for special irritation is that, in almost all instances in the past, the United States has moved in favor of right-wing or oligarchic or military elements. This is a record, and reputation, that is difficult to overcome. The task of the United States, therefore, is complicated partly by history, partly by the ingrained Latin-American fear of a manipulation that might not know where to stop. This was illustrated in the case of the Dominican Republic, where there was acceptance of the United States decision to employ a fleet to end the Trujillo dynasty, but acceptance only because the fleet was anchored outside territorial waters and, technically, did not violate Dominican sovereignty. Here was a clear example of "good" intervention removing an evil dictatorship.

It can be argued that the intervention would still have been considered "good" even if U.S. Marines had stepped ashore temporarily, so long as progress was the result. It can also be considered as something of an ironic fact that it took the country of this former dictatorship, in its first free expression of opinion in more than three decades, to point up dramatically the urgent need to make changes in the social structure of nearly every one of the republics. The man the Dominicans chose as president, Juan Bosch, defeated his opponents not only because he stood for major reform, beginning with agrarian reform, but because he offered hope in a philosophy that discarded conservatism. Bosch was of the left, of the moderate left. It was encouraging that the fledgling democracy chose him as a leader, because it now stood a chance of staving off Fidelismo.

At the height of the Cuban blockade crisis last year, and in the reappraisals that followed it, attention was paid mainly to the firmness with which the United States dealt with Soviet encroachment in the hemisphere and the removal of missile bases. Lost sight of was the fact that Fidelismo itself had not altered. Fidelismo begins more as a symptom, a reaction against adverse conditions, than as a conscious ideology. As soon as the immediate missile tension disappeared, the hemisphere was reminded that chronic social and economic problems, pushed momentarily into the background, had not vanished; Andean Indians lived as primitively as ever; Brazil's wildly spiraling inflation testified to government mismanagement and indifference. The withdrawal of rockets and Soviet military technicians from Cuba was matched by a United States guarantee, with some provisos, against invasion of the island. (Nonetheless reports persisted that armed Russian formations were still present in Cuba.) But Cuba itself was now relatively unimportant. No matter how the Cuban question was ultimately resolved, no matter what happened to Castro as an individual, the key demands remained in almost all the other republics.

What I am getting at is this: the Alliance for Progress is severely handicapped and unable to push firmly for radical changes. The clock truly indicates "one minute to midnight," and only decisiveness and firmness can form the basis for a policy of stimulating change in the hemisphere. "If I were President of the United States," said Julio Vivas, a leading Nicaraguan commentator, "I would say, 'to hell with the oligarchies. I am going with the people, to create the kind of revolutions that are necessary for social democracy.' "

Is there any alternative that offers a chance, any alternative to social democracy? My estimate, broadly, is that there is no alternative, that if nations continue to be directed, as many of them are at present, by faltering leaders, the certain outcome will be chaos. Fidelismo as such may not flash up immediately, even with the connivance of outside forces. But hunger and discontent carry the germs of political instability and unpredictability. There is a Juan Bosch in every country, ready to work on the side of moderation and optimism. Unfortunately, either through the tight command of the oligarchy, or dishonesty in election practice, or perversion of militarism, the Bosches are not being given a chance in the countries that stand close to the explosion point. Almost all the "revolutions" that have taken place up to now are meaningless, because the majority of the people have received no benefit from them.

The principle of moderate socialism, once it is understood by the United States as the only hope for Latin America, involves acceptance also of another fundamental credo: the need to help *liberal* forces, truly reformist movements that would hasten land distribution and offer the people a promise that democracy is possible and, simultaneously, beneficial. As a first step there should be no hesitation such as marked the debate between the two ambassadors, one saying that countries might receive Alliance grants even without prior assurance of reform, the other contending that Washington must hold back its money unless there is a guarantee it will be used properly. My own feeling is that the United States should be dogmatic in following the rigid rule: No reform, no money. I would go further and say: No dealings with militarists.

An attempt to combine both these rules was made in Peru last year. During the presidential election there, the United States ambassador, James Loeb, openly supported candidate Haya de la Torre, the old leader of the APRA party. At one time, a generation ago, APRA was considered leftist and reformist; latterly hardly more than moderate. But by comparison with other candidates, Haya de la Torre was a "liberal," untainted by corruption and worth supporting because he offered hope, instead of gloom, to millions of Peruvians. However, because of a long-standing feud between APRA and the army, military men plainly were not going to let him take office. Loeb threw a victory party for Haya de la Torre when it seemed he was winning, but before the count was confirmed. The army promptly warned Loeb that it was not satisfied with the way voting had been conducted and was going to declare the election invalid. Loeb in turn threatened that in such an event the United States would cut off aid. When a *junta* did assume power, the United States suspended diplomatic relations and stopped Alliance and military assistance.

It was a forthright move by Washington. There had been criticism, just four months previously, that the United States had stood by and done nothing when an Argentine military group evicted the Frondizi civilian government.

Now the stand in Peru was hailed both in Latin America and in the rest of the world as a courageous Kennedy act. However, old exigencies—or what were supposed to be practical considerations—prevailed. Peru was a supporter of United States policy on Cuba and therefore had to be catered to; Peru, with its social structure frozen for four centuries, could snap wide open in an incalculable revolt if economic conditions were allowed to deteriorate without United States aid. And so Washington retreated. Within a month it recognized the *junta,* and before much longer Alliance and military aid were back to normal.

Here was a sad example of constructive "intervention" that failed, because of the timidity, the uncertainty, the unfamiliarity surrounding a theoretically bold stand. One can only wonder how much longer now will be delayed the very revolt that United States aid is supposed to forestall. One can also wonder if resumption of support for an oligarchic regime was due to the same mentality that chronically has led the Central Intelligence Agency and the State Department toward right-wing forces in what they believe is the proper course in fighting communism. One of the troubles is that the State Department still prefers a government that is friendly to it, regardless of what this means internally to the country in question. Even the existence of Castro has not yet fully opened State Department eyes; the United States, as late as 1963, backed tyrants, such as Somoza in Nicaragua, telling them—it is true—to behave better than in the past, but, in the fundamentals, changing nothing. The longer a Somoza is allowed to function and to drain his land of wealth and dignity, the shorter will be the road for a Castro.

The United States is frankly committed to a policy dedicated to the overthrow of Castro. This policy, since the Khrushchev-Kennedy exchanges that resolved the missile crisis, is more concerned with subverting and strangling the Cuban regime through economic, psychological, and political methods than by physical attack. It is quite obvious that the C.I.A. has had a hand in planning and directing maneuvers against Castro. Oddly, C.I.A. appears able to function when its target is "communism." There is no evidence of its ever having gone into action against a regime labeled as "militarist" or "oligarchic."

The United States is accused of meddling or muddling, no matter what it does. In former days, the cry, almost exclusively, was that Washington gave its support only to venal dictatorships representing United States business and strategic interests. Today the cry just as often is uttered by right-wing Latin Americans—wealthy defenders of an old society—who say that Alliance demands for reforms are crude invasions of established customs and practices. It is clear that regardless of the fashion in which Washington conducts itself, it will be condemned heatedly by one faction or another. It is equally clear that even the lack of "intervention"—that is, indifference to a state's problems—can be interpreted as influencing the directions of that country, since the United States then can be accused of insensitivity, cruelty, or other evils. And Russia? It would not possess these evils, some men would say.

There is, then, no simple formula. In one instance, "intervention" is considered "good," in another it is "bad." But as a general directive, intervention has to be on the side of the liberal forces, the liberal democrats, the social democrats, the men who are willing to stimulate Alliance objectives. These men are not always available with large followings; but where they are, as in Chile, they should be encouraged as the counterforce against outright Fidelistas. Where they lack physical strength but have sentiment behind them, they should be assisted by other Latin Americans trained in the science and dedication of revolution. The Communists are constantly accused of sending provocateurs to foreign lands. Democratic revolutionaries, missionaries of the Alliance for Progress, could emulate this example by setting up their own school, based, say, in Mexico, which has the longest and most successful example of revolution in Latin America, and training men in skills needed to overthrow undesirable regimes.

The emphasis, of course, should be on bloodless revolutions; but, where these are not possible, the United States must be prepared to foment physical upheaval in order to install governments with reformist lines. These suggestions, it must be repeated, are made only in a sense of desperation and because all other measures are failing in Latin America. A school for revolutionaries is not entirely far-fetched; its graduates would be acceptable if they were Latin Americans, known to be working in the best interests of fellow Latin Americans. The United States would be doing the financing and encouraging from behind the scenes, just as in the past when it manipulated events to ensure the establishment in Central America of regimes sympathetic to its interests. Again one could only wish that the C.I.A. might participate with a more progressive instinct than it has shown in the past.

The principle of nonintervention is a myth; the United States has always intervened in Latin America when it thought it necessary; it has, in fact, a duty to its own people to do so when it feels threatened. It has intervened when there was doubt as to the justice of such action; it would be much more honest to intervene on the side of honor and decency.

Index

I 333TFI 950 6045
89 24 BR